P9-AGO-332

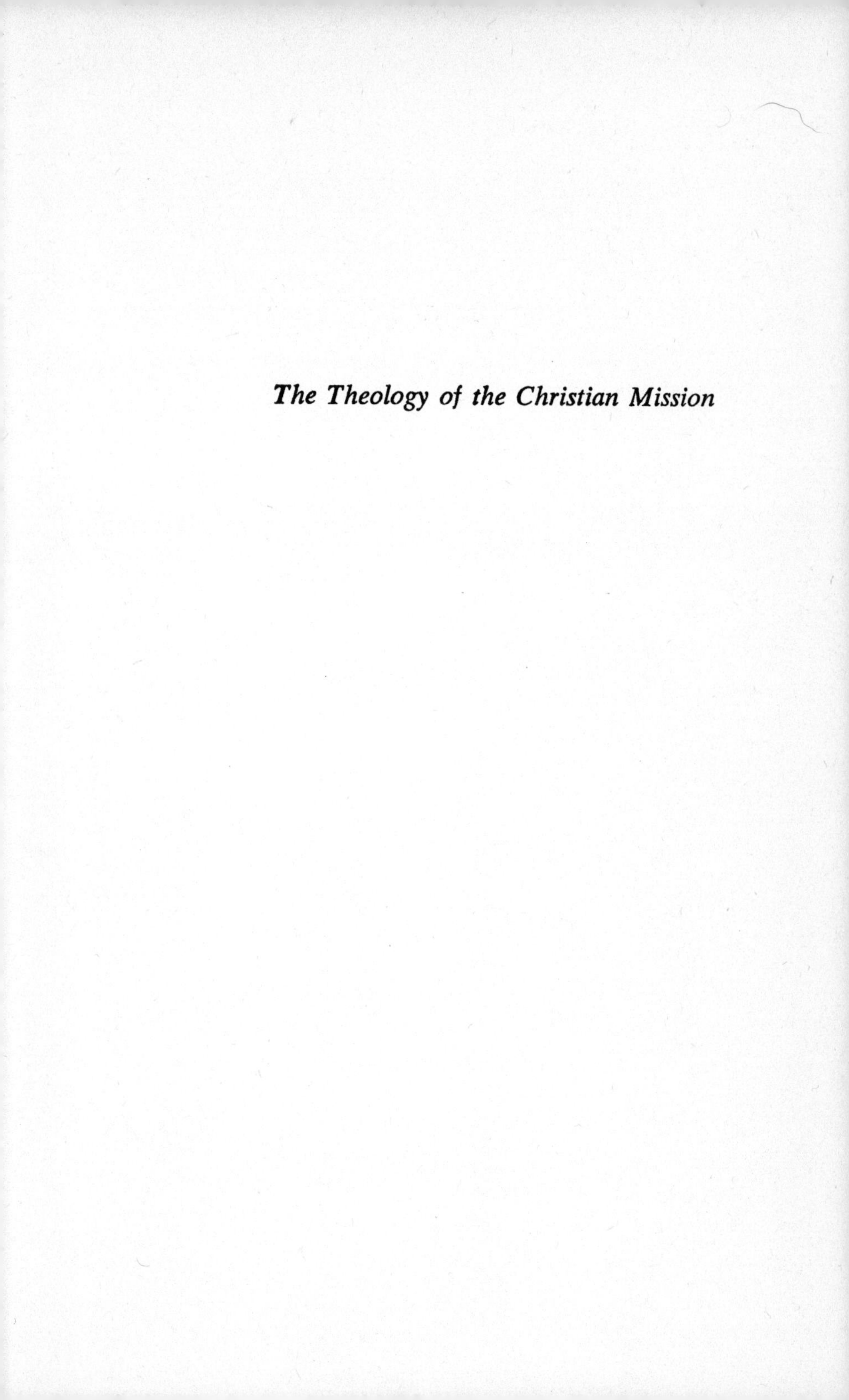

The Theology of the Christian Mission

THE THEOLOGY OF THE CHRISTIAN MISSION

Edited and with an Introduction by

GERALD H. ANDERSON

SCM PRESS LTD
BLOOMSBURY STREET LONDON

First British edition 1961
Printed in the United States of America

Dedicated
To all those who labor as missionaries
in His name. . . .

An endless line of splendor,
These troops with heaven for home,
With creeds they go from Scotland,
With incense go from Rome.
These, in the name of Jesus,
Against the dark gods stand,
They gird the earth with valor,
They heed their King's command.

Onward the line advances,
Shaking the hills with power,
Slaying the hidden demons,
The lions that devour.
No bloodshed in the wrestling—
But souls new-born arise—
The nations growing kinder,
The child-hearts growing wise.

What is the final ending?
The issue, can we know?
Will Christ outlive Mohammed?
Will Kali's altar go?
This is our faith tremendous—
Our wild hope, who shall scorn—
That in the name of Jesus,
The world shall be reborn!

Vachel Lindsay
(1879–1931)

CONTRIBUTORS

Wilhelm Andersen, Professor of Systematic Theology, Augustana-Hochschule, Neuendettelsau, Germany.

Gerald H. Anderson, Professor of Church History and Ecumenics, Union Theological Seminary, Manila, Philippines.

Christian G. Baëta, Senior Lecturer in Divinity, University College of Ghana, Legon (via Accra), Ghana; Chairman of the Ghana Christian Council and of the International Missionary Council.

Karl Barth, Professor of Theology, University of Basel, Basel, Switzerland.

R. Pierce Beaver, Professor of Missions, Federated Theological Faculty of the University of Chicago, Chicago, Illinois.

Ernst Benz, Professor of Church History, University of Marburg, Marburg, Germany.

Johannes Blauw, Secretary of the Dutch Missionary Council, Amsterdam, Netherlands.

A. C. Bouquet, Sometime Lecturer in the History and Comparative Study of Religions, University of Cambridge, Cambridge, England; and recently on the faculty of Andhra University in India.

Oscar Cullmann, Professor of New Testament Studies, University of Basel, Basel, Switzerland, and the Sorbonne, Paris, France.

F. N. Davey, Director of the Society for Promoting Christian Knowledge, London, England.

Paul D. Devanandan, Director of the Christian Institute for the Study of Religion and Society, Bangalore, India.

L. Harold DeWolf, Professor of Systematic Theology, Boston University School of Theology, Boston, Massachusetts.

F. W. Dillistone, Dean of the Cathedral, Liverpool, England.

Masatoshi Doi, Professor of Church History and Ecumenics, Doshisha University School of Theology, Kyoto, Japan.

William Richey Hogg, Professor of World Christianity, Southern Methodist University, Perkins School of Theology, Dallas, Texas.

Hendrik Kraemer, Sometime Professor of the History of Religions, University of Leiden, Leiden, Netherlands; and late Director of the Ecumenical Institute, Bossey, Switzerland.

Harold Lindsell, Dean of the Faculty and Professor of Missions, Fuller Theological Seminary, Pasadena, California.

Franklin H. Littell, Professor of Church History, Southern Methodist University, Perkins School of Theology, Dallas, Texas.

Donald G. Miller, Professor of New Testament, Union Theological Seminary, Richmond, Virginia.

Lesslie Newbigin, Bishop of the Church of South India, and General Secretary of the International Missionary Council.

Frank Wilson Price, Director of the Missionary Research Library, New York, New York.

Floyd H. Ross, Professor of World Religions, Southern California School of Theology, Claremont Graduate School, and Blaisdell Institute for Advanced Study of World Cultures and Religions, Claremont, California.

Alexander Schmemann, Professor of Church History and Liturgical Theology, St. Vladimir's Orthodox Theological Seminary, New York, New York.

Andrew V. Seumois, O.M.I., Professor at the Institute of Missiology, Propaganda Fide University, Rome, Italy; and Consultant of the Sacred Congregation for the Propagation of the Faith.

Paul Tillich, University Professor, Harvard University, Cambridge, Massachusetts.

Max Warren, General Secretary of the Church Missionary Society, Church of England, London, England.

G. Ernest Wright, Parkman Professor of Divinity (Old Testament), Harvard Divinity School, Cambridge, Massachusetts.

ACKNOWLEDGMENTS

Grateful acknowledgment is made to Basler Missionsbuchhandlung G.m.b.H., Basel, for permission to publish, in English translation, *Auslegung von Matthäus 28, 16–20* by Karl Barth; to the *Occasional Bulletin* of the Missionary Research Library, New York, for permission to reprint, after revision by the author, "The Theology of Missions" by Paul Tillich, which originally appeared in the issue of August 10, 1954 (Vol. V, No. 10); to Cambridge University Press for permission to reprint "Eschatology and Missions in the New Testament" by Oscar Cullmann from *The Background of the New Testament and Its Eschatology* (1956), edited by W. D. Davies and D. Daube; to The Macmillan Company for permission to use the poem "Foreign Missions in Battle Array" from *Collected Poems* by Vachel Lindsay, copyright 1913; and to the Division of Christian Education of the National Council of Churches of Christ in the U.S.A. for permission to quote from the Revised Standard Version of *The Holy Bible,* copyright 1946 and 1952.

Each author is responsible for only those views expressed in his own essay.

FOREWORD

The theology of the Christian mission is no longer a subject only for specialists or enthusiasts. It has become a subject in which everyone who wishes to reflect seriously about the task of the Church in our time must interest himself. For the Church is now, in a sense which has not been true for many centuries, in a missionary situation everywhere.

The immense enterprise which usually goes by the name of foreign missions took its rise in a period when the word "Christendom" represented a limited and fairly well-defined part of the inhabited world, and when for centuries the Christian Church had been almost completely isolated from the other great religious cultures of the world. Christendom had become a self-contained society, concerned with its internal problems, and barely conscious of the existence of the rest of the world except for the constant presence on its border of the great culture of Islam which provided the barrier against contact with the religious cultures of India and China. The forms of church life, and the presuppositions of Christian thought, were all shaped by the experiences of this self-enclosed existence. At the beginning of the seventeenth century, when the evangelization of the greater part of the human race had not been begun or even thought of, Bishop Lancelot Andrewes could give thanks for "the more than marvellous conversion of all the world to the obedience of faith." Christendom had become a largely isolated and self-contained enclave of humanity.

Foreign missions were a breaking-forth from that enclave into a strange new world. Their rise was part of that whole explosion of the human spirit which has carried the debris of Western Christendom into every corner of the world to shake the ancient structures of society and to create new forms of thought, of personal and family life, of commerce and statecraft. Of course they were much more than this. They were, and are, part of the continuing signs of the presence of the new creation in Christ. But, like every other part of the Church's being, they were and are also part of the secular history of their time. And the time in which they took their rise and developed their characteristic patterns of thought and practice has now ended. This ending is not a mere termination but a fulfillment; it is an ending which causes one who understands to look forward in hope.

In one sense this is obvious. The foreign missionary movement has reached a kind of fulfillment in the existence of indigenous Christian churches in almost every country of the world. The Gospel has reached "the ends of the earth." While there are great areas of the world in which Christian witness is pitifully weak or almost nonexistent, yet there are not—in the old sense—"regions beyond." Christendom is no longer a small and clearly defined sector of the inhabited world; it exists in dispersion, in a multitude of communities, most of them small minorities, scattered throughout the human race. The old picture of the missionary as one who sallies forth from a geographically defined Christendom into the outer world of barbarous superstition is no longer valid.

In another sense, also, the era in which modern missions took their rise has ended. The cultural explosion which has carried Western ideas of science, commerce, and politics (whether in their Marxist or "democratic" forms) into every part of the world has also had a kind of fulfillment. These ideas, and the explosive human forces which they release, are no longer the exclusive property of the West. They have become—or are rapidly becoming—the common property of mankind. The dynamism of Western society is being matched and exceeded by the new societies appearing in Asia, Africa and other so-called "areas of rapid social change." The winds of change no longer blow all in one direction. In the nineteenth century these winds often helped to fill the sails of the missionary ship venturing into strange waters and among strange people. Sometimes the navigators became perhaps a little too expert at making use of these winds. Today they are as likely as not to blow the other way, and the missionary has to learn the art of navigating against the prevailing wind. If, in seeking to learn, he remembers that the greatest of missionaries had intimate experience of changing winds and knew much of their perils, he may be encouraged and emboldened; but that will not alter the fact that he has painfully to rethink many things which his predecessor took for granted.

It is at such a moment that the Church has the invitation and the opportunity to learn again that her history is *not* simply part of the secular history of her times. She faces a radically new situation, and nothing will suffice save radical rethinking of the nature of her mission. Such rethinking must include both a realistic understanding of the new facts with which the mission has to deal, and a humble return to the source of the mission in the Gospel. It must take both the Bible and the daily newspaper seriously. If it does, we can expect that the Church will be shown the new forms which must be taken for this new day by the mission which is the same from Christ's coming to his coming again.

For, while in one sense the events which now confront us are the fulfillment of the missionary movement of the past centuries, in another sense they challenge us with an awe-inspiring sense of the greatness of the unfinished task. To anyone who understands the Gospel, the task of world-evangelization must surely be even more demanding and compelling than it was to the great missionary pioneers of the eighteenth and nineteenth centuries. But it is a task which has to be differently conceived. Today the mission field is everywhere, and the home base is wherever the Church exists. Today the pagan world is no longer something away over the horizon; it is here in the midst of us. Even the good Christian congregation which faithfully gave its yearly offering to foreign missions finds itself having to face for the first time the question whether it is really true that there is salvation in no other name than that of Jesus. We live in one world in which the competing faiths, no longer separated and insulated by distance, jostle one another in every city and even in the minds of ordinary Christians. Today the question of the theology of the Christian mission is a question that —whether recognized or not—knocks at the door of every congregation.

The essays which follow represent very varied approaches to this central question. Certainly not all of them will carry the assent of any reader. May they serve to stimulate everyone who reads them to play his own part in the task of helping the Church in our day to rediscover in the Gospel the source and nature of her mission to all nations.

LESSLIE NEWBIGIN

London

CONTENTS

PART III CHRISTIANITY AND OTHER FAITHS

PART IV THEORY OF THE MISSION

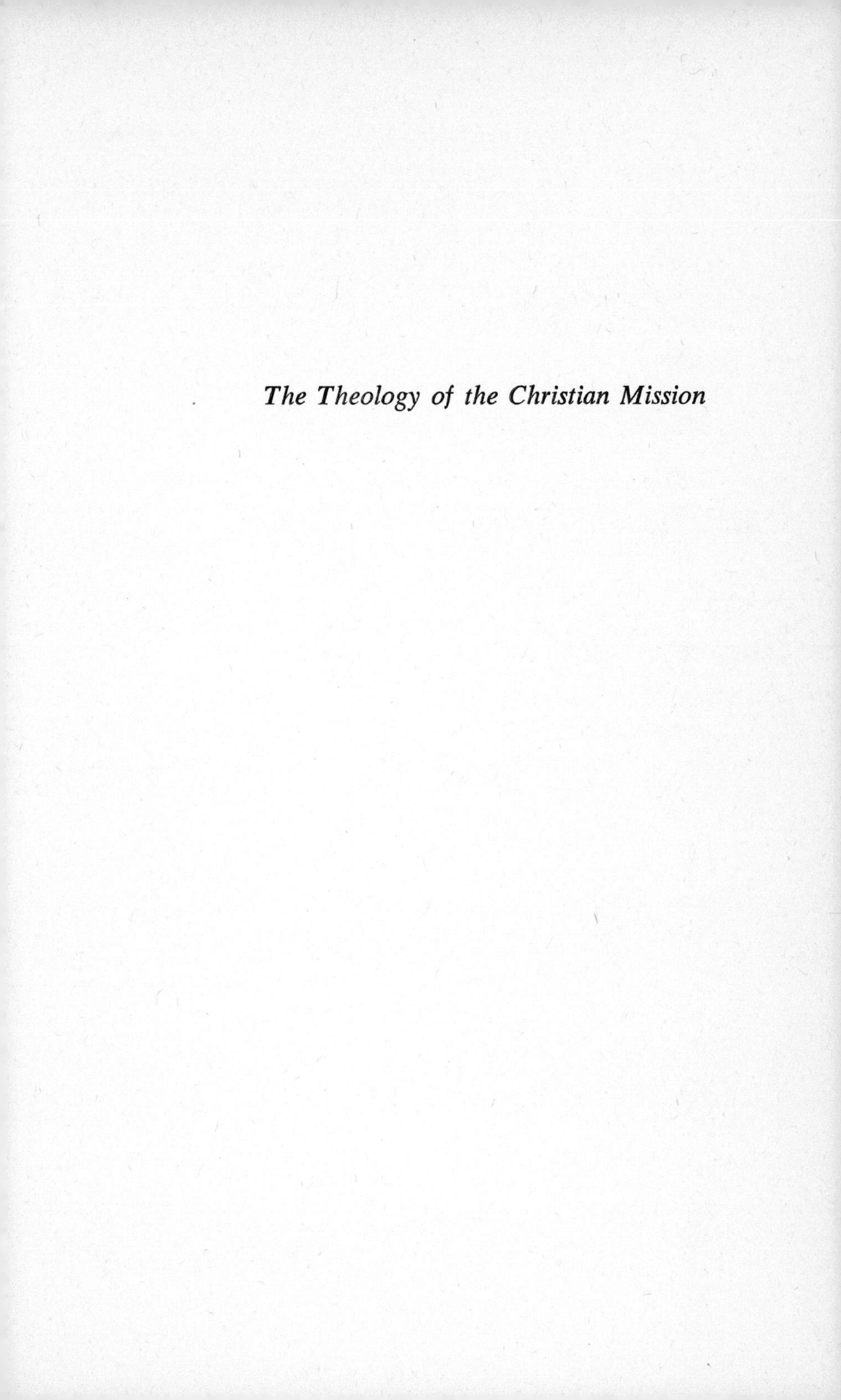

The Theology of the Christian Mission

INTRODUCTION

The Theology of Mission among Protestants in the Twentieth Century [1]

BY GERALD H. ANDERSON

In his book *What Present-Day Theologians Are Thinking* Daniel Day Williams suggests that one of the major issues which "may well dominate much of theological thought as we move into the second half of the twentieth century" is the relation of Christianity to culture and other religions.[2] The reasons for this are well known. The resurgence of non-Christian religions, the shift of cultural and political power in the world, and the rise of an indigenous ecumenical church have so transformed the setting for Christian missions as to cause confusion among Christians concerning their proper attitude and approach to men of other faiths. The underlying principles and theological presuppositions for the Christian mission have been called into question and Christians are challenged to rethink the motives, message, methods, and goals of their mission.

In face of this confusion there is surprisingly little creative theological endeavor available for guidance. As recently as 1951, in a confidential report to a group of American theological scholars, a missionary leader said, "When we turn to mission and theological libraries in search of material on the theology of missions, we almost draw a blank." This situation is not new. Wilhelm Pauck, the church historian, has pointed out that "with the possible exception

[1] The word Protestant is used here to include Anglicans, although many in communion with the Church of England strongly disclaim that title.

[2] (Revised edition; New York: Harper & Brothers, 1959), pp. 5–6.

of the early Church, whose theology was decisively shaped by the missionary spirit, no part of Christendom has produced major theological responsibility and creativeness in connection with evangelistic endeavors." [3] Christian theological endeavor has been more concerned with introspection, with intra-Christian relations, than with the interrelation of Christianity and other faiths. Too often those most interested in the nature of the Christian faith have been those least interested in its relation to men of other faiths. The result, in the words of an astute observer, is that "the Christian community is at the moment theologically unequipped for living in the twentieth century, with its pluralistic mankind." [4] The fundamental task, therefore, of the missionary enterprise today is to clarify the nature and meaning of its being. This must be done in the realm of theological thought, not only to increase effectiveness in presenting the Gospel to the world, but also to give Christians a deeper understanding of what their task *is* in the world.

I

In approaching this important undertaking it is helpful to begin by surveying some of the trends and factors in the development of the theology of mission thus far in the twentieth century. One is that there has been a progressively deepening thrust, despite brief periods of recession, toward a fundamental reformulation of the theology of mission. This may be seen, to some extent, in two ways: (1) by the progressively deepening confrontation of Church and mission with theology, which may be discerned most clearly, in the Protestant tradition, by the questions dealt with in the series of great international missionary gatherings; (2) by the progressive narrowing of the gulf between Church and mission, from 1900, when the missionary enterprise was considered by many to be primarily the responsibility of missionary societies rather than the churches, until the present-day integration of Church and mission, as seen in the proposed integration of the World Council of Churches and the International Missionary Council.[5]

[3] "Theology in the Life of Contemporary American Protestantism," *Religion and Culture: Essays in Honor of Paul Tillich,* ed. Walter Leibrecht (New York: Harper & Brothers, 1959), p. 278.

[4] Wilfred Cantwell Smith, "Christianity's Third Great Challenge," *The Christian Century,* April 27, 1960, p. 506.

[5] This must be qualified by saying that this narrowing has been more true in Britain and on the Continent than in America. In the United States,

This first trend may be illustrated with an analogy in which the progressive historical development of the theology of mission thus far in the twentieth century may be thought of in terms of a spiral staircase in a seven-story building, with a landing at each floor level between flights of stairs. Each landing represents one of the major international missionary gatherings, with the steps between landings indicating the important events and publications which occurred between meetings. These meetings served to stimulate interest, to sharpen the issues, to focus world attention on the developments which occurred in the intervening years, and to indicate the way forward to further possible lines of development in the discussion.

With this analogy in mind one can follow the developments in the theology of mission by descending the staircase, beginning from the landing on the seventh floor. On this landing, which represents the Edinburgh Conference of 1910, the first truly world missionary conference, the major question being put to the missionary enterprise was simply "How missions?" Edinburgh was primarily concerned with strategy, and most participants seemed to take for granted that the Great Commission of Christ (Mt. 28:19) was the only basis needed for the missionary enterprise.[6] It came at a time when missionary endeavor was at a high point of enthusiasm, and the missionary obligation was considered a self-evident axiom to be obeyed, not to be questioned.

The second landing in the descent of the staircase represents the Jerusalem Conference of 1928, where the issues and discussion might be summarized with the question "Wherefore missions?" At this international missionary gathering the theology of mission was given primary consideration under the title "The Christian Life and Message in Relation to Non-Christian Systems of Thought and

---

at least since 1837, the general pattern has been one of denominational, rather than independent, missionary societies. On the other hand, there has been a tremendous growth of independent and nondenominational missionary societies within American Protestantism in the twentieth century. This counterdevelopment in America has considerable significance for the theology of mission. Also, it remains to be seen whether the integration of the W.C.C. and the I.M.C. will bring about structural changes at the national and local level in those areas where missionary societies have remained outside and independent of the churches.

[6] This does not minimize either the historical significance of Commission IV at Edinburgh or the continuing worth of its report on "The Missionary Message in Relation to Non-Christian Religions."

Life." Secularism and syncretism were seen as the two major threats to Christian missions, and discussion was oriented around a consideration of goals toward which the missionary enterprise should be directed. But, while the Jerusalem Conference did bring the whole question of theological presuppositions to the fore, it did not penetrate the issue to any significant degree.

The third landing in the descent toward a deeper understanding of the Christian mission represents the Tambaram, Madras, meeting of 1938, where the major question was "Whence missions?" At Madras the missionary enterprise realized that it must reconsider its roots. This led to a discussion of the nature of revelation, its locus and authority, as the key issue in determining the relationship and approach of Christianity to non-Christian religions. This discussion was cut short by the outbreak of the Second World War.

By the time the fourth landing is reached, the Whitby meeting of 1947, the question being asked is "Whither missions?" The Christian mission at Whitby was defined in terms of evangelism and was seen by members of an indigenous world church as "Partners in Obedience." There was little advance at Whitby beyond what had already been achieved at Madras toward a deeper understanding of the basis and nature of the Christian mission, but Whitby *was* an advance in that it recognized the urgent need for a deeper study of this whole complex of issues and took the first step toward launching a major ecumenical study of "The Missionary Obligation of the Church."

Discussion of this topic takes the reader down the steps to the fifth landing, to the Willingen meeting of 1952. There the issues were seen at the level of "Why missions?" And although Willingen was unable to adopt an agreed statement on "The Missionary Obligation of the Church," it did have immeasurable significance for the theology of mission in that it considered the theological presuppositions for missions at a deeper level and within a broader context than had been the case at any previous meeting. The thoroughgoing nature of the discussion at Willingen, together with the inability to arrive at an agreed point of conviction, caused the missionary movement further to realize that the theology of mission required high priority for depth study. This conclusion was seconded by the World Council of Churches in the years immediately following Willingen, and by the time one descends to the sixth landing, to the Ghana Assembly of 1957–58, he finds the missionary enterprise asking itself the most radical question in its history, "What is the Christian mission?"

In an effort to answer this question one descends to the main floor of the theology of mission, which should be reached at the Delhi Joint Assemblies of the International Missionary Council and the World Council of Churches in 1961, where it is expected that these two great bodies will be integrated and give major attention to the nature of the Christian mission.

There is an additional factor, however, needing to be recognized and dealt with before the missionary enterprise can have a clear understanding of its task. The Christian mission is so inextricably related to the nature of the Christian Gospel that it is necessary to go even deeper in this building, into the basement and to the foundations, to a deeper understanding of the Gospel itself, before the theology of mission can be adequately formulated. There are indications that there may be many stories beneath the ground floor, dealing with the nature and meaning of the Christian Gospel, and needing equally careful examination in order to secure the proper foundation support for the surface structure.

II

A second factor in the development of the theology of mission during the twentieth century has been the diversity of Protestant attitudes toward men of other faiths.

At the beginning of this century a large part of the missionary movement, influenced by the spirit of Dwight L. Moody's revivalism, had a passion for souls that stemmed from an emphasis upon the rapidly approaching judgment day and a strong sense of obligation to save the heathen from eternal damnation. Yet at the Edinburgh World Missionary Conference in 1910 agreement was reached on "two very notable points":

> The first of these is the practically universal testimony that the true attitude of the Christian missionary to the non-Christian religions should be one of true understanding and, as far as possible, of sympathy, . . . that the missionary should seek for the nobler elements in the non-Christian religions and use them as steps to higher things, that in fact all these religions without exception disclose elemental needs of the human soul which Christianity alone can satisfy, and that in their higher forms they plainly manifest the working of the Spirit of God.
>
> But, along with this generous recognition of all that is true and good

in these religions, there goes also the universal and emphatic witness to the absoluteness of the Christian faith.[7]

The threat of materialistic secularism to all religions in the years following Edinburgh, 1910, brought about a strengthened reaffirmation of the Edinburgh position at the Jerusalem Meeting of the International Missionary Council in 1928.[8] The Jerusalem Statement on the Christian Message began with the Christocentric affirmation:

> Our message is Jesus Christ. He is the revelation of what God is and of what man through Him may become. In Him we come face to face with the Ultimate Reality of the universe; He makes known to us God as our Father, perfect and infinite in love and in righteousness; for in Him we find God incarnate, the final, yet ever-unfolding, revelation of the God in whom we live and move and have our being.[9]

The Statement continued, with regard to the Christian attitude to non-Christian systems of thought and life:

> We rejoice to think that just because in Jesus Christ the light that lighteth every man shone forth in its full splendor, we find rays of that same light where He is unknown or even is rejected. We welcome every noble quality in non-Christian persons or systems as further proof that the Father, who sent His Son into the world, has nowhere left Himself without witness.[10]

The attitude expressed at Jerusalem, however, did not go unquestioned. Considerable misgiving was expressed by European missionary leaders at the meeting concerning what they believed to be a tendency toward a syncretistic approach to the non-Christian religions. Dr. Karl Hartenstein, the noted Missions Director from

[7] "General Conclusions" in The Report of Commission IV: *The Missionary Message in Relation to Non-Christian Religions, Vol. IV* of *The World Missionary Conference, 1910* (Edinburgh and London: Oliphant, Anderson & Ferrier; New York: Fleming H. Revell Company [1910]), pp. 267–68.

[8] A more elaborate study of the development of the Christian attitude toward non-Christian religions in this period would take into consideration the influence of humanitarianism, democratic thought, Biblical criticism, liberal theology, the Social Gospel movement, the First World War, and theological reaction on the Continent.

[9] "The Council's Statement" in *The Christian Life and Message in Relation to Non-Christian Systems of Thought and Life,* Vol. I of *The Jerusalem Meeting of the International Missionary Council* (New York and London: I.M.C., 1928), p. 402.

[10] *Ibid.,* p. 410.

Basel, later dealt with the subject from the perspective of the continental "Theology of the Word," giving special emphasis to the eschatological attitude, in his study of the Christian mission as a theological problem.[11]

In 1932 the discussion was stimulated and the issues were sharpened when the Laymen's Foreign Missions Inquiry issued *Re-Thinking Missions,* the Report of its Commission of Appraisal, which William Ernest Hocking served as chairman. This valuable Report suggested that the aim of missions is "to seek with people of other lands a true knowledge and love of God, expressing in life and word what we have learned through Jesus Christ"; [12] that "the Christian will regard himself as a co-worker with the forces which are making for righteousness within every religious system"; [13] that "the relation between religions must take increasingly hereafter the form of a common search for truth"; [14] and that the missionary "will look forward, not to the destruction of these [non-Christian] religions, but to their continued co-existence with Christianity, each stimulating the other in growth toward the ultimate goal, unity in the completest religious truth." [15] This approach departed sharply from the more traditionally held concept of missions, the role of the missionary, and the relation of Christianity to other religions. As such, the Report stimulated recognition of the missionary problem as a theological problem and provoked basic rethinking of the issues involved, but was itself widely criticized for its tone of optimism and relativism.

A more radical departure came in 1934 with the publication of *Christian Missions and a New World Culture* by Archibald G. Baker, Professor of Missions at the University of Chicago. Baker took a culture-centered approach and suggested that the function of missions is to serve as the agent for a cultural synthesis by means of the interpenetration or cross-fertilization of cultures. He maintained that all religions "emerge in the same process which has been working through the ages," the only differences in them being

[11] Karl Hartenstein, *Die Mission als theologisches Problem* (Berlin: Furche-Verlag, 1933).

[12] *Re-Thinking Missions: A Layman's Inquiry After One Hundred Years* (New York: Harper & Brothers, 1932), p. 326.

[13] *Ibid.*, pp. 40 and 327.

[14] *Ibid.*, p. 47.

[15] *Ibid.*, p. 44.

differences in accomplishment and character.[16] The center of reference for missions, according to Baker, should be Jesus Christ, but the process for fulfillment is joint deliberation and cooperation with non-Christians, abandoning all claims to absolutism and finality. This approach was not representative of any large group within the missionary enterprise, but it was a thoughtful presentation that must be given recognition.

Hugh Vernon White, Secretary for the American Board of Commissioners for Foreign Missions, presented a position corresponding to *Re-Thinking Missions* in his book *A Theology for Christian Missions* which appeared in 1937. White said that the service of man should be the regulative aim of missions, and that it should be carried out through witness and friendship, through the conquest of selfishness, and reverence for "the sanctity of human personality." [17] He believed that Christianity was the best religion in the world, but did not deny that there are truths and values in other religions.

Professor Hendrik Kraemer, in his book *The Christian Message in a Non-Christian World,* introduced a new dimension to the discussion and provided a reply to the position represented in *Re-Thinking Missions*. Written at the request of the International Missionary Council for its meeting at Tambaram, Madras, in 1938, this classic study stressed the idea of a radical discontinuity between the realm of "Biblical realism" and the whole range of non-Christian religious experience. Dr. Kraemer took the position that all non-Christian religions, philosophies, and world views are "the various efforts of man to apprehend the totality of existence," whereas the Christian revelation, which is absolutely *sui generis* and remains hidden except to the eye of faith,

> asserts itself as the record of God's self-disclosing and re-creating revelation in Jesus Christ, as an apprehension of existence that revolves around the poles of divine judgment and divine salvation, giving the divine answer to this demonic and guilty disharmony of man and the world.[18]

[16] (New York and Chicago: Willett, Clark and Company, 1934), pp. 291–92.

[17] (New York and Chicago: Willett, Clark and Company, 1937), pp. 36–41, 71.

[18] (Published for the International Missionary Council by Harper & Brothers, New York and London, 1938), pp. 113–14.

Allowing that God does shine through the works of His creation and through the conscience of man, Dr. Kraemer emphasized that "this 'general revelation' can only be effectually discovered in the light of the 'special revelation,' " and therefore is itself an object of faith.[19] The only basic point of contact with the non-Christian religions, he said, is the missionary worker.[20]

The Tambaram, Madras Meeting of the International Missionary Council in 1938 issued a Statement on "The Faith by Which the Church Lives" that declared unequivocally:

> We believe that Christ is the Way for all, that He alone is adequate for the world's need. . . . We are bold enough to call men out from them [other religions] to the feet of Christ. We do so because we believe that in Him alone is the full salvation which man needs.[21]

The Statement acknowledged also, however, the good in other religions:

> We see and readily recognize that in them are to be found values of deep religious experiences and great moral achievements. . . . We do not think that God has left Himself without witness in the world at any time. Men have been seeking Him all through the ages. Often this seeking and longing have been misdirected. But we see glimpses of God's light in the world of religions, showing that His yearning after His erring children has not been without response.[22]

There was again, and even stronger than at Jerusalem, a feeling of misgiving on the part of some delegates, mostly among those from the Continent, concerning what they felt to be the neglect of some vital principles of the Gospel. These members submitted a separate statement to the meeting, expressing their concern and emphasizing the importance of maintaining a sense of discontinuity together with an eschatological attitude when considering the Christian approach to other religions.

Following the Madras meeting, this discussion, centering around

[19] *Ibid.,* p. 125.

[20] *Ibid.,* p. 140. Dr. Kraemer's later book, *Religion and the Christian Faith* (London: Lutterworth Press, 1956), was essentially a restatement, with new material and broader perspective, of the same basic position presented in this earlier book.

[21] "Findings of Tambaram Meeting" in *The Authority of the Faith,* Vol. I of *The Tambaram Madras Series* (Published for the International Missionary Council by Oxford University Press, London, 1939), p. 200.

[22] *Ibid.,* pp. 200–01.

the two concepts of "Biblical realism" and "discontinuity," was carried on to a further stage in Volume I, a symposium entitled *The Authority of the Faith,* of *The Tambaram Madras Series.* Professor Kraemer, supported by an essay from Karl Hartenstein, restated the case, clearly and succinctly, for "Biblical realism" and "discontinuity." Other views were presented by T. C. Chao, David G. Moses, A. G. Hogg and Karl Ludvig Reichelt, with Walter Marshall Horton and H. H. Farmer taking a mediating position.

During the Second World War important contributions came from Godfrey E. Phillips and Edmund Davison Soper. Phillips, who was Professor of Missions at Selly Oak College in Birmingham, England, said that the view which suggests that non-Christian religions are merely the product of human striving and in no way an answer to divine inspiration and initiative

> seems to lack sympathy, as if we were to rebuke some terrified lost child looking for its mother for pride in the assumption that it can find her. Probably the child was naughty to get lost, but its present attempt to find her is due not to naughtiness but to something within which it has from its mother. The note in many a non-Christian prayer is not of self-confidence but of wistful yearning for what it is intuitively felt that only divine grace can grant.[23]

Soper, in his book, *The Philosophy of the Christian World Mission* (1943), described Kraemer's position as "uniqueness without continuity," and Hocking's position as "continuity with doubtful uniqueness," while his own position he gave as uniqueness with continuity.[24] This book remains as a representative exposition of the viewpoint held by a large segment of American Protestantism.

Since the war there has been increasing participation in this discussion by scholars from the so-called younger churches, and a renewal of interest on the part of scholars in the West. Also there has been a resurgence of the orthodox or conservative evangelical tradition, which is commonly, though not always correctly, referred to as "Fundamentalism." Christians in this tradition argue for the plenary inspiration of Scripture and limit the ground of religious authority to the Bible. They recognize no real values in

[23] *The Gospel in the World, A Re-Statement of Missionary Principles* (London: Gerald Duckworth and Company, 1939), p. 79.

[24] (New York: Abingdon-Cokesbury Press, 1943), pp. 223, 228.

other religions, and are apt to believe in a literal hell to which men without Christ, both those who have rejected him and those who have never heard of him, are doomed. The evangelicals have been a constant source of missionary effort in the twentieth century, and today approximately one third of the total Protestant missionary endeavor is administered by agencies that are rooted in this tradition and do not cooperate with either the World Council of Churches or the International Missionary Council.

The situation today, in the words of Victor E. W. Hayward, Research Secretary of the International Missionary Council, is that "the great debate as to the way in which Christians ought to regard the great non-Christian faiths has reached stalemate rather than agreement." [25] The major issues, despite a renewal of interest and discussion, have not been resolved. If anything, they have become more crucial.

The most promising developments for a breakthrough to a new understanding of the relationship of Christianity and the non-Christian religions have come from the ecumenical study projects launched since 1954 by the International Missionary Council in cooperation with the World Council of Churches. One has been the establishment of a number of "Centers for the Study of Non-Christian Religions" in various parts of the world.[26] The purpose of these "Centers" is to make "on the spot" studies of the actual religions in their contemporary forms and expressions, and to try to understand them as the living faiths of men who are struggling against the tensions and temptations of life in the modern world. The "Centers" also want to assist the churches in working and witnessing relevantly in their own situations.

Working in close cooperation with the "Centers" is a study known as "The Word of God and the Living Faiths of Men." This is a study of:

[25] "Long Term Missionary Studies of the I.M.C.," *International Review of Missions,* XLIV (July 1960), p. 316. It is not uncommon today to find nearly all of the attitudes surveyed here within a single church or denomination. For a recent indication of this see: S. Paul Schilling, *Methodism and Society in Theological Perspective* (New York: Abingdon Press, 1960), pp. 158–59.

[26] There have been, of course, important "Centers" concerned with the relationship of Christianity to other religions prior to this, such as Karl Ludvig Reichelt's *Tao Fong Shan Institute* at Hong Kong.

— the nature of the living faiths of men and the elements in them of appeal and power;
— the nature of the Word of God which is addressed to men who live by these faiths;
— the nature of the relation between the Christian message and these faiths;
— the way in which the Church may be enabled to communicate this Word to those who live by these faiths.

A significant development in this study is that it has differed from the earlier discussions of Christianity and the non-Christian religions in that it has not opposed Christianity and the other religions as such to one another. Instead, it has

> made a basic distinction between the Gospel and all religions. This distinction presupposed that the important point of concern is not with religious systems as such but with religious man and especially with men under the proclamation of the Gospel. The important result of this distinction is that the starting point is anthropological, that is with man — however conditioned by his religion and history and environment. Thus, in the first instance at any rate, the problems of the comparison of truths of one system with truths of another are transcended because the center of attention is not these truths but the human being himself.[27]

A third study that should contribute to a new understanding of the relationship between the Gospel and the religions is the study of "The Theology of Mission." [28] The central focus of this study is: "What does it mean in theological terms and in practice in this ecumenical era, for the Church to discharge its mission to all the nations?" This study includes the Biblical and theological basis and goal of mission, together with a theological evaluation of the existing structures expressing the missionary responsibility of the churches and of those which are emerging.[29] More specifically, the

[27] "The Bossey Meeting on 'The Word of God and the Living Faiths of Men,' " *Bulletin* (Geneva: World Council of Churches Division of Studies), IV (April 1958), p. 25.

[28] Other ecumenical studies also of significance in this realm are: "The Theology of Evangelism," "The Lordship of Christ over the Church and the World," "The Life and Growth of the Younger Churches," and the W.S.C.F. study and teaching program on "The Life and Mission of the Church."

[29] See the *I.M.C. Assembly Minutes,* Ghana, 1957–58, pp. 46–47, Report of Committee I.

study is concerned with such questions as: [30] (1) What is the Biblical meaning of "the nations," and the theological significance of "the ends of the earth"? (2) What are the meaning and practical implications of the Christian claim that there is salvation "in no other name"? (3) What is the relation between history and "salvation-history"? (4) What is the relation between the Gospel and human cultures?

The basic issues for consideration in all these studies are: (1) How should we understand the urgency of mission in terms of theology today? (2) How should we understand the uniqueness and ultimacy of the revelation of God in Jesus Christ? (3) How can we in the presentation of the Gospel relate it dynamically to the cultural life of a nation without compromising the essential nature of the Christian faith?

It is hoped that out of these studies and a renewal of the missionary confrontation in theology there might come not only a deeper understanding of the relationship between the Gospel and the religions, but also a more adequate theological perspective for the Christian mission today.

III

A third trend that is discernible as the theology of mission has developed in the twentieth century is that the direction of orientation is leading toward a *theocentric* point of view in thoroughgoing trinitarian perspective. A major cause for confusion in missions today has come from the inadequacy of the various attempts to formulate the theology of mission in recent years. There have been attempts from the culture-centered, man-centered, revelation-centered, eschatology-centered, kingdom-centered, Bible-centered, Church-centered and Christ-centered points of view. While all of these attempts have stressed various aspects of Christian doctrine that are essential for the missionary enterprise, it seems that when any one of them has been made the central point of focus and orientation for the theology of mission, it has proven inadequate for the task, tending to narrow the scope of the mission and causing it to go astray. It remains now for a major attempt to be made at formulating the theology of mission from the view of *radical trinitarian theocentrism.*[31] When it comes, this approach may plant

[30] "Long Term Missionary Studies of the I.M.C.," *op. cit.*, p. 312.

[31] A contribution in this direction is Georg F. Vicedom's *Missio Dei:*

the seed—but only God gives the growth—for a new flowering of missionary endeavor in our time.

It is hoped that the essays which follow, coming as they do from a wide range of scholars who differ in many respects, may help to bring into focus a more catholic and well-rounded trinitarian point of view that will increase our understanding of the Christian mission today.

Einführung in eine Theologie der Mission (München: Chr. Kaiser Verlag, 1958).

PART ONE

THE BIBLICAL BASIS

The Old Testament Basis for the Christian Mission

BY G. ERNEST WRIGHT

The rootage of the Christian mission in the faith of Israel may be discussed from several perspectives, of which three in particular are here mentioned. The first centers in the assembling of the texts which portray the redemptive relation existing between the Chosen People and the peoples. A second and deeper level of discussion centers in the doctrine of God which the Old Testament presents as an integral and exceedingly vital part of the Christian doctrines of the Trinity, the Incarnation, Atonement, and Ecclesia, of which the mission of the Church is one important element. A third level, closely allied with the second, might proceed from a discussion of the offense of the Old Testament for the missionary enterprise, an offense deriving both from the contemporary Church's misunderstanding of the Old Testament and from the offense inherent in the very nature of the Gospel itself.

I

H. H. Rowley, in his small volume *The Missionary Message of the Old Testament,* has performed a worthwhile service in assembling what might be classed as the various "missionary texts" of the Old Testament.[1] He affirms that "Moses was the first missionary

[1] (London: Carey Press [1945]). See also Alfred Bertholet, *Die Stellung der Israeliten und der Juden zu den Fremden* (Freiberg und Leipzig:

of whom we have any knowledge," for God had sent him both to save Israel and to lead them to worship Him, to the end that in Israel "all the families of the earth will bless themselves" (i.e., find blessing).[2] Visions of this goal are to be glimpsed in a large number of passages, especially in the Psalms and Prophets. The following motifs predominate: In the days to come all nations shall stream to Jerusalem as the religious capital of the world. There they shall bow before the Lord, sing praises to Him, learn of His righteousness and acknowledge His universal rule. There God will be enthroned; and there He will judge the peoples with equity, and bring peace to replace the sword.[3] God's claim to sovereignty over the whole world, a universal rule that He will one day bring about, is never doubted but triumphantly affirmed again and again in appropriate contexts. These are especially in passages which relate creation and history, in prophetic views of "the last

---

J. C. B. Mohr, 1896); J. Hempel, "Die Wurzeln des Missionswillens im Glaube des Alten Testamentes," *Zeitschrift für die alttestamentliche Wissenschaft,* Vol. LXVI (1954), pp. 244–72; Max Löhr, *Der Missionsgedanke im Alten Testament* (Freiberg und Leipzig: J. C. B. Mohr, 1896); Hartmut Schmökel, *Jahwe und die Fremdvölker* (Breslau: Maruschke und Berendt, 1934); E. Sellin, "Die Missionsgedanke im Alten Testament," *Neue allgemeine Missions-Zeitschrift,* Vol. II (1925), pp. 34–45, 66–72; W. Staerk, "Ursprung und Grenzen der Missionskraft der alttestamentlichen Religion," *Theologische Blätter,* Vol. IV (1925), pp. 25–37. For additional bibliography see especially Joachim Jeremias, *Jesus' Promise to the Nations* (London: SCM Press, 1958), pp. 76–79, whence the above citations were derived; and *Bibliography of the Theology of Missions in the Twentieth Century,* compiled by Gerald H. Anderson (2nd ed. rev. and enlarged; New York: Missionary Research Library, 1960), pp. 1–10.

[2] Gen. 12:3; 18:18; 28:14; 22:18; 26:4. Following Hermann Gunkel, *Genesis* (Göttingen: Vandenhoeck und Ruprecht, 1922), p. 165, Rowley gives a minimal (and nontheological) interpretation of these words. Yet they play a central role in the Genesis theme of the Promises to the Patriarchs, and a radically reductionist interpretation is scarcely in keeping with the theological content of the Yahwist and Elohist works as a whole. Cf. the broader interpretation of S. R. Driver, *Genesis* (London: Methuen [1906]), p. 145; Gerhard von Rad, *Das erste Buch Mose* (Göttingen: Vandenhoeck und Ruprecht, 1949), pp. 14 ff., 132 ff.; Walther Zimmerli, *1. Mose 1–11: Die Urgeschichte* (Zürich: Zwingi-Verlag [1957]), pp. 295, 421; and the present writer, *The Old Testament Against Its Environment* (London: SCM Press, 1950), pp. 51–52 and note 13.

[3] E.g., 1 Kings 8:41 ff.; Is. 2:2–4; Mic. 4:1–4; Is. 11:1–9, 19:23–25, 56:6–7, 66:18–24; Jer. 3:17; Hab. 2:14, 20; Zeph. 3:9–10; Zech. 9:9–10; Ps. 22:27–28, 47:6–8, 67, 68:28–32, 72:8–17, 86:9–10, 102:15–22.

days," and in the psalms which reflect the celebration of God's universal rule in relation to the office of the Davidic king (i.e., the royal and "enthronement" hymns).

As to the mission of Israel in the world, the Old Testament, of course, gives no united voice, except on the fact of the mission and on the necessity of becoming and remaining a loyal "people of God." [4] The deepest penetration into the method of the mission appears in the Books of Jonah and Second Isaiah. The former undoubtedly sees in the figure of the unwilling prophet the Chosen People herself who attempt to escape from God's calling of them for an important responsibility in the redemption of the world. In the figure of "servant of the Lord" Second Isaiah presents the people of God with an eloquent and deeply moving portrayal of their mission, one fulfilled in Christ and become the pattern for the Church's life in the world. Not only has the servant suffered for his own sins (Is. 40:2, 42:18–25), but he has vicariously borne in his body the wounds inflicted by the world's evils (52:13–53:12). Moreover his present mission is that he continue his humble mien before the world ("a bruised reed he will not break") and serve as a mediator of the redemptive righteousness of God, of "a covenant to the people, a light to the nations, to open the eyes that are blind" (42:1–7). In the crisis of world history the servant is God's witness in the trial of the nations, His chosen agent to testify that the Lord of history and the meaning of history is the God of Israel, beside whom "there is no saviour" (43:8–13). Consequently, for the servant to assume that his essential task is self-salvation and the restoration of his people to their land is too trivial, too "light," an understanding of his calling. God has appointed him "a light to the nations, that [the news of] my salvation may reach to the end of the earth. . . . I have kept you and given you as a covenant to the people . . . , to say to the prisoners, 'Come forth,' and to those who are in darkness, 'Appear' " (49:5–9).[5]

It is in Second Isaiah, therefore, that the finest missionary texts

[4] On the importance of this last emphasis in both testaments, see the writer, *The Biblical Doctrine of Man in Society* (London: SCM Press, 1954), pp. 125 ff. The roles of missionary and martyr are important but passages about them are not as frequent as admonitions to *exhibit the fruits of loyalty* before the world.

[5] The recent revival of the individual, as opposed to the collective, interpretation of the figure of the servant, whether considered as resting on a mythological or "ideal" basis, does not commend itself to this writer: see

in the Old Testament appear. The people of God as both His elect and His servant in the crisis of the empires is a picture of poignant power, and through Christ must lie at the very center of the Church's self-understanding. It cannot be emphasized too strongly, however, that the terms "elect" and "servant" in Second Isaiah and in Biblical theology as a whole do not connote primarily a substantive or ontological status. Numerous problems have surely arisen in the history of the Church because the Bible has been misinterpreted at this point. Instead, the primary emphasis in the terms was understood to be verbal, having to do with function or mission, not status. The latter was simply for the sake of the former, and could be withdrawn at any time when the mission was betrayed.

II

At a different level of discussion, however, one could well point to the significance of the canon of Scripture for the Christian doctrine of God. The trinitarian formula in one sense can be understood as an attempt to state in the language of the Greco-Roman world the complexity of the divine self-revelation in the Scripture as a whole. For all three "persons" of the Trinity the Old Testament reveals much, without which the Church would be so impoverished as to be easy prey to idolatry. In the Old Testament faith is a gift to a people living amidst the basic idolatries of mankind. There God reveals Himself as the sole saviour against the multitude of rival claims to knowledge, security, and wisdom in ancient and respected religious cultures. The Old Testament's radical devaluation of all earthly powers breaks the natural man's easy adjustment to the "natural" order, including particularly his adjustment by the institutional means of cult and state which so easily become the vital links between earth and heaven. In this sense it can be

---

Sigmund Mowinckel, *He That Cometh* (New York: Abingdon Press [1954?]), Chap. VII; I. Engnell, "The Ebed Yahweh Songs and the Suffering Messiah in 'Deutero-Isaiah,'" *Bulletin of the John Rylands Library,* Vol. XXXI (1948), pp. 3 ff.; and C. R. North, *The Suffering Servant in Deutero-Isaiah* (London: Oxford University Press, 1948), especially Chap. X. For a defense of the more usual view in modern scholarship, see H. H. Rowley, *The Servant of the Lord and Other Essays* (London: Lutterworth Press, 1952), Chaps. I and II; James Muilenburg, *Interpreter's Bible,* Vol. 5 (New York: Abingdon Press, 1956), pp. 406–14; and the writer, *ibid.,* Vol. I (New York: Abingdon Press, 1952), pp. 373–74; *The Old Testament Against Its Environment* (London: SCM Press, 1950), pp. 60–68.

claimed that the Old Testament is the Church's bulwark against the "natural" powers that invade and weaken, where they do not destroy, her faith.[6]

For certain other facets of the Old Testament's revelation of God we may point to the theological inferences drawn from or seen to compose the real meaning of the event of the Exodus. In the earliest period of the nation's life in Palestine the spring and fall nature festivals had been "historicized" as celebrations of God's act of deliverance from Egyptian slavery and His leading and feeding of Israel in "the great and terrible wilderness." With this theme is associated the conquest of Canaan, understood, not as Israel's victory, but God's gift of a land to the dispossessed who were outside the protection of law. The sacraments of worship were commemorations of events which had been interpreted as the gracious deeds of God. The events had created the community, and their celebration served the purpose of community renewal. The pagan festival was by contrast an acted rite or cultic drama, in which the primordial security in nature was achieved and the basic rhythm of nature on which life is dependent was continued. The drama was not primarily a celebration but a rite which recreated the event of nature and secured again its benefits. It had its setting in magic and dealt with the elemental forces of life, reproduction, and death in nature. The Old Testament sacrament by contrast centered in particular events in history and brought community renewal through meditation on God's action, common worship, and renewal of commitment. This is surely the soil in which the sacrament of the Lord's Supper is to be understood, though in the history of its interpretation and celebration there would appear to be a poorly adjusted conflict between the two basic conceptions to which allusion has been made.

In any case, the celebration of the Lordship of God by historical narration meant ultimately that the Bible as a religious literature would center, not in ritualistic, spiritual, or ethical teachings, but in the history of a people who were on the crossroads of the world in the first great era of imperialism. Theology thus produced an interest in history and in historical tradition, until even the creation is represented as simply the beginning of historical time and

[6] Cf. The writer's article on this topic in *International Review of Missions,* Vol. XL (1951), pp. 265–76; and his *God Who Acts* (*Studies in Biblical Theology,* No. 8; London: SCM Press, 1952), Chap. I.

of the Lordship of God over time. Furthermore, the association of God with particular events in time and place brought meaning into history and resistance to every attempt to convert the faith into a philosophy. Time thus is more than a cyclical or rhythmic framework of human existence; it is more akin to purpose in history. When Jesus affirms according to Mark 1:14 that "the time is fulfilled and the kingdom of God is at hand," he is speaking of the salvation of God which is being effected in history, which began with Abraham and is "filled full," completed, in Christ. The canonical "time" of God's purpose is surely the setting of the incarnation. God in Christ is an event in history, in "time" and space. He is an *action* of God, and to emphasize the ontological aspects of the divinity of Christ at the expense of his active, functional relation to God and to God's "time" or purpose in time, is surely in some measure to miss the point.

One may suggest, therefore, that it is the Old Testament's presentation of the nature of God's self-revelation which, on the one hand, keeps the eye focused on what is central in the Incarnation, and, on the other, reveals with clarity the setting of the Church's mission. God's active Lordship over His creation, over all "times" and places, His actively prosecuted claim to sovereignty over all men—this is the only setting in which the Church's mission and the individual Christian's vocation in the world is meaningful. In a sense it is because God has a mission and has placed Christ at the center of it that the Church exists at all or that the question of the Church's mission is even raised. The Old Testament basis for the Christian mission must surely center, then, in its doctrine of God, in its revelation of the nature of the first Person of the Trinity and of the very ground of the Trinity itself. This is the God who is determined to be *Lord,* and not simply the philosophical Absolute or First Cause or the Ineffable in whom we are absorbed and "saved" *from* history.

Central to God's action in history is His election, His choosing, His formation and commissioning of a new community: "I will be your God, and you shall be my people." The language whereby the meaning of this election was made clear was that of Covenant, a particular type of treaty well-known in ancient times. God's action was a free, unmerited gift which drew Israel to Him, as one is indeed drawn to a gracious Giver. The bond between God and people was thus established in a gracious act which pulled from the recipients a gracious response, or, where the response was otherwise, gave rise to feelings of guilt, infidelity, betrayal of personal relationship. The language which gave expression to this bond, and the requirement of fidelity implicit within it, was adapted from a certain type of covenant in the realm of international law, that is, from vassal treaties of the second millennium B.C.[7] In this form God appears not as a king among kings, but as a suzerain, a "King of kings and Lord of lords," who enters a special relationship with His vassal. He identifies himself to the vassal as one whose gracious acts should lead the vassal to keep the covenant, not because of legal necessity, but because he wishes to be gracious in return. The rights or prerogatives of the suzerain are then specified, and the vassal is left free to order his own life within the framework which the prerogatives of the Ruler specified. Thus in the Biblical text the Ten Commandments specify the will of the Lord, the elemental bounds within which the people of the Lord must live. These commandments alone are called the "Words" of God and considered to be direct revelation. All other laws are mediated; they are the "ordinances" (*mishpatim*), most of which we know to have arisen in judicial decisions which have been preserved to become precedents. A clear distinction thus exists between the Decalogue and all other laws of a mediated nature. The former may be described as the legal policy of the new community, within which it is free to order its life by the adoption of a variety of specific legal procedures ("ordinances"). Old Testament law was never meant to be constitutional law; the original Mosaic covenant was an order of freedom, freedom to live within the boundaries determined by the Lord, which were a denial of the right to serve other lords and the requirement of internal peace within the community. Judaism arose in the postexilic period as a reform movement based on the collection of the variety of legal materials in an atmosphere of delayed eschatology, and their interpretation as the *Law* or constitution within which every step was to receive regulation. In the New Testament Jesus and Paul revert to the older Israelite conception of the Covenant, jumping over as it were the Judaistic reformulation.

The political symbol of the ruler in special treaty with his people

[7] See George E. Mendenhall, *Law and Covenant in Israel and the Ancient Near East* (Pittsburgh: Biblical Colloquium, 1955; reprinted from *The Biblical Archaeologist,* Vol. XVII [1954], pp. 26–76).

stands behind the Old Testament's confessions of faith and provides the structure of the language of the faith. In this context "truth" is not primarily an idea or ideal, but an acknowledgment of God's covenanted claim upon us, a fidelity in commitment and action so that mind and will function together under a commission or vocation. God as Ruler in the form of commanding general is He who would make the world His kingdom, and the convolutions of history are to be understood in this light. God the Ruler as Judge, setting exterior standards of right to which men and nations are responsible, is the dominant form under which He is presented in prophecy. As the Lord, Shepherd, and Father of His people, God is also their Saviour, their Rock and Fortress, He who blesses and forgives.

In other words, the covenant language is wholly symbolic, and truth is understood within the frame of reference that language provides. Here again the very language of the faith prevents its complete conversion into a philosophy, an ethical system, a sacramentalism, or a mysticism. It is held within history, and the truth it envisages is not, therefore, the same truth which another religion with a totally different symbolic apperception of reality may seek or promise. This is one way of affirming that the way to Christ must be through the faith of Abraham, not through the other religions. While it may be held that the Biblical language must be continually translated into the tongues of the contemporary world, yet that language itself sets limits to these attempts, creates tensions, and causes a return to Scripture before a new attempt is made. The basic Old Testament symbols of the active sovereignty or kingship of God and His fatherhood over His people appear to be so integral to the Christian understanding of truth that they can never permanently be set aside. Theologically, it may be said that God has chosen to reveal Himself within these historical forms, that while He Himself is independent of them, He has nevertheless given Himself thus to us and does not intend that we shall really know Him in the Church by means of the nonhistorical, nontemporal, nonsymbolic. While a tension exists between the real and the symbol, we are only given the latter, and for Biblical man this was clearly sufficient as the guide to life.

Finally, we have only the space to mention the fact that the Exodus gave rise to a language which was central to the Bible as a whole: for example, "deliver," "redeem," "salvation," "bring out," "lead forth," "mighty acts," "signs and wonders," and the like. The event became a nucleus around which a whole cluster of meanings adhered which influenced the nature of prayer and piety, and which always kept before the worshiping community the direction of God's action and the nature of His righteousness. The prayers of Israel, as a result, were firmly rooted in the great variety of life's problems, tragedy, sin, frustration. God's saving action in the past became the ground of hope and trust that salvation could be known as a present experience in history, and not solely as a future event beyond current history, as was the case in later Jewish apocalypticism. This element in the Israelite's faith in the living God, as much as any other, is the soil which made possible the New Testament's reinterpretation of Judaism's apocalyptic hope so that in Christ it could become both "here" and "not yet." Christianity in this sense was able to rescue the hope of the Jews from the realm of historical embarrassment and to reform it as the context of the Church's life.

The righteousness of God, furthermore, was seen to be the ultimate power at work in history to deliver or to save the weak, the oppressed, the poor, the enslaved, the dispossessed. It is not a distributive justice, but a zealous action on behalf of the weak, a redemptive action for earth's needy, regardless of their social status. Here, then, was the ground of hope in history, that what is now present is not what shall be, that we can lift up our hearts to the Lord who alone gives power to the faint and makes them mount up with wings like eagles. And as God is righteous, so His people are to be righteous. This meant that weakness and poverty were not to be made into a source of profit by the strong (cf. Ex. 22:25–27 in the earliest Israelite teaching collection of legal precedents). The commandments to love God and neighbor (Deut. 6:5; Lev. 19:18) had their setting originally in this type of legal and community context. The meaning of economic life was not profit, but the love and service of the neighbor as our obedience to the Lord.

The special concern for the poor was an integral part of the earliest legal corpora in Israel, and furnished part of the background for the prophetic announcement of God's controversy with Israel for her failure to maintain a just order. The prophetic proclamation of God's judgment furnished the means whereby Israel's destruction at the hands of Mesopotamian imperialism was understood. Central to the Bible is God's creation of a new community in which the individual finds his true humanity.[8] The ethic of this community, therefore, is not merely the private affair of individuals but is at the same time a social ethic for which the community as a whole bears responsibility. And there will be no peace where the Lord is disobeyed. The Old Testament's proclamation of the righteousness of God, of the community's responsibility for obedience as a community, of history as God's struggle, not only with the nations, but with his Chosen People for unrighteousness—all this is surely a vital and integral part of the Church's Gospel and self-understanding, of its view of history, of its understanding of man, and of its mission in the world. Could it be said that one of the difficulties of the missionary effort in the past has been the temptation to view the Gospel as a matter of individual conversion by proclamation and education, while the corporate aspects of the Church's life were largely left unexamined, only to become identified with a particular secular ethos in the Western world?

Other aspects of Old Testament theology, including especially its anthropology, are here omitted for lack of space, and some readers may feel them more important than what is here written. Yet the theocentric emphasis, which alone can give adequate theological meaning to the canon of Scripture, seems to me to be the real setting of the Church's mission, and without it there would be no mission. If this is true, then the Old Testament's revelation of the God who is the Father of Jesus Christ is a vital part of the Scriptural basis for the Church's mission. That basis is not primarily an injunction to the Church to preach the Gospel to the world, though this is certainly part of it. Instead it is the doctrine of God, the God who Himself is the mission.[9]

[8] This is the central thesis of the writer's monograph, prepared with the aid of an ecumenical committee in Chicago, *The Biblical Doctrine of Man in Society, op. cit.*

[9] See further Emil Brunner, *Die Unentbehrlichkeit des Alten Testamentes für die missionierende Kirche* (*Basler Missionsstudien,* No. 12; Stuttgart und Basel: Evang. Missionsverlag, 1934). The theme of this brief essay is as follows: "The Church stands or falls with the Old Testament, as it likewise stands or falls with Jesus Christ. Without the Old Testament there is no Jesus Christ. . . . Jesus takes form not only on Palestinian, but on Old Testament soil. . . . The Old Testament is related to the New Testament as is the beginning of a sentence to the end. Only the whole sentence, with

III

In spite of what has here been said, however, it is not assumed that numerous questions do not remain. Indeed, the Old Testament has always been and will always remain something of a problem to the Church, and certainly to the Church's mission. While at any one period there have been various levels of misunderstanding in the interpretation of the Old Testament, the question is nevertheless posed as to whether the *essential* offenses of the literature must not be considered as an integral part of the Gospel's offense in the world.

The most common impression concerning the Old Testament is that for the Word of God it is a very inadequate book, with blood on so many of its pages and with faulty moral examples so numerous as to enable Christians by its means to excuse almost any action they may care to take. This problem is particularly acute, however, for those who expect of Scripture primarily a series of ideals, or who impose upon it a doctrine of inspiration which God did not design it to bear. If the Old Testament proclaims God's sole Lordship over history and His role as the righteous redeemer of history, then one would expect history to be portrayed as it is, with heightened apprehension of its real nature, rather than simply as in ideal one would like it to be. Here all men stand revealed as they are, the object of both God's judgment and salvation. Sin is here taken so seriously that wherever God touches it, blood is understood to flow. This is true when men rebel against God, when God punishes by holding men accountable for their acts, when God's representative or elect fulfills his (or its) mission in the world, or even when rites of atonement are undertaken. Evil is so serious a matter that blood, understood as the seat of life, must be spilled both because of it and in atonement for it.

One phase of this problem which commonly is thought to be most acute is the Conquest of Canaan. Here God is presented as

---

beginning and end, gives the sense." Brunner then expounds his thesis by means of the Old Testament offices of prophet, king, and priest. Jesus as the Christ is the Word of God, the King in whom God's kingdom is come, and the one in whom the right offering by the right priest is brought. The message of the cross is completely incomprehensible apart from the Old Testament. Indeed, the revelation of the love of God in Christ could only be mystically-sentimentally or esthetically grasped, apart from the Old Testament.

the Commanding General of a war of conquest. Two things in particular may be noted. One is that "the wars of Yahweh" (in the Conquest) are interpreted within the institution of Holy War, a particular institution of the premonarchial days of Israel. It was a part of that history, and, one might say, an institution which God used to gain His historical ends. If God is Lord of history, one cannot assume that He withdraws when the conflicts of men become bloody. Hence the Lordship of God is even here to be affirmed, and at the same time the context of historical evil in which that Lordship is seen to be at work by mediate means, using people as they are to effect His ends. God's election does not deliver His servant from history, nor even, it appears, from the ambiguities in all historical action. The authority of the Bible lies primarily in its truth about God, but its focus in history prevents that authority from being transferred to absolutize anything in the human scene, including even His elect people's testimony to Him.

Still another area of difficulty which Christians have encountered in the Old Testament is the problem of the laws and the Law. Is not the Old Covenant filled with so many laws as to make it a religion of works, which in Christ is set aside for freedom under grace? Or as Protestant oxthodoxy was at one time inclined to say: Is not the Old Covenant the proclamation of the law of God which led men to despair and thus prepared them for the proffer of grace in Jesus Christ? The interpretation of the Old Testament as a legal document which stands at the opposite pole from the New Testament is a misunderstanding, derived particularly from the books of Romans and Galatians. Yet these epistles of the Apostle Paul are to be understood as polemic against Judaism, not as an exposition of the relation of the Old to the New Testament. As already pointed out, the Pentateuchal laws were the legal procedures adopted by a people who were living within the covenant. The rubric "ordinances," given them, and the fact that they were mediated, was Israel's way of indicating the difference existing between them and the Decalogue. The latter alone was the "Words" of God. With this distinction clearly in evidence between legal policy and procedures, it can further be said that the whole structure was given Israel, not to lead her to despair, but as a guide to life for a people whom God had already saved and redeemed. It is precisely the genius of the original Mosaic covenant that obligation was tied to the recital of God's saving acts, that *didache* (teaching) was seen to follow from *kerygma* (proclamation), that obedience was placed within the context of response to gracious, redeeming activity. Judaism, on the other hand, created from the variety of scattered legal materials a constitution, so that covenant became the gift of the Law and obedience to that constitution. It can thus be argued that Paul's attack on the Judaism of his time was in a sense a reformulation in Christ of the original intention of God in Israel. In any event, Law and Gospel cannot be considered an adequate formula for the understanding of the relation between the Testaments, because it falsifies the revelation of God to Israel.

Finally, it is often claimed that the exclusivism of the Old Testament's claim, based upon the doctrine of God's jealousy and wrath, makes it difficult for the Church to enter a viable relationship with people of other religions. We live in an age of tolerance, when it is necessary for mankind to live together without undue friction, and it is being claimed that the Christian religion is not a help but a hindrance to mutual understanding. Its exclusive claims and its lack of tolerance, which appear to divide it into many camps, each in competition with the others, hardly furnish a setting for the unifying of mankind. Modern Christianity in the multiplicity of its missionary forms [10] is an enemy to itself, and, more important, to the achievement of one world.

From one perspective, namely the sectarianism of the churches, the charge against the Christian mission is surely true. The churches as institutions have gone far to absolutize their external forms, so that the element of exclusivism in the Gospel, which belongs to God alone, is transferred to externals. On the other hand, there is adequate evidence that major Christian groups understand full well the prophetic indictment against all religious forms and piety which are anchored anywhere but in God Himself. Hence the contemporary churches are now suffering and must expect to suffer the judgment of God. Among the evidences of this is the very fact that their evangelizing efforts do not meet with more success, and

[10] For example, before the Second World War there were some ten American denominations sponsoring missionaries in Japan. By 1959 there were eighty-five. Sixty per cent of the missionaries thus sent were working outside the bounds of established indigenous churches. (Data supplied by T. F. Romig, Secretary for Personnel, Ecumenical Mission and Relations, United Presbyterian Church in the U.S.A.)

that the figure of Jesus Christ in Scripture is more respected universally than the Church's attempts to preach and to teach him. The Church's mission has always been more hampered by the churches themselves than by Biblical difficulties.

At a deeper level, however, there can be no doubt that the Biblical witness demands an exclusivism of faith, and that particularly so when the God and Father of Jesus Christ is known as the God before whom all other gods are idols. The absolute claims to sovereignty on God's part, His determination to be God and God alone, surely set limits on the tolerance of Christians in matters of syncretism, that is, in the reinterpretation of Biblical faith in such manner as to relieve the tension between it and another religion. Yet it is the radical Lordship of God which for the Christian actually makes possible the breaching of the barriers which divide the world. The reason is that the Christian is (ideally) created by God as a humble person who faces another human being as a brother in need like himself, not as a subject to be proselytized. He knows that he cannot make converts; only God himself can do that. He must share what has been given him, but it is God who validates it. He is a servant of God to the needy, not an imperialist or a righteous patriarch who with gracious condescension assists the unfortunate. He is one also who has a keen eye to discern God's work by the Holy Spirit, knowing that the charisma of God cannot always be channeled into the organizational bounds in which he has been reared. Indeed, at a given moment in history it may not be God's will to enlarge the numbers of converts, but possibly instead to reform another religion from within, and that especially where no community of Christians exists to replace an old one being broken.

The Biblical View of Man in His Religion

BY JOHANNES BLAUW

During the past three decades we have become more and more aware of the fact that it is impossible to speak of "the Biblical view of religions." The words "religion" and "religious," in the true sense, do not occur in the Bible, nor does any equivalent word appear. This may be, on the one hand, an indication that the Bible is not at all interested in religious systems and ideas as such. On the other hand it may be a reflection of the fact that the religious world in Biblical times was rather uniform in outlook and intention, despite local differences.

When speaking about the Biblical view of man, we are stressing here the fact that the Bible is interested in man; man in his concreteness as a living being on earth. But what about the addition of the phrase "in his religion"? Is it possible to speak about religion *in abstracto?* Professor Heinrich Frick reminded us some years ago that "religion is real only in religions." [1] In saying this he warned us not to operate with ideas, but only with realities. Undoubtedly he was right, and if I myself had chosen the title of this short essay, I would rather either have chosen an expression other than "in his religion," or have simply crossed it out.

"In his religion," in this connection, cannot mean anything but

[1] Heinrich Frick, *Vergleichende Religionswissenschaft* (Berlin und Leipzig: Walter de Gruyter, 1928), p. 62. "Religion ist wirklich nur in Religionen."

a more precise definition of man. A man without "religion" is a contradiction in itself. In his "religion" man gives account of his relation to God. His religion is reaction upon the (real or pretended) revelation of God. Man is "uncurably religious" because his relation to God belongs to the very essence of man himself. Man is only man as man-before-God.

Man before God

The first and most fundamental Biblical view of man is found in the first chapters of Genesis. Here the well-known words of Genesis 1:26–27 are of far-reaching importance, for they give us the clue to the whole story of man and mankind. The two features of primary importance are:

(a) Man is a creature, completely dependent upon his Creator like all other creatures, and yet at the same time entirely different from all other creatures. He is not the top of a creation pyramid, but a creation *sui generis,* bearing a secret that is only *his* secret.

(b) Man's secret is that he is created "in our image, after our likeness." This expression means (*a parte Dei*) that man is a reflection of God, a mirror, *speculum Dei;* and (*a parte hominis*) that man is a follower of God, called to have dominion over every living thing.

There is something of the glory and majesty (*kabood*) of God upon man, yet man is not, definitely not, a god himself, but a creature. This does not mean that there is a "dialectical" relation with God. Being a creature is not the opposite or a weakening of man's likeness to God. On the contrary, his being a creature of God (like everything else) strengthens and qualifies his dignity as a reflection and follower of God. The one cannot be understood without the other.[2] Man is *creature before God* and only as such can he bear and maintain his humanity. One cannot cut off "the image of God" as if man could be God's creature *without* this image.[3] Man's humanity *is* his relation to God. This relation includes (but is not identical with) man's responsibility to respond when God addresses him.

It seems to me undeniable that the picture presented in Genesis

[2] Cf. man's dignity in Psalm 8 with man's humility in Psalm 131.

[3] It seems to me that the Old Testament picture was allowed to fade in older systematic theology when the doctrine of the image of God was restricted to the status *integritatis,* in opposition to Genesis 5:1 and 9:6.

1, which is a deep and sharply formulated credo, alludes to the deification of man and the world. This was common to old Eastern patterns of religion, and is common at all times to every man in the world. This fact becomes particularly clear in view of Genesis 3, where we find man's reaction to the high place and holy task (Gen. 2) given to him by his Lord and Creator and where there is a definite distinction made between God as Creator and Lord on the one hand, and man as creature and servant, bound to responsibility and obedient service, on the other hand.

In Genesis 3 the basic temptation for man is set forth as the temptation for man to exceed the bounds that have been set for him, which are precisely the bounds that indicate his humanity! He is so near to God as creature and yet not content to act as privileged creature. Instead, there is a (willingly accepted) suggestion that this privilege of being created as man in communication with and dependent upon God is not man's *treasure* but his *deficiency*. In the story of the serpent we are confronted with the temptation of man to bring God and himself to one common denominator. The servant of God becomes a magician, seizing the opportunity held out to him "to be as gods."

Even the disappointment from failure in this seizing act does not suffice to cure man from his intention to exceed his bounds, as is made clear by the words in Genesis 3:22, "then the Lord God said, 'Behold, the man has become like one of us, knowing good and evil.' " The dividing line between God and man has been ignored, and shall be ignored. Now the humanity of man is endangered (Gen. 4, 6, and 7) because the divinity of God is denied. "Every living thing"—the dominion of man—is influenced by man's disobedience, and even the waters of the flood do not cleanse men from the desire to be like gods and to act like gods in self-assertion (Gen. 11).

On the other hand—and this is even more important for the Biblical understanding of man in his religion—God does not give up His claim upon man. He, unlike man, is not unfaithful. Man remains for Him the image of God and His creature. In other words, man's view of God may have changed, but God's view of man does not change. When man gives up service, God does not give up man as His servant. When man no longer considers himself a creature, God nevertheless treats him as His creature. When man hides himself from the presence of the Lord, God does not hide

Himself from the presence of man. All this is guaranteed, after the flood, in the covenant that is established between God and man and every living creature (Gen. 9:12–13). The covenant remains intact even when man in a new combined effort exceeds his bounds (Gen. 11), despite the fact that the covenant takes the special form of a covenant with *one* man (Abram) and *one* nation (Gen. 12:1–3).

The history of Israel is the history of God's action by which and through which He maintains the covenant with man as *the creature before God*. This means: (a) that man as creature cannot have God or the world at his disposal, but instead is entirely dependent upon the Lord of creation; and (b) that man will always be connected with God, not because he desires to, or is able to enter into connection with God, but because God maintains man in his humanity, that is, in his "deficiency," which *remains* his "treasure" in the eyes of the Creator. This covenant, connection, and communication with God is man's "treasure" in the eyes of God. The will to save, on the part of the God of Israel, is one with His will to create.[4]

Israel before God

The Biblical view of man as *man before God* can only become really articulate if we turn to the Biblical view of God as the God of Israel. The following two examples illustrate that the kernel of the Biblical message concerning man is: to be *different* from and to be *connected* with God.

The first example comes from Exodus 3:7–14, where the name of Yahweh as the God of Israel is explained. "God said to Moses, 'I am who I am.' " This is not a name that has dogmatic or philosophical significance. It is not an ontological statement. It means: I shall be present as I shall be present (Martin Buber); or, I will manifest myself to be that which I will manifest myself to be (G. von Rad).

This means that God will never be absent or remote from Israel. But it also means that God is not "at the disposal" of Israel, for He is the free Lord who will never be rendered into the hands of men. Man cannot live without God, and he need not live without

[4] Cf. W. Eichrodt, *Das Menschenverständnis des Alten Testaments.* (Zürich: Zwingli-Verlag, 1947), pp. 27–34; especially p. 32: "So ist also der Erlöserwille des Gottes Israels mit seinen Schöpferwillen eins."

God; but he will never have the chance to use God merely to serve his human purposes, despite the fact that this is the hidden desire of the human heart.

In this respect it is surprising to compare the third chapters of Genesis and Exodus: the history of Israel is not to be a reiteration of the history of man in the Garden! The name of Israel's God is a proclamation against man's exceeding his creaturely bounds, and at the same time a promise of God's permanent presence. The name of God is in itself a protest against man's mastery of God for human purposes. And is *this* not one of the most common tendencies in human religion: to serve God in order to have God serve man and his desires? Certainly this was the case in the religions that confronted Israel.

The second example is found in 1 Samuel 15:1–26 (following 1 Samuel 13:1–14) where Saul is rejected as king of Israel because he was disobedient to the Lord of Israel. The declaration of Samuel (15:23) is important: "For rebellion is as the sin of divination, and stubbornness is as iniquity and idolatry." Saul did not refuse to serve God (verse 20), but he did refuse to serve God in the way that the prophet of God had showed to him. Serving God in your own way is serving God for your own purposes, and that is the same as the original sin.

It is significant that the examples chosen here indicate a turning point in history. On the eve of liberation from Egyptian slavery (Ex. 3) and on the threshold of the Davidic dynasty (1 Sam. 15) man is reminded of the fact that he cannot trade with God, he cannot dispose of Him as the first man in Genesis 3 tried to do.

In later times the Prophets unmasked man's religiosity as being not just a desire for God, but a desire to *have* a god, to possess him, to have him for their own, at their disposal. In the famous and somewhat cynical passage of Isaiah 44:6–23 we find a rather detailed description of the way in which man proceeds with his gods. We see him, the fabricator of idols, as a *pseudo creator* (of pseudo gods, verses 9–11); as a *religious zealot* who toils and moils in order to get the finest god he can produce according to his cultural and social status (verses 12–14); as a *blind self-deceiver* who makes a god from the unproductive leftovers of raw material (verses 15–20). Man, whose humanity exists in his relation to God, whose existence is and can only be an existence *coram Deo,* cannot live without a god before him. But the only real God is the living God who remains true to Israel even when she has been untrue to Him. The way in which God acts with and within Israel will prove to be the great démasque of the gods and the shame of those who trusted them (verses 21–23). We should also refer here to the significance of the second commandment which forbids the making of images of God, because it is forbidden to make use of the power of God, to "catch" Him in images.

Israel has been elected to represent the *true* man, the right man, in a world where men refuse to recognize God as God and to serve Him as His humble creatures. Israel represents the right man because she has been elected to serve the only true and living God. The failure of Israel, according to the Prophets, is a disgrace to Yahweh and therefore God shall save Israel and restore her to true service, because the world is to know that He is the Lord.

A picture of the real man, the real Israel, is given by the prophet Jeremiah in 31:33–34:

> "I will put my law within them, and I will write it upon their hearts; and I will be their God, and they shall be my people. And no longer shall each man teach his neighbor and each his brother, saying, 'Know the Lord,' for they shall all know me, from the least of them to the greatest, says the Lord; for I will forgive their iniquity, and I will remember their sin no more."

This is the full counterpart to man's sinful longing: "Make us gods who shall go before us" (Ex. 32:23).

Another picture, still more penetrating, is given in the so-called songs of the servant of the Lord, who both represents and replaces Israel. He represents the right Israel and therefore also the right man. In him the Biblical view of man culminates (Is. 42:1–7, 49:1–7, 50:4–11, 52:13, 53:12). It is also the culmination of the expectation of the Messiah. The mystery of the Lord's servant is an indication that the mystery of man remains veiled until the real man, the "son of man" according to another prophecy (Dan. 7:13–14), will appear.

The Man Jesus

There is no doubt that Jesus regarded man in the same way as the Scriptures of the Old Testament to which he referred so often. Man, for Jesus too, was man only in relation to God. The name "sinner" is an indication that man is man-before-God, and the proclamation of the kingdom of God means that man stands over against his King and Judge.[5] Man as creature has not fulfilled his duty and will be judged unless he repents and turns to him who proclaims the new kingdom of God.[6]

Certainly Jesus restricted himself and ordered his disciples to restrict themselves to the lost sheep of the house of Israel (Mt. 10:6), in accordance with the "oikonomia tou mysteriou" (Eph. 3:9) which was the hidden policy of God revealed in Christ. But Christ "knew all men and needed no one to bear witness of man; for he himself knew what was in man" (Jn. 2:25). For him, man was both the creature who could not escape God and the one who yet was always trying to escape obedience to God. Man was pretending a righteousness that was in fact defective. Over against this, Christ is the right man, the man of Jeremiah 31 and the Servant of the Lord.

Man before Christ

The writers of the New Testament did not view man in general terms, but only in connection with the Gospel of Christ. There is no "general anthropology" in the New Testament. There is only man in the concrete situation of being confronted with Jesus Christ. There are very few references to man "in his religion." One of them is Romans 1:18–32 where we are reminded of Genesis 3. Men can know God because God has shown Himself to them (verse 19), and they do know Him (verse 20), but they suppress the knowledge of Him with imaginations that cause their foolish hearts to be darkened (verse 21). The only proper response on the part of men to that which had been shown to them, would have been praise and thanksgiving to God for His eternal power and deity (verse 20). Instead, they became futile in their thinking, preferring their imaginations to reality, and thereby living as fools in an imaginative world where the creature takes the place of the Creator (verses 22 and 23). Since the creature is no longer understood as creature, the powers inherent in creation gain dominion over man, who originally was destined to dominate these powers (verses 24–25). God, seeing His honor perverted by dishonor, gave men

[5] Werner Georg Kümmel, *Das Bild des Menschen im Neuen Testament* (Zürich: Zwingli-Verlag, 1948), p. 12.

[6] Werner Georg Kümmel, *Verheiszung und Erfüllung* (Zürich: Zwingli-Verlag, 1950), p. 86.

up to impurity, dishonorable passions, and a base mind (verses 24, 26, 28).

We see here the darkest picture possible of man. It does not mean that all men come to such a state, but it is an illustration of what is meant by "the wrath of God is revealed from heaven against all ungodliness and wickedness of men who by their wickedness suppress the truth" (verse 18). It shows the need of man for the Gospel of Christ as the power of God for salvation (verse 16). Certainly it is possible to say other things about man, such as in Romans 2:13–16, which suggests that every man, whether he be Jew or Gentile, knows the difference between good and evil and will be judged according to this knowledge. But here too stress is laid on the fact that God will judge the secrets of men by Jesus Christ (verse 16) and that all men are sinners. This is not a view of man that can or will be accepted by everyone. It can only be accepted before Christ. In and through him it becomes clear that man is a sinner, that he lives with his imaginations, that he worships and serves the creature more than the Creator. In this connection it is important to notice that in Romans 1:18–32, and even more in Romans 3:23, is the suggestion that man has lost the image of God; a suggestion that was never made in the Old Testament.[7] Here "he abolishes the first in order to establish the second" (Hebrews 10:9), which is the new man in Christ (cf. Eph. 4:24). "In thy light do we see light" (Ps. 36:9); "I have come as light into the world, that whoever believes in me may not remain in darkness" (Jn. 12:46).

Positive or Negative?

Is not this Biblical view of man too hard and one-sided? Are there not still other passages in the Bible that correct the picture given thus far? [8] I know of no more positive statement concerning man than the statement that he is the image and servant of God. I know of no more negative statement than the statement that he refuses to be a servant and wishes "to be as gods" or to use God (or rather gods) for his own ends. I know of no more exciting

[7] Cf. Genesis 5:1, 9:6, and Psalms 8:5.

[8] The often quoted words of Malachi 1:11 are a negative judgment of Israel rather than a positive judgment of the nations. Nevertheless, the positive way in which this negative judgment is stated should not be underestimated.

message than the message that in Christ the real man and the real relation with God has been restored. These are the realities in the Biblical view of man, over against which it is only a regression to speak about "human possibilities." In my opinion the Bible is not interested in questions like "continuity or discontinuity." [9] The great continuity is the continuity of God's love for man, revealed first in Israel and then in Jesus Christ. The great discontinuity is man's permanent striving to *have* a god rather than to *serve* God; to claim independence when he is completely dependent. The light which the Bible throws on man in his religion, or religiosity, penetrates deeply into the hiding places of human existence.

It is only in the light of this Biblical view of man that we can try to approach the great religions of men for the encounter of the Gospel and the religions. What this means for a theological criticism of these religions can only be stated here in the form of several theses, which may be too apodictic after such brief analysis of the position of man.

1. A theological criticism of religion(s) must take into account that man in his religion is the man who—for better or for worse—is related to God. Religion is and religions are always signs and confessions of this undeniable fact. Therefore it is important for us to have an understanding of the religions in order that we may be able to *hear* in them the answer of men to God's question, "Man, where art thou?" The answers given in the various religions are always *human* answers, and we must seek to *understand* these answers if we are to understand the man in and behind the religions.

2. In a sense we can say that religions are the result of the fact that God maintains man as man, in His image and as dependent creature. God gives men the opportunity to create and formulate their own answers. He does not interfere as He did with Abraham, Israel, and the Christian Church. He allows all nations, as in times past, to walk in their own ways (Acts 14:16) and to do their own thinking.[10]

3. It is only in the light of Jesus Christ and in the power of the Holy Spirit that the ways of men in their religions are seen to be *imaginations.*

[9] Cf. the famous debate at the Tambaram, Madras Meeting of the International Missionary Council in 1938.

[10] Romans 1:21—"dialogismoi": R.S.V.—"thinking"; K.J.V.—"imaginations"; Luther—"poetry."

4. Only Jesus Christ is from above. We are all men saved or to be saved by him, and to be saved time and again from our imaginations. "Christian" imaginations are seven times worse than other religious imaginations (Mt. 12:43–45). Therefore it is the privilege of Christ and his Spirit to convince man and the world of sin and judgment (Jn. 16:8–11). We are his messengers and must remain faithful to him and his message. We remember his words, "I did not come to judge the world but to save the world." (Jn. 12:47). To help people discover the deep and hidden process of thinking in the light of the Gospel means to help a neighbor who is in exactly the same position as we are; as sinners who fall short of the glory of God (Rom. 3:23). Only in solidarity with man can we give him the bread of life and be identified as ambassadors of Christ.

5. While we may agree that the Bible does not know about and is not interested in religious systems as such, we must not draw the false conclusion that the Bible is interested only in "man" and not in "his religion." The way in which many parts of the Old and New Testaments are formulated shows a vivid interest in, and often a reflection upon, *the religious position of man.* This is not because his position is considered either to be right or wrong, but simply because man can hear the Gospel only in terms of his own religious position. Therefore it is important to have a real knowledge of the religions of man, not only because of general interest, but in order better to be able to articulate the Word of God which is for all men, as the Word of God for *this* man in his particular religious position.[11]

6. By going as far as possible with man into his religious home, its atmosphere and vocabulary, perhaps the way may be opened for a new understanding both of "this religion" and "this gospel." It is only through the Church gathered out of all nations that "the manifold wisdom of God might now be made known to the principalities and powers in the heavenly places" (Eph. 3:10).

7. In full recognition of the Biblical view of man as sinner against God, it is necessary to consider at greater length than has been possible here the question whether or not the statement of St. Paul in Colossians 1:15–20, concerning the reconciliation of

[11] Consider, for instance, the use of the term *kyrios* for Jesus Christ, which was taken from the idiom of the religion(s) in New Testament times; and the use St. Paul makes of Stoic terms and ideas, such as in his Areopagus speech.

all things to Christ, has any significance for the religions. I would venture only to put it as a question: Do we not fall short of the glory of Jesus Christ if we exclude from "all things" mentioned in Colossians 1:20 the extremely rich heritage of the manifold religions by assuming that they *cannot* be reconciled to him? Or are we, in suggesting this question, already on the way (the old way of Genesis 3 and Romans 1) toward exchanging "the excellency of the knowledge of Christ Jesus our Lord for things which are to be counted as dung"? (Cf. Phil. 3:8 K.J.V.) If this be the case: *pereat mundus, vivat Rex Iudaeorum!* [12]

[12] From the extensive literature on Biblical anthropology see especially: Joachim Jeremias, "anthropos" in *Theologisches Wörterbuch zum Neuen Testament,* begr. v. G. Kittel, hg. v. G. Friedrich, I, p. 365 ff.; the monographs by Eichrodt and Kümmel already mentioned above; *Das Menschenbild im Lichte des Evangeliums: Festschrift Emil Brunner* (Zürich: Zwingli-Verlag, 1950); Reinhold Niebuhr, *The Nature and Destiny of Man* (2 vols.; New York: Charles Scribner's Sons, 1941, 1943); Bertil Gärtner, *The Areopagus Speech and Natural Revelation,* translated by Carolyn Hannay King (Uppsala: Gleerup, 1955).

Eschatology and Missions in the New Testament *

BY OSCAR CULLMANN

Does the expectation of the end paralyze the missionary impulse? Does it divert our attention from the task of preaching the Gospel here and now? It is sometimes said that this "hope" has an inhibiting influence upon Christian action; is this true? To give an affirmative answer to these questions would mean that "missions" —on the grand scale—would have been possible only because the eschatological hope had gradually faded. In point of fact, the missionary enterprise of the Church is often represented as a kind of "second best"—something which has been substituted for the unrealized hope of the kingdom of God. If this were true, then the Church has carried on its mission because it has been obliged to renounce eschatology.

Such ideas are due to a mistaken conception of early Christian eschatology. It is of course true that in the early Church there was a tendency to distort the Christian hope, which diverted the attention of Christian people from the sphere of present duty, as for instance at Thessalonica, in the time of Paul, and one hundred years later, in Asia Minor, in Montanism. But in the New Testament itself this tendency was explicitly rejected and condemned as heretical. The genuine primitive Christian hope does not paralyze Christian action in the world. On the contrary, the proclamation of

* Translated by Miss Olive Wyon.

the Christian Gospel in the missionary enterprise is a characteristic form of such action, since it expresses the belief that "missions" are an essential element in the eschatological divine plan of salvation. The missionary work of the Church is the eschatological foretaste of the kingdom of God, and the Biblical hope of the "end" constitutes the keenest incentive to action.

It is the purpose of this article to show that this thought can be traced throughout the New Testament, and is deeply rooted in New Testament eschatology.

The close relation between Christian action and the expectation of the end comes out in two prominent characteristics of New Testament eschatology: (a) we do not know when the end will come; (b) although the end lies in the future, the present is already part of the period which begins with the death and resurrection of Christ.

(a) This first point is connected with the fact that the very heart of Biblical eschatology is its emphasis upon the divine omnipotence. Nowhere is this stressed more strongly than in the doctrine of creation and in the eschatological hope. Eschatology is the new creation. The last day will appear at God's command, uttered with the same divine authority as the primal word: "Let there be light!" Both are the sovereign act of God. This means, however, that no human effort or knowledge will enable us to ascertain when the kingdom of God will come.

We cannot achieve the coming of the kingdom of God by our own action: *we* cannot "bring in" the kingdom of God. The whole witness of the New Testament is so clear on this point that no further proof is needed. Then does this mean that all that is required from us, in response to the eschatological hope, is a passive attitude and not a stimulus to action? By no means! For it is only those who are firmly convinced that the kingdom comes from God who are given the courage to work here and now, whether success or failure be their portion. If we believed that the coming of the kingdom depended on us, when confronted by failure we would inevitably despair. But we can work joyfully and courageously, not in order to "hasten" the coming of the kingdom, but because we know that the kingdom comes from God.

On the other hand, no human effort will enable us to know when the kingdom of God will come. At this point, even Jesus himself, during his life on earth, had to confess: "But of that day or that hour no one knows, not even the angels in heaven, nor the Son, but only the Father" (Mk. 13:32). It is very significant that the New Testament emphasizes this point: that the Son does not know when the kingdom will come, when it lays so much stress on the fact that no one knows the Father "except the Son . . ." (Mt. 11:27). This ignorance of the "day and the hour" is, however, a spur to Christian action, to "watchfulness": "Watch therefore, for you do not know on what day your Lord is coming" (Mt. 24:42). We are in the position of the householder who does not know when the thief will come (Lk. 12:39), or in that of the bridesmaids who do not know when the bridegroom will come, and must therefore keep their lamps trimmed and burning all night long (Mt. 25:1 ff.). It is true, of course, that Jesus expects his death and resurrection to be of decisive significance for the fulfillment of God's purpose, for the end he has in view; and indeed, since the first Easter it has been a fundamental conviction of the Church that the end has already been "introduced" by this fundamental saving event. But the Church is also aware that the "new creation" has not yet been realized. Thus, for the Church, seen in the light of the Resurrection, it is true that "the day of the Lord will come like a thief in the night" (1 Thess. 5:2); hence she too must "watch" and "not sleep, as others do." Because the day of the Lord is always near, there should be no feverish agitation about its coming, as though the "time" mattered to us; on the other hand, it is the duty of every Christian to "watch," sustained by hope.

(b) This brings us to the second characteristic of New Testament eschatology, which is indeed the basis of Christian action. The end is not yet, it is true, but since the Resurrection has taken place we know that the decisive event leading to the end has already happened. The end may seem to be delayed, but this should cause no disappointment, doubt, or despondency. When faith in the Resurrection is strong, it breeds a firm conviction that the royal sovereignty of Christ has already begun, and that it will be exercised for a period of unknown length until Christ "delivers the kingdom to God the Father after destroying every rule and every authority and power" (1 Cor. 15:24). Thus it is a mistake to think that eschatology has nothing to do with the present day, and, therefore, that it has a paralyzing effect upon Christian action. Indeed, it is rather the other way round, because the kingdom of God has actually come nearer, with Christ, than would have been the case if all had been left to the usual course of events. From the chronological point of view, something has happened: the present "age" has taken a great leap forward. We are reminded that God is Lord of time. We have entered the final phase of this "age," which will end with the return of Christ.

One eschatological element has, however, already been realized, which points clearly to the fact that we are already living in and from the end, although the end itself still has to come: the Holy Spirit. He belongs to the future, for God has given us "his Spirit in our hearts as a guarantee" (2 Cor. 1:22); we have "the first fruits of the Spirit" (Rom. 8:23). The miracle of Pentecost was rightly interpreted by Peter (Acts 2:17 ff.) when he appealed to the passage in the prophet Joel: "And in the last days it shall be, God declares, that I will pour out my Spirit upon all flesh." This, however, is more than a foretaste; the Spirit is already part of the fulfillment. The risen Lord himself points this out when his disciples ask him when the kingdom will come (Acts 1:6–8). He says: "You shall receive power when the Holy Spirit has come upon you." In his reply to their question he points out that it is not for them "to know times or seasons which the Father has fixed by his own authority." But they will now receive the Holy Spirit. This means that the end has already dawned, although this "age" is still present. Within this period there is a stage—of undefined extent—which still forms part of "this present age." Thus our relation to eschatology is different from that of mankind at other periods in world history: "Children, it is the last hour," says the writer of the First Letter of John (2:18).

We are living in an interim period which already belongs to the end, and yet still forms part of "this present age." Thus, with Albert Schweitzer, we may describe the ethic which belongs to this period as an "interim ethic," but not in the sense that it was only valid for the first century A.D. For the "interim period" is still going on. The future, it is true, still influences this ethic, but it is also influenced by that element of the future, which is partially realized in the present, namely, the Holy Spirit. The Holy Spirit, who guarantees that one day our sinful bodies and the whole material universe will be re-created by him, enables us here and now to take the old law seriously, with all that this involves, and to fulfill it. Under the impulse of the Holy Spirit the eschatological summons to action: "Repent!" is seen in the right light. It is because the kingdom has come nearer to us, and, in the Holy Spirit, is, in part, already here, that it is now possible for us to act in a Christian way.

It is the presence of the Holy Spirit which makes the action of the Church, as such, eschatological. The Church itself is an eschatological phenomenon. It is in the center of the present lordship of Christ. It was constituted by the Holy Spirit at Pentecost. That is why the task of the Church consists in the proclamation of the Gospel to the whole world. This is the very essence of the Holy Spirit's work, and the meaning of the miracle of Pentecost, when, quite suddenly, all present understood one another. Precisely in the period to which we belong—between the Resurrection and the return of Christ—it is the duty of the Church to go out "into all the world, and preach the Gospel to every creature," looking toward the end. That is why the disciples' question to the risen Lord: "Will you at this time restore the kingdom to Israel?" receives this answer: "It is not for you to know times or seasons which the Father has fixed by his own authority. But you shall receive power when the Holy Spirit has come upon you; and you shall be my witnesses in Jerusalem and in all Judea and Samaria and to the end of the earth" (Acts 1:7–8).

The Holy Spirit, and the world mission: these are the "signs" of the final phase, determined by the future, in which we stand. Does this mean, however, that the kingdom of God will come only when all men have been converted? If that were so, then its coming would depend on man, and the divine omnipotence would be ignored. On the other hand, the conviction that evil will be intensified during the last days is part of Christian eschatology. All that matters, however, is the fact that the Gospel should be preached to all nations. Evidently, God means that everyone should have an opportunity of hearing the Christian message; therefore the call to repentance must be made to all. But the coming of the kingdom does not depend upon men's acceptance of the call. This view contains the strongest incentive for human decision, and yet the divine sovereignty is not in the least impaired. The proclamation of the Gospel to all nations itself becomes a "sign" of the end, an integral element in the eschatological divine plan of salvation.

We must examine these ideas more closely; first of all, we must investigate their origin in Judaism, in order that we may have a clearer grasp of the novelty and the theological significance of the New Testament conception.

Pre-Christian Judaism has a sense of "mission," it is true, but not as the precondition of the messianic kingdom. But we also find another conception which prepares the way for the New Testament doctrine of the Church's mission as a "sign" of the end, which is, at the same time, corrected by it. In Judaism there were constant efforts to calculate the "date" of the messianic kingdom. We cannot here go into details about the various calculations and conclusions to which they led. Again and again these efforts proved abortive, for the kingdom of God did not "come" on the dates which had been calculated beforehand. During the New Testament period there arose a view, often expressed in the Talmud and in the apocryphal books, that the kingdom of God would not come until Israel as a whole had repented. In this connection, this question often appears in the Talmud: "Who is preventing the Messiah's appearing?" To estimate the New Testament conception of the mission aright, we note that it is significant that within Judaism, according to Rabbinical texts, there were two different schools of thought, which answered the question in different ways, and in so doing both broke away from the idea of the divine omnipotence, which, however, is the constitutive element in eschatology as a whole. The school of Eliezer gave up any attempt to calculate the date. It taught that the Messiah will come when all Israel has repented. This, however, makes the coming of the kingdom dependent on the moral attitude of man, and this impairs the doctrine of divine sovereignty. The coming of the kingdom is no longer a divine, sovereign act. The opposite school of thought insists upon fixing a date, namely, the year A.D. 240, when, apart from man, the end of the world will come. The leader of this school of thought does not answer the question: "What prevents the Messiah's appearing?" by saying: "Israel has not yet fully repented," but "the time has not yet come." This view, however, also impairs the idea of divine sovereignty, because it links the coming of the Messiah with this element of calculation which depends upon human effort.

In the New Testament eschatology, on the other hand, the divine sovereignty is fully maintained, in so far as neither by his action nor his knowledge can man know when the kingdom will come. This is taken seriously in the particular conception of "mission" which we are here examining, according to which the end will not come until the Gospel has been preached to all nations. Before I present the evidence for this view, I will indicate two other lines of thought within Judaism which more directly prepared the way for the Christian conception of "mission" as the eschatological "sign" (or "promise"): (i) Elijah will preach repentance in the last days (Mal. 3:1; Ecclesiasticus 48:10, 11); and (ii) there is the other view, according to which the kingdom will come when the number of the elect has been completed (1 Enoch 47:4; 2 Baruch 30:2; 4 Ezra).

Now we come to the New Testament textual evidence. We must begin with the two parallel passages in the Little Apocalypse, Mark 13:10: " 'And the gospel must first be preached to all nations' "; and in Matthew 24:14: " 'And this gospel of the kingdom will be preached throughout the whole world, as a testimony to all nations; and then the end will come.' " In both passages note particularly the clear chronological definition: in Mark "first" (after this comes the passage about the appearance of Antichrist). In Matthew it is still clearer: "then the end will come"; and this "end" is likewise ushered in by the appearance of Antichrist. In both passages the mission is mentioned as a divine "sign," along with the eschatological woes: wars, famines, cosmic catastrophes, persecutions, etc., and the intensification of evil in men. Thus it appears that the coming of the kingdom does not depend upon the success of this "preaching," but only upon the fact of the proclamation itself.

We find further evidence for the same view in the Book of Revelation (6:1–8). In this passage it is clear what the second, third, and fourth riders mean. In each instance the reference is to one of the characteristic eschatological "plagues" which are personified by these mysterious figures. Their outward appearance corresponds with the destructive task which they fulfill upon earth. But what does the first rider mean? Many and varied interpretations have been suggested. First of all, we must note that the description of this first rider has no connection with the sinister aspect of the other three. On the contrary, he is a rather radiant figure; he is seated upon a white horse, and when we remember that white is always represented as a heavenly quality, it makes us question the theory that this first rider, like the other three, also had to pour out an eschatological plague upon the earth. Even the crown with which he is adorned gives him rather the air of a force for good. Finally, it is said of him: "He went out conquering and to conquer." But the verb "to conquer" (in Revelation) does not carry with it the negative sense of "conquering by violence," but, on the contrary, it describes the quality of God's action. Therefore it is very improbable that, as is usually said, this first rider must mean some military power, like Rome or Parthia. To me this seems out of the question, because this rider would then have the same task as the second rider, who sits upon a red horse and, of whom it is said explicitly: "its rider was permitted to take peace from the earth, so that men should slay one another."

Who then is this first rider? This becomes clear when we compare this passage with the similar passage in Revelation 19:11 ff. in which a rider on a white horse also appears. There the explanation is given: "Behold a white horse! He who sat upon it is called Faithful and True, . . . and the name by which he is called is The Word of God." In other words, it is his task to proclaim the Gospel to the world. This must also be the mission of the first rider, and indeed it fits in with the description of him. What, then, has the preaching of the Gospel in the world in common with the task of the other three riders? It also is a divine "sign" (or "promise") of the end, and, as a final offer of salvation, it runs parallel with all those horrors, which are indeed connected with the evil in man. Further, in other passages in this book the necessity for the summons to repentance before the end is emphasized. In 11:3 the "two witnesses" are mentioned (Elijah and Moses) who prophesy. In 14:6–7 is the picture of the angel with the "eternal gospel," who addresses a final appeal to repentance "to every nation and tribe and tongue and people."

The fact that the proclamation of the Gospel as an eschatological "sign" is not a peripheral phenomenon, comes out very clearly in the passage in Acts 1:6–7 which has already been quoted. Here, the risen Lord tells his disciples: "It is not for you to know times or seasons." Why? "The Father has fixed [them] by his own authority"; hence we have no business to pry into His mysteries; the "time" of the coming of the kingdom is known to Him alone, and is under "his own authority." But there is one thing the disciples can be sure of: that they must proclaim the Gospel to all the world, until that "day" comes. This duty is laid upon them by the gift of the Spirit, which they have received. The period between the Resurrection and the unknown "day" of the Lord's return must be filled with the missionary preaching "in Jerusalem . . . and to the end of the earth." For this is the era of "grace," granted to mankind: it is God's will that all men shall have the possibility of hearing the Gospel. Here, too, this allusion to the world mission before the end comes is not stated primarily as an imperative but as an indicative, as an eschatological statement: "You shall be my witnesses." It is God who through His messengers gives us this "sign," which offers the Gospel to the world. In all this the apostles are only the instruments through whom the eschatological plan of salvation is carried out.

But this view is also expressed in a missionary command in the famous words at the end of Matthew's Gospel: "Go therefore and make disciples of all nations." This command also applies to the final phase of this "age," which, as we know, is strictly limited. This comes out very plainly in the promise which is linked with the command: "I am with you always, to the close of the age." This is not a vague chronological statement like "always" (as we usually interpret it), but is a clear reference to the eschatological character of the missionary enterprise, which must take place precisely in this form, before the end of the age, and itself gives its meaning to this age.

In Pauline thought the missionary motive, as the precondition of the coming of salvation, permeates the whole theology of the apostle, and is intimately connected with his sense of missionary vocation. Paul's sense of vocation is clearly influenced by eschatological ideas; this comes out in his conviction that he is an instrument of the eschatological plan of salvation. This is shown very clearly, first of all, in Romans 9–11. These chapters are a very apt commentary on the words in Mark 13:10: "'And the gospel must first be preached to all nations.'" In chapter 10 the apostle emphasizes the fact that God is indeed carrying out His own plan, precisely as He intends, but that our human responsibility is equally clear. For all have the opportunity of hearing the Gospel (Rom. 10:14 ff.). "But how are men to call upon him in whom they have not believed? . . . And how are they to hear without a preacher?" Opportunity must be given to all to hear the Gospel. The Jews have already had it; "but they have not all heeded the gospel," hence the call now goes forth to the Gentiles before, finally, the Jews will enter the kingdom. So the word of the Gospel, which must first of all be proclaimed to the Gentiles, has a particularly concrete meaning in Pauline terminology, in which the main emphasis is certainly upon the word "Gentiles." But the chronologically-eschatologically determined character of the "missionary message" as a "sign" of the "end" is here also quite evident. Only Paul regards this "sign" first of all, so to speak, from "within," that is, from the angle of his apostolic vocation as an instrument of this plan (of salvation). When he speaks of the divine eschatological plan, Paul continually emphasizes the fact that his calling is especially to the Gentiles. In Romans 11, where he speaks of the "mystery" of that divine plan, he mentions his own office: "Inasmuch then as I am an apostle to the Gentiles, I magnify my ministry" (Rom. 11:13).

In the Epistle to the Colossians, 1:22–29, he underlines the close connection between his personal "office" and the divine plan of salvation (the "divine office," verse 25), which is related to "this mystery among the Gentiles" (verse 27, K.J.V.). When we remember that Paul knows he has been "integrated" into a divine plan, whose fulfillment depends upon the coming of this kingdom, we understand better the "necessity" (1 Cor. 9:16) laid upon him to "preach the gospel," as a "debtor" both to Gentiles and to barbarians (Rom. 1:14). He regards himself as Christ's prisoner on behalf of the Gentiles (Eph. 3:1). It is from this point of view that we understand more fully his eagerness to go to new places, where the Gospel has not been proclaimed, from Jerusalem to Illyria, and when his work is finished in that part of the world, he intends to turn toward Spain. The time is short: "Woe to me if I do not preach the gospel!" (1 Cor. 9:16).

From all this it seems very probable that in the much disputed passage in 2 Thessalonians 2:6 ff., *καὶ νῦν τὸ κατέχον οἴδατε*—"you know what is restraining him . . ." with the following reference to the Antichrist, there is an allusion to the proclamation of the Gospel as a "sign" of the end. When we consider that this conception of the missionary message can be traced right through the whole of the New Testament, as we have seen, this hypothesis is as probable as any hypothesis can be. Usually the passage is taken to refer to the Roman Empire. But we can find no other passage in support of the view that the state, the manifestation of the Antichrist, delays the end. On the contrary, both in Jewish and in primitive Christian apocalyptic, the Antichrist is usually represented as some kind of Satanic empire. Precisely in 2 Thessalonians 2:4 it is described in images taken from the Book of Daniel, which there certainly refer to Syria. Can it be that in the very passage where Paul alludes to the Antichrist in these "images," at the same time he would have introduced the state as that which "restrains" the Antichrist? If this is what he means, he would have brought strange confusion into the realm of eschatological ideas, since in the same passage he would have spoken of the state as the opponent of the Antichrist, and as a Satanic power.

On the other hand, a great deal could be said for the view, suggested first of all by Theodore of Mopsuestia and by Theodoret, and later on by Calvin, according to which "what is restraining him" in 2 Thessalonians 2:6 is the eschatological missionary message. At first the Greek verb for "restraining" had a temporal meaning in the sense of "retarding," "delaying." Here the allusion is to the "time," or "date" of the coming of the kingdom of God. Nowhere, however, is there a relation of this kind between the state and the "time" when the end is expected to come; we have, however, seen that there is (a relation) of this kind between the preaching of the Gospel to the nations and the question of the "date" of the *parousia.* According to the Synoptic passages in Mark 13:10–14 and Matthew 24:13–15 the Antichrist appears after the preaching of the Gospel to the Gentiles, just as in 2 Thessalonians 2:6 ff. he will appear after "what is restraining him" has been removed.

Further, this assumption is directly connected with that Jewish Rabbinic question, "Who is preventing the appearing of the Messiah?" which we have already mentioned. We have already seen that the most usual Jewish answer to that question was: "the repentance of Israel which is not yet complete," and this answer points clearly toward the Christian view of the eschatological necessity for the proclamation of the Gospel to the "heathen," and it is corrected by it, in so far as here the essential element is the call to repentance.

The whole context in which the passage (2 Thess. 2) occurs also supports the idea of a relation with the preaching to the Gentiles, and shows why the Gospel must be preached to all nations before the appearance of Antichrist. In 2:9–12 we read of those "who are to perish, because they refused to love the truth and so be saved"; and in 2:13–14 Paul sets—against those who reject the preaching of the apostle—the readers themselves, and of them he says: "God chose you from the beginning to be saved. . . . To this he called you through our gospel." The whole of the preceding chapter, too, deals with the relation between eschatological events and the acceptance or rejection of the Gospel which they have heard:

> We are bound to give thanks to God always for you, brethren . . . because your faith is growing abundantly, and the love of every one of you for one another is increasing. . . . This is evidence of the righteous judgment of God, that you may be made worthy of the kingdom of God, for which you are suffering . . . when the Lord Jesus is revealed from heaven with his mighty angels in flaming fire, inflicting vengeance upon those who do not know God and upon those who do not obey the gospel of our Lord Jesus.

We could almost regard this as an allusion to the proclamation of the Gospel to the heathen, in this connection, if it were not included in the allusion to "what is restraining him."

In the same passage there is first the neuter (2:6 ff., "*what* is restraining him"), then the masculine (*he who* now restrains). If "*what* is restraining" is the missionary message, then it is probable that "*he* who restrains" or withholds is the apostle himself. This would fit in well with what we have said about St. Paul's deep sense of missionary vocation, which indeed is influenced by that eschatological conviction that the Gospel must be offered to the non-Christian world. The question of Paul's speaking of himself in this way in the third person should not cause any difficulty, since elsewhere he uses the third person in speaking of the grace granted to him (2 Cor. 12:2).

Even if this interpretation of 2 Thessalonians 2:6 ff.—which has a solid foundation, and could be further supported by passages from early Christian writers of the first and second centuries—should not be correct, there are other New Testament passages which would give sufficient evidence for the fundamental insight of faith that the missionary enterprise is the work of God, which His servants are carrying out during the final period of this age, in which we are living. For this final period is a time of grace, which God in His mercy has granted us for repentance. This view springs out of the nature of New Testament eschatology. It leaves the doctrine of divine omnipotence unimpaired, since it does not make the coming of the kingdom of God dependent upon man, and excludes all human calculations. On the other hand, it greatly intensifies the responsibility of man in view of the eschatological period of grace, and finally gives the Church its peculiar commission, namely, in God's name to carry the Gospel to all nations. This is the eschatological saving work in the period between the Resurrection and the return of Christ. From every point of view, this was, theologically speaking, a deep and fruitful conception, which, alas! was soon forgotten, and only sporadically reappears as a missionary motive.

Like all other "signs," that of the missionary enterprise cannot be limited to this or that generation. For it is characteristic of this final period, in which we are living, that it forms a unity, and that as a whole it is characterized by "signs." But we can never say, "this is the final hour" in which the "sign" will appear. This means that the Reformers were wrong when they thought they could get rid of "missions" by saying that the Gospel had already been proclaimed to all nations by the apostles. Rather, it is of the essence of a "sign" that to the very end it should appear in each generation which belongs to the present final phase of this "age." This means, however, that the missionary obligation covers the whole time which remains, right down to the unknown final end, and that each generation anew must proclaim the Gospel to the "heathen" of their own day, without wondering whether their ancestors before 1900 had had an opportunity of hearing it. Hence, in every generation the Church must carry on the apostles' work and proclaim the Gospel to all nations, so far as is humanly possible at any given time.

An Exegetical Study of Matthew 28:16–20 *

BY KARL BARTH

Now the eleven disciples went to Galilee, to the mountain to which Jesus had directed them. And when they saw him they worshiped him; but some doubted. And Jesus came and said to them, "All authority in heaven and on earth has been given to me. Go therefore and make disciples of all nations, baptizing them in the name of the Father and of the Son and of the Holy Spirit, teaching them to observe all that I have commanded you; and lo, I am with you always, to the close of the age." MATTHEW 28:16–20

Here we have part of the New Testament testimony about events that took place during the forty days after Easter.

Let us recall what happened in those days according to the New Testament record. It was during this period that the purpose of Jesus' life and death, and with it the mission of his followers, could for the first time be seen, heard, and grasped by men. It was the time of the Son's coming in the glory of the Father, ushering in not more and not less than the approaching end of this world and the beginning of a new one. "To them he presented himself alive after his passion by many proofs, appearing to them during forty days, and speaking of the kingdom of God" (Acts 1:3). It became manifest in those forty days that neither the proclamation of God's king-

* Translated by Thomas Wieser.

dom at hand, as first heralded by John the Baptist and later by Jesus himself, nor the miracles and signs accomplished by Jesus were empty words. The petition "Thy kingdom come" had not been uttered in vain after all; "this generation," the generation of those alive at the time, was indeed not to pass away before "all these things" had taken place as foretold by Jesus according to Mark 13:30. It became manifest that some of the people who gathered around Jesus actually did not taste death before they had seen the kingdom of God come with power (Mk. 9:1). The disciples truly were not to go through all the towns of Israel before the Son of man came (Mt. 10:23). Now he came, and now "all these things" happened. Peter's confession at Caesarea (Mt. 16:16), at the time premature, was now proven to be right and necessary. "You are the Christ, the Son of the living God." Right and necessary, therefore, was the name "Lord," *kyrios,* which the disciples had given to their master. It became manifest, in other words, that the *eschaton* had really begun. All these things were revealed when Jesus, after his death and burial, rose from the tomb and appeared to his followers anew, thereby "coming again" already then and there. He appeared to them not in order to continue his ministry of teaching and healing so to speak during the second part of his earthly life, but to disclose the hitherto hidden purpose of his life and death to his followers and to give them the charge of proclaiming his Lordship and the kingdom now manifest before their eyes. This is, very briefly, the content of the Easter stories at the end of the four Gospels, at the beginning of the Book of Acts, and of 1 Corinthians 15. This is the *fact* of Easter.

Two preliminary observations about the form of these stories will facilitate our understanding.

1. We must be quite clear that these accounts relate a *real event* in space and time, and not just some thought or idea. They speak of an empty tomb (Mt. 27:62–66, 28:11–15), and of the newly visible, audible and touchable body of Jesus (Lk. 24:39 f.; Jn. 20:24 f.; 1 Jn. 1:1). These characteristics are all mentioned within the context of the story of Jesus and his followers, even of the history of the world (Pontius Pilate!). Christ's appearance is in itself an historical moment, marking the end of all preceding, and the antecedent and the turning point of all coming events. To speak here of a "myth" would be to confuse categories. Easter is an absolutely *unique* event. We must immediately specify that this

unique event is the beginning of a new heaven and a new earth (Rev. 21:1; 2 Pet. 3:13), of the Last Day, of the glory of God in the flesh (Jn. 1:14). It is the presence of the *eschaton.* Such an event could only be described in incomplete and contradictory terms, such as are used in the Easter narratives. Think of the relationship between the reports of Matthew and Luke, or of the Synoptics and John, or of the Gospels and 1 Corinthians. It is impossible to construe from these reports a history in our understanding of the term. The topographical and chronological precision is lacking. There is no clear differentiation of the various scenes and no corroboration by impartial witnesses of the events described. These narratives are recounted not in the style of history but, like the story of creation, in the style of historical saga. The content bars any attempt at harmonizing. All these narratives deal no doubt with a common subject and are in basic agreement. Yet each of them needs to be read independently, as a unique testimony of God's decisive word and intervention at the turning point of the eons. Quite obviously each narrative needs to be consulted to clarify the others.

2. These texts speak of an "historically" inconceivable event, but do not mean that this event was subsequently interpreted or construed, much less invented by the faith and piety of the Church. They unequivocally refer to an event which laid the foundation of, and gave shape to, the faith of the emerging Christian community. The crux of it was that Jesus' presence among his own revealed God to them. This revelation in Jesus' presence, placing the faithful in the center of time, disclosed to them the past and the future will and work of God. It is therefore both a recapitulation of the history of Israel, culminating in the earthly life of Jesus, and an anticipation of the history of Jesus' reign in the Church and in the whole world. God's action, past and future, was present in those forty days as if it were still going on, or already going on.

One more preliminary remark about Matthew 28:16–20 as it relates to the other Easter stories. Two sets of narratives are to be distinguished among them.

1. The stories of Jesus and the women. These underscore the manifestation of the *fact* of the Resurrection (the empty tomb) and the *identity* of the risen Lord with the crucified (28:1–6 and 9). Add to it the charge to the women to tell the disciples what they had seen (28:7–8 and 10). This charge is particularly significant

because, according to Mark 16:8, the women "said nothing to any one for they were afraid" and, according to Luke 24:11, their words seemed to the disciples "an idle tale." Incidentally this particular role of the women in relation to the disciples may be interpreted as an analogy of the relationship between the historical community of Israel and the now emerging Christian community of the end of time.

2. The stories of Jesus and the disciples. Here again the manifestation of the *fact* and of the *identity* (28:17–18; Lk. 24:37 f.; Jn. 20:19 f.) is important. However, it is overshadowed by the charge to the disciples to go and tell the world what they had seen (28:19; Lk. 24:27; Jn. 20:21). The passage about Jesus and the disciples is missing in Mark's original text. Mark 16:9–20 is a later addition. The charge to the disciples is validated by the pouring out of the Holy Spirit. John 20:22 indicates that the fourth evangelist understood Easter and Pentecost as one and the same event. In content, they most certainly belong together. Easter together with Pentecost, Pentecost together with Easter, constitute the gathering of God's people at the end of time.

Our text clearly belongs to this second set of narratives about Jesus and his disciples. Parallel texts are Luke 24:36–49 and John 20:19–29. In addition Luke 24:13–35 relates the incident on the road to Emmaus; Luke 24:50–53 and Acts 1:4–12, the Ascension; John 21:1–23, the appearance at Lake Tiberias and the conversation with Peter. The Gospel according to Matthew, which offers the most coherent account, relates only the one appearance of Jesus before his disciples. To this we now turn our attention.

Verse 16

"The eleven disciples" (also Lk. 24:9, 33) are the first twelve of Jesus' followers, whose number is temporarily diminished by the loss of Judas. They embody and represent the Israel of the end of time. These "eleven"—according to Biblical arithmetic!—equal "twelve," for even in their incompleteness they account for the totality of Israel. 1 Corinthians 15:5 explicitly mentions Jesus' appearance to the twelve. Judas could not impair the full number.

". . . went to Galilee . . ." Significantly, Matthew leads Jesus' history back to the place of its origin (Mt. 4:12–17); to the Galilee of the Gentiles, to the people who walked in darkness and have seen a great light. The history of the end stands in continuity with the

previous events in the life of Jesus and the history of Israel, which in turn point to the end. (Luke transposes this scene to Jerusalem, to the life center of Israel, which is seen here—Lk. 24:47—as the point of departure for the eschatological proclamation to all nations.) Note how the two narratives, topographically incompatible and with different theological emphases, nevertheless agree in substance.

"*. . . to the mountain . . .*" What mountain is referred to here—the mountain of the transfiguration or that of the Sermon on the Mount? (Cf. B. Weiss.) It might be better not to identify it geographically and merely think of a mountain opposite Mount Zion to the north.

"*. . . to which Jesus had directed them.*" According to verse 7 it was the angel, according to verse 10 it was Jesus himself, by means of the women, who directed the disciples, "his brethren," to go there. The order must have gone to the disciples, since now the eleven turn up. The combination with the appearance to the five hundred brethren (1 Cor. 15:6), as proposed by Olshausen and Schlatter, seems therefore unlikely.

Verse 17

"*And when they saw him . . .*" This seeing (ἰδόντες) implies that the revelation of the fact of Jesus' resurrection and of the identity of the risen Lord with the crucified, earlier accorded to the women, is now to be granted to the disciples as well. The expression "he came" (προσελθών) in verse 18, however, suggests for the time being a certain distance and objectivity of this revelation.

"*. . . they worshiped him,*" as did the women in verse 9, and as all shall do again at the Ascension (Lk. 24:51). Thomas' confession, "my Lord and my God," serves as a necessary commentary. Worship is offered in the presence of the revealed God. Jesus encountered them as God, and they encounter him now as worshipers.

"*. . . but some doubted*"; as in Luke 24:37 f. and John 20:24 f. (Thomas has suffered great injustice at the hands of exegetes. His insistence upon touching the body of Jesus to relieve his doubt is quite normal and apostolic!) Older exegetes (Starke, Rieger, Olshausen) found it inadmissible to ascribe the doubt to the asposstles, and accordingly assumed the presence of others. But this is improbable in the light of verse 17. J. Weiss finds the phrase linguistically crude, disruptive, isolated, and "against the temper of this harmonious ending." Yet the comparison with Luke and John indicates the necessity of the element of doubt even for Matthew. Calvin correctly interpreted: worship and doubt have a common cause; the servant figure of the man Jesus was garbed in the glory of God. Revelation always has a *terminus a quo* and a *terminus ad quem.* Veiled, it arouses doubt; unveiled, it commands worship. All of us waver again and again between the two. Rieger is therefore right when he says that this sentence was included "as a reminder that faith requires struggle. Don't be surprised if your belief is a continuous conquest of unbelief." This element of doubt to be conquered by faith is represented here by "some" (οἱ δέ), as in John by Thomas, and in Luke by almost all apostles. Only the gift of the Holy Spirit puts an end to the struggle and casts out doubt. Doubting apostles and a doubting church *after* Pentecost truly have no place in the New Testament. *Spiritus sanctus non est scepticus,* said Luther. But here the apostles are only at the beginning. They stand in the shadow of the death of Christ. They reenact the doubtful role they displayed at the time of the Passion.

Verse 18

"And Jesus came and said to them": with these words Matthew perhaps hints at the event of Pentecost, not mentioned elsewhere in his record. It is at any rate certain that when Jesus drew near the objective revelation was subjectively appropriated. Bengel comments, *"eo ipso dubitantibus fidem faciens."* By approaching them Jesus awakened faith in the doubters! This, then, is the "sequence" to the doubting in verse 17 which J. Weiss missed.

" 'All authority in heaven and on earth has been given to me.' " According to the *"therefore"* (οὖν) of verse 19, this affirmation of power is the objective presupposition on the part of Jesus for the immediately following imperative. As the one described in verse 18, Jesus has the power and authority to address the disciples the way he does in verse 19. Hence the disciples' carrying out of the charge will not at all be determined by the excellency and strength of their own will and work; nor will it be jeopardized by their deficiencies. Behind the command of verse 19 stands the commander himself, Jesus, as described in verse 18. He assures the execution of the command over against both the disciples' weakness and any interference by a third party.

ἐξουσία means "right and power" and corresponds to the Latin term *potestas.* The parallel is only seemingly missing in Luke. The fact that Jesus is invested with the highest authority as a guarantee for his command is also attested by Luke inasmuch as Jesus is there both the content and the interpreter of the Scriptures. According to Matthew's version, Jesus' prophecy to the high priests (26:64) has now been fulfilled, "Hereafter you will see the Son of man seated at the right hand of Power, and coming on the clouds of heaven," and with it Daniel 7:14, "To him was given dominion and glory and kingdom." The kingdom is truly his, and he will deliver it to the Father (1 Cor. 15:24). God has highly exalted him and bestowed on him a name above every name, the name of *kyrios,* that at this name every knee should bow, in heaven and on earth and under the earth (Phil. 2:9 f.). He disarmed, according to 1 Corinthians 15:24 even destroyed, the principalities and powers and made a public example of them, triumphing over them in him (Col. 2:15). He is "far above all rule and authority and power and dominion, and above every name that is named, not only in this age, but also in that which is to come." God "has put all things under his feet" (Eph. 1:21–22). "The kingdom of the world has become the kingdom of our Lord and of his Christ, and he shall reign for ever and ever" (Rev. 11:15). What does all this mean? It means that the divine claim to all things created in heaven and on earth is, very concretely, Jesus' claim; the divine authority is Jesus' authority; the divine acting, ruling, and judging is Jesus' affair. As the holder of this ἐξουσία Jesus stands behind the command in verse 19; he is the authority to those whom he sends out, and as such guarantees the implementation of the command to the disciples as well as against interference of third parties. Those who accept the command fall under this ἐξουσία; they are responsible to and covered by this authority.

All authority in heaven and on earth! This affirmation is exclusive. Objectively speaking, there is no authority besides the authority of Jesus. All power, all right, belongs to Jesus. Remaining are only principalities and powers already subjected to him, of which he is the head (Col. 2:10). There are therefore no such things as natural law and natural power, asserting their own domain over against Jesus', deserving homage, trust, fear, and obedience in their own right. Thus it is impossible to postulate, on the basis of the ἐξουσίαι (Rom. 13:1 f.) a secular power instituted by God alongside the kingdom of Christ, a political realm that would not be included in the kingdom of Christ.

But who is the holder of such ἐξουσία? Because all authority has been "given" to him we are prevented from thinking in the abstract of an eternal, nonincarnate Son of God, of the λόγος ἄσαρκος. To him authority need not be given; he holds it from eternity to eternity. The New Testament constantly speaks of this Son of God, yet never abstractly. The eternal Son is always man at the same time. Of him our text speaks. To the man Jesus is given the ἐξουσία. The man Jesus is the commanding Lord in verse 19.

That all authority has been "given" to him must however not be interpreted to mean that he received it only in his resurrection. Such an assumption is refuted by a number of very clear texts in the Gospels where the affirmation made in verse 18 undeniably refers to Jesus before his death. " 'All things have been delivered to me by my Father' " (Mt. 11:27). "The Father . . . has given all things into his hand" (Jn. 3:35). Jesus knew "that the Father had given all things into his hands" (Jn. 13:3). " 'Thou hast given him power over all flesh' " (Jn. 17:2). "He taught them as one who had authority" (Mt. 7:29). " 'The Son of man has authority on earth to forgive sins' " (Mt. 9:6). See also Matthew 21:23 f. ἐξουσία is given to the man Jesus as divine authority can alone be given to a human creature. Only when man prays for it, believes in God, is obedient to Him, is it given as free grace. Because God's free grace is eternal, authority is given everlastingly; potentially in God's design to create and save the world, actually in the incarnation of the Word. "Er ist ein Kindlein worden klein, der alle Ding erhält allein." By forgiving sins and accomplishing signs and miracles, Jesus made at least a partly visible use of his authority long before his resurrection. There was never a time when he was devoid of it. His "emptying himself" (Phil. 2:7) was nothing but the hiddenness of his majesty, caused by human blindness. What he achieved in the state of utmost weakness, his death upon the cross, was truly a manifestation of his might. "Sa divinité se tenoit pour un peu de temps comme cachée, c'est à dire elle ne démonstroit point sa vertu" (Calvin). In the Resurrection, however, Jesus reveals himself to the disciples as the one who held, holds, and will hold all authority, a fact that had hitherto been hidden from the disciples as well as from the world. It is of this revelation of the risen Lord that verse 18 speaks.

Verses 19–20a

This is the crucial affirmation of the whole text. It is the charge and commission of the risen Jesus, the authority for which was asserted in verse 18.

"Go therefore and make disciples . . ." Make them what you yourselves are! Have them learn here, with me, where you yourselves have learned! Call them into the twelve of the eschatological Israel! Let them share in its place and task in the world!

We have already noticed the strangeness of Biblical arithmetic. The twelve are designed to be countless. In the same manner as Jesus "made" apostles from the first disciples (Mk. 3:14–15), the apostles are called to make apostolic Christians of all others. The kingly ministry of the Messiah is here entrusted to the first disciples constituting the king's troops.

The sweeping imperative, "Go therefore," rests on the authority which is given to Jesus. As soon as his authority is announced in verse 18 there follows the charge, "make disciples!" The reminiscence of the "sending" in Matthew 10 and of its parallel in Mark 16:15, " 'Go into all the world and preach the gospel to the whole creation,' " largely obscures the peculiarity of our text. The same reality is envisaged here as in chapter 10. Yet there it appears in its implicit and hidden form, while here in its explicit and visible form. In both instances the founding, through Jesus' word, of the *apostolic* Church is envisaged. It is the Church that receives the apostles' word and actively transmits it. " 'As the Father has sent me, even so I send you' " (Jn. 20:21). This apostolic Church, existing not for itself, but "for Christ," on behalf of him (2 Cor. 5:20), is the decisive event of the *eschaton* that has broken into time. The existence of the new community consists not only in the apostles' preaching of the Gospel and their fellow men's listening. It is constantly renewed as the listeners themselves become "apostolic" and, as new disciples, begin to proclaim the good news. Consequently the charge is not only κηρύξατε but μαθητεύσατε, "make disciples." John 17:20–23 might well be the appropriate commentary to this charge. " 'I do not pray for these only, but also for those who are to believe in me through their word, that they may all be one; even as thou, Father, art in me, and I in thee, that they also may be in us, so that the world may believe that thou hast sent me . . . and hast loved them even as thou hast loved me.' "

And now the great problem of our text:

"*. . . all nations . . .*" πάντα τὰ ἔθνη. On the basis of these words the text is called "the great commission." What does "all nations" mean?

It means, first of all, *people* from among all nations who are received into discipleship. They become significant for the existence of their respective nations because the nations now come within reach of the apostolate and its proclamation and receive their concealed center through the Christian community living in their midst. Note the αὐτούς, which occurs twice. It cannot refer to ἔθνη. Not the nations as such are made disciples. This interpretation once infested missionary thinking and was connected with the painful fantasies of the German Christians. It is worthless.

"All nations" means, furthermore, people from Gentile lands, from the *goyim*. This does not exclude Israel. Her right of the first-born, her *dignitas primogeniturae,* as Calvin called it, remains unimpaired. Yet the disciples are summoned to go out to the Gentile people and nations. For now the eschatological Israel shall appear, the people gathered by the Messiah who appeared at the end of time. This is the new eschatological community. It is gathered from among the Jews and Gentiles. The doors and windows of the house of Israel, so far closed, must open. The apostles' mission is "to the Jew first and also to the Greek" (Rom. 1:16). Accordingly, Mark 16:15 states, " 'Go into all the world and preach the gospel to the whole creation.' " Matthew expresses the same idea, only in more concrete terms, when he speaks of "all nations." Through this mission the community of Jesus becomes manifest in his resurrection as the universal community. It is the eschatological Israel, the Israel which receives into its life and history the chosen ones from among the Gentiles. In fact it had never been anything else. Even during his life before death Jesus had never given it any other foundation than that which now became apparent: not as a special community within Israel, and hence not as a new form of the previous Israel in history, but as the Israel of the end of time, fulfilling the destiny of the historical Israel, as "a covenant to the people, a light to the nations" (Is. 42:6, 49:8). It is important to see this. Already the relationship to verse 18 and its parallels rules out any limitation of Jesus' dominion. How could he, to whom all power is given, have ever intended founding a pious little Jewish club? The name of the "Son of man" is the name of him whom "all peoples, nations, and languages" shall serve (Dan. 7:14). The field where the Son of man sows the good seed is the world (Mt. 13:38). The ransom for many (ἀντὶ πολλῶν Mk. 10:45) and the shedding of blood for many (ὑπὲρ πολλῶν) certainly imply Jesus' identification with the suffering servant of God in Isaiah 53 (see in particular verses 11–12). Of him it is said, " 'It is too light a thing that you should be my servant to raise up the tribes of Jacob and to restore the preserved of Israel; I will give you as a light to the nations, that my salvation may reach to the end of the earth' " (Is. 49:6). "He shall be exalted and lifted up, and shall be very high. . . . So shall he startle many nations; kings shall shut their mouths because of him" (Is. 52:13 f.). From the very beginning Jesus calls his disciples "the salt of the earth" and "the light of the world" (Mt. 5:13–14). Already John the Baptist had proclaimed that God would raise up children to Abraham from the stones (Mt. 3:9). Jesus himself spoke of the many that will come from east and west and sit at table with the patriarchs (Mt. 8:11); of the angels whom the Son of man shall send out at the Parousia to gather his elect from the four winds, from one end of heaven to the other (Mt. 24:31; see also 25:31 f.); of the servants that will go out to the streets and gather all they find, both bad and good (Mt. 22:9 f.); even of the testimony his disciples will bear also before the Gentiles (Mt. 10:18).

Jesus at first kept this universality of the new community relatively hidden, as he did with the power and authority given him (verse 18), and with the name of Messiah (Mt. 16:20). Why? The previous, historical, Israel had not yet run its course before Jesus' death. His life had not yet been spent as a ransom for many. Not everything was ready yet. The table had not been set. The guests could not yet be invited. Israel was not yet fully prepared to fulfill its eschatological mission. Aware of this "not yet," Jesus understood his mission to be—temporarily—to the lost sheep of the house of Israel. But even as he pronounced this rule, he made an exception (Mt. 15:24). In the very strange passage of Mark 4:10–12 an even stricter rule is announced. Initially he did "not yet" address himself directly and properly to the whole people of Israel, but only to his disciples. Aware of this "not yet" he charged his disciples to go—temporarily—nowhere among the Gentiles and to enter no town of the Samaritans (Mt. 10:5). This "not yet" again overshadows the relative seclusion of the primitive apostles in Jerusalem. They had first to overcome their reluctance to get in touch with the Gentiles (Acts 10), and finally entrusted Paul with the mission to the Gentiles (Gal. 2). Nevertheless, while this "not yet" casts its shadows even over the time after Easter, it was in fact overcome. The great turning point in history had since been marked. The "delivering" of Jesus to the Gentiles, foretold in the second and third announcements of his imminent suffering, had taken place (Mt. 27:2). This event separates the times. Now the eschatological Israel begins. Jesus' rejection by the Jews becomes the offer of grace to the Gentiles. In the rejection and death of its Messiah, the history of Israel has reached its end and goal; the hidden church of Jews and Gentiles awaits its revelation. The messianic Israel is in fact revealed by the words of verse 19. What does it matter if the revelation was apparently not fully realized right away? The number twelve of the eschatological Israel is even externally again complete by the addition of Paul. The activity of the apostles must set in with this very revelation: "Make disciples of all nations."

This "all nations" in no way contradicts the earlier teaching and practice of Jesus. The narrow path within Israel had to branch out into the wide world of all nations, and the inroad into the wide world had to begin as the narrow path within Israel. "Salvation is from the Jews" (Jn. 4:22). From the *Jews*—this is the first, limited, and hidden form of the eschatological community, represented by the eleven. Salvation *comes* from the Jews—to the Gentiles—this is its second, unlimited, and manifest form, represented by the eleven plus one.

To say that the primitive apostles acted as if they had not heard the Great Commission (J. Weiss, Klostermann) is misleading. Already the eleven, as Jesus saw and addressed them, are the eleven plus one who shall carry out the mission. The Church as a body will obey the command: its proclamation, first exclusively addressed to Israel, is immediately understood by the Jews of all lands in their own language (Acts 2:6 f.). Spread by Paul, the twelfth apostle, it becomes the message to the Gentiles.

It is therefore not necessary to draw upon the assumption of a "backward projection on the part of the later Church" (Klostermann) in order to explain verse 19. Nor do we have to declare the commission as "interpolated," to justify the mission to the Gentiles by the "supra-Jewish substance of the Gospel," and to find its Magna Charta in the history of "early Christian missions" (J. Weiss). As recapitulation and anticipation, revealing the hidden reality of the eschatological community, the Great Commission is truly the most genuine utterance of the risen Jesus.

". . . baptizing them in the name of the Father and of the Son and of the Holy Spirit." The making of disciples is achieved by baptism and teaching.

Baptizing is the priestly function of objectively introducing others into the realm of God's reign. Initially it is the function of Jesus himself. Yet here he transmits it to his first disciples after he had them taste in advance the fruit of his sacrificial death—at the Last Supper—and then had suffered death.

Baptizing in a *name* meant, in the Jewish custom of the day, to administer to someone a cleansing bath intended to certify a state to be attained. A Gentile slave, for instance, was administered baptism as a sign of his liberation when he left. Baptizing in the name of the Father and of the Son and of the Holy Spirit means to give to someone the cleansing bath which certifies to him and to others that he belongs to this God. Father, Son, and Holy Spirit, then, are for him what the name of the triune God really stands for. He in turn has to confess and to confirm that he belongs to this God.

Some special observations:

1. If the *BD* reading * βαπτίσαντες ("after having baptized them") were correct, the administering of baptism would only be a secondary task to laying the groundwork for the primary task of teaching.

2. The text does not propose a liturgical formula to be used for baptism (as maintained by Zahn). Baptism "in the name of Jesus Christ" (Acts 2:38) therefore does not speak against the authenticity of the text (as has been suggested by J. Weiss).

3. Stress is laid, not on the act of baptizing itself, since cleansing rites attesting initiation were a current Jewish practice of the time; rather, the emphasis is on the particular kind of baptism the disciples are asked to administer. A Gentile becomes a disciple when

* A reference to two Greek manuscripts: *B—Codex Vaticanus; D—Codex Bezae Cantabrigiensis.*

he is assured of his belonging to the Father, Son, and Holy Spirit.

4. The external act of baptizing is a *signum pro re*. The disciples are commanded, and therefore they expect to be able, to bring about the state of affairs to be certified. By the intermediary of the disciples the Gentiles shall be joined with those who belong to the Father, the Son, and the Holy Spirit, thereby becoming themselves disciples. Luke 24:47 explains the meaning of this incorporation. Repentance and the forgiveness of sin shall be preached to the Gentiles in Jesus' name. They become disciples as sinners who, set free by God and thankful to God, are wrenched from the separation from God.

The command to baptize is to be understood in the same light. It is the transferral of the messianic power of Jesus, the priest of all men, to Peter. "I will give you the keys of the kingdom of heaven" (Mt. 16:19), a most genuine word of the risen Lord. Genuine and very significant, furthermore, is the invocation of the name of the triune God at the very moment when the universal existence of the apostolic Church at the end of time is revealed. This is the only place in the New Testament where this name is invoked with such simplicity (cf. 1 Cor. 12:4–6; 2 Cor. 13:13; 2 Thess. 2:13–14; Eph. 4:4–6; 1 Pet. 1:2).

"*. . . teaching them to observe all that I have commanded you.*" As baptism constitutes the existence and the nature of discipleship, teaching constitutes the ways and works of the disciples.

"Teaching," *διδάσκειν*, is the function of the prophet and teacher by preaching and instruction. Now Jesus appoints his disciples to this teaching office. To become a Christian means to become a Christ to others by participating in Christ's kingly, priestly, and prophetic ministry. The apostles accede to this ministry after passing through the crisis, i.e., through their failure during the Passion when their apostleship, humanly speaking, had become utterly discredited. They had failed in *τηρεῖν*, in observing what Jesus had commanded them. Yet without inquiring into the validity of their conversion (see, however, Lk. 22:32), Jesus freely entrusts them, the undeserving, with teaching the Gentiles this "observance," and with guiding them in the ways and works of disciples. (*τηρεῖν* means "to keep," "to preserve," to protect something entrusted to one's care.)

". . . all that I have commanded you." What did Jesus command them to do? To follow him, in order "to be with him" (Mk. 3:14).

They are to live within the earthly confines of the kingdom of God and to submit to the order of life established there. All this not as an end in itself, for the sake of their own personal morals and salvation or of the well-being of society, but that the order of service be preserved which he had given them, his heralds and apostles. All "baptized" become *eo ipso* subservient to this order of service, the very foundation of the Christian community. They in turn need to be called to acknowledge, to keep, and to confirm their belonging to the Father, the Son, and the Holy Spirit. They need to be nurtured in this service in order that their works may become those of disciples and a Christian community may exist in the world. It exists only where the things commanded by Jesus are "observed." This nurturing of the Gentiles who, by baptism, become servants of the triune God, is the task of the apostles. As the witnesses to Jesus' life and resurrection, they are entrusted with the task for all times and in all places. All others receive it only from them, secondhand. The apostles, and they alone, are called to teach in the Church. For there is no room in the Church for any other object of τηρεῖν but the one commanded by Jesus to the apostles. What they have been commanded, they must teach without omission, the whole content of the order of service. This is the New Testament affirmation of the self-sufficiency of the Scriptures, the crossroad where we must part from the Roman Catholic Church. Teaching in the Church can only be repetitive of apostolic teaching.

There remains one more question with regard to verses 19–20a. What about the explicitly stated task (Mt. 10:8 f.) to heal the sick, to raise the dead, to make clean the lepers, to cast out evil spirits? We know from Acts and from several Letters that such special "gifts," though not widespread, were not lacking in the later Church. Nevertheless, the part of Jesus' commandment dealing with doing signs has been fulfilled and become superfluous with the Resurrection of Jesus, the sign of signs. Signs may happen again. But they cannot be postulated as essential marks of the eschatological community. In its past, the forty days, as in its future, the Second Coming, this community is surrounded by the one "sign of the Son of man." When in Mark 16:17 ff. the gift of "accompanying" signs is declared to be an almost indispensable attribute of faith, it only shows the noncanonical character of that text. The task of the apostles, and therefore also of the apostolic

Church, consists in baptizing and teaching in the light of this sign—in the light of Easter morning, in the light of "the hope laid up for you in heaven" (Col. 1:5).

Verse 20b

"And lo, I am with you . . ." The Church of the *eschaton* which broke into time and now is manifest and recognized is not left alone. Its founder possesses not in vain all authority in heaven and on earth (verse 18). "Where two or three are gathered in my name, there am I in the midst of them" (Mt. 18:20). Jesus himself, with all his power and authority, stands behind the apostles when they carry out his command and commission. "He who hears you hears me" (Lk. 10:16). "So every one who acknowledges me before man, I also will acknowledge before my Father who is in heaven" (Mt. 10:32). *Ergo nunquam plane exspirabit ecclesia christiana* (Bengel). This is why the Christian Church can never speak or act on its own authority and for its own cause. The self-seeking and self-exalting idea of the Roman Catholic Church is thereby attacked at the very roots.

"I am with you" is, according to Genesis 28:15; Judges 6:12; Haggai 1:13, the affirmation of the immediate presence of God. In making it, Jesus once more says who he is. "I am *with you."* This is not to say that he will always be with his people in the same way as he is now. These forty days are unique, only to be compared with the return in glory which, rightly understood, begins already with the forty days. However, the Church between Ascension and Second Coming is not without a master. And because the Church is in the world, the world is not without a master either. The Church has no right to consider the world as "masterless," merely neutral or even hostile, or else it has not grasped Jesus' "with you."

"I am with you": in remembrance of my past life, death and resurrection, I speak and act today. In the Holy Spirit I fill and rule the present, any present, with my word. I will come with the future, any future. I stand at the door and knock. With my past, my present, and my future I shall be with you evermore.

This is the *promise* of the risen Lord, covering the time beyond the forty days. It is the point of departure for the subsequent events at the end of time. As the apostles receive and grasp this promise and stand on this firm ground, they are the rock on which Jesus builds his church, stronger than the gates of Hades.

"*. . . to the close of the age.*" We must reckon with three different times or ages. From creation to the appearance of Christ: the time as it passes, and is actually past, with the appearance of Christ. From Christ's appearance to his return in glory: the *eschaton* as revealed in Christ's resurrection. From his return in glory into eternity: God's own eternal time in which the temporal is suspended. Accordingly, "to the close of the age," of this age, must signify until the time when the *eschaton,* ushered in with the appearance of Christ, will have run its course, when the universe will be subjected to God's reign, when the distinct reign of Christ will come to an end, and God will be everything to everyone (1 Cor. 15:27 f.). Because of Jesus' presence, the sum and substance of our text, the Great Commission of the risen Lord to baptize and evangelize is valid throughout the days of this "last" age.

Pauline Motives for the Christian Mission

BY DONALD G. MILLER

Why missions? This question is on the lips of most secular people concerning the work of the Church to the ends of the earth. The "why?" of some is sympathetic: Why do these nice but naive people waste their lives in discomfort and loneliness, vainly toiling at futility? The "why?" of others is antagonistic: Why should efforts be made to change men's religion? After all, are not all religions essentially alike, all headed in the same direction? And are not religions culture-conditioned, each having developed in its own milieu as befitting the needs of its own adherents? And do not missions, in the light of present world tensions, interfere with good international relations? Isn't there enough, too, for each church to do in its own land without setting forth to evangelize other lands? And isn't there a profound Pharisaism, a distasteful spiritual pride, an unwholesome taint of religious superiority, lying behind the whole idea of missions? These and similar questions are fervently voiced by countless onlookers as the Church seeks to fulfill her mission in the world. But more—these same questions are frequently raised by many within the Church.

These objections are not to be taken lightly. Especially where they inadvertently are criticisms of missionary method rather than of the mission itself, the Church should penitently stand under their judgment and seek to mend her ways. But in so far as they strike at the heart and seek to deal a deathblow to the Church's mission, they summon to a reexamination of missionary motives.

Motive is defined as "any consideration . . . moving the will." [1] If the will of the Church is to be moved to pursue the mission task before her, she must reexamine those "considerations" which initially turned the Church out toward the whole world. All of the objections stated above, save interference with international relations, were as valid in the first century as in the twentieth.[2] And yet, "the history of the New Testament is a history of missions." [3] We turn to Paul, the greatest missioner of them all, to search for the motives which made this so.

The Self-Revelation of God

To Paul, mission was involved in the fact that God had revealed Himself. Paul was "a Hebrew born of Hebrews" (Phil. 3:5). To him, Israel was God's "people," "the natural branches" of the tree of God's promise into which the Gentiles had been "grafted" (Rom. 11:17 ff.). His description of them even after he became a Christian—"They are Israelites, and to them belong the sonship, the glory, the covenants, the giving of the law, the worship, and the promises; to them belong the patriarchs, and of their race, according to the flesh, is the Christ" (Rom. 9:4 f.)—indicate that Paul's faith was not a reaction against Judaism but an outgrowth of it. The Church, according to Paul, was the true Israel, the heir of ancient Israel's mission. What Paul knew, therefore, of the God who had revealed Himself in the history of His people was basic to his understanding of his mission as a Christian.

1. *The revelation of God as one* is the ultimate foundation on which mission rests. If there is but *one God,* then He is the *God of all men.* How early a clearly defined monotheism developed is debatable, but it is now plain that its roots go back into the earliest stages of Israel's history and underlie her whole development.[4] The patriarchal stories interpret God's call of Abraham from a missionary perspective: "in you all the families of the earth will be blessed" (Gen. 12:3, R.S.V. margin). Amos brought non-

[1] *Webster's New International Dictionary,* second edition, unabridged (Springfield, Mass.: G. C. Merriam Company, 1947).

[2] Cf. Robert E. Speer, *Some Living Issues* (New York: Fleming H. Revell Company, 1930), pp. 224 ff.

[3] John Bright, *The Kingdom of God* (New York and Nashville: Abingdon-Cokesbury Press, 1953), p. 257.

[4] Cf. John Bright, *op. cit.,* pp. 24 ff.; H. H. Rowley, *The Faith of Israel* (London: SCM Press, 1956), pp. 71 ff.

Israelite peoples into the purview of God's purpose (Amos 9:7). The writer of 1 Kings records the purpose of the building of the Temple: "that all the peoples of the earth may know thy name and fear thee, as do thy people Israel" (1 Kings 8:43). The implications of monotheism are most clearly set forth by Second Isaiah: "there is no other god besides me. . . . Turn to me and be saved, all the ends of the earth! For I am God, and there is no other" (Is. 45:21 f.).

It is clear that Paul's concern to take the Gospel to the whole world was rooted in this aspect of his heritage. He insisted that the Gentiles were the heirs of God's grace because God is one: "Is God the God of Jews only? Is he not the God of Gentiles also? Yes, of Gentiles also, since God is one" (Rom. 3:29 f.; cf. also Rom. 10:12; 1 Cor. 8:4 ff.; Eph. 4:6). Were there no other motivation, belief in one God who is thereby the God of all men lays on the Church an inescapable obligation to mission. The one God is God of all.

2. Neither Paul nor the Old Testament writers, however, arrived at this merely as the conclusion of a syllogism. They were not philosophers speculating about the nature of God and the relevance of this to life. Their monotheism rested ultimately on the fact that *God had revealed Himself as Lord.* His Lordship rested on the dual facts of creation and redemption. Although patently creation precedes redemption, yet it seems quite likely that it was through His redemptive activity that God revealed Himself as Creator.

At the Exodus God had made Himself known as a compassionate, saving God. Moses was commissioned in this fashion: "I have seen the affliction of my people who are in Egypt, and have heard their cry because of their taskmasters; I know their sufferings, and I have come down to deliver them" (Ex. 3:7 f.). The psalm commemorating the Exodus event exults: "The Lord is my strength and my song, and he has become my salvation" (Ex. 15:2). The covenant was renewed to Moses with the words: "The Lord, the Lord, a God merciful and gracious, slow to anger, and abounding in steadfast love" (Ex. 34:6). Micah voiced the common conviction of the prophets when he termed the Exodus and what followed "the saving acts of the Lord" (Mic. 6:5). Second Isaiah encouraged his forlorn people with these words: "But now thus says the Lord, he who created you, O Jacob, he who formed you, O Israel: 'Fear not, for I have redeemed you; I have called you by name, you are mine' " (Is. 43:1). In the history of His people, God had revealed Himself as a God of sheer grace and mercy.

But in so doing, He had manifested His power over all the forces of nature and over all the supposed gods who were identified with the forces of nature: "on all the gods of Egypt I will execute judgments: I am the Lord [Yahweh]" (Ex. 12:12). God's redemptive activity demonstrated Him as Yahweh (Ex. 3:14), "He who causes to be what comes into existence."[5] He was the one who "in the beginning . . . created the heavens and the earth" (Gen. 1:1). As maker and redeemer, then, Yahweh is Lord. To Him all that is belongs. Nature exists to serve His purposes. Man is a creature made to live under the loving will of his Creator.

The Lordship of the redeeming God Paul believed to have been manifested finally in Jesus Christ. Out of many examples, one may serve to make this clear. In Romans 10:13, Paul quotes Joel 2:32: "every one who calls upon the name of the Lord [Yahweh, in Joel] will be saved." This word about the Lordship of Yahweh he applies directly to Jesus: "if you confess . . . that Jesus is Lord . . . you will be saved" (Rom. 10:9). But in addition to God's Lordship in redemption, His Lordship in creation is also manifested in Jesus: "in him [Jesus] all things were created, in heaven and on earth, visible and invisible, whether thrones or dominions or principalities or authorities—all things were created through him and for him" (Col. 1:16). "Jesus is Lord," as the agent both of creation and redemption, is the earliest Christian creed.

Every rebellion, therefore, against God's will, and all indifference to the claims of His love made known in Christ, is a challenge to His rightful Lordship. Those who do not acknowledge Christ's Lordship are "alienated from the life of God" (Eph. 4:18), "enemies" who need to be "reconciled to God" (Rom. 5:10). Christian conversion, then, is a radical break with a world hostile to God and a decisive transference "to the kingdom of his beloved Son" (Col. 1:13). There can be no truce between the kingdom of Christ and alien forces. It is Christ's purpose to subdue all enmity to God, to destroy "every rule and every authority and power," including death, so that "God may be everything to every one" (1 Cor. 15:24 ff.). Those, therefore, who accept God's Lordship in Christ

[5] Cf. W. F. Albright, *From the Stone Age to Christianity* (Baltimore: Johns Hopkins Press, 1940), pp. 197 f.

cannot remain quiescent in the presence of any challenge to it. In Athens, Paul's "spirit was *provoked* [παρωξύνετο, "pricked," "irritated," "exasperated"] within him as he saw that the city was full of idols" (Acts 17:16). He was stirred to action to bear witness to the Kingship of Christ established at the Resurrection and to be made final at the last judgment (Acts 17:31). The idolatries, the rivals of Christ's Lordship, in our time are different in form from those of ancient Athens but quite the same in essence. Acknowledgment of Christ's Lordship means mission, witnessing to that Lordship until "every knee should bow, in heaven and on earth and under the earth, and every tongue confess that Jesus Christ is Lord" (Phil. 2:11).

The Nature of the Gospel

Mission is involved in the very nature of the Christian Gospel.

1. This may be seen first in *its nature as revelation.* In the Bible, God is never the object of contemplation. He is the subject who initiates action to make Himself known. By His very nature as God, He "sits above the circle of the earth" (Is. 40:22), of whom no "image" can be made (Ex. 20:4) nor any "likeness" imagined (Is. 40:18, 46:5), whose "thoughts" are beyond all human thoughts (Is. 55:8 f.), and upon whose "face" man may not look and live (Ex. 33:20). He cannot be discovered by man's search, but is to be known only when He discloses Himself. Yet He is One who does disclose Himself, who "speaks," whose "word . . . goes forth from [His] mouth" and does "not return . . . empty" but accomplishes what He purposes (Is. 55:11).

Paul shared this Old Testament view. He was convinced that "the world did not know God through wisdom" (1 Cor. 1:21), and that those who were outside the group to whom God had made His self-disclosure simply did "not know God" (1 Thess. 4:5). He was equally convinced that God had made himself known in Jesus Christ, who had come not as the end product of human searching but as God's gift to man, initiated and carried through by Him alone. The "mystery" of God's righteousness and wrath, the "secret and hidden wisdom of God" concerning man's salvation and glorification, "kept secret for long ages," is "now disclosed and . . . made known to all nations" (Rom. 1:17 f.; 1 Cor. 2:7 ff.; Rom. 16:25 f.). The revelation was not the mere impartation of a new set of religious ideas to match or replace those of other men, but rather God's gift of Himself to men in the objective, concrete, historic reality of His Son. True revelation is "the direct, temporally located self-manifestation of God, valid for all men," which functions as "God's judgment *on* man, as God's active relationship *to* man, and His long-suffering dialogue *with* man." [6]

The fact of such a revelation is an unproved and unprovable assumption, but counter views rest on a similar undemonstrable basis. The assumption of revelation is the only objective criterion of truth which is not at the mercy of human subjectivity. How is the truth of a religion to be determined? It is mere subjective assumption to say by the height of its spiritual values, for another may assume that material values are superior to spiritual values. The measuring rod of unselfish altruism may be countered by one who insists that altruism is "the root illness of man" and that "it is the morality of altruism that men have to reject." [7] The degree of mysticism, too, is a purely subjective measuring rod, for it may just as handily be argued that mysticism is an escape from reality which should be avoided at all costs. At long last, subjective judgments may be reduced quite largely to what one happens to prefer.[8] To posit the fact of God, however, and to hold that because God is God He can speak to man, and that in Jesus Christ He has done so, is an assumption, but it rests on a possible act of God outside man which, if true, has a greater degree of objectivity than rival assumptions. If this assumption has any validity, the criterion of truth becomes not what one prefers but what God has revealed.

God's self-disclosure, then, is final truth which is the criterion of all truth. Christianity is thus a universal religion which by its very nature as revelation is impelled to mission the whole world. It cannot come to terms with any syncretistic tendency to amalgamate the good in all religions, on the theory that all religions are simply adaptations of one general species. Its aim is not to supplement other religions, but to supplant them. This can be considered arrogance only by those who misunderstand the nature of revelation, and can *be* arrogance only by Christians who do not understand their own faith.

As an empirical religion, Christianity stands alongside other

[6] Cf. Hendrik Kraemer, *Religion and the Christian Faith* (Philadelphia: The Westminster Press, 1956), pp. 19 and 347.

[7] Ayn Rand, *Time,* February 29, 1960, p. 94.

[8] Cf. Hendrik Kraemer, *op. cit.,* chapters I and II.

religions, partial, time-conditioned, fallible. The historic Christian Church is not the criterion of final truth, but Jesus Christ. In full humility, therefore, and in full recognition of how far historic Christianity has failed either adequately to embody or to witness to the truth in Christ, the Church, as the bearer of final revelation, is inescapably impelled to witness to all men. The witness must be made in full recognition of the fact that the Gospel "is as responsible for those who proclaim it as it is for those to whom it is proclaimed. It is the advocate of both." [9]

2. That mission is involved in the nature of the Gospel may be seen, too, in *its nature as proclamation.* The very word "gospel" means "good news," and news must be "heralded." The nature of revelation as God's objective action in the history of Israel and in the life, death, and resurrection of Jesus Christ demands that these events should be told. "Faith comes from what is heard" (Rom. 10:17). "And how are [men] to believe in him of whom they have never heard? And how are they to hear without a preacher?" (Rom. 10:14). To believe that in Jesus Christ God has spoken His full and final word to all men lays on the believer the responsibility of bearing witness to this and of seeking to persuade others to a like faith.

This is not a mere matter of propagandizing others, or of seeking to dominate their thinking by overwhelming pressures. It is rather a question of obedience to the Lordship of Jesus Christ. "Grace means bearing witness to the faithfulness of God which a man has encountered in Christ, and which, when it is encountered and recognized, requires a corresponding fidelity toward God. The fidelity of a man to the faithfulness of God—the faith, that is, which accepts grace—is itself the demand for obedience and itself demands obedience from others. Hence the demand is a call which enlightens and rouses to action; it carries with it mission, beside which no other mission is possible." [10]

3. The *nature of the Gospel as invitation* also means mission. From the question of God to man in the Garden of Eden, "Where are you?" (Gen. 3:9), to the thrice-repeated "Come" on its last page (Rev. 22:17), the Bible is the record of one great search on the part of God for man. God is the great "extrovert" who has

[9] Karl Barth, *The Epistle to the Romans* (London: Oxford University Press, 1933), p. 35.

[10] *Ibid.*, p. 31.

turned Himself out toward man in relentless love. "When Israel was a child, I loved him . . . How can I give you up, O Ephraim?" (Hos. 11:1, 8), is a refrain which haunts every movement of the Old Testament symphony. But the love God had for Israel was His love for the world. "God so loved the *world* that he gave his only Son" (Jn. 3:16) is simply the Old Testament refrain in a New Testament key.

No one grasped more clearly than Paul the nature of the Gospel as invitation, God's summons to the whole world to be reconciled to Him. Paul knew the radical nature of this unbelievable invitation because he knew the radical nature of man's situation. Man is "estranged and hostile" to God, an outright "enemy" (Col. 1:21; Rom. 5:10). But God has acted in love which could not be destroyed by man's enmity. Entirely apart from anything man could do or desires to do, God has *"reconciled* to himself" all men "by his grace as a *gift,* through the redemption which is in Christ Jesus" (Col. 1:20; Rom. 3:24). If the very nature of the Gospel is the active seeking of God's reconciling love, then to believe *this* gospel is, in our measure, to be the active agents of this reconciling love to others.

The Nature of the Church

The nature of the Gospel determines the nature of the Church. As Emil Brunner has said, "The Church exists by mission, just as a fire exists by burning." [11] Without flame, no fire; without mission, no Church!

1. This is clear when the Church is seen as the *body of Christ* (Eph. 1:22 f., 4:4 ff.; 1 Cor. 12:12 ff.). A "body" is the organ of expressing the will of its head, the active agent by which the impulses and desires of the head are given concrete form. The Church, then, is that body which exists to give continuous expression to the will of God in Jesus Christ.

As such, the Church is the true heir of ancient Israel. Through Second Isaiah, God speaks of Israel as "the people whom I formed for myself that they might *declare my praise*" (Is. 43:21). That this declaration was not mere verbalizing but concrete action is made clear in that Israel was given "as a covenant to the people, a light to the nations, to open the eyes that are blind, to bring out

[11] Emil Brunner, *The Word and the World* (London: SCM Press, 1931), p. 108.

the prisoners from the dungeon" (Is. 42:6 f.). This is echoed in the New Testament in Peter's description of the Church: "But you are a chosen race, a royal priesthood, a holy nation, God's own people, that you may *declare the wonderful deeds* of him who called you out of darkness into his marvelous light" (1 Pet. 2:9).

Paul, too, described the Church as those who "shine as lights in the world" (Phil. 2:15), and by example and precept insisted that it was the Church's business "to make the word of God fully known" as the fulfillment of God's having "made manifest to his saints" the riches of the mystery of Christ (Col. 1:25 ff.). But in one place he particularly connects the Church with this task, when in speaking of "the eternal purpose which [God] has realized in Christ Jesus" he insists that it is "through the church" that "the manifold wisdom of God might now be made known" (Eph. 3:9 ff.). The redeeming work of God in Christ is now to express itself through Christ's body. "To be a member of Christ's body is to be involved with Him in all His concerns. . . . The Church is to be responsible for all those for whom Jesus assumed responsibility." [12]

2. Mission, too, is involved in the nature of the Church as *servant of the Servant*. A servant does not determine his own tasks. They are set for him by another. His service does not rest on his own initiative, or desire, or the advice of others. It consists in doing the bidding of a master. So it is with the Church. But in this instance, the Master himself was the great Servant. "I am among you as one who serves"; "For the Son of man also came not to be served but to serve"—these sum up Jesus' ministry in his own words (Lk. 22:27; Mk. 10:45). Hence, for the Church to serve this Master is to be a servant of the Servant.

This concept is involved in the very idea of apostleship, which lay behind all of Paul's missionary effort. The great Apostle—the one "sent" to speak and act on behalf of God who sent him—was Jesus Christ (Jn. 3:17, 6:29, 8:42, 17:3; Heb. 3:1). But as the Father had "sent" him, he in turn had "sent" the apostles (Jn. 17:18, 20:21). In most of Paul's letters he describes himself as an apostle, and in Galatians he vehemently defends his apostleship (Gal. 1:1 ff.). In his deepest consciousness he was convinced that Christ had "sent" him to herald the Gospel (1 Cor. 1:17). The Church, however, is heir to this apostolic mission. Paul was

[12] Donald G. Miller, *The Nature and Mission of the Church* (Richmond: John Knox Press, 1957), p. 74.

aware that his own apostolic mission was to be Christ's servant in building a church through whom "the manifold wisdom of God might now be made known": a "household of God, built upon the foundation of the apostles and prophets" which was to be "a dwelling place of God in the Spirit" (Eph. 3:10, 2:19 ff.).

But how was this apostolic mission to be carried out? Paul frequently associates with his calling as an apostle the words "slave" (δοῦλος) and "servant" or "minister" (διάκονος) (Rom. 1:1; Phil. 1:1; 2 Cor. 4:1; Gal. 1:10; Eph. 3:7 ff.). Since Jesus was a Servant, the Church's ministry is to be the channel through which he may still serve the world. This service is the expression of Christ's love for the world. "For the love of Christ controls us," Paul wrote. This is not love *for* Christ, but rather *the love Christ had for the world* which led him to die in order to "reconcile" men to God by bringing them into a "new creation" (2 Cor. 5:14 ff.). The "ministry of reconciliation" is now "given" to the Church. Christ, who loved and still loves the world, is now expressing his love to men through the service of the Church. "So we are ambassadors for Christ" (2 Cor. 5:20).

The Church's service is to express the passion of the Servant. Paul boldly stresses this by rejoicing in his sufferings; for, said he, "in my flesh I complete what is lacking in Christ's afflictions for the sake of his body, that is, the church. . . . Him we proclaim . . . that we may present every man mature in Christ. For this I toil, striving with all the energy which he mightily inspires within me" (Col. 1:24 ff.). And he summons the Church to have the servant "mind" which "you have in Christ Jesus, who . . . emptied himself, taking the form of a servant" (Phil. 2:5 ff.). The Church is never more the Church than when it is the servant of the Suffering Servant, in "the sustained, determined act of announcing the good news" of his suffering love, until every knee bows and every tongue confesses that he is Lord.

3. The Church is involved in mission also as *"debtor" to all men.* "I am under obligation," said Paul, "so I am eager to preach the gospel" (Rom. 1:14 f.). The obligation did not stem from anything which those to whom he preached had given him. He was not paying back a debt, but passing on to them something which God had given him for them. As a servant of Christ Paul was a "steward of the mysteries of God" (1 Cor. 4:1). A steward was one who handled that which did not belong to him, the resources

of his master. And if his master's graciousness led him to make gifts to others, it was the steward's business to see that the gifts were delivered. Paul was under obligation to all men, therefore, because he held the Gospel in trust for them. God had given him "grace and apostleship to bring about obedience to the faith for the sake of his name among all the nations" (Rom. 1:5). If he did not pass the Gospel on to others, he was keeping back that which belonged to them, and was thus recreant to his duty.

The missing persons bureau of a large city recently broadcasted a plea for knowledge of the whereabouts of a missing lady. Her father, from whom she had been separated years before, had died in a foreign country and left her a sizable estate. The frantic plea was for someone to locate her and give her the news of her good fortune, so that she could acquire her inheritance. Without owing her a debt in the sense of having received anything from her, whoever knew her whereabouts and had the knowledge of her legacy was under obligation to inform her of it, though he may never have seen her before. Likewise the Church, knowing of the rich inheritance left to all men by God, is under obligation to pass on the news to all. "For necessity is laid upon me," said Paul. "Woe to me if I do not preach the gospel!" (1 Cor. 9:16). To know the Gospel, therefore, is to be obligated to mission.

The Predicament of Man

The need of man is justification for mission. Paul viewed man's need not from a human perspective, inspired by psychological and sociological analyses. His whole understanding of man was theological. Jesus Christ was for Paul the measure of man's depravity and his glory. To measure man by what Jesus was as a man is to see how far short of God's glory man has fallen (Rom. 3:23). Yet the fact that in Jesus God became man reveals the glorious fact that man may become the dwelling place of God, the temple of His Spirit (1 Cor. 3:16 f.; 6:19; 2 Cor. 6:16; Eph. 2:21).

1. *The futility of man's life in alienation from God* motivated Paul to offer man Christ's deliverance. Paul shared the radical view of man's alienation from God voiced in the Old Testament. Created as a creature to live under the sovereign will of a loving Creator, man had sought to be independent of God and thus to be equal to Him (Gen. 3). Made in the "image" of God, man was

unwilling to be a reflection of the divine nature; he aspired after deity itself. The paradox of man's lot is that, thus aspiring to deity, he rather fell under the power of the demonic. "For although they knew God they did not honor him as God or give thanks to him, but they became futile in their thinking and their senseless minds were darkened" (Rom. 1:21). Men became subjected to "the prince of the power of the air" (Eph. 2:2), fell under "the dominion of darkness" (Col. 1:13), became "slaves to the elemental spirits of the universe" (Gal. 4:3), victims of "death" (Rom. 5:12). To Paul these descriptions were not the philosopher's proud attack on human stupidity, implying that man could do better if he would only choose to do so. This was rather a description of the radical dislocation within man to which all are victims, himself included. "Wretched man that I am! Who will deliver me. . . ?" was the confession of his own futility apart from Christ (Rom. 7:24).

But this futility of man's Adamic nature has been overcome by Jesus Christ, the "last Adam" (1 Cor. 15:45). "He has delivered us from the dominion of darkness" (Col. 1:13), he has overcome death (1 Cor. 15:20 ff.), and he "delivers us from the wrath to come" beyond death (1 Thess. 1:10). Through this deliverance he has overcome man's alienation from God, restoring him to his rightful sonship and sending "the Spirit of his Son into our hearts, crying, 'Abba! Father!' " (Gal. 4:6). It is the duty and privilege of the Church to answer the human cry, "Wretched man that I am! Who will deliver me. . . ?" with the ringing answer: "Thanks be to God through Jesus Christ our Lord!" (Rom. 7:24 f.)

2. Paul also was motivated to mission by the fact that *man is under divine judgment*. In dealing with the human predicament, Paul insists that "the wrath of God is revealed from heaven against all ungodliness and wickedness of men" (Rom. 1:18). If this were but an isolated statement, it might well be dismissed. But Paul refers to this concept over and over again, always in the most serious vein (Rom. 2:5 ff., 9:22; Eph. 5:6; Col. 3:6; 1 Thess. 2:16). Some have sought to avoid the implications of this by holding that the wrath of God is an "impersonal" thing, "an inevitable process of cause and effect in a moral universe." [13] It is more Biblical to think of wrath as "a personal activity of God . . . the eternal

[13] C. H. Dodd, *The Epistle to the Romans* (London: Hodder & Stoughton, 1932), pp. 23 f.

reaction against evil without which God would not be the Moral Governor of the world." [14] God's wrath is never in conflict with His love. The opposite of love is hatred, not wrath. Divine wrath is God's holy love in action against sin.

Furthermore, to indicate that God's wrath was not merely the impersonal operation of a moral law which is the nemesis of evil in this life, Paul speaks of a hardening of heart which does not acknowledge that "God's kindness is meant to lead . . . to repentance," and is "storing up wrath . . . on the day of wrath when God's righteous judgment will be revealed." "Wrath and fury," rather than being impersonal forces, are contrasted with "glory and honor and immortality" and "eternal life" (Rom. 2:4 ff.).

Although we move in the area of mystery here, and although universalism is an inviting prospect, it is difficult to see how Paul could have taken God's wrath so seriously if he felt that ultimately all men would be saved. Hendrik Kraemer seems to be moving on truly Pauline grounds when he writes:

> "Hardening of heart" is in Greek σκληροκαρδία, "kardiosklerosis." It is a terribly clear word to express that this is a hopeless lethal case. The more so, when we remind ourselves that in the Bible "heart" is man in the totality of his being. These cases exist, just as there exists the mystery of Judas. Without minimizing in the least the Biblical teaching that the gospel . . . is meant for the whole world, we should not lose sight of the important marginal flashes the Bible throws on the mystery that man can get by his own acts into an irretrievable situation, and that God puts the seal upon it by *making* it irretrievable.[15]

To do all that can be done to dissuade men from such an irretrievable course is a part of the motivation to mission. As this discussion has indicated, it is by no means the only motive, and if it were withdrawn, there would be ample motivation for the Church's mission. But that this is *one* motive which we would do well to ponder seems inescapable. Paul worked constantly under the stimulus of this motive, and even kept always before his mind the solemn fact that he, too, was to be judged at the last day. "Therefore, knowing the fear of the Lord, we persuade men" (2 Cor. 5:11).

[14] A. M. Hunter, *Interpreting Paul's Gospel* (Philadelphia: The Westminster Press, 1954), p. 79.

[15] *Op. cit.*, p. 380.

The Gospel According to St. John and the Christian Mission

BY F. N. DAVEY

The Gospel according to John has played a decisive part on many occasions when the Church's conception of its mission was in doubt, in recent as well as former times. More than any other book of the Bible, it caused Christian theologians of the West to return to the study of Christian sociology, and to insist that Christian social action must be governed by the Christian revelation of God. During the critical years of "the new theology" and the apparent triumph of liberalism, when everyone was questing for the "Jesus of history," it protested by its presence in the New Testament against the identification of "history" and "theology," and affirmed that theology must exist in its own right. As the subject of several notable commentaries, it has helped to show how theology may answer the questions which history leaves unanswered, and has inevitably come more and more into the center of New Testament study as that study has recovered its authentic preoccupation with theology. The result of putting it into the hands of learned students, whether of the great religions of Asia or of Judaism, has not seldom been their conversion to the faith of Christ. It has spoken authoritatively alike to those drawn to mysticism and to those schooled in philosophy. It is not surprising that at the Tambaram Conference in 1938 it was claimed that "the all-embracing activity of Jesus Christ, as well before as after his incarnation, found in the

Gospel of St. John, is of the greatest importance with regard to world mission work."

Yet, is it right to speak of "the Johannine approach to the world mission of the Church," as though this Gospel had a conception of Christ, or a conception of man, or a conception of the Holy Spirit, altogether different from those found in the rest of the New Testament; or as though this Gospel alone defines and justifies a particular missionary assumption and technique? The question must be examined, not so much in order to assess the relation of the Fourth Gospel to the rest of the New Testament as it is understood today, a quarter of a century after the Tambaram Conference, as to define once again (as the Church must continually try to do) the ways in which the Christian Gospel may be shown to be relevant to the thinking of those still without Christ in the world.

Twenty-five years ago the Fourth Gospel was commonly studied in contrast to the three "Synoptic Gospels." These were held to share a common point of view, precisely in distinction to that of the Fourth Gospel. At that time, their "authors" or "redactors"—those responsible for their final shape—were regarded as the least important factor in their composition. Even though it was becoming accepted that nowhere in the Synoptic Gospels could the student identify history that was not already selected and recounted under the influence of prior "interpretation," this "interpretation" was held to represent—particularly if recognizable in more than one of the supposedly separable strands of Synoptic tradition—the common mind of the Church in very early (indeed, in apostolic) times. Here, it was maintained, was sufficient basis for the study of the mind of Christ; sufficient basis, therefore, for presenting Christ to the world today. The Fourth Gospel, it was conceded, might also contain material of similar significance; but in practice it was left on one side, as representing the mind of only part of the Church, in an age almost entirely removed from direct apostolic influence.

Since those days a very considerable reassessment has taken place. Dr. C. H. Dodd has taught that the Fourth Gospel follows Mark in many respects more directly than do Matthew and Luke, and has "a close affinity with the apostolic preaching." Hoskyns has affirmed that the Fourth Gospel is the first and best commentary on Mark. On the other hand, the first three Gospels have increasingly come to be studied for their individuality—not so much for the sources that appear to lie behind them as for their author's or redactor's patent intention and purpose. The common idea that the first three Gospels preserve (no doubt in fragments and disorder) what might be described as "photographs" of the Jesus of history, whereas the fourth is a "portrait," has given way to the recognition that all four Gospels are best regarded as portraits. No doubt there are differences of form—the first three Gospels, for instance, share an episodic style conspicuously different from the allusive continuity of the fourth. But a difference that matters more is the difference in the deliberate intention of the author. Professor C. K. Barrett has summed it up as follows:

> Each of the evangelists begins his work by tracing back the activity of Jesus to its origin (ἀρχή): Mark to the work of the Baptist and the baptism of Jesus, with the descent of the Spirit and the divine pronouncement, Thou art my Son; Matthew and Luke to the birth of Jesus from a virgin; John to the creation, and beyond it. Each intends to prepare his readers for understanding the ensuing narrative; Jesus can be understood only as Messiah, as Son of God, and as Logos. *John alone, however, gives the narrative about Jesus an absolute theological framework.*[1]

This difference must be borne in mind even when the fundamental unity of the New Testament is being emphasized—as has also become common during recent years. The fundamental unity of all four Gospels consists in their common preoccupation with the self-revelation and redemptive achievement of God, with the good news of His unique and ultimate act of salvation, with which —and this too is equally true of all of them—the life, death, and resurrection of Jesus are essentially and inextricably connected. Their portraits of Jesus may be said to differ inasmuch as each wrote in a particular situation in the history of the Church, and to the best of his ability and understanding presented Jesus so as to show how, in him and by him, and through his death and resurrection, God's mercy and truth offered all men all that they needed in that particular situation. To men with the burden of Old Testament prophecy ringing in their ears, with an intense expectation of the promised Messiah of God, with their eyes looking for the first sign of God's kingdom come on earth; to men crying out for the vindication of God's justice, for the unleashing of His compassion, the Marcan introduction should have been enough. For those

[1] *The Gospel According to St. John* (London: S.P.C.K., 1955), p. 125.

familiar with Jewish-Christian controversy, or who, while knowing the Old Testament, were far removed from the atmosphere of Messianic expectation, Matthew and Luke open with the account of the birth of Jesus. Wise men worship the Holy One of God, to shepherds the wonder of his birth is revealed—scenes anticipating, perhaps, the scenes with which both these Gospels end, when the disciples worship the risen Christ. The theological understanding of Jesus implied for the readers of Mark by messianic allusions is not heightened in Matthew and Luke—that would be impossible—it is safeguarded by a more obviously theological definition of his person. The potential misunderstanding, that he became Messiah "by adoption" at the Baptism (no doubt unthinkable to the author of Mark) is at the same time precluded. It remained for the Fourth Evangelist to make the theological definition of Jesus unmistakable in a world so vague and various in its conceptions of divinity that even the fact of virgin birth might not seem to constitute an absolute claim to Godhead. In Professor Barrett's words: "The only perspective in which the work of Jesus, and his relation to the Father, could be truly seen and estimated was that of eternity." Jesus is therefore presented as "the Word who was in the beginning with God, who himself was God."

Although St. Paul did not name Jesus the Word of God, he reached a similar Christology by what seems to have been a similar process. In his Epistle to the Colossians he has moved away—not from the historical Gospel delivered by Christ to the apostles—but from the presentation of that Gospel in such terms as might have seemed relevant only to Jews nourished on the Old Testament Scriptures. It is perhaps possible to show how St. Paul learned by experience to begin where his readers or hearers were; to start from their intellectual apprehension—true or false—of the revelation of God. However this may be, when writing to the Colossians he appears to be fully aware that, owing to the conception of the universe they shared with much of the hellenistic world, they were doubtful whether Christ could have power to save except in the lowest of the spheres by which men believed the earth to be surrounded. Surely there were higher powers intervening between man and the ultimate Godhead. St. Paul takes cognizance of their conception of the universe, their cosmogony, only in order to insist on the ultimate authority of Christ. To accept him as possessing restricted authority is to misunderstand him altogether. Rather, he alone is the truth to which even men's false and shadowy conceptions point, for he alone is the truth of God.

St. Paul and the Fourth Evangelist agree, but not because they were speculative theologians who naturally used the language of contemporary syncretistic philosophy. They were anything but speculative theologians. They agree because they were consciously concerned to show the absolute implications of the Christian faith that Jesus *is* the Gospel and that the Gospel *is* Jesus, to men familiar with the jargon of religion and philosophy that was popular for many years throughout much of the Roman Empire. When the Gospel is offered to men, it is Christ himself who is offered to them, and received by them. But, to be confronted by Christ is to be confronted by God, nothing less. Jesus, then, is the beginning and the end; the first creator and the final judge; the ultimate truth both of God and of humanity. Truly man as well as truly God, he mediates between God and man, offering us true knowledge of God, salvation from sin and death, eternal life in union with God. It follows that there is no genuine insight or authentic experience of man of which Jesus Christ is not the true meaning and the ultimate fulfillment. And it follows also that even where man is groping after a half-truth, or is imprisoned in a false interpretation of life and the world he lives in, Christ is still the truth to which it should be possible to direct his eyes, if not by analogy, yet at least by contrast; if not by arguing directly from men's actual conceptions, yet at least by repudiating them so as to bear witness to the truth.

Dr. Dodd has suggested that the Fourth Gospel was not written for Christians but for intelligent, educated people in the Greco-Roman world, conversant with contempory syncretisms of Jewish religion and Greek thought, men of respectable morality and humane idealism, in an attempt to lead them on from what they already accepted, to correct their ideas and finally redefine them in terms of the Gospel of Christ crucified and risen. Others prefer to think that the Fourth Gospel was written for Christians acquainted with the tradition represented for us in the three Synoptic Gospels, but in danger of misunderstanding it, in an attempt to make them see the full implications of what they were ignoring or limiting through overfamiliarity and superficiality. Both these approaches to the Fourth Gospel are relevant to the Church's missionary task. But, whatever readers the Fourth Evangelist had consciously in mind, and whatever assumptions of his may have conditioned his method, what is even more relevant is his apprehension that Jesus reveals and makes accessible the truth and grace of God to men, in the world they live in, so as to make sense both of that world and of their own lives in it. When everything possible has been done to discover the background of such great Johannine terms as "word, life, light, truth, way"; when we have found, or failed to find, parallels to the Evangelist's references to birth, water, wind, eating, drinking, meat, darkness, death; the fact remains that in each case it is the fundamental human experience connected with the imagery that provides the most illuminating clue to the Evangelist's purpose. The vocabulary in which the Jesus of the Fourth Gospel speaks about himself and about God is furnished by the essential pattern, by the raw material, of ordinary human life.

This does not mean that mere consideration of the context and conditions of human life in the world leads automatically to the contemplation of the truth of God. Perhaps it should mean that, and would mean that in an unfallen world. But men as this Gospel knows them are in the darkness which does not apprehend the truth. Even such a man as Nicodemus, for instance, has no inkling of the meaning of Christ's conversation about birth, water, and wind. To be in darkness is to interpret such things as having meaning only in themselves, in their actuality. A religious man can show himself to be in darkness by his attitude to material things. On the other hand, Jesus reveals the truth of God by showing in himself the true meaning of such things—and this always involves, implicitly if not explicitly, his life, death, and resurrection. A supreme example of this, in this Gospel, may be found in its theme of life. True life—to which all life should bear witness—is new life from above: life originating from and located in God. Such is Jesus' own life. But even his own life can be misapprehended as though it were something originating in time and space, something existing—though temporarily only—in its own right and strength.

Through death then must the origin and nature and locus of his life be laid bare, and the true origin, the true nature, the true locus of all life be revealed. At that point, reached historically because the clash between his life-giving ministry, summed up in his raising of Lazarus, and the blindness of the Jews is ultimate, his words, "I am the resurrection and the life" begin to be fully apprehensible to those with faith. Apprehension remains the gift of God. It can be described only as the achievement of the Holy Spirit bestowed upon his disciples through Jesus Christ's death and resurrection. But—and this is most striking—this apprehension illuminates the whole life which Christian men and women have to live in the world while yet being not of the world. In their living of this life in faith, the Holy Spirit reveals to them the meaning both of Christ's life and of their own. It is not simply that through Christ's death they have seen human life pointing beyond itself to eternal life with God. In seeing it thus pointing beyond itself they have seen (though only by faith) human life established and revealed in its full meaning; its truly amazing meaning; its *glory*.

According to the Fourth Gospel, the raw material of human life furnishes the essential Christian vocabulary because, through his life, death, and resurrection, Christ rules out the worldly, materialist, or exclusively humanist interpretation of life—not in the interests of some dualism, as though reality is to be found in the realm of ideas or through spiritual ecstasy, but in the interests of a true understanding—better, of an authentic living—of life as it is. Life in this world is therefore the more fully understood the more fully it is interpreted by reference to Christ crucified and risen. To put this the other way round, Christ crucified and risen is the key to all life, and through the Holy Spirit we see all life marked with his cross and consummated in his resurrection. It is usually assumed that when the author of the Fourth Gospel wrote:

> He was in the world,
> and the world was made through him,
> yet the world knew him not.
> He came to his own home,
> and his own people received him not

he was already thinking of the historical advent and rejection of Jesus. Of course he could not help thinking of it—it was the source of his whole understanding of the Gospel. But he also had in mind the eternal "advent" of Christ, in his creation and government of the world, as well as his particular "advent" to "his own" people through the prophets and seers and all those to whom a true insight had been given. God confronts man, through Christ, first in the pattern of creation and history, secondly in the calling and history of Israel, thirdly, in his coming in flesh and blood. But it is this third "coming" which enables the author of the Fourth Gospel—and which should enable us—to discern in his other two "comings" the absolute truth, the unique grace, of God in Christ.

For some people some words of the Prologue of the Fourth Gospel justify what has been called the particular Johannine approach to missionary work: "The true light that enlightens every man was coming into the world." Can this be rightly interpreted in terms of hellenistic religion and the Logos be thought of in a Stoic manner, so that there may be seen in this verse "a reference to a general illumination of all men by the divine reason, which was subsequently deepened by the more complete manifestation of the Logos in the incarnation"? Professor Barrett raises this question only to reject it. To "lighten" can indeed mean "to illuminate inwardly," but it is more in keeping with the rest of the Gospel to render it "to shed light upon," "to bring to light" and so to expose to judgment. St. John 3:16–21 deserves careful consideration. To build upon some supposed hellenistic reference a theory that the Word of God is to be encountered particularly, albeit dimly, in the various religious systems of mankind, seems precarious. The "life" is "the light of men" because it brings to judgment: because it exposes the disastrous, humanocentric, materialistic, "darkness" which imprisons men by nature, and strikes at its very roots wherever it may be found—not only in paganism, in Islam, Buddhism, or Hinduism, but in Israel—even in the Church of God! But this exposure to judgment is not destructive either in motive or (through Jesus Christ) in effect. The Word of God judges only that he may save: he lays bare only that he may clothe; he kills only that he may make alive.

It remains to sum up some of the points that seem to arise from this brief glance at what in the Fourth Gospel seems relevant to the mission of the Church.

1. The opposition with which the Fourth Gospel (in common with the rest of the Bible) is concerned is the opposition between the truth of God and the darkness in which sinful men are in bondage. That darkness may manifest itself in false religions, but that is symptomatic only of a more universal, a more fundamental, darkness, rooted in man's inability to see in relation to God the world, his existence in the world, and the whole pattern and material of life. The fundamental opposition is between the truth and grace of God, and the darkness as a result of which sinful man everywhere enthrones himself in the place of God.

2. On the other hand, the truth and grace of God in Christ are

apprehensible everywhere *by faith;* for by faith life and the things and events of life are seen by men in their true relation to God. Because Christ made and governs the world, any true discernment, anywhere, of the meaning of life is a triumph of the Holy Spirit of God, whether Christ himself is or is not acknowledged by name.

3. Men's eyes may be opened in discernment of the truth anywhere in human life; and, since religion is part of life, some men may find true discernment in a particular religion, however primitive, however crude. Indeed, because some religions at least consciously attempt to see life related to God, the opportunity for true discernment may perhaps be greatest when man is trying to be religious. Yet there too the possibility of self-deception also appears to be most prevalent, and most fatal.

4. The Christian Church, in preaching the Gospel, must start where men are. In trying to preach Christ to those of other faiths it will no doubt be well to try to build by analogy and by contrast upon such discernments of the truth as they seem to find in their religion. Yet it will be better still to try to present Christ as the meaning of the whole of their life; to show how any real grasp or understanding of God's world cries out for judgment—for the devastating interpretation and the merciful fulfillment which only the life, death, and resurrection of Jesus Christ can supply.

5. The Fourth Evangelist knew of no approach to the world essentially different from that of St. Paul, or indeed of the New Testament writers in general. Like them, he preached Christ and him crucified. But he clarified the apostolic approach in at least one respect. He showed that there is no situation of man, no experience of man, no authentic part of human life, which, when truly understood, does not point beyond itself toward Christ, and which, when so apprehended, does not, through the death and resurrection of Christ, become a great occasion of hope, a precious means of rejoicing in the glory of God. The Christian missionary task is to communicate such an understanding as that. Once communicated it is irresistible, for it is the earnest of the Holy Spirit of God.

PART TWO
HISTORICAL STUDIES

The Rise of Protestant Missionary Concern, 1517–1914

BY WILLIAM RICHEY HOGG

The Reformers evidenced no concern for overseas missions to non-Christians. Indeed, three centuries elapsed before Protestantism at large even began such outreach. Why? This and related questions here claim our attention.

Our approach relates to "foreign missions," not because these alone define the mission entrusted by God to his covenanted people, but because in the main through them Protestantism discovered the full missionary dimension of the Church. To attempt to examine this multiform and much-debated development briefly is both presumptuous and frustrating. Necessary generalizations require detailed qualification that is here impossible. Adequate documentation would triple the pages allotted. Yet the task requires doing.

The rise of Protestant missionary concern must be seen against the background of Christendom, the *corpus Christianum,* the ideal of a vast, unified, transnational Christian society. Many profess to see the *corpus Christianum* most fully realized under Pope Innocent III (d. 1216). Yet even in the thirteenth century the notion of Christendom was specious. The forces that shattered the idea and disclosed its unreality were growing long before the Reformation, gained major strength in the nineteenth century, and by the end of 1914–1945 were everywhere acknowledged—but not by all.

The impossibility of any longer assuming that missions proceed from a Christian West and take the Gospel and benefits of "Christian civilization" to the non-Western, non-Christian world is a major key to the crisis of the Christian mission in mid-twentieth century.

The main stages in the struggle for religious liberty provide this chapter's chronological divisions. The periods involved also coincide with major epochs in Protestant thought and missionary development. Increasingly after 1789, freedom of religion came to be understood by many as freedom from religion. This has contributed to acceptance of a "post-Christendom" age and major reshaping of contemporary thought on the Christian mission.

Roman Catholic Missions at the Time of the Reformation

For a thousand years prior to the Reformation the Roman Catholic Church through its monastic orders had conducted missions. In 1305, writing to Rome from Peking, the Franciscan John of Montecorvino declared that the apostles had never visited these regions. In 1492 Columbus reached America, the Spaniards completed the expulsion from their homeland of the Moors, and discovery via the sea lanes, already well begun, was launched on a global scale. By 1555 the Society of Jesus, the greatest missionary order of all, was fifteen years old, Xavier was already dead, and Roman missionaries labored in North and South America, Africa, Asia, and the islands of the seas.

Three great forces account for this missionary vigor.

First—the papacy. As Vicar of Christ, the pope represented universal authority and symbolized the universality of the Church. Innocent III had declared that Christ "left to Peter [and thus to the popes] the governance not of the Church only but of the whole world." Boniface VIII in 1302 in the bull *Unam Sanctam Ecclesiam* set forth the highest claim made for papal power. On the eve of the Protestant Reformation, in transnational outlook, universal authority, and exercise of effective dominion, the pope stood unique. Thus, in 1493 Alexander VI in his bull *Inter Cetera* could divide the world between Spain and Portugal for both trade and missions and require the Catholic monarchs to bring the people of the newly discovered lands to the Catholic faith. In 1537 Paul III in the bull *Sublimis Deus* emphasized that part of the meaning of the Great

Commission in relation to non-Westerners is that "all are capable of receiving the doctrines of faith." A few years later Rome began the experiments, lasting for more than a half century, that led in 1622 to the founding of the Propaganda [1] with its supervision of all Roman missions.

Second—monasticism. The orders were the missionary agencies of the Roman Catholic Church. The monks were its missionaries.

Third—the monarch. For hundreds of years Christian rulers had provided the financial means and protection for missions in their territories. They understood this to be their Christian duty, and their contribution had been a major factor in Christianity's spread through Northern Europe. As one result, people had been brought to the faith *en masse* as the monarch's subjects rather than as individually responsible persons.

The Period of the Reformation, 1517–1555

In 1555, thirty-eight stormy years after Luther (d. 1546) posted his famous "Ninety-five Theses," the Peace of Augsburg was drawn, incorporating the principle of *cuius regio, eius religio* ("whose region, his religion"). The ruler of a territory determined its religion. For the first time in Western Christendom a church—the Lutheran—other than the Roman Catholic was given equal recognition in law. By 1555, Calvin (d. 1564) had gained complete mastery in theocratic Geneva.

Luther.—To document in detail the Reformers' amazing lack of a theology of missions would require a small book, but to this problem considerable attention already has been given.[2]

[1] *Sacra Congregatio de Propaganda Fide,* Congregation for the Propagation of the Faith.

[2] Gustav Warneck, *Outline of a History of Protestant Missions from the Reformation to the Present Time,* translated from the Seventh German Edition by George Robson (Edinburgh and London: Oliphant, Anderson & Ferrier, 1901). The final German edition appeared in 1913. Chapters I and II provide the baseline from which all subsequent studies proceed. Unfortunately, Warneck is poorly documented. A recent and most useful investigation is Johannes van den Berg, *Constrained by Jesus' Love: An Inquiry into the Motives of the Missionary Awakening in Great Britain in the Period between 1698 and 1815* (Kampen: J. H. Kok, 1956). This doctoral dissertation from a conservative Dutch scholar is remarkably thorough and in its Chapter I provides a splendid survey, well documented, of studies on the subject. See also K. S. Latourette, *A History of the Expansion of Christianity* (7 vols.; New York: Harper & Brothers, 1937–45). The

Here the briefest summary is in order. Some have charged that all the Reformers assumed the Great Commission had been fulfilled by the apostles. Luther knew that the Gospel had not been spread through the whole world in the first generation of the Church, yet this seemed to mean little to him. *His* part of the world had received the Gospel. For all practical purposes, the Great Commission had been fulfilled. After the apostles, says Luther, "no one has any longer such a universal apostolic command, but each bishop or pastor has his appointed diocese or parish." [3]

Luther knew well the presence of the Moslem Turks in Hungary. He refused the approach of the Crusades, but he urged Christian rulers to fight the Moslem advance. Yet it seems not to have occurred to him that any Christian in positive witness should reach out to these Moslems. The Turks' Christian prisoners should bear witness to their captors, but this exhausts Luther's concern for a Christian approach to the Moslems.[4]

One searches in vain in the *Works of Martin Luther* [5] for any exposition of Matthew 28:19–20 or Mark 16:15 that would hint at the Church's responsibility to move beyond Christendom. This silence is in notable contrast to expressed papal understanding of the Great Commission. Even more striking is the contrast between Luther and the Anabaptists, who made the Great Commission binding upon every baptized Christian and who were choosing and sending missionaries as they could.[6] Warneck sees Luther's understanding of election and eschatology making impossible any concern for missions Van den Berg not altogether convincingly disagrees.

The Other Reformers.—Similarly, one searches John Calvin's *Institutes* and commentaries without finding any positive recognition of a theology of missions. Examination of Zwingli, Bucer, John Knox, and Melanchthon produces the same negative report. To be

---

reader who wishes to pursue the question would do well to compare Warneck, J. van den Berg, and Latourette and the larger literature to which they point. For much in this chapter the writer is considerably indebted to these three scholars, but documentation will be kept to a minimum.

[3] Quoted by Warneck, *op. cit.*, pp. 14–15.

[4] *Martin Luthers Werke,* Weimarer Ausgabe (*Heerpredigt wider den Türken,* 1529).

[5] *Ibid.*, or the shorter Philadelphia Edition, 1943.

[6] See Franklin H. Littell's chapter, "The Free Church View of Missions," note 14.

sure, Luther's doctrine of salvation and of the priesthood of all believers, and Calvin's theology with its inherent activism, concern for the extension of the kingdom, and emphasis upon the responsibility of the elect for humanity and society, have missionary implications (and were later appealed to), but the Reformers did not link these with missionary obligation. Here a prayer for the heathen's conversion, there an interest in a handful of Christians outside Christendom—but the overwhelming and well-nigh unanimous evidence points in the Reformers to no recognition of the missionary dimension of the Church.

Why the Lack?—Latourette lists six causes contributing to this absence of missionary concern. Protestantism's struggle to establish itself, its involvement in the wars of religion, the Reformers' eschatology, the indifference of Protestant rulers to spreading the faith, the absence of Protestant missionary machinery, and the relative lack of contact with non-Christian peoples by predominantly Protestant countries until the latter part of the seventeenth century.[7] Important as these are in the total picture, they do not altogether account for a theological deficiency. The Reformers provide scant explicit evidence for an answer. Yet one ventures to suggest several reasons.

First, the Reformers completely rejected the papacy, not least because to them it represented the height of sinful human pretension. They denied its universal claim and all that flowed from it. In so doing, they eliminated a major sixteenth-century missionary motivation and produced skepticism concerning Roman missions themselves. They disowned the methodology of "papal missions" with mass admissions to the faith all too frequently forced by the conqueror's armed power. That the Reformers' treatment of Anabaptists and others is equally damning does not diminish the force of their rejection. Moreover, no small factor in the Reformation's accomplishment was the surging dynamic of nationalism. This provided widespread popular support for the Reformers' renunciation of the papacy. Restive under papal dominion, new nationalism, when freed from that control, focused powerfully upon the internal needs of the native land.

Second, the Reformers repudiated monasticism. The Catholic parishes had no developed sense of missionary responsibility, but the elite in the monasteries understood and responded to the mis-

[7] Latourette, *op. cit.*, III, pp. 25–28.

sionary implications of the papacy. The Reformers disavowed the double standard of Christian life implied in the distinction between parish Christian and monk and also monasticism's "works-righteousness." Theologically and practically for the Reformers this meant denying anything comparable to Roman missions.

Moreover, the Reformers (and the papacy) thoroughly rejected the Anabaptists, their enthusiasms, their views on church and state, their attempt to "restore" the New Testament church, and their insistence that the Great Commission is binding upon each Christian. So great was the "danger" the Anabaptists seemed to pose that they were nearly wiped out.

Each of these repudiations involved denying a missionary ideal viewed either as false or as seriously defective. Moreover, with parishes devoid of missionary responsibility, attitudes congenial to the notion that the Great Commission had been fulfilled by the apostles, and "corrective" theologies emphasizing God's sovereignty, election and man's inability to shape his salvation, the Reformers, perhaps understandably, may have been incapable of seeing or espousing a theology of missions.

Allied with the above, there is also a more positive factor that helps to explain the Reformation's myopia toward missions. Emphasis upon the Bible, the priesthood of all believers, the full responsibility of each Christian under the Gospel, and fulfillment of one's Christian calling where he is placed, meant a recovery of meaning for local congregational life. Later these concerns led to new forms of response to the Gospel's universal claim and the Church's unity,[8] but initially, from the standpoint of mission and unity, they seemed to be severely limiting.

The Age of Protestant Scholasticism, 1555–1689

In Britain the Toleration Act of 1689 allowed Dissenters personal religious liberty. The battle was far from won, but the essential principle of religious freedom was established. In the years between the Peace of Augsburg and the Toleration Act, Protestant scholasticism and orthodoxy prevailed. Protestant theologians re-

[8] See John T. McNeill, *Unitive Protestantism* (New York: Abingdon Press, 1930), and his "The Ecumenical Idea and Efforts to Realize It: 1517–1618" in Ruth Rouse and Stephen C. Neill, *A History of the Ecumenical Movement: 1517–1948* (Published on behalf of the Ecumenical Institute Château de Bossey by S.P.C.K. in London, 1954).

fused to recognize the new thought currents swirling about them and sought only through medieval methodology to elaborate sound doctrine. This sterile period eventually produced two strong reactions.

Theological Developments.—Meanwhile, two developments in Calvinism emerged that in quite different ways influenced the rise of Protestant missionary concern. First, the Synod of Dort in 1619 marked the triumph over Arminianism of an extreme Calvinism that prevailed widely and worked effectively to throttle missionary endeavor. Second, the Westminster Confession of 1647, a major restatement of Reformed doctrine, in its Articles I and IV makes clear that "the holy Scripture . . . is the Word of God." The Bible was no longer the vehicle of the Word, but was equated with the Word itself. As one result, one hundred fifty years later men could point to the Great Commission and call for missionary obedience precisely because God's Word says, "Go."

Missions Pro and Con.—In this period several men saw and advocated the Christian's responsibility for foreign missions. The English Puritan Thomas Sibbs (d. 1635) sounded an early call.[9] Hadrian Saravia (d. 1613), a Dutchman who turned Anglican and died while Dean of Westminster, maintained the continuing validity of Matthew 28:19 and applied it to the whole Church. From Geneva in 1592, Theodore Beza (d. 1605) sharply attacked and denied Saravia's interpretation. Johannes Gerhard of Jena (d. 1637) later attacked Saravia and "proved" that through the apostles the Gospel had been conveyed to all and that the Great Commission had been fulfilled and was no longer binding.

In 1651 Count Truchsess challenged the Wittenberg theological faculty to acknowledge that Matthew 28:19 still required obedience. The Faculty refuted the judgment and insisted that the apostles had taken the Gospel to the world. If any race had forgotten or failed to respond, it deserved eternal punishment. Christian laymen and pastors were not called to be missionaries!

From 1664 Baron von Weltz urged his fellow Lutherans to carry the Gospel to unbelieving nations and proposed forming a missionary society. Von Weltz died as a missionary in Dutch Guiana, but in Germany he was widely attacked. Von Weltz was the first of many who came to acknowledge Roman Catholic criti-

[9] Martin Schmidt, *The Young Wesley: Missionary and Theologian of Missions* (London: Epworth Press, 1958), pp. 5–11.

cisms of Protestantism's lack of missions. But this recognition simply inspired Protestant theologians further to justify and proclaim their negative attitude.[10] Meanwhile, Oliver Cromwell and John Comenius, the Moravian,[11] also proposed launching missions, but there was no response.

The Age of the Enlightenment, Pietism and the Awakenings, 1689–1789

Drafted in 1789, the first article of the Bill of Rights of the United States' Constitution sets forth equal freedom for all religions. The same ideal was caught up in the French Revolution of 1789 and thenceforward became the policy in most European nations and in the so-called "secular states" among today's new nations. In the years between the drafting of the Toleration Act and the Bill of Rights a decisively new climate was created for Protestant missionary thought.

A Mechanistic Universe.—Introverted Protestant scholasticism was cut off from the world. Mere mention of the names of Copernicus, Kepler, Galileo, Harvey, and Newton reminds one that there were those in the preceding age who by their knowledge of astronomy, physics, and medicine made possible a mechanistic understanding of the universe that brought much in the Bible into serious question. Reflecting philosophy's accommodation to the new knowledge were Descartes, Hobbes, and Spinoza. Revelation scarcely seemed tenable. At the same time Northern Europe's Protestant nations had just begun their imperial encirclement of the globe.

Protestant Rationalism.—Within Protestantism the results of all that had transpired in geographical discovery, science, philosophy, and theology since the Reformation were twofold. The first was the emergence of a strong rationalistic strain within Protestantism. In Germany this was designated the Enlightenment (*Aufklärung*). It began with Leibniz (d. 1716), interestingly an advocate of missions in part because of his knowledge of Jesuit work in China. The *Aufklärung* culminated in Kant (d. 1804). He provided the transition to the liberal theology of the nineteenth century. In England a major outgrowth of this rationalism was Deism, or "natural

[10] For all the above see Warneck, *op. cit.*, pp. 20–40, 50, and J. van den Berg, *op cit.*, pp. 16, 23, 24.

[11] Rouse and Neill, *op. cit.*, pp. 88–91.

religion," best expressed in Tindal's *Christianity as Old as the Creation* (1730). Tindal held that Christianity's principles can be deduced by any reasonable people anywhere.

Pietism.—The second result was the development in the eighteenth century of Evangelical piety. Emerging almost simultaneously in Germany, Britain, and the Thirteen Colonies, and reflecting Lutheran, Anglican, and Calvinistic backgrounds, these pietistic movements were of similar temper. In striking fashion they interacted and influenced one another. They made possible the burgeoning of Protestant missions in the nineteenth century.

(A) Germany. Pietism in Germany began with P. J. Spener (d. 1705), who from 1670, in reaction against the sterility of prevailing Lutheran Orthodoxy, began founding cell groups and emphasizing Bible study, fellowship, and Christian *experience*. Thus emerged the little church within the Church (*ecclesiola in ecclesia*). On Spener's death, his close friend A. H. Francke (d. 1727) succeeded him. This Pietism of Halle did not become a sect, but remained a movement within Lutheranism and attracted many educated and influential people.

A teacher at the University of Halle and a close friend of Leibniz, Francke set forth a world view and missionary concern quite new in Lutheranism. At the suggestion of a Halle-trained adviser, Frederick IV of Denmark sought missionaries for his Danish colonies and found his only volunteers at Halle. Thus began the Danish-Halle Mission in 1705, which in 1706 sent out Ziegenbalg and Plütshau as the first Lutheran missionaries to India. Francke stood solidly behind the mission. His great dream was a Universal Seminary in which Lutherans, Eastern Orthodox, and others could be trained for missions throughout the world.[12]

Count N. L. von Zinzendorf (d. 1760) gained his missionary zeal from Francke. Some years later remnants of the old Moravians settled on Zinzendorf's estates in Saxony and there in 1722 built their village, Herrnhut. Zinzendorf's missionary vision and German Pietism deeply influenced the Herrnhutters. Within five years the Moravians reconstituted their church, with the entire community accepting missionary responsibility. Whole families went overseas as self-supporting missionary units. Within several decades Moravian missions were at work in Russia, Southern Asia, Africa, the Caribbean lands, North America, Greenland, and Labrador. A

[12] *Ibid.*, pp. 100–01.

whole church in mission with warmhearted zeal was something new in Christian history.

(B) The Thirteen Colonies. John Eliot (d. 1690), a Puritan pastor in Massachusetts, conducted a major mission among the Indians in New England. He learned the Indians' language and translated the Bible into their tongue. As some hundreds of Indians were converted, Eliot formed them into communities exemplifying the Calvinistic-Puritan theocratic ideal. Directly confronting "savages" ignorant of the Gospel, Eliot, with a Calvinist's concern for men's souls, became a vigorous and thoughtful missionary. He appears to have been the first to refocus the various elements in Calvinism so that that theology's inherent missionary power, hitherto thwarted and obscured, could emerge. His work inspired financial support in Britain and began to open men's eyes to Christian missionary responsibility.[13] Eliot's biographer, Cotton Mather (d. 1725) engaged in considerable and significant correspondence with the Halle Pietists, whose influence was also felt in New England.[14]

The Great Awakening arose in the Thirteen Colonies in the 1720s and had as its outstanding native-born leader, Jonathan Edwards (d. 1758). A theologian, philosopher, and pulpit orator, Edwards against the indifference of his day reinterpreted Calvin and sought for evangelical conversion among his hearers. Like Eliot, Edwards had worked among the Indians. Moreover, David Brainerd (d. 1748), a young protégé of Edwards, had burned himself out in five years as a missionary among the Indians. Engaged to Edwards' daughter, Brainerd died at the age of thirty in Edwards' home. Edwards' biography of Brainerd (1749) influenced Carey, Martyn, and others. Among the several results of the Great Awakening and related revivals were missions to Negroes and Indians and the considerable development of Christian higher education.

A young friend and student of Edwards, Samuel Hopkins (d. 1803), pursued and modified his mentor's thought. He was spokesman for the New England theology that had developed with full awareness of the American aborigines and that modified a widely

[13] Warneck, *op. cit.*, pp. 48, 49; J. van den Berg, *op. cit.*, pp. 23–28 *et passim.*

[14] Ernst Benz, "Pietist and Puritan Sources of Christian World Mission," *Church History*, Vol. XX (1951).

restrictive understanding of Calvinism so as to free it to make an appeal for conversion to all men. Hopkins' "disinterested benevolence," encouraging sacrifice of self for the greater glory of God, placed missionary motivation in a new context and enabled its author to look forward to the time when Christianity would spread throughout the world.[15]

In the Thirteen Colonies for the first time Calvinists in large numbers encountered non-Christian "natives." This then unique American experience caused them to re-examine their theology. Indeed, Calvinism's transplantation to American soil brought striking change. Among Calvinism's leading interpreters were those who had perforce been missionaries among the Indians. Their theological presuppositions led them to see that Christians must proclaim the Gospel among *all* men so that the elect from every nation can respond and show forth their election to the greater glory of God.

(C) Britain. In the eighteenth century the Evangelical Awakening became the most potent force in Britain's religious life. The majority of the predominant figures in the Awakening were Anglican, chief among them John Wesley (d. 1791). The Awakening issued in Anglicanism's Evangelical wing and through the Wesleys in Methodism. It also influenced other churches. Wesley's Arminian theology emphasized that Christ had died for all and that men everywhere could respond and receive the gift of life. From the deadness of Deism, Britain's people were brought by the Evangelical Awakening to a mighty spiritual quickening.

This much-described Awakening transformed England religiously and then socially. For nearly a century it influenced and was influenced by developments in Germany and America. John Wesley,[16] George Whitefield, and Jonathan Edwards symbolize this amazing interpenetration. Evangelical piety, concerned for men's souls and for those without the Gospel, through the entire eight-

[15] Latourette, *op. cit.*, Vol. IV, p. 78, and *Christianity in a Revolutionary Age* (New York: Harper & Brothers, 1958), Vol. I, p. 196; J. van den Berg, *op. cit.*, pp. 83, 84, 101. See also James S. Udy, *Attitudes Within the Protestant Churches of the Occident Toward the Propagation of Christianity in the Orient—an Historical Survey up to 1914*. Unpublished Ph.D. dissertation, Boston University, 1952, pp. 218–29.

[16] Schmidt, *op cit., passim.*

eenth century was conditioning a people. On the eve of the nineteenth century, when the missionary seed was planted in this well-prepared soil, it brought forth abundant fruit.

Colonial Missions.—In the period just surveyed several missionary ventures emerged. The Danish-Halle Mission and the missions conducted by the Dutch East India Company reflected the pre-Reformation idea that the ruler is responsible for Christianity in his territory. Two Anglican agencies, the Society for Promoting Christian Knowledge (1699) and the Society for the Propagation of the Gospel in Foreign Parts (SPG; 1701), arose in part from the impulses of German Pietism, but operated within a colonial context and thus reflected pre-Reformation conceptions. Although these Anglican societies were primarily for *British* colonists, from the outset they reached to Negroes and Indians (American and Asian). These several ventures attracted little enthusiasm and by the century's close were considerably less than vigorous. Interestingly, one notes, the only element in sixteenth-century Roman Catholic missions *not* rejected by the Reformers was the monarch's responsibility for Christianity and missions in his territories. On this foundation were built most of the missionary agencies before Carey.

Eruption of the Protestant Missionary Idea, 1789–1815

The above dates encompass the French Revolution's beginning and Napoleon's defeat at Waterloo. The sharply contrasting social and political emergents in France and in Britain in these two and a half decades were the natural issue of forces that had been mounting in the preceding century. Britain's Evangelical Awakening provided the crucial difference.

That Awakening also decisively influenced the course of the Christian mission.

William Carey.—William Carey, the British Baptist cobbler, stands as the pioneer and great symbolic figure of the beginning of modern Protestant missions. There were Protestant missions and missionaries before Carey's time; but, with the Moravians a major exception, these were colonial, were sometimes state-supported, and in large part reflected Augsburg's *cuius regio* principle. The Moravians' challenge to mission went unheeded, for the Herrnhutters addressed the Enlightenment's spiritual coldness. But sixty-five years later, when Carey summoned Christians to missionary obedience, he spoke to hearts stirred by the Evangelical Awakening. The response that issued then has continued to grow.

The examples of Eliot, Brainerd, the Moravians, and the Roman Catholics, Jonathan Edwards' *An Humble Attempt to Promote an Explicit Agreement and Visible Union of God's People Through the World, in Extraordinary Prayer, for the Revival of Religion, and the Advancement of Christ's Kingdom on Earth,*[17] Captain James Cook's *Voyages,* the influence of the Anglican Thomas Scott, Bible study, geographical and ethnographical research, his own evangelical concern, the weight in his heart produced by the unconverted near at hand—these coalesced in Carey to make him a man of unshakable and zealous missionary conviction. All this found expression in his *An Enquiry into the Obligations of Christians to Use Means for the Conversion of the Heathens*—the "charter of modern missions." [18]

Among a group of strict Calvinistic Baptists, some of whom had been reading Edwards and found their Calvinism thereby modified, and at Carey's urging, in 1792 there was formed The Particular Baptist Society for the Propagation of the Gospel amongst the Heathen. The title honored the older Anglican body but significantly added "amongst the Heathen." Its purview was universal, not colonial. Supported by church members, the society made its first grants to the Moravians and in 1793 sent Carey and the physician John Thomas to India. The rest is history.

Carey supported himself in Bengal. There he cared for his insane wife twelve years before death released her from her suffering. A self-taught linguist and scientist, Carey translated the Bible into several Indian tongues, launched training for Indian ministers, stimulated social reforms, and through his botanical research gained a Europe-wide reputation.

Carey did not use the term "foreign missions." He knew only one mission to be carried out on *all* fronts. He knew there should be only one missionary agency for all, but recognized the practical and denominational difficulties in his day. He urged a decennial

[17] 1748. The only work cited in a note in Carey's *Enquiry.*

[18] For a brief description of Carey's *Enquiry* and his ecumenical views on missions see W. R. Hogg, *Ecumenical Foundations* (New York: Harper & Brothers, 1952), pp. 5–8, 17.

world missionary conference to encourage unity and to encourage an over-all, coordinated approach to the Christian mission.

Founding of Missions.—Carey's first letter from India stimulated the formation of the interdenominational London Missionary Society (LMS) in 1795. Edwards' influence and that of an Anglican chaplain in Sierra Leone—this colony for freed slaves was itself an outgrowth of Evangelical concern—also played a part. In 1799, Anglican Evangelicals loyal to "the church principle" founded what became the Church Missionary Society (CMS) and thus drew Anglican participation away from the LMS. Also in 1799 the Religious Tract Society was formed, and five years later the British and Foreign Bible Society began its work. In 1817–1818 the Wesleyan Methodist Missionary Society took shape.

The impulses thus released quickly spread. In 1798 the Netherlands' Missionary Society was begun. New missionary societies grew up in Scotland. In New England, influenced by the theology of Edwards and Hopkins, Samuel J. Mills, Adoniram Judson, and other students were responsible for the emergence of the American Board of Commissioners for Foreign Missions in 1812. Judson went to India and en route his study caused him to accept the Baptist view on believers' baptism by immersion. He and several others were baptized by Carey in Calcutta. To support these new Baptist missionaries, the American Baptists in 1814 began their society. By 1821, American Methodists and Episcopalians had established their mission boards. The cumulative effect of these events encouraged the formation of regional missionary societies in Germany, and by mid-century there were nine, all sprung from Pietism. Other societies arose in Scandinavia.

Protestant Missions Cover the Earth, 1815–1914

In the years between Waterloo and Sarajevo, Protestant missions, in Latourette's phrase, experienced their "Great Century." Theologically, that century began with F. D. Schleiermacher (d. 1834) who, influenced both by Pietism and Kant, was optimistic about man and rejected Biblical literalism. The century also saw the rise of Biblical criticism. Albrecht Ritschl (d. 1889) marked the century's close. Distrusting metaphysics, rejecting Schleiermacher's foundation of "religious feeling," and starting with the Gospel as determined by "scientific history," he saw Christianity primarily as ethics. Faith leads to realization of the kingdom—humanity at its highest bound together by loving action. Thus, by the century's end optimism about man's capabilities for progress was influencing wide segments of Protestantism, including some in its foreign missionary outreach.[19]

Missionary Motivation.—Yet one must guard against assuming that a prominent motif in nineteenth-century theology was all-determinative for missions in this period. The Protestant world did look to Germany for leadership in theology, history, and Biblical studies, and German scholarship exercised real influence. But there were several schools of theological thought in Germany, some very conservative. Significantly, Germany's missionary outreach came mainly from those of conservative background.

Nineteenth-century Protestant missionary motivation is a vast and complex subject.[20] Although motives and understanding were modified from decade to decade, a strong and recurring eschatological strain among the Germans viewed foreign missions as the fulfillment of a condition needed for the Lord's return. Although both men were British Evangelical Christians, contemporaries, and worked in China, Hudson Taylor, founder of the China Inland Mission (the first great "faith mission"), was from a different background and differed sharply in theology from the Baptist Timothy Richard, who had strong social concern. Those of the SPG and of the missionary bodies that grew out of the Oxford Movement and Anglo-Catholic revivals had a different motivation from either Taylor and Richards or the German Lutherans.

Wide acceptance in many denominations of the Westminster Confession's interpretation of the Scriptures often gave appeal to the Great Commission's unchallengeable authority. The Moody revivals in the United States and Britain, the Student Christian Movement, the Student Volunteer Movement with its frequently misunderstood watchword, "The Evangelization of the World in This Generation" [21]—all of which are intimately related—had enormous influence in the final quarter of the century. These produced an unprecedented outpouring of lives from universities for service over-

[19] Cf. James S. Dennis, *Christian Missions and Social Progress* (3 vols.; New York: Fleming H. Revell Co., 1897–1906).

[20] Several doctoral dissertations of the scope and thoroughness of J. van den Berg's *Constrained by Jesus' Love,* and tracing specific developments in the period, would be of tremendous worth.

[21] John R. Mott, *The Evangelization of the World in This Generation* (New York: Student Volunteer Movement for Foreign Missions, 1904).

seas. Between 1887 and 1900, for example, the number of missionaries under the CMS tripled.

Colonial Expansion.—One must also record the considerable importance for missions of the high-water marks of Western European colonial expansion. In mid-century, China and Japan were opened to the West. In the final quarter the European powers divided Africa among themselves. At the same time, Korea was opened, and a few years later the Philippines came under American control. Here was the peak of Western impact upon the non-Western world.

Anglican missions flourished in British colonies, Reformed missions in Dutch colonies, Lutheran missions in German territories, and Roman missions in the possessions of Latin European countries. Yet, as Latourette has shown, Protestant missions in this period were more independent of governments—and more critical of colonial policies—than in any century since the fourth. Indeed, by 1910 probably a majority of the Protestant missionaries were at work in lands in which their home governments had no control. This was new in Christian history.

Other Factors.—When the Great Century began (1815), several hundred persons would amply have accounted for the total Protestant missionary force. When it ended (1914), there were some 22,000 missionaries—half of them women. Single women comprised more than one-fourth of all missionaries. Moreover, the emergence of the unmarried women missionaries occurred mainly within the century's final three decades.

By 1900 almost every church recognized that missions are the responsibility of the churches and of all Christian people—a remarkable transformation within a century's time. In the process, Protestantism *de novo* built up its missionary agencies. (In a notable parallel development voluntary societies for the support of Roman missions also emerged.) One outstanding result of this was the planting of Protestant churches among almost every people.

Missionary evangelism includes the spoken and the written word. Yet many peoples among whom missionaries labored had no written language. Accordingly, to help men read the Bible, missionaries reduced hundreds of languages to writing (in Romanized script), taught people how to read, and by 1910 had translated the Scriptures into more than five hundred tongues. This process went on vigorously in the twentieth century. The first literature for newly literate peoples has been the Gospels. The full meaning of this one fruit of modern Protestant missions may be much clearer three centuries hence.

Education and medicine provided the two major forms of Christian missionary service. By 1910 Protestant missionary secondary and higher educational institutions enrolled 180,000 students in Asia, Africa, and Latin America. Of the 86 institutions of college or university grade, enrolling some 8,600 students, India and China together had the majority, with India alone providing 58 per cent of the students. Medical missions appeared in the second half of the century. They sometimes provided the only Christian witness allowed or possible. By 1910 more than one thousand missionary doctors served overseas—one third of them women. The large majority of hospitals and dispensaries were in China and India, which lands also had the outstanding medical-training institutions.

Denominationalism and a variety of interpretations of the Gospel were part of this outreach. There was growth in nondenominational and "faith missions." Yet in remarkable fashion there was widespread and growing cooperation among Christians "on the mission field." There was new concern for the Church, its nature, its ministry, and its unity. Moreover, missionary conferences were establishing a pattern of cooperation that helped to shape "Edinburgh, 1910," and contributed to the development of national Christian councils a few years later.

On the eve of World War I, when mankind passed from the nineteenth century into the twentieth, the World Missionary Conference at Edinburgh in 1910 symbolized Carey's hope and reflected the most dynamic and creative forces in a century of missionary endeavor. Moreover, "Edinburgh, 1910" stands as the root symbol of the Ecumenical Movement in the twentieth century. The crucial significance of these two inseparable facts will become increasingly clear in future generations.

The Free Church View of Missions

BY FRANKLIN H. LITTELL

Until fairly recently it was common practice for Protestant historians to present the history of Christianity and its expansion within the framework of a traditional and ethnocentric periodization. Thus, early church history would be discussed within the context of the Mediterranean matrix, shifting from the synagogues of the Diaspora to the Latin-speaking world of the Pax Romana. As centuries went by, the center of Christendom shifted from the Mediterranean area to the Holy Roman Empire. The shift to the north was confirmed and completed by the Reformation of the sixteenth century. Thereafter, Western Europe—and perhaps even the German Empire—was taken for granted as the center of Christendom.[1] Missions, when presented at all, were treated from the

[1] In the *Handbook der Kerkgenschiedenis* of J. N. Bakhuizen van den Brink and J. Lindeboom, published at The Hague by D. A. Daamen's Uitgeversmaatschappij, 1946, in two volumes, the churches of Great Britain and North America are given a brief treatment together (p. 328 f.): ecumenical concern and missions receive thirty pages (p. 363 f.), but the discussion still centers in Germany, Switzerland, the Netherlands. The famous and much-printed *Kompendium der Kirchengeschichte* of Karl Heussi, published in many editions, the 10th here used (Tübingen: J. C. B. Mohr, 1949), is even more ethnocentric, with brief treatment of "Protestantism outside Germany" (pp. 491–506) and "World Missions" (pp. 513–15). Although Friedrich Loofs was better informed on non-European Christianity, his *Grundlinien der Kirchengeschichte* (2nd ed.; Halle: Max Niemeyer, 1910) is centered in German Protestantism, giving two pages to the

"center" outward. The missionary churches were handled as minor deposits of European church life.

Within the last few decades, however, church historians have been brought to the conclusion that the "younger churches" of America, Africa, Asia and the islands of the sea can no longer be discussed as provinces of European Christendom. There are several reasons for this return to more ecumenical and universal perspectives in the writing of church history. In two World Wars and two types of totalitarianism (Nazism and Communism), the self-satisfaction of the European religious establishments was thoroughly shaken and the disillusionment of the "new Christians" very great. Moreover, the disenchantment with European Christendom came at the end of the "Great Century" of the founding of new churches, at a time when the leaders of the "younger churches" were beginning to be aware of a certain self-consciousness and independence of white, West European cultural forms. Finally, it has been plain since the 1928 *Interpretative Statistical Survey of the World Mission of the Christian Church*[2] that the center of support for Christian expansion has shifted from Western Europe to the Free Churches. Not only are the large majority of Protestant missionaries supported by the Free Churches in Great Britain and America, with the latter widening the gap steadily, but the change of pace has been marked in Roman Catholicism and Judaism as well. The major proportion of support for Roman Catholic undertakings has come from the United States since before the First World War. The shift of Jewish culture and civilization to the New World was completed during Hitler's control of the old centers of Christian civilization.

With the end of the nineteenth-century culture religion on the Continent, a new period of church history is at hand for Western Europe, the former center of world Christianity. It is frequently termed, especially by those who have made a study of totalitarian-

---

churches in North America in the nineteenth century. In the 10th "improved" edition of Hans von Schubert's *Grundzüge der Kirchengeschichte* (Tübingen: J. C. B. Mohr, 1937) edited by Erich Dinkler, the discussion centers entirely in German-speaking Christianity. Other examples could be given, but four of the best European handbooks by four of the great church historians have been chosen.

[2] Edited by Joseph I. Parker and published by the International Missionary Council in New York.

ism in its various phases, the "post-Christian era" or the "post-Constantinian period." [3] The newer experiments in the disciplines of discipleship, lay movements which endeavor to capitalize on the lessons in discontinuity learned during the church struggle with Nazism,[4] have broken both in theology and educational method from the comfortable old identification of Western civilization with "the Christian religion." In doing so, they have found a heartening response from the members of the churches of Asia and Africa. As instruments of evangelism, movements such as the Kirchentag and Evangelical Academies have been greeted by the leaders of the "younger churches" with an enthusiasm and fraternal warmth no longer accorded the traditional style of Western-controlled missions. In sum, there are many sections of the earth today where the planting of Christian churches is welcome if the Church be the *ecclesia viatorum* of the New Testament, but unwelcome if the Gospel be identified with the peculiarly Western style of *corpus Christianum.*

The old periodization of church history, which culminated in the Reformation of the sixteenth century, left the strong impression that the last four centuries have been a time of steady decline—at best but a sequel to the main act of the play. Yet the Protestant state churches were anything but missionary, and the real epoch of modern Christian universalism did not begin until the rise of Pietism on the Continent and the Evangelical Awakening in the British Isles. Most important of all for a new view of church history, the "Great Century" of the Christian movement was the nineteenth century.[5] During this period, to be bracketed generally from the

[3] See the author's discussions of this point in "Die Bedeutung des Kirchenkampfes für die Ökumene," *Evangelische Theologie,* Vol. XX (1960), pp. 1–21; Guy F. Hershberger (ed.), *The Recovery of the Anabaptist Vision* (Scottdale, Penna.: Herald Press, 1957), pp. 119–34; "Totalitarismus," in *Weltkirchenlexikon* (Stuttgart: Kreuz-Verlag, 1960), cols. 1466–69. Hereafter, *WKL:* coedited with Hans Hermann Walz.

[4] See "Akademien, Evangelische" and "Kirchentag, Deutscher Evangelischer" in *WKL:* cols. 21–24, 727–30; also, the author's "Can America Adopt the Evangelical Academy?" in *The Christian Scholar,* Vol. XLIII (1960), pp. 39–45.

[5] The concept of the "Great Century" has become common coin as a result of the impact of the work of Kenneth Scott Latourette: *A History of the Expansion of Christianity* (N.Y. & London: Harper & Bros., 1937–45), Vols. IV, V, VI; see also his "New Perspectives in Church History," *The Journal of Religion,* Vol. XXI (1941), pp. 432–43. Two major studies of

Congress of Vienna (1815) to the beginning of the First World War (1914), more missionaries worked in the field, the Bible and basic Christian literature were translated into more tongues, the support of the Christian movement was spread over a broader base, more people were reached in more organized ways, than in any other period of church history. If a primary test of the Christian faith be its universality, the decades which preceded the World Missionary Conference at Edinburgh (1910)—the first of the great contemporary ecumenical conferences—were far more critical in shaping the Christian Church than those decades which culminated in the Peace of Augsburg (1555) and the Treaty of Westphalia (1648).

Certainly this is true for the "younger churches" of Asia, Africa, and the islands of the sea. Wise observers have come in recent studies to compare their situation to that of the "younger churches" to which Paul addressed his pastoral letters. The new churches of these areas, planted or watered during the Great Century of expansion, are much nearer to the New Testament and early Church than they are to the style of coercive religion which dominated most of Christian Europe from the era of Constantine, Theodosius, and Justinian to the age of the French Revolution. "Christendom," as defined in medieval political theory and reconfirmed in the teachings of the great Reformers, has been a concept ill-fitted to the situation and needs of the newer churches. From the perspective of the members of the "younger churches," having of necessity no other weapons for their spiritual warfare than those ordained by Scripture, being totally dependent upon the guidance of the Holy Spirit for government and the voluntary giving of members for support, there is little real difference in effect between Martin Luther's "Address to the Christian Nobility of the German Nation" (1520) and Richard Hooker's "The Laws of Ecclesiastical Polity" (1594 ff.). The "younger churches" are "Free Churches," and they belong to a different period of church history than do those which represent some coloration or other of establishment.[6]

Professor Latourette's work in relation to the theology of history have been published by Professor Ernst Benz of Marburg: "Weltgeschichte, Kirchengeschichte und Missionsgeschichte," in *Historische Zeitschrift* (1952), and "Kirchengeschichte als Universalgeschichte: Das Lebenswerk von K. S. Latourette," in *Saeculum* (1950).

[6] See articles in *WKL:* "Freikirchen," "Volkskirche," cols. 434–35, 1563–64.

In a very real sense, the major issue now confronting the American churches can be summarized in this formulation of issues: Is Christianity in America to be understood as a province of European Christendom, with the cultural and ecclesiastical adjustments of the Old World awkwardly adapted to the cultural, religious, and legal pluralism of the New, or are the American churches in truth "younger churches"? At the present time the American churches are still uncertain as to the answer to that question. Indeed, the whole development of a self-conscious American style of churchmanship has been very slow, as indicated—among other things—by the fact that "American Church History" has been taught only recently in some theological faculties and is still largely neglected by the majority. As recently as 1956, the newly elected president of the American Society of Church History was moved to comment in his inaugural paper: "We cannot forever solve the problem of a right approach to church history by setting aside the experience of the American church as an anomaly." [7]

How shall the American churches understand the planting of God's Word in the New World? For the first American theologians, the problem was relatively simple. The American churches, like the political entities, were but deposits of European culture and religious life. In the New England "standing order," as well as in the colonies where the Church of England was established, religion was regarded as the capstone of culture and the cement of society. The Christian Indian villages of John Eliot (1604–90) were perhaps the most representative attempts in Puritan missionary statecraft, since the break of the converts from their tribal society was as complete as their religious transformation. Both transitions were conceived in vigorously theocratic terms, with fourteen towns of "Praying Indians" organized in terms of Exodus 18:21 ff. The words of the Covenant adopted at Natick, 1651, state clearly the blending of civil and religious affairs:

We doe give up ourselves and our children unto God, to be his people. He shall rule us in all our affairs, not only in our religion and affairs of the church, (these we desire as soon as we can, if God will.) but

[7] Leonard J. Trinterud, "The Task of the American Church Historian," *Church History,* Vol. XXV (1956), pp. 3–15, 9. See also Richard C. Wolf's report on the teaching of church history in American seminaries—"Recover Our Protestant Heritage!" in *The Christian Century* for April 30, 1952.

also in all our works and affairs of this world, God shall rule over us. The Lord is our Judge. The Lord is our Law-giver. The Lord is our King.[8]

The end of King Philip's War (1675–76) found the Christian Indian villages desolated. Many hundreds shared the fate of their unbaptized fellow Indians, who were sold off as slaves in the West Indies when the "rebellion" was shattered. As later with the Christian Indian settlements of the Moravians ("Gnadenhütten," scene of a massacre of Christian Indians by white men, 1782), neither the Indian tribes who stayed pagan nor the white society which identified "Christian religion" with European civilization was able to understand and trust the members of these early Christian missionary villages.

When the colonial state churches collapsed at the time national independence was established (1776–89), church membership in America fell to its true proportion of the population. As customary with disestablished churches, which normally claim in their previous position of privilege to embrace practically the whole population, the sudden shift to a system of voluntary membership and support revealed the hollowness of the earlier claims to comprehension. Confronted by a mass exodus from the churches, once the compulsory feature was removed (as late as 1819 in Connecticut, and 1833 in Massachusetts), Christian leaders were confronted by a problem of home missions of major proportions. The answer was given by the development of those techniques of mass evangelism which have, more than anything else, given the characteristic stamp to American church life. The statistics tell the story: at the end of a century and a half of strenuous work in home missions, church membership on a voluntary basis, church attendance, church giving for all purposes, has reached the highest peak both absolutely and proportionately in the whole sweep of church history.[9] Roman Catholicism and Judaism, as well as Protestantism, have had their whole style of religious association and life shaped by the emer-

[8] Given in O. Bacon, *A History of Natick* (Boston: Damrell & Moore, 1856), pp. 21 f. As Eliot put it, "I find it absolutely necessary to carry on civility with religion." John Eliot, "Letters of Eliot," Series 3:IV *Collections of the Massachusetts Historical Society* (Boston: Charles C. Little & James Brown, 1846), p. 88.

[9] See the discussion, with statistical reports, in the author's *The Free Church* (Boston: Starr King Press, 1957), pp. 116 f.

gence of a pattern of *voluntaryism* and *pluralism* utterly new in religious history.

This pattern, which the great church historian Philip Schaff saw already emerging in the latter part of the nineteenth century, is based on the separation of the civil covenant from the religious covenant(s). (The familiar terminology, "wall of separation of church and state," is faulty.) As late as the struggle over the Virginia Statute of Religious Freedom (1785), patriots as distinguished as George Washington and Patrick Henry argued that an established church was essential for a stable commonwealth. In many states, particularly among the former thirteen colonies, there are residual elements of Protestant privilege to this day. It is this factor which gives particular coloration to the tensions in the Southeastern states, where Protestantism has continued in its position of privilege and semiestablishment right into the twentieth century. Protestant compulsory chapel was maintained at the (state) University of South Carolina until the end of World War II, and the salary and office of the (Protestant) Chaplain are still maintained with state funds today. The dominant Protestant churches in the Southeast, socially if not always legally privileged, are today subject to strong temptation to adopt a "nativist" line in opposition to Jews, Roman Catholics, immigrants generally. The volume of material flooding the area from the "Protestant underworld" is very great, and more respectable organizations such as "Protestants and Other Americans United" receive a response out of proportion to the merits of their case. A century ago, as industrialization was bringing cultural and religious pluralism to the New England and Middle Atlantic states, Abraham Lincoln wrote a friend his judgment on Protestant culture religion:

> Our progress in degeneracy appears to me to be pretty rapid as a nation. We began by declaring *"all men are created equal."* We now practically read it "all men are created equal, *except negroes."* When the Know-Nothings get control, it will read "all men are created equal, except negroes, *and foreigners, and catholics."* When it comes to this I should prefer emigrating to some country where they make no pretense of loving liberty.[10]

[10] Letter to Joshua F. Speed of Kentucky, 1855; quoted in Carl Sandburg's Centennial Address to Congress (February 12, 1959), "Lincoln, Man of Steel and Velvet," *The National Geographic Magazine,* Vol. CXVII (1960), pp. 239–41.

In terms of religious liberty, the "younger churches" of the United States are maturing into the conviction that that service only is pleasing to God which is voluntary and uncoerced. As Philip Schaff put it, "the glory of America is a free Christianity, independent of the secular government, and supported by the voluntary contributions of a free people." He further declared that "this is one of the greatest facts in modern history." [11] The next step beyond voluntaryism is, however, willingness to accept the implications of cultural and religious pluralism for the relations between fellow citizens, and for the style of the Christian mission.

Significantly enough, it has been in the area of the Great Plains that the frank acceptance of voluntaryism and pluralism has been institutionalized. From the University of Minnesota to the University of Oklahoma the religious concerns of the state universities are expressed in offices of Coordinators of Religious Activities or Directors of Religious Affairs, with multifaith patterns of group cooperation, counseling, "Religious Emphasis Weeks," "Panel of Americans," and so on. In a growing number of cities, Roundtables of Christians and Jews carry on the mutual concerns of American Catholics, Jews, and Protestants who have learned that they can be cordial fellow citizens and still worship at different altars. Although in the Atlantic coastline states (and especially in the Southeast) the old claims to Protestant privilege still hang on, and although on the west coast (particularly in California and Washington) there has been institutionalized some of the anticlericalism of the French Revolution and Tom Paine, in the area of the plains states a new and significant pattern of civil and religious cooperation is emerging. In terms of Protestant history, it is significant that this is the area where through the great revivals and mass evangelism the masses were won back to the churches on a purely voluntary basis.[12]

[11] *Germany: its Universities, Theology, and Religion . . .* (Phila. & N.Y.: Lindsay and Blakiston, and Sheldon, Blakeman & Co., 1857), p. 105.

[12] Note the studies by Will Herberg, especially *Protestant-Catholic-Jew* (New York: Doubleday & Co., 1953); Winthrop S. Hudson, *The Great Tradition of the American Churches* (New York: Harper & Brothers, 1953); Timothy L. Smith, *Revivalism and Social Reform* (N.Y. & Nashville: Abingdon Press, 1957). On the characteristic "activism" of American churches, Smith comments: "Lay leadership, the drive toward interdenominational fellowship, the primacy of ethics over dogma, and the democratization of Calvinism were more nearly fruits of fervor than of reflection" (p. 8).

Will the dominant American churches come to understand their status as "younger churches," with the large majority of their membership *"new* Christians," or will they increasingly revert to the pretensions of white, privileged, culture religion? The answer to this question will determine whether they continue to use the form of address which Reinhold Niebuhr has condemned as "moralism." "Moralism" is that style of preaching and proclamation in which the Protestant churches "speak to the world as though it were the church" (W. A. Visser't Hooft). Those churches which conduct themselves in this way have an entirely different view of Christian missions than those which accept the whole world as their parish, which recognize the truth of the great statement by Hendrik Kraemer in *The Christian Message in a Non-Christian World.* Addressing himself to the crisis in Christendom of the old style, Professor Kraemer wrote:

> Nothing can demonstrate more clearly that *the Christian Church, religiously speaking, in the West as well as the East, is standing in a pagan, non-Christian world, and has again to consider the whole world its mission field, not in the rhetorical but in the literal sense of the word.*[13]

This is to return to the essential genius of the approach of the Free Churches to Christian missions. At a time when Protestant state churches still held to a territorial definition of Christian religion, nonmissionary in character, the forerunners of the modern Free Churches set out to restore church life patterned on the New Testament and early Church. Among their central teachings were lay initiative, voluntary discipline, and literal acceptance of the Great Commission as binding upon every baptized Christian. The "restitution" (Anabaptism) or "restoration" (Alexander Campbell) of the True Church, the Church before "the fall," involved a basic rethinking of the whole missionary imperative.[14] At a time when members of European state churches were selling Africans as slaves and maintaining that they had no souls, and shooting the natives of the South Sea islands for the sport of practicing on run-

[13] (New York: Harper & Brothers), pp. 16–17.

[14] For detailed study of the "restitutionists'" view of the Great Commission, see the author's "The Anabaptist Theology of Missions," *The Mennonite Quarterly Review,* Vol. XXI (1947), pp. 5–17: "Protestantism and the Great Commission," *The Southwestern Journal of Theology,* Vol. II (Fort Worth, 1959), pp. 26–42; Chapter IV in *The Anabaptist View of the Church: An Introduction to Sectarian Protestantism* (Boston: Starr King Press, 1958).

ning targets, "restitutionists" (Quakers, Moravians, Baptists, and others of the "Left Wing of Protestantism") were sending missionaries to the farthest lands of the earth and gathering in the "first fruits" of the peoples.

Whether or not the Free Church fathers were naive and non-historical in their effort to restore primitive Christianity, the fact is that their descendants in the "younger churches" find themselves today in a period of church history remarkably like that of the early Church. Mystery religions abound; Montanist and Gnostic sects are everywhere apparent; persecution of the Biblical faith is more widespread than ever before. Cast back into the early Church situation, the Gospel must go into the arena of public life and thought and triumph through the quality of its voluntary discipline, the power of its preaching and witness, the steadfastness of its discipleship. The political powers which so long served to suppress the opposition and support the Christian religion are either unfriendly or neutral. The "Constantinian era" is at an end.

For the Free Churches, and those who accept the implications of the present status of Christianity throughout the world, a new period of church history is at hand.

The Evolution of Mission Theology among Roman Catholics

BY ANDREW V. SEUMOIS, O.M.I.

Systematic research in the field of mission theology is a relatively recent development, beginning largely in the twentieth century.[1] Studies were made in earlier times on various questions pertaining to mission doctrine,[2] especially during the sixteenth and seventeenth centuries,[3] but they were not sufficiently systematic and complete. When the theological aspect of the mission did receive attention, it was only according to the mentality of the period; viz., in terms of the missionary duty of the religious Orders and of Christian rulers, the bounds for intervention of the "secular arm" in the spiritual conquest, the directions to follow in case of persecution, and the qualities and privileges of missionaries. Much attention was given also to moral casuistry, especially concerning the administra-

[1] This essay is a revision of the writer's article "L'évolution de la théologie missionnaire au vingtième siècle" in the symposium *Scientia Missionum ancilla* (Utrecht: Dekker en Van de Vegt, 1953), pp. 54–65.

[2] The anonymous treatise "De Vocatione omnium Gentium," composed around 450 (Migne, *Patrologia Latina,* T. 51), cols. 647–722, can be considered the first essay in mission theology. Some scholars have suggested authorship by Prosper of Aquitaine or Pope Leo the Great.

[3] A special place of significance must be given to the volume written by Thomas a Jesu, O.C.D. (Díaz Sánchez), *De Procurande salute omnium Gentium* (Antwerp, 1613), 926 pp., which was a notable effort of synthesis.

tion of the sacraments, as met with—or supposed to be met with—by missionaries in their work.

Furthermore, the few books concerning mission doctrine were not easily accessible to those who went as missionaries. Recall the complaint of Antony Erington, an Irish Franciscan at the end of this period (1672), when he said:

> It seems perfectly strange and hardly credible that while the arts and sciences are providing the books required for their students, the apostolic work of propagating and planting the faith is so lacking in treatises that new missionaries, who have to emigrate to far distant lands, are not able to obtain a single book that could serve them as a faithful companion and guide on all occasions.[4]

This complaint was still valid at the beginning of the twentieth century. In the writing which marked the launching of the modern missiological movement, Father Robert Streit, after noting that mission literature had already received some consideration from such sciences as ethnology, added:

> We would like to be in a position to point out that such consideration has also been given to missions by the theological branches. In fact, however, a short inventory of contributions to mission studies in this field, from the Catholic side, shows what seems to be a vacuum. . . . It certainly would be useful to investigate the missionary question with dogmatic accuracy in scholarly books and articles.[5]

Thus, theological study of the mission apostolate presented itself from the beginning as one of the primary tasks of the modern mis-

[4] Antony Erington, *Missionarium, seu opusculum practicum de Fide propaganda et conservanda* (Rome, 1672), p. 4. A bibliography concerning the period 1502–1909 can be found in the first volume (fundamental and general part) of the *Bibliotheca Missionum,* compiled by R. Streit and J. Dindinger (Münster: Aschendorff, 1916), xi + 24 + 877 pp.; and a short one in the first volume (doctrinal missiology) of *La Chiesa Missionaria* by S. Paventi (Rome: Unione Missionaria del Clero in Italia, 1949), pp. 146–67.

[5] Robert Streit, *Die deutsche Missionsliteratur* (Paderborn: Schöningh, 1907), p. 6 (previously published in the review *Der katholische Seelsorger,* 1907, Heft 6–9). Concerning the role played by Father Streit as initiator of the modern missiological movement, see: Johannes Pietsch, *P. Robert Streit, O.M.I., Ein Pionier der katholischen Missionswissenschaft* (Schöneck/Beckenried, Schweiz: Administration der Neuen Zeitschrift für Missionswissenschaft, 1952), 56 pp.; also my *Introduction à la Missiologie* (Schöneck/Beckenried, Schweiz: Administration der N.Z.M., 1952), pp. 445–53.

siological movement. But while Streit was desirous of a careful and progressive theological elaboration for missiology, Dr. Joseph Schmidlin, who joined the missiological movement in 1910, seemed to be in great haste. Moreover, Schmidlin was a controversialist. He ran head on into the famous book of mission theory *Evangelische Missionslehre,* by the German Protestant scholar Gustav Warneck,[6] and was pleased to find there such definite propositions as well as fine material for controversy. He adopted the plan and methods used in that work, took up its various questions, and reproduced, in great part, the ideas presented by Warneck together with what had already been written from the Catholic side. In so doing, Schmidlin became the first Roman Catholic author of a theology of mission.[7] His work, however, was very hasty and largely polemical, and its method—like the one used by Warneck—was unsuited for any systematic deepening of mission doctrine. Very briefly, the purpose of missionary activity, according to Schmidlin, is "the christianization of the non-Christians" (pagans, Mohammedans, Jews, and, in a merely accidental way, the Eastern Orthodox Christians, because of their Islamic surroundings). The primary scope of mission is individual conversions, and because the newly converted people require an ecclesiastical organization, the establishment of a local self-sufficient church is considered as a secondary scope, or as a social corollary of the primary end.

Schmidlin's book met with some success in Germany. Its principal parts were presented in digest by Peter J. Louis,[8] and by the seminarians of Hoeven in 1924.[9] The polemical trends, however, of Schmidlin's *Missionslehre,* which suited him, soon had to disap-

[6] Schmidlin's dependence on Warneck has often been brought to light. See: Hans Schärer, *Die Begründung der Mission in der katholischen und evangelischen Missionswissenschaft* (Zollikon-Zürich: Evang.-Verlag, 1944), 44 pp.; Olav G. Myklebust, *The Study of Missions in Theological Education,* Vol. I (Oslo: Egede Instituttet, 1955), p. 294; Pierre Lefebvre, "L'influence de Gustav Warneck sur la théologie missionnaire catholique," *Nouvelle Revue de Science Missionnaire,* 1956 (4), pp. 288–94.

[7] *Katholische Missonslehre im Grundriss* (Münster: Aschendorff, 1919; 2nd ed., 1923), 468 pp.; English translation, *Catholic Mission Theory* (Techny, Illinois: Mission Press, S.V.D., 1931), 544 pp.

[8] *Katholiche Missionskunde: Ein Studienbuch zur Einführung in der Missionswerk der katholischen Kirche* (Aachen: Xaverius Verlag, 1924; 2nd ed., 1925), 271 pp.

[9] *De Katholieke Missie in Wezen en Ontwikkeling* (Hoeven: Groot-Seminarie, 1924), 348 pp.

pear.[10] This is especially clear in the second publication from the Hoeven seminarians, which, while still adopting the plan and ideas of Schmidlin, deliberately omitted the controversial aspect.[11]

At this point, when the science of missions was not always clearly distinguished from missionary propaganda and was marked by a kind of impulsive enthusiasm, the next stage of development was that of encyclopedism. The thought was that all aspects of missiology could be dealt with in a satisfactory, if not exhaustive, fashion within a single volume. Hence came the "manuals" of missiology.[12]

The manuals revealed the importance of searching for a clearer division of the areas in missiology, and when scholars finally arrived at a certain precision in defining the proper area belonging to the theology of mission, it became clear that much of Schmidlin's *Missionslehre* had to be superseded. His book had been influenced by the concrete situation which shaped the missionary enterprise and activity in the early part of this century. Many of his considerations were merely an apology for this special situation, or were a methodological explanation of the particular framework, resulting from influences of the psychological, sociological, and cultural order, which was molding the missionary function at that time, but was not essential to it. Beyond these apologetical or methodological features, the real theological study which remained in the book consisted almost exclusively of statements dealing with the notion of Christian mission and its supernatural motivation. This explains the fact that many manuals restricted their mission theology almost exclusively to a study of the definition and "motives" of the Christian mission.

The majority of the manuals, in dealing with the concept of mission, departed from Schmidlin, preferring instead the thesis of

[10] J. Beckmann, "Der Einfluss der Missionswissenschaft auf die Beziehungen der christlichen Konfessionen," *Katholisches Missionsjahrbuch der Schweiz, 1958* (Freiburg: Akadem. Missionsbund, 1958), pp. 28–35.

[11] *De Katholieke Missie,* I, *Missieleer* (Hoeven: Groot-Seminarie, 1933), 155 pp.

[12] See, for instance, U. Mioni, *Manuale di Missionologia* (Milano: Ed. "Vita e Pensiero," 1921), 536 pp.; and C. Carminati, *Corso di Conferenze missionarie. Compendio di Missiologia* (Bergamo, 1928), 400 pp. These two manuals are not scientific, but are intended for missionary propaganda. For encyclopedism see J. E. Champagne, *Manual of Missionary Action* (Ottawa: University Press, 1947), 840 pp.

Grentrup, as endorsed and popularized by Pierre Charles. For them the specific purpose of the missionary function is the planting of the Church in every region where she is not yet fully established. The criterion is one of geographical order, and is concerned with the regional status of the church organization. When the new regional church is sufficiently established with her own hierarchy and means, the missionary activity is finished.

The manuals followed Schmidlin, however, in dealing with the foundations of the mission, but they elaborated on the positive side of things. Schmidlin was an historian. As such he was naturally inclined to formulate a theology of mission according to the patterns of an historiography, using the textbooks of theology as the sources. The task, as he saw it, was simply to examine the textbooks one by one and extract all that could be more or less related to the mission. From this procedure he arrived at a first "foundation" of the mission with the treatise *De Deo Uno,* saying that it is because of the oneness of God that missions strive against polytheism and pantheism.[13]

Such considerations were far from a genuine theology of the mission apostolate,[14] and the manuals were rooted in Schmidlin's way of presenting the theological aspect. They were, therefore, unable to enter the realm of systematic mission theology, despite their efforts to the contrary. This was not only due to their defective methods, but also resulted from an almost exclusive restriction of the material object of mission dogma to the "motives" for the missionary task. Of course, the manuals were not silent about the subject, the object and the finality of mission, especially when seeking to define the missionary function, but they did not give adequate theological analysis in these areas. Perhaps it was due to the fact that they relied largely on Schmidlin's *Missionslehre,* which had developed these points methodologically, but not theologically.

The manuals, furthermore, were inadequate because they were premature. Before encyclopedism could be substantially helpful,

[13] Schmidlin, *Missionslehre,* 1923, *op. cit.,* pp. 70–71.

[14] The specific theological justification of the missionary function of the Church cannot be found in the motives for one particular activity of the missionaries. Since the struggle against polytheism is only one point in the whole range of mission activity, and is not even properly mission activity because this is common to the whole ministry of the Church, no real and genuine theology for the missonary function can be found along such lines.

it was necessary that more research and writing of monographs be done on the individual topics of fundamental importance in mission theology. It was particularly important that there be a more precise definition of the nature, the object, and the method of systematic mission theology.

Important advances have been made along these lines in recent years and valuable bibliography on the various topics is readily available.[15] In fact, the numerous problems pertaining to the introduction of missiology, which is of crucial importance for a coherent study in the various fields of missiology, have occasioned a great amount of research, discussion, and writing.[16] In 1952, with all of this material to draw upon, the present writer prepared his book *Introduction à la Missiologie,* which sought to deal with the various aspects of the introduction to missiology in a systematic and coherent fashion.[17] The size of this book may seem enormous, considering the fact that it is only an introduction, but it seemed preferable to take into account all the opinions and developments in this field in order to provide a clear picture of exactly what the situation is at the present time.

It is important to recognize that theological studies are not based upon invented ideas, but upon *revelation.* They must always rely upon revelation and should never deviate from it. For an harmonious elaboration of systematic missiology, therefore, it is necessary to produce critical studies in the field of Biblical missiology, and, secondarily, in patristical missiology. Since the time of Streit's

[15] An annual bibliography of books and articles in missiology is published in the Dutch quarterly *Het Missiewerk* in the last issue for each year. More elaborate is the annual publication *Bibliografia Missionaria* (Vol. XXIII for 1959), compiled in Rome (Ed. Unione Missionaria del Clero d'Italia), which also gives reviews of the more important publications. A good selection of titles is also mentioned in the quarterly bibliography of the *International Review of Missions.*

[16] See: Joseph Schmidlin, *Einführung in die Missionswissenschaft* (Münster: Aschendorffsche Verlagsbuchhandlung, 1917), vi + 208 pp.; 2nd ed., 1925, v + 188 pp.; G. B. Tragella, *Avviamento allo Studio delle Missioni* (Milano: Pontificio Istituto Missioni Estere, 1930), 95 pp.; Alphons Mulders, *Inleiding tot de Missiewetenschap* ('s- Hertogenbosch: Teulings'Uitg., 1937), x + 225 pp.; (2nd ed.; Bussum: Paul Brand, 1950), 267 pp.; A. Perbal, *Lo Studio delle Missioni,* "Orizzonti Missionari" (Roma: Ed. U.M.C. 1946), 177 pp.

[17] Andr. V. Seumois, *Introduction à la Missiologie, op. cit.*

inaugural booklet,[18] there have been numerous valuable studies in both these fields. In Biblical missiology there has been a variety of publications bearing upon the economy of the primitive Covenant, the mission theology of the Mosaic Covenant (with special emphasis on the question of the contrast between particularism and universalism), the missionary idea in the Psalms and among the Prophets, and, finally, upon the missionary idea in the New Testament—the missionary figure of Christ, the theological aspects of the missionary activity of the Apostle to the Gentiles, and the kerygmatic witness according to Acts. In the vast field of patristical missiology there are also many studies available. Some examine the mission doctrine of a particular group of Church Fathers. Others are concerned only with one Father in his missionary aspect. This is particularly true of studies of Augustine, John Chrysostom, Ambrose of Milan, Clement of Rome, Clement and Cyril of Alexandria, Origen, Ephraem the Syrian, Cyril of Jerusalem, Caesarius of Arles, and Gregory the Great.[19] Others present a study of one particular point of mission doctrine in light of the whole tradition of the first centuries. This is what the present writer sought to do in studies dealing with missionary adaptation, the lay apostolate, and missionary prayer according to the tradition of the early Church.[20] Although the patristical documents are interesting primarily for the area of practical missiology, they also

[18] Robert Streit, *Die Mission in Exegese und Patrologie* (Paderborn: Schöningh, 1909), 30 pp. (previously published in the review *Der katholische Seelsorger,* 1909, pp. 296–306, 346–50, 400–07, 445–53).

[19] A selection of titles from this field would include: Paul Andres, *Der Missionsgedanke in den Schriften des heil. Johannes Chrysostomus,* "Missionswissenschaftliche Studien," Heft 8 (Hünfeld: Verlag der Oblaten, 1935), xv + 196 pp.; Jean Mesot, *Die Heidenbekehrung bei Ambrosius von Mailand,* "NZM Supplementa," Heft 7 (Schöneck/Beckenried, Schweiz: Administration der NZM, 1958), xi + 153 pp.; A. Paulin, *S. Cyrille de Jérusalem catéchète,* "Lex Orandi," Nr. 29 (Paris: Ed. du Cerf, 1959), 256 pp.; J. Wang Tch'ang Tche, *Saint Augustin et les vertus des païens* (Paris: Beauchesne, 1938), viii + 194 pp.; J. Zameza, *La conversión del mundo infiel en la concepción del "Totus Christus" de San Agustín,* "Biblioteca Misional del Seminario de Misiones," Nr. 2 (Burgos: Seminario de Misiones, 1942), 97 pp.

[20] See *La Papauté et les Missions au cours des six premiers siècles. Méthodologie antique et orientations modernes* (Louvain-Paris: "Eglise Vivante," 1953), 224 pp.; "L'apostolat laïc de l'antiquité selon les témoignages patristiques," *Euntes Docete* (Rome), 1952, 126–53; "Missionary Prayer in the Early Church," *Worldmission* (New York), 1953 (3), pp. 283–308.

bring matters of great interest to the area of systematic missiology.

What about this area of systematic missiology (dogmatic and moral)? It is mission theology in the strictest sense. It is concerned with the theological elaboration of mission. At the end of the Second World War scholars still noted a lack of serious studies in this field for several reasons.[21] The deficiencies of the approach established by Schmidlin were matched by a near vacuum of ideas for a more proper orientation. There was skepticism from missionaries who were unwilling to delve into theory and doctrinal principles. There was a degree of proud contempt from some theologians, perhaps very competent in traditional scholastic disputations, who were not inclined to leave the sphere of speculation in order to devote doctrinal study to the complex ecclesiological realm of missionary realities. Now the spirit of things has changed. Missionaries everywhere are seeking for an elaborated systematic theology of mission that will help guide them in the difficult apostolate they bear in the name of Christ and the Universal Church. Theologians are increasingly interested in mission questions, because of the greater emphasis given to ecclesiastical, ecumenical, and apostolic problems.

The first problem to be solved in systematic missiology concerns the concept of mission. Schmidlin defined missionary activity, as noted above, according to the statement of Warneck, empirically based on the ideas commonly held at that time. In an effort to correct this incomplete and inaccurate delimitation, Grentrup in 1925 gave as the specific object of missions the planting of the Church in every country where it is not yet fully established.[22] This theory was endorsed and divulgated by many, especially by Pierre Charles, who made the mistake, however, of minimizing the factor of conversion as well as the virtue of charity in the

[21] See P. de Menasce, "Polarité de l'activité missionnaire," *Neu Zeitschrift für Missionswissenschaft,* 1945 (2), pp. 81 and 87; Alph. Mulders, *Missie en Wetenschap* (Utrecht-Nijmegen: Dekker, 1946), p. 9.

[22] Theodorus Grentrup, *Jus Missionarium* (Steyl, Holland: Typographia domus Missionum a S. Michaele Archang. nuncupatae, 1925), pp. 1–12. He had already expounded this view of mission in 1913 in "Die Definition des Missionsbegriffes," *Zeitschrift für Missionswissenschaft,* 1913, pp. 265–74. Schmidlin presented his view as early as 1911 in his essay "Die katholische Missionswissenschaft," *Zeitschrift für Missionswissenschaft,* 1911, pp. 10–21; and this concept was further expounded in his *Einführung in Missionswissenschaft, op. cit.,* pp. 11–24, and in his *Missionslehre, op. cit.*

course of his argumentation.[23] His use of a mold to illustrate his central thesis was unfortunate, for the point he was illustrating is indeed true and traditional in the Church.[24]

Discussions on this matter were numerous, and they monopolized most of the energy in the field of systematic missiology for a long while. For several years now, however, the issue has been settled by what is nearly unanimous agreement concerning the essential lines of definition for the missionary function.[25] The understanding is that mission activity is a specific task, quite distinct, in the ecclesiastical ministry. No salvation is possible outside the Church, but there are normal and suppletory ways for justification. The ordinary ecclesiastical ministry is twofold: *pastoral* (for the care of the faithful in the Church), and *apostolic* (for the conversion to the Church). Many kinds of apostolate can be distinguished, but missionary activity is a specific field of the apostolate aimed at bringing the Church to souls where she is not yet established, in order to bring souls to the Church, i.e., implanting the Church in a new area so that a new particular (regional) church may be set up, live, and grow in an autochthonous way by her own personnel and means.

Although there is widespread agreement on this point, there has still been some problem outside missiological circles with language, particularly in France since 1943, with regard to the term "mission." This has come about because of a misunderstanding of the precise meaning of mission activity and an inability to distinguish this function from other forms of apostolate. Despite the

[23] Pierre Charles, *Les Dossiers de l'Action Missionnaire* (Nr. 36–38, 1926–28; 2nd ed. Louvain: Editions de l'Aucam, 1939), Vol. I fasc. 1, pp. 16–32. Also his *Missiologie: Etudes, Rapports, Conférences,* I (Louvain: Ed. de l'Aucam, 1939), 304 pp.; and *Etudes Missiologiques* (Bruges [Louvain]: Desclée De Brouwer, [1956]), pp. 16–43.

[24] See the writer's essay "La Mission 'Implantation de l'Eglise' dans les documents ecclésiastiques," pp. 39–53 in *Missionswissenschaftliche Studien; Festgabe Dindinger* (Münster: Metz, 1951), 440 pp. ("Veröffentlichungen des Instituts für Missionswissenschaftliche Forschungen.")

[25] Andr. V. Seumois, *Vers une définition de l'Activité Missionnaire* (Schöneck/Beckenried, Suisse: Nouvelle Revue de Science Missionnaire, 1948), 46 pp. ("Cahiers de la Nouvelle Revue de Science Missionnaire," Nr. 5.) Translated into German by Joseph Peters, *Auf dem Wege zu einer Definition der Missionstätigkeit* (Gladbach [München]: B. Kühlen Kunst und Verlagsanstalt, 1948), 64 pp. Portuguese translation in the review *Portugal em Africa,* 1948.

opinion of some,[26] this misuse of terms [27] has not affected the reality defined as the implanting of the Church regionally.

The question of the moral constitutive foundation of mission can be considered solved.[28] A special organic study has been devoted to the missionary duty of the Church and to the whole area of systematic missiology dealing with missionary efficiency *in ordine causalitatis principalis.*[29] The theological shape of the particular indigenous church is a matter that has attracted much attention and occasioned substantial study.[30] This issue is of

[26] J. C. Hoekendijk, "L'Eglise dans la pensée missionnaire," *Le Monde non chrétien* (Paris), 1951 (Oct.–Dec.), p. 427. Attempts to confuse the concept of mission apostolate have been made by the journal *Parole et Mission* (Paris), which began in 1958 and is preoccupied with emphasizing a Theology of the Word especially directed toward the apostolate in the dechristianized milieux of France. This journal presents also some legitimate missionary articles, and then tries to force an analogy between the real mission countries and lands with a dechristianized social milieu where the Church is still geographically implanted, making an identification of the two. It applies the wrong and vaguely analogical expression "espaces humains" to the situations of social milieux, thereby increasing the chance for confusion between the apostolate of social milieux and the proper missionary task. Such isolated attempts at confusion have, however, remained without success in missiological and missionary circles; and the Sacred Congregation "de propaganda Fide" has shown no inclination to extend its missionary jurisdiction to those dechristianized "espaces," which are left in the care of the apostolic activity, not of the proper missionary action.

[27] Edouard Loffeld, "Notre concept de Mission," *Le Bulletin des Missions* (Bruges), 1951, pp. 91–108. Gillès de Pélichy, "Qu'est-ce qu'un pays de Mission?" *Le Bulletin des Missions,* 1952, pp. 1–11.

[28] Ign. Omaechevarría, "La caridad en la teología misionera," *Missionalia Hispanica* (Madrid), 1951 (24), pp. 523–89; Andr. V. Seumois, "La Charité Apostolique, fondement moral constitutif de l'activité missionnaire," *Nouvelle Revue de Science Missionnaire,* 1957, pp. 161–75; 256–70.

[29] Andr. V. Seumois, "L'Anima dell'Apostolato Missionario," *Studi Missionari,* Nr. 1 (Milano: Editrice Missionaria Italiana, 1958), 220 pp. One gentle reviewer (Waigand, *Neue Zeitschrift für Missionswissenschaft,* 1959, p. 313) said this work "can be considered as a modern treatise on grace."

[30] J. Frisque, "La Mission et l'Eglise particulière," *Eglise Vivante* (Louvain), 1949, pp. 389–412; Ed. Duperray, "L'implantation des Eglises autochtones," pp. 75–86 in *Colonisation et conscience chrétienne,* "Recherches et débats," Nr. 6 (Paris: Fayard, 1953); Edouard Loffeld, *Le problème cardinal de la missiologie et des missions catholiques,* "Publications de l'Institut de Missiologie de l'Université Nimègue," Nr. 4 (Rhenen, Holland: Editions Spiritus, 1956), xx + 416 pp.

primary importance in mission doctrine because the missionary, who brings the Church Universal with the essential factors of her divine constitution, must, however, tend to the planting of new particular churches, fully autochthonous. The whole matter of lay missionaries has been provided now with a solid theological framework,[31] and several other issues of doctrinal import have been widely discussed in articles, for which only an extensive bibliography could give account. Problems of a more comprehensive nature regarding the apostolate in general have not been explored as yet to any great extent, but they are questions of great value for a deeper penetration into the question of what constitutes the missionary function. Some studies have been published concerning the kerygma and conversion,[32] but there is still no theology of the generic questions concerning the apostolate as such.[33]

Normative missiology, studying the juridicial figure of mission organization in conformity with the norms of doctrine (being a study of theological order—*theologia rectrix*—like the whole of ecclesiastical law), is now being treated integrally.[34] Sooner or later

[31] For a discussion of this issue and references to the related bibliography, see the writer's articles: "Lay Missionary Organization," *Worldmission,* 1951 (4), pp. 78–87; "Notion du laïcat missionnaire," *Eglise Vivante,* 1951, pp. 177–90; "Fonction du laïcat missionnaire," *Neue Zeitschrift für Missionswissenschaft,* 1951, pp. 173–83, 282–93; "Vocation au laïcat missionnaire," *ibid.,* 1952, pp. 211–29.

[32] André Rétif, *Foi au Christ et Mission* (Paris: Le Cerf, 1953), 185 pp.; Jos. Gewiess, "Die Bekehrung nach dem Neuen Testament," (pp. 7–21) in *Ecclesia Apostolica,* Jahrbuch des Katholischen Akademischen Missionsbundes 1949–50 (Münster: Regensberg, 1950); Laurenz Kilger et al., *Die Neuheit des Lebens als Ziel und Frucht der Weltmission,* Missionsstudienwoche, 1956 (Münster i.W.: Intern. Institut für missionswissenschaftliche Forschungen, 1957), 287 pp.

[33] In addition to the questions of kerygma and conversion, a theology of the apostolate should deal with the meaning of apostle in the New Testament, the precise concept of apostolate, the position and value of the catechumenate and the indirect apostolate, the social aim and the eschatological accomplishment of the apostolic function. Some views have been given by A. M. Henry, *Esquisse d'une théologie de la Mission,* "Foi Vivante" (Paris: Ed. du Cerf, 1959), 248 pp.

[34] Note the following reference books in normative missiology: M. Gérin, *Le gouvernement des Missions* (Quebec: Université Laval, 1944), xxiv + 256 pp.; X. Paventi, *Breviarium Iuris Missionalis,* "Bibliotheca Missionalis," Nr. 4 (Rome: Officium Libri Catholici, 1952), 294 pp.; C. Sartori, *Iuris Missionarii elementa* (2nd ed.; Rome: Libreria S. Antonio, 1951), 160 pp.

these studies should allow for a simplification of the ecclesiastical law in force in missions by the constitution of a special missionary code that will be discreet and flexible enough to permit necessary adaptations. The law which is in force is largely the Codex of the constituted Latin Church, which has been accommodated to the younger churches in the process of their establishment through a series of norms which have come about as exceptional legislation. A proper mission code that would be binding in all mission territories, together with another code of a real ecumenical range for all the churches already established, should permit a readjustment of the universal expression of the Church on a world-wide scale.

Practical missiology, scientifically theological, covers the study of mission spirituality and mission methodology. Spiritual missiology is still not provided with a fully elaborated exposition, but a fundamental orientation of a plainly apostolic spirituality, quite different from the egocentric and devotionalistic trends of the last centuries, has been established.[35]

Mission methodology is very much associated with a deepening of mission theology. Study conferences or congresses which gather missiologists and missionaries for an examination of various mission method topics, more and more reserve the opening lectures for a doctrinal statement or a review of practice on the topic during the first centuries.[36] Publications on problems of mission method

[35] These recent developments have been sanctioned in the last two mission encyclicals, *Fidei Donum* of Pius XII in 1957 and *Princeps Pastorum* of John XXIII in 1959.

[36] Cardinal Agagianian, Prefect of the Sacred Congregation for the Propagation of the Faith and Patriarch of the Armenians, sanctioned this tendency in his paper that was presented at the World's Fair in Brussels, August 14, 1958, on the topic "Mission and Civilization" ("L'Eglise et le progrès des collectivités économiquement sous-développées," *La Documentation catholique* [Paris: Bonne Presse, 1958], 1317–24). The 1957 and 1958 Missiology Weeks at Burgos were devoted to the problem of adaptation, and started with a study on the theology of mission adaptation (*La Adaptación Misionera* [Burgos: Instituto de San Francisco Javier para Misiones, 1959], xl + 479 pp.). The writer presented introductory papers of this nature at the Missiology Week of Louvain in 1954 where the theme was devoted to the question of schools in missions, speaking on "Aspects théoriques et historiques de l'enseignement dans les missions" (*Questions scolaires aux Missions, 24ᵉ Semaine de Missiologie Louvain* [Louvain: Desclée De Brouwer, 1955], pp. 12–42), and in 1959 at the "International Study Week on Mission and Liturgy" in Nijmegen, Holland.

are also beginning to follow this pattern,[37] so it can be said that there is a tendency toward doctrinal readjustment and a fresh rethinking in the light of early tradition. In the words of Cardinal Costantini, the trend is toward "a reform that restores the liberty and methods of apostolic times to mission activity." [38]

[37] A good bibliography is given by Hernández A. Santos, *Adaptación Misionera* (Bilbao: Ed. "El Siglo de las Misiones," 1958), 617 pp.

[38] C. Costantini, *Va e annunzia il Regno di Dio* (Brescia: Morcelliana, 1943), Vol. II, p. 24.

PART THREE
CHRISTIANITY AND OTHER FAITHS

Ideas for a Theology of the History of Religion *

BY ERNST BENZ

One of the urgent tasks of contemporary theology is to formulate a new theological understanding of the history of religion. This involves new insight into the position of Christianity within the general religious development of mankind and a new conception of the relationship of the history of religion to salvation-history (*Heilsgeschichte*). The urgency of this task has been caused by the profound changes in the general situation of Christianity in the world, by the great transformations within the non-Christian religions, and by the universal changes in religious consciousness which have arisen in the twentieth century.

In this situation the traditional schemata of the theological evaluation of the history of religion are no longer adequate; indeed, they begin to endanger the claim of the Christian revelation to truth. These traditional schemata can be reduced to two basic types.

The first is represented by the doctrine of absolute discontinuity between Christianity and the non-Christian religions, between the God who reveals himself in the Old and New Testaments and the gods of the various religions. This schema has found its modern expression in dialectical theology. It maintains that the various

* Translated by Joseph Cottrell Weber.

religions are the efforts of man to justify himself before God; a way of self-justification which does not save man from his guilt and self-centeredness, nor from being lost. The history of religion from this point of view is the history of the religious dreams of mankind in which man dreams of saving himself but is unable to lift himself up from his sickbed. He is awakened out of his dreams only by the revelation of the true word of the true God. Christianity is the crisis of all religions. It is the revelation of the "wholly other" God, who utters His divine verdict upon the self-made gods of man.

The second schema is represented by the Logos theology of the Apologists and is found today especially in Roman Catholic mission theology. Logos theology attempts to place the general history of man and religion in a more positive relationship to Christian salvation-history which has its backbone in the Old and New Covenants. It begins with the idea that there are seeds of the divine Logos in the heathen environment of the Old Testament; in Indian, Persian, Egyptian, and above all in Greek, "philosophy." Sparks from the burning bush have fallen on the land of the heathen. The divine Logos, who spoke through the mouth of Moses and the prophets, called forth some perception of the light in the non-Judaic world before He became man in Jesus Christ and appeared in his completeness and fullness.

Both these schemata, confronted with the development of our modern consciousness of history and of religion, lead to absurd consequences. Both separate the history of mankind from salvation-history. Both conceive of salvation-history as an arbitrary improvisation which no longer makes possible any meaningful relation between the history of all humanity and salvation-history.

The first schema, the assertion that Christ is the crisis of all religions (in the words of a Buddhist philosopher, the "theology of flying saucers,") can no longer be upheld in a world situation where Christianity is reproached by the non-Christian religions for its guilty entanglement in the colonial and economic expansion of the European and American West.

The second schema, the traditional Logos theology and its modern versions, proves itself to be a theological ell which is too short to measure our modern consciousness of history. It limits salvation-history before Christ to the events of the Old Testament and the happenings in the general history of man which accompany these events, thereby limiting salvation-history to the development of religious consciousness within this segment of history. Traditional Logos theology regards the development of the history of mankind and of religion as essentially closed with the birth of Jesus Christ and the appearance of the Christian Church. It ignores the history of religion after Christ, in as far as this history is not identical with the history of the Christian Church. Two important new tasks arise here for a Christian view of the history of religion.

The first task consists in bringing our contemporary picture of human development, including prehistoric times, into a meaningful relationship with the Christian understanding of salvation-history. The traditional Christian picture of the course of salvation-history is built upon the ancient Jewish chronology, which believes that world history took place in an extraordinarily brief period of time. According to the Jewish computation of time the date of the creation of the world is not so far distant in the past. In terms of the Christian calendar it took place in the year 3761 B.C. According to the calendar which was accepted in the Byzantine imperial church, Christ was born in the year 5509 after the creation of the world. Into such a picture of history as this the theologians of the ancient Church sketched a schema of salvation-history which had its backbone in the history of the Jewish nation, which saw its fulfillment in the incarnation of the Son of God in Jesus Christ and in the Christian Church, that reckoned with the speedy return of Christ and believed that the epochs before and after Christ were held together through the schema of promise and fulfillment.

The problem of whether and to what extent the general history of mankind in the epoch before the election of the Jewish people (as the real bearers of salvation-history) can be understood as salvation-history arose already for Jewish thought and then more so for Christian thought. This question was answered with the idea of the first covenant, before the election of Abraham, between God and Noah, the father of all human generations who survived the flood. Jewish theology based the universality of salvation-history upon this idea, and the Christian Church held onto it for a positive relation between salvation-history and the general history of mankind. The Apologists thought of the revelation in Jesus Christ as the fulfillment of the universal development of humanity.

This beginning, however, remained static and did not keep pace with the general consciousness of history. The cleavage between the traditional mythological picture of history in the Bible and the modern consciousness of history appeared for the first time with the discovery of America. It seemed absolutely impossible to fit the fact of the existence of such huge continents into the traditional picture of history in Christian doctrine. Christian theologians attempted to explain the origin of the newly discovered peoples in two ways. Some wanted to keep the traditional schema of history by explaining the population of America as the progeny of the ten lost tribes of Israel. Others, to whom this theory seemed too adventurous, considered it necessary to develop the idea of the existence of preadamites, an explanation which came under severe ecclesiastical condemnation.

The cleavage between the traditional picture of salvation-history and the modern consciousness of history has deepened to the degree that the knowledge of prehistory (prehistoric times) and early history has increased. The task of connecting the modern view of human history with the Christian conception of salvation-history becomes even more urgent when we realize that the retention of the traditional historical-theological conceptions goes against the very content of the Christian Gospel. A God who has left man to the power of demons, to the service of idols, magic, and sorcery, and who improvised a salvation-history which could be appropriated by a very small and arbitrary selection of mankind only after thousands of human generations died in sin and went to hell, has more similarity to the God of Marcion or to the Devil than to the God of the New Testament.

Christian theology today cannot escape the task of bringing the knowledge of the tremendous phases of the development of human religious consciousness in prehistory and early history into a meaningful relationship with the theological concept of salvation-history. The modern understanding of prehistory and history demands from theology a modern theodicy. The claim to universality of Christianity will be fulfilled only when it is shown that the universal history of religion and the development of the religious consciousness of man in all of history stand in a meaningful relationship to Christian salvation-history. The Christian understanding of man and his history as salvation-history cannot exclude the prehistory and early history of man. Either the saying is true that God "did not leave himself without witness" (Acts 14:17) even in the thousands of generations of archaic humanity, or we must relinquish the belief in a salvation-history and the claim of the Christian message of salvation to universality.

A second task for Christian theology results from the fact that the history of religion continues *post Christum*. Christian theology has not done justice to this fact; indeed, it has ignored it. Even where Christian theology attempted to establish a positive relationship to the non-Christian religions in the manner of the Logos theology of the Apologists, it started from the assumption that the history of religion had already found its fulfillment, its suspension and historical conclusion. In this view there cannot be a history of religion after Christ, after the fulfillment of time.

Nevertheless new world religions have appeared *post Christum*. Some of them can still—with some difficulty—be explained by the traditional theological picture of history. The first world religion which opposed the Christian Church with new holy books, with a new institution and a claim to universality was Manichaeism in the third and fourth centuries. But the apologists of the Christian Church opposed it as a Christian heresy rather than a new religion.

Even Islam was not understood as a new religion. It challenged the Christian claim to be the fulfillment of all the prophecies of salvation. It accepted the previous stages of revelation of God in Moses, in the Prophets, and in Jesus, but believed them to be surmounted and consummated by the final revelation in the prophet Mohammed. Christian theology fitted Islam into its picture of history by an eschatological explanation. It saw in Islam the fulfillment of the final prophecies of the coming of the false prophet (Rev. 19:20). And after Islam began to spread over the areas of the earliest Christian missions by means of holy war, its advance was interpreted as the fulfillment of those plagues and afflictions which had been prophesied for the final sifting of the Church by John in the Apocalypse.

For nearly a millennium Islam remained the only non-Christian religion with which Christianity had to deal. It engaged Islam in a fight of life or death, and the opposition to Islam became the model for contact and polemic with other non-Christian religions. The Asiatic religions in India, China, and Japan were discovered only at the beginning of the seventeenth century. Even today one attempts to explain these religions eschatologically. The obvious analogy between Buddhistic and Roman Catholic forms of worship and institutions caused the first Jesuit missionaries in China and Japan to interpret Buddhism as a countermeasure of the devil, who used the forms of expression of the Catholic Church to seduce the peoples of Asia by an anti-Christian church of the devil and to keep them away from the true Church of Christ.

The recognition of an independent development of the history of religion beside and outside of Christianity came only gradually. In its expansion Christianity came into contact with all the living non-Christian religions and encountered their opposition. Christian theology must deal with the fact that the history of religions still continues to develop in great variety. The great world religions have not been any more willing than Christianity to remain static in the same forms with which they began. They have gone through an astonishingly diverse internal development in which many varied forms and degrees of religious experience and theological exposition have found expression. These in turn have led to the most varied types of religious forms of social expression. They have also, to a large degree, determined the general political, social, and cultural development of the Asiatic peoples. All of the great Asiatic religions, in the same manner as Christianity, have brought forth new sects and new schools of thought in the course of their historical development and their adaptation to the various national structures. These sects and schools represent new forms of religious consciousness and religious ethics.

All the great religions have influenced one another to a great extent wherever they have come into contact. After Islam had taken up a considerable inheritance from Christianity in its gospel, its piety, and its devotional forms, it entered the domain of Hinduism in the subcontinent of India and created new religious forms of expression. New forms have originated also in Hinduism. They appeared partly as reform movements, but also partly took on the character of a new independent religion, like Jainism. New religions, like Sikhism, have arisen in India out of a combination of Hinduism and Islam.

Buddhism, which first appeared in the fifth century before Christ as a reform movement within Hinduism and which later was driven from India through the reaction of Brahmanism and the coming of Islam, has gone through a multiplicity of variations and even up to the present has called into life new forms of religious experience and social structures.

Christianity itself has in no small way contributed to this further development of the non-Christian religions. The missionary attack by Christianity has led to an intensification of activity on the part of the great non-Christian religions in Asia, and these religions have copied some of the methods for their renewal from the Christian mission. Buddhism and Hinduism have partly adopted the practice of the Sunday preaching service and have developed methods of religious education which are copied from Christianity. Likewise the modern Hindu and Buddhist lay and youth organizations, and above all their various social institutions, have copied from the corresponding organizations and institutions of Christianity.

The fact that the history of religion goes on becomes especially obvious and appears as an urgent theological problem where new religions are formed within the best organized working areas of the Christian mission. This is the case above all in Japan.[1] A series of new revelatory religions (religions based on revelation) have appeared there since the middle of the last century. These have attracted millions of followers, while the Christian mission in spite of all its efforts scarcely has acquired its first half million of believers of all confessions. These new religions are noteworthy because they appeal to new revelations—some of them in the form of a new incarnation of God in the person of their founder—and because they put into effect a series of specific Christian claims in their social ethics. Besides such new religions based on revelation a series of syncretistic religions have appeared, which, like the Caodai Religion in Vietnam, consciously take up Christian doctrine and ethics and the "integration" of all previous historical religious forms.

The facts that the history of religion continues after Christ and that the Christian Church and the Christian mission are drawn into this current of universal development of the history of religion should no longer be ignored theologically. A theological conception of salvation-history cannot bypass the fact that the history of religion continues *post Christum*. This fact must be brought into a meaningful relationship to Christ's claim to be the fulfillment of time. It is important to examine the question of whether and to what extent the very dynamic and mobile history of religion *post*

[1] For further information on this point see the essay by Masatoshi Doi.—Ed.

Christum stands in a direct or dialectical relationship to the history of Christianity and of the Christian Church and to the history of the Christian mission and its expansion.

The answer to the two questions that have been asked concerning a new view of the history of religion cannot be found in the development of a new schema from the traditional presuppositions of Western theology in place of the old dogmatic schema—be it the schema of "absolute discontinuity" or the schema of Logos theology. Two new ways offer themselves to us.

First it is well to reflect the fact that the view of an exclusive claim to absoluteness (*Absolutheit*) which is generally accepted as the self-evident presupposition of Christian dogma is not the only self-evident and determinative attitude to be found in the New Testament. The New Testament knows, rather, a series of indications of a completely different conception of the relationship of the Christian Church to the non-Christian religions.

Acts 14 portrays how the miraculous healing of a cripple by the Apostle Paul causes the people of Lystra to see in the Apostles Barnabas and Paul the epiphany of the gods Zeus and Hermes, and how the people, led by the priest of the temple of Zeus, prepare to honor the Apostles cultically by a great sacrifice of flesh and flowers. Paul wards off this honor shown to divinity with the words:

> Men, why are you doing this? We are also men, of like nature with you, and bring you good news, that you should turn from these vain things to a living God, who made the heaven and the earth and the sea and all that is in them. In past generations he allowed all the nations to walk in their own ways, yet he did not leave himself without witness, for he did good and gave you from heaven rains and fruitful seasons, satisfying your hearts with food and gladness.

Père Jean Daniélou, the only modern Roman Catholic theologian who has dealt with the problem of the theology of the history of religion with any acuteness, has made this passage the basis for his doctrine of the *révélation cosmique,* the cosmic revelation. Paul emphasizes here the continuity of the self-witness of the living God throughout the whole series of human generations, and Paul expressly includes his own generation. This continuous self-witness of the living God is an expression of His love. It is completely off the track here to speak of an absolute discontinuity between Christianity and the history of religion before Christianity. In this passage all humanity appears under the sign of the continuity of the self-witness of the one God who is Lord of creation and of salvation-history.

Jesus expresses himself very clearly in regard to the claim of absoluteness by orthodox Christians. At the end of a series of sayings on the theme "by their fruits you shall know them," Jesus says in Matthew 7:21–23:

> Not every one who says to me, "Lord, Lord," shall enter the kingdom of heaven, but he who does the will of my Father who is in heaven. On that day many will say to me, "Lord, Lord, did we not prophesy in your name, and cast out demons in your name, and do many mighty works in your name?" And then will I declare unto them, "I never knew you; depart from me, you evildoers."

Such a saying is quite surprising, for usually the possession of such gifts of the spirit as prophecy and exorcism appears as a sign of election to the kingdom of God. But this saying of "Lord, Lord"—the insistence upon an orthodox Christology, upon the prestige of correct belief—appears here apparently as a negative attitude of the spirit. It cannot even be compensated for by the exercise of such superb charismata as prophecy and exorcism.

The only commentary to this obvious deprecation of charismata is the hymn to Agape in the First Letter to the Corinthians. Here also the usually highly praised charismata are disapproved of as they are measured against the norm of Agape. With increasing intensity the charismatic feats—from talking in tongues to the offering of oneself—are presented. Then if they are not motivated by Agape, they are radically rejected. The lack of Agape, the lack of love for our fellow men, is the real characteristic of this self-conscious saying of "Lord, Lord." This lack is the reason why simply saying "Lord, Lord" does not lead into the kingdom of God and why all gifts of the spirit are useless if they are related simply to saying, "Lord, Lord." The lack of Agape makes allegiance to Christ simply a formal, dogmatic claim to absoluteness, which claims for itself the whole truth and all salvation. It creates an attitude of lovelessness toward those who do not accept this claim—a lovelessness that comprehends in itself the whole range of negative components that are the opposite of love: presumptuousness, contempt, disdainfulness and arrogant condescension.

Jesus promises that even those who have never heard of him, heathen and non-Christians, who to their own surprise turn out to be Christians because they have fulfilled the command of love, will be received into the kingdom of God and will sit at table there with him. This promise forms the complement to the exclusion of those who simply cry, "Lord, Lord." The most powerful of these sayings is found in Matthew 25:31, where Jesus describes the coming of the Son of Man at the last judgment and reveals the criterion with which men will then be judged. According to this promise of Jesus many heathen who did not know Christ at all will be chosen by the Son of Man to be subjects of the kingdom. The criterion which determines the consignment of men to the kingdom of God or to outer darkness is not a definite doctrine about Christ, not a recognition of the Christian claim to absoluteness, nor is it even a knowledge of the historical figure of Jesus, but it is the fulfillment of the commandment of love toward the least of our human brethren. In the final judgment it becomes clear that a formal claim to absoluteness does not exist; the prestige of Christians is not taken into consideration. Many non-Christians in the generations of mankind before and after Christ conducted themselves as children of the kingdom of God without knowing Christ. There are children of the kingdom not only within the congregation of those who confess Jesus Christ, but also within all of humanity and in all times until the end of time.

Similarly one can see in the prophecy of the coming of the kingdom of God in Luke 13:29 ff. that many will be rejected who consider themselves to be the rightful followers of Jesus and who claim the fellowship of the table (personal fellowship) with him. They insist that they have personally received their doctrine from Jesus. Instead of them, however, others are received into the kingdom and deemed worthy to sit at the table with the Son of Man: "And men will come from east and west, and from north and south, and sit at table in the kingdom of God." Not even the sacramental fellowship of the supper guarantees that nominal Christians belong to the kingdom of God. On the other hand many heathen who never came into contact with Jesus Christ are permitted to enter into the kingdom. In this passage also that which counts in the decisive moment, namely in the final judgment, is not the theological prestige of the Christian claim to absoluteness, but the fulfillment of the commandment of love toward the least of our brethren. This fulfillment of the commandment of love is found also outside of the Christian congregation. Salvation-history is realized not only in the area of organized congregations and confessional groups, but in the whole range of the history of religion. Salvation-history is human history.

This point of view is especially significant in the contemporary situation because the strongest argument against the exclusive Christian claim to absoluteness is precisely the history of the Christian Church and the history of its mission. The bright side of the history of Christianity is accompanied by a shadow of error and misdeed which often obscures the light. The "night of history," of which Franz von Baader speaks, was often identical with the night of Christianity. Today more than ever the followers of the non-Christian religions point to this dark side of church history as an important argument against the exclusive claim to absoluteness of Christianity. A work like Professor Thomas Ohm's *Asiens Kritik am abendländischen Christentum* [2] shows that this criticism can no longer be overlooked, but must be taken by Christianity as an occasion for a sincere self-examination. Professor Friedrich Heiler has summed up the result of such a critical self-examination of the Christian claim to absoluteness in the light of church history with the words: "Every exclusive view which sees in Christianity the only saving revelation of God has thereby finally collapsed."

A second way of a new approach seems to me to consist in directing the question of a Christian understanding of the non-Christian religions to those Christian personalities who have themselves grown up in a living experience and knowledge of a non-Christian religion and then have become Christian out of personal conviction. The exclusive judgments of non-Christian religions have up to now been made chiefly according to a fixed theological schema by theologians who did not know the non-Christian religions from within. But what do the great Christian converts say who have come out of a personal experience of Hinduism or Buddhism? This question has hardly been asked, let alone investigated. The great religious personalities of the Asiatic religions have characteristically expressed their recognition of the relation of religions to one another in figures and parables and not in abstract concepts. A pious follower of Mahayana Buddhism compares the relation of various religions to the pure light of the moon which is reflected by all the waters of the earth: by the muddy puddle of rain water, by the crystal-clear mountain lake,

[2] (München: Kösel, 1948).

and by the boundless sea. Sarojini Naidu, a spiritual leader of Hinduism, compares the different religions "to the different colors in a beautiful piece of opal." The great Mongolian Mangu (Mongka) Khan, grandson of Genghis Khan, compares the various religions as different ways of God to the different fingers on the same hand. In the Buddhistic Pali-Canon is found the famous parable of the blind men and the elephant. The parable of the three rings, which Lessing used in his *Nathan der Weise,* also has an Oriental origin. All of these parables of non-Christian origin aim at a harmonization and comparison of all religions within the context of a universal and inclusive idea of religion. It is characteristic that no such figurative visions of the relationship of Christianity to the non-Christian religions have originated in Western Christianity. I have found only one attempt to place a Christian parable over against the Buddhistic parables, and this came from an Asian Christian, the late Toyohiko Kagawa. He made use of an old Japanese proverb in which Zen Buddhism expressed its conception of the equality of all religions with these words: "Every way leads to the goal; every religion is good. Do not many paths lead to Mount Fuji?" This saying is very vivid for the Japanese, who know the various pilgrim paths which lead to the summit of the holy Mount Fuji, with their stations along the way, which are climbed annually by thousands of pilgrims. Kagawa was reared a Buddhist and was a believing Buddhist before he turned to Christianity. He takes this proverb which suggests: "Although many ways lead to the summit, we see the same moon from the summit; therefore why should Jesus Christ be our only leader?" and answers it in the following way:

> Buddhism, Omoto, Tenri and Islam, all of these religions are good. All contain truth and guidance. But some stop at the sixth resting place on the mountainside, some at the fourth and some become tired and rest even before they have passed the first station. Many rest at the second and some reach only the third. Buddhism may bring us to the ninth resting place, but because it stops there I do not choose Buddhism. I choose Christianity because I want to climb to the top.

This parable is surprising because it shows that Kagawa counts not only the great classical religions like Buddhism and Islam among the "good religions," but also some of the so-called "new religions" of Japan, like Tenri and Omoto which stem from new divine revelation and were founded only in the middle of the nineteenth century. Kagawa demonstrates that he wishes to apply this parable to the total religious development of mankind *ante Christum* and *post Christum.* The decisive point of importance in the parable is that it gives up the traditional formulation of the Christian claim to absoluteness in its exclusive form, yet avoids a complete relativism of religions. All religions are "good" in so far as they strive for the transcendent reality of God and have one final goal in view, but the individual religions attain or arrive at different stations on the way to that goal. They have higher or lower experiences and perceptions of the transcendent reality. Christianity alone leads to the summit of the experience of God and mediates the final fullness of the knowledge of God. Actually it is amazing that Kagawa assigns such a high rank to Buddhism, which he says out of his own experience leads man to the next to the last station under the summit, the ninth station. Everyone who has climbed Mount Fuji knows that the stretch between the eighth and ninth stations is the steepest and most difficult part of the climb. At station nine one has the worst part of the climb behind him. But it is only Christ who leads to the summit, to the experience and the view of the full self-disclosure of divine love. There are different degrees and levels in the encounter between the various religions and the transcendent One. These steps are disclosed in the history of religion. But in Christ the heart of God is disclosed.

The last instance known to me of an approach to a Christian theology of the history of religion which attempts to overcome the traditional claim to absoluteness and to push on to an inclusive understanding of the history of religion from the standpoint of salvation-history stems from Rudolf Otto. Thanks to his remarkable intuitive ability at identification he was personally very close to Eastern thinking and its figurative manner of expression. He writes in his *Vischnu-Nārāyana, Texte zur indischen Gottesmystik:*

> I am convinced that Christianity is decisively superior to other special forms of religion, not on the side of its many disputable historical accretions, but rather in terms of its specific ideal content; its highly individualized type of unique spirit. Its relationship of superiority to other religions is not that of truth to falsehood, but rather as Plato to Aristotle; not as master to slave, but as the first-born to his brothers.[3]

[3] (Jena: E. Diederichs, 1917; 2. Aufl., 1923), p. 155.

The Resurgence of Non-Christian Religions

BY PAUL D. DEVANANDAN

This is an age of widespread religious revival. Other religions beside our own have become strangely conscious of a new life. The ancient people of Asia are passing through revolutionary social changes; they have made rapid advance as independent nations; and they have turned to their ancestral religions with a new hope. They realize that a good deal of their national culture is closely related to their religious ideas, and that a cultural reintegration is impossible without a religious reconstruction. Thus, in recent times, the ancient religions of Hinduism, Buddhism, and Islam have become very real forces in the life and thought of the Asian people.

These resurgent faiths are in fact determining factors in the national and international outlook of modern man today. Whatever form the revival of religion may take, whether in the case of the intellectual, the common man, or the illiterate villager, it finds expression in a new sense of pride which is sensitive to criticism or disapproval. Non-Christians everywhere make the claim "our religion is as good as any other." Sometimes they go further and add, "if not actually in some ways better than other religions."

At the same time, this new religious temper is keenly aware that religion can be a disastrous source of division within a nation and among nations. Modern man is therefore anxious to avoid religious rivalry. We live in a world that is both tired of war and fearful of an imminent breakout of another world war. Religion has caused many wars in past history. Although in recent times we have not seen wars of religion, people suspect religious enthusiasm as a possible source of international controversy. So they hold that in order to prevent war and ensure world peace religions must come to some peaceful settlement.

Moreover, this general resurgence of religions in the plural is bound up with modern man's quest for understanding the real nature and significance of religion, of religion in the singular, of religion underlying religions. The dominant creative urge of this atomic age, contrarily enough, is to build on lasting foundations. Thoughtful men, therefore, affirm the transforming power of spirit over the downward drag of things. In a world where temporal, material values seemingly threaten the reality of eternal, spiritual good, they find assurance in religious faith.

Another characteristic development is the trend to discover a common formula of belief, though not a formulated creed, comprehending the diverse forms of these historic faiths. This is true of Hinduism and Buddhism in particular. There is a determined effort to include what until now had been described as "lower forms" of these religions, so that renascent, historic faiths have become, in a sense, catholic and unitary. Also, each of them makes the claim independently that it has the answer to the world's ills, and it is broadly hinted that Christianity has failed to cure them. Consequently a new emphasis is placed on a "world message" and on "missionary work." Finally, in every case, resurgent non-Christian religions have become socially conscious. Keen interest is taken in reform of social institutions which retard the development of the individual person and the realization of justice in social relations. This emphasis has resulted in a new understanding of personal values, a new stress on creative action and a new interest in contemporary history.

Opposition to Christian Claims

Resurgent non-Christian religions differ widely one from another in their basic credal affirmations. But they are all agreed in their opposition to the missionary expansion of Christianity; for obvious reasons. They disapprove chiefly of the proselytizing activity of Christians. Christian missionaries were the first to question the religious adequacy of other faiths. The sting in all this propaganda was the deliberate intention to make people repudiate, as wholly worthless, the faith in which they had been brought up. In retaliation, there was need to show that these historic religions, which had been for centuries closely identified with the cultural heritage and the social fabric of these lands, were very much alive, and still furnished the sustaining drive to true national well-being.

At first encounter, therefore, resurgent religions tended to be violently apologetic. They were all the time on the defensive. This reaction was in part also due to the fact that the Western powers who dominated Asian countries professed the Christian faith. The Arya Samaj movement in Hinduism represented this phase in Hindu resurgence. Theravada Buddhism in Ceylon and in Burma is still in this stage of resentment. But there is a further stage in the development of non-Christian apologetics. This is when resurgent religions set forth the claim not only to regional self-sufficiency, but to universal acceptance. The contention now is not that other religions are inadequate in comparison to theirs, but that whatever other religions profess to offer is also to be found in their own creed, if only it is rightly interpreted.

Therefore the plea that, as Christians, we should not strengthen the reactionary forces of a divisive exclusivism but help the growth of a comprehensive outlook of universalism. In an age of many religions, they suggest, we should give up all talk of mutual exclusion, and find a formula of comprehension which will make for unity in diversity. Every religion in fact possesses what had been regarded so long as peculiar to other religions; nevertheless we should preserve the characteristic identity of each religion as a separate historical phenomenon. Doctrinal differences based on traditional concepts held through many centuries of past history will persist. What vitally matters is the dynamic of faith undergirding these concepts, making them relevant to present life and meaningful in contemporary human history. In consequence, renascent faith consciously or unconsciously reformulates beliefs that in a previous generation had meant something very different. For instance, such words as *Karma* and *Maya* to the modern Hindu, or *Metta* and *Nibbana* to the modern Buddhist, and, in a different degree, *jihad* and *kismet* to the modern Moslem, now convey new meanings. There is a "newness" about these doctrines so restated which makes them challenging and relevant to all people.

Common Ground of Humanity

Another thing common to resurgent world faiths today is their concern for man. An overwhelming sense of compulsion to reckon with modern man's predicament is expressed in all their restatement of beliefs. Has religion an answer for problems of human distress in want, disease, and oppression? Can the dynamic of faith be mobilized to create a just social order, a true community of people, a world in which human rights are guaranteed? This has called for new emphases in the religious beliefs of all historic religions. So much so that a humanistic corrective to other-worldly mysticism and a conscious sense of human solidarity as against ethnic separatism characterize all resurgent faiths. Consequently they all claim to be basically alike despite differences, because they all seek to put meaning to our common humanity and ensure the worth of human values. Therefore also the call for interreligious cooperation.

Christians should seriously heed this invitation. In our times the impact of secularism, the anxious despair of many men in dire need of food, clothing, and shelter, creates real problems. We face them every day and everywhere. They all stem from the deep longing to find some meaning in our very existence. We stand on the common ground of humanity, then, when we talk together of these concerns that we share as Christians and non-Christians. It is our common humanity that provides both the framework and the context of our conversation. We share a multitude of common concerns which all eventually turn upon the quest for the true meaning of life and the final destiny of man. In fact, at such times we cease to be conscious that we are Christians and Hindus or Buddhists and Moslems. And we will discover for ourselves the disarming challenge of the claim:

> There is indeed a frontier, but it does not lie between the Christian man and the non-Christian man, but within both. . . . The heathen or Gentiles are those for whom God has acted and still acts, but God's saving action has not yet reached them. They are people who live in opposition. But—and it is a big but—the line does not run between Jew and Gentile, between heathen and Christian, but within each. The unredeemed "old man" of the New Testament, is to be found in me, a Christian; it is a possibility and a fact in me, in exactly the same terms as the unredeemed "old man" is to be found in the non-Christian. For

we, in large measure, are heathen still. We need to be converted as does the Hindu.[1]

This is a hard saying, but it brings us up against a very real issue which we often lack courage to face. Renascent non-Christian faith in our day puts it up to us to "Try your own selves, whether ye be in the faith." Are we ourselves involved in all this New Creation, experiencing in the deep within of ourselves the birth-throes of the New Man in Christ?

Fighting on Three Fronts

Thinking Christians of this generation, especially those in Asia, need to give serious thought also to the peculiar difficulties of present day non-Christian leaders. We do not sufficiently appreciate their predicament. They find themselves, at the same time, fighting on three fronts, as it were. At one point, they are up against the unwillingness of Christians to admit that the resurgence of their ancient faith is sure evidence of its vitality and its present worth. They are baffled by the failure of Christian evangelists to see in them allies and fellow crusaders in the fight against the common enemy of skeptism and materialism. At another point, leaders of resurgent religions in Asian lands find that, in their own country and among their own people, their plea for reformation of traditional beliefs and practices is met by reactionary orthodoxy with the charge that the faith of the fathers is betrayed. At a third point, they encounter revolutionary movements of secularistic humanism which would have nothing at all to do with the ancestral religion, because they see in it only the time-old forces of traditional evil which have made for human degradation and social injustice.

The charge of orthodoxy against the leaders of resurgent religions is invariably leveled against the tendency of modern temper to be receptive to new truths. This is regarded as a dangerous compromise, motivated by an opportunism which overstresses the exigent and the temporal to the neglect of the eternal and the abiding. Moreover, orthodoxy disapproves of the reformers' disregard of traditional practices and long-accepted religious observances. The modern emphasis on the "inwardness" of spiritual experience in worship to the neglect of the "outward" expression in worship is denounced as a move in the wrong direction. For it may even-

[1] *Religion and Society,* Vol. VI, No. 1 (1959), pp. 69 ff.

tually lead to a total abandonment of the claims of all religious sanctions, and result in the unbelief of irreligion. There is again a suspicion on the part of orthodoxy that the modern trend to place more regard on the good life, and the widening conception of what is good, is to accept the values of contemporary thinking on man and society. The natural conservatism of orthodoxy still cleaves to standards of right and wrong, of ideals of human relations, which had been established in times past when social thinking and human relations were conditioned by circumstances which limited the outreach of social relations to a much narrower area of life. Today the ties that bind mankind together form a complicated network which encompasses the whole world. Moreover, what binds men together in a new sense of solidarity are material things and civic concerns, both of which have acquired global significance. These economic and political factors play an important role in the ordering of human relations. This is why modern man feels the need for widening his conception of the good life to include material things and thought forces, and for regarding political and economic relations as also belonging in the realm of the spirit.

The secularist disapproval of the resurgence of religion is for another set of reasons. To the secularists all religion is outmoded, because essentially religious beliefs and practices are of the nature of unscientific superstitions which convey no meaning to the rational mind. Therefore they would regard all religion as irrelevant in the circumstances of life today. In fact, they would maintain that any revival of religion is a retrograde step in that it is an attempt either of reactionary ignorance to block progress or the deliberate device of vested interests to prevent the liberation of the masses. It may be that some secularists are willing to concede that religion can be permitted to exist as a private possession for the time being, but they look forward to the time when it would be dispensed with altogether as both unnecessary and invalid.

In their battle against orthodoxy on the one hand, and secularism on the other, what support can leaders of non-Christian resurgent religions expect from the Christian evangelist? Are there issues here which the discriminating insight of prophetic Christian faith can regard as issues in which Christian evangelists should also be concerned? Would any effort to strengthen the forces of renascent religion to that extent imply that the preaching of the Gospel suffers by default or compromise? These are some of the questions that need to be squarely faced. At the same time, we may not expect Christian thinking to be wholly agreed in its answer. A group of Christians in India spent some time together giving serious thought to "The Christian Approach to Renascent Hinduism." In formulating their findings they have stated:

> God works in the world which is His world; the Lordship of Christ includes all men and all human situations, and the Christian is therefore privileged to know that every place is his home and every man is his brother. . . . Our easy assumption that God works among us Christians alone is plainly and openly called in queston by the creativeness which has been given in our own country to those outside the Church. Such creativeness is from the God and Father of our Lord Jesus Christ whether it be found as moral creativeness in Sarvodaya or as scientific creativeness in the sphere of building up the nation. The word of reconciliation in Christ which has been given to us for transmission to others needs to be spoken into all situations; for every creative power of man has possibilities for both good and evil. We can only speak this word if we accept in mind and heart that these gifts of creativeness are from God.[2]

Interpenetration of Specific Doctrines

Christian thinking regards all religions as more or less unitary systems. So it denies that there can be any real interpenetration of particular doctrinal beliefs; not certainly to the extent that it can change the organic whole of any religious system. Nevertheless, it seems true that the outburst of newness of life and release of unexpected power in the resurgent non-Christian religions is due to the somewhat strange and almost irrational additions of contradictory beliefs from other creeds, and from Christianity in particular. Closer examination shows that invariably the addition is from corresponding religious categories. In renascent Hinduism, for instance, the doctrine of the world as a present reality, the validity of creative effort in the here and now, and the recognition of a divine purpose as conditioning human history are all the consequence of the interaction of religious thought in terms of corresponding doctrinal affirmations in Hinduism and Christianity. The same can be also said of certain new emphases in renascent Buddhism and Islam.

Characteristically Christian truths, abstracted from the accepted

[2] *Ibid.*, pp. 79 ff.

pattern of the Christian creed, are found now in the context of non-Christian religious thought. They are woven into the very texture of corresponding doctrinal beliefs and religious categories, undoubtedly enriching them with a new meaning content and life. How far have such additions to specific doctrines, and their consequent restatement, transformed the total creed of non-Christian systems? We do not know. It is too early in the day to furnish an answer. But this much is certain. On the one hand, it has resulted in an inward unsettlement, and some heart-searching inquiry. On the other hand, it has also led to a noticeable stiffening attitude of unfriendliness to Christian evangelism. What must give us concern, however, is that while certain Christian truths are received and appropriated with eagerness by resurgent non-Christian religions, the total claims of the Christ are rejected. For it is realized that accepting his total claims would mean giving up the whole of the ancestral faith as altogether invalid.

There is one other matter we need to consider in this connection: the religious vocabulary which we have perforce to employ both as Christians and non-Christians is the same. We use the same words to convey different meanings. Unless Christians know the meaning content of words which we use along with non-Christians, how can we make clear to others where we differ? Especially is this so in many modern movements within Hinduism, where words used in different sense for similar concepts have come to acquire a noticeable Christian flavor. While we are warned of the danger of syncretism by such traffic in words, should that fear drive us to equally great danger of withdrawal and isolationism? In the providence of God it is quite possible that by making it necessary for us as Christians to witness to His works, as we understand them, in the words of the religion of others to whom we seek to communicate the Gospel, there may be a purpose which we have yet to fathom.

The Central Issue

It is at this point that we come up against the central issue raised by renascent non-Christian religions: Is the preaching of the Gospel directed to the total annihilation of all other religions than Christianity? This is of crucial concern to our generation in Asia and Africa. Will religions as religions, like nations as nations, continue so to be, characteristically distinguishable, in the kingdom when God's redemptive act in Christ Jesus is consummated? In the final gathering up of all that is of this world, we believe there will be a total transformation of what now is. We will not be able to distinguish in the "New" what there is of the "Old." Therefore it is not for us to indicate what will be preserved, and in what manner. For the New Creation is not to be regarded as so totally new in that the old is wholly destroyed. Or else, God's activity in the here and now is meaningless and futile. That surely cannot be our belief. If God's redemptive activity in Jesus Christ is a fact with which we should reckon in every human situation, it is not so much by total destruction that He manifests His power but by radical renewal. That is why the Gospel we proclaim is the Good News of the Resurrection, the hope of the New Creation.

It is passing strange that in the parable of the talents, the servant who faithfully preserved the one talent given him by the Lord is severely dealt with. As Christians, we stress the "giveness" of the doctrine, and we do right in so doing. Whatever is true is of God and from God. But the very faithfulness of the servant who zealously safeguarded the one talent came in for harsh condemnation. Faith possesses and profitably utilizes what is given—and to that extent runs a risk. At the same time, faith has no illusion about the "possession" as something "given," to be put to use and increase. Our Lord's words are: "To him who has will more be given, and he will have abundance; but from him who has not, even what he has will be taken away" (Mt. 13:12). And he may well be talking of faith which increases with the abandon with which one is willing to adventure in assured trust that He who hath "given" can well protect His gifts, if we speculate with it in His name.

Christian faith should learn to distinguish between the Christian hope of the fulfillment of God's promise of the kingdom, and the non-Christian claim that all human desire to reach out to God will eventually be fulfilled. Fulfillment in the second sense would mean that progressive realization of a more or less continuous process which can be traced back to the past, perceived in the present, and finally realized in the future. But fulfillment in the former case would mean that because the final end is so totally assured it is in reality a present fact. Though still of the future, God's promise is being revealed in the present, however incompletely, to those who dare to live in that hope here and now. For present history, to the discerning eye of faith, is not the fulfillment of the past but the realization of the future! So it was to the Seer of Patmos.

> Then I saw a new heaven and a new earth; for the first heaven and the first earth had passed away, and the sea was no more. . . . And I heard a great voice from the throne saying, "Behold, the dwelling of God is with men. He will dwell with them, and they shall be his people, and God himself will be with them and be their God." . . . And he who sat upon the throne said, "Behold I make all things new."
>
> Revelation 21:1, 3 and 5

Christian Presuppositions for the Encounter with Communism

BY FRANK WILSON PRICE

The amazing and alarming twentieth century in which we live may be described in many ways. We shall not be far amiss if we characterize it as the century of Communist power. In the Russian Revolution of 1917 Marxism, which for seven decades had been only a provocative revolutionary philosophy, seized the reins of government and began to press its challenges and demands upon the whole world. Today nearly a billion people are under Communist rule, and another billion find themselves deeply stirred by Communist promises, pressures, appeals, or threats. The polarization of this global struggle and the resulting cold war between the United States and Soviet Russia affect every nation, large and small. As a dynamic force flowing from the brain and personality of Karl Marx, as a radical and compelling body of ideas, as an organized political system, and as a new kind of universal faith, Communism claims the attention, and it would like to claim the allegiance, of all mankind. To this end it employs every possible instrument and ally—modern science and technology, foreign trade and technical aid, anticolonial sentiment, national spirit, racial pride, the urge of undeveloped areas toward rapid industrialization and higher living standards, infiltration and astute propaganda, an aggressive expansion policy, and of course impressive military might.

In the nineteenth century the great ethnic religions seemed to be the chief barriers to the spread of Christianity. Today these religions, many of them undergoing revival, intertwined with national heritage and culture, and inspired by patriotic fervor, are still resistant to the Christian Gospel, although they welcome better understanding and more sympathetic approaches. Christianity now finds its most militant opposition, its most severe test, not from other ancient faiths, but rather in its encounter with contemporary Communism. All the living religions of the world, we may add, are being challenged by Communist power.

What presuppositions does the Christian disciple or the Christian Church hold in this momentous encounter? With what convictions and in what mood and spirit shall we enter upon the critical meeting? It must be said that the circumstances under which Christians and Marxists come together today are not the same in all places. The daily contact of a Chinese Christian with his Communist regime and environment is quite different from the casual encounter of a Western Christian with a Communist visitor from the Soviet Union, or from the meetings of Christians and Communists in countries wooed but not yet dominated by Marxian ideas. The encounter takes on a different character in a democracy where free speech and worship are permitted, from what it does in a totalitarian state where the Christian citizen is suspected of being reactionary or disloyal. We need to keep in mind the varying dimensions of Communist–Christian dialogues and meetings, and at the same time look for some basic principles upon which Christians everywhere may unite, even when their governments face each other in unfriendliness or hostility.

The points which I now suggest come from personal thinking and study and also out of the experiences of Christians in many lands. They arise from our common search for Biblical and theological light upon the perplexing way before us.

1. As Christians we start from our faith, our faith in God, Creator, Judge, and Redeemer. In the divine–human relationship God takes the initiative; He made us for a purpose; He seeks us when we go astray; He yearns to save us. He has come into our time and space, into the history of mankind, through Jesus Christ, the Eternal Word or Truth expressed in human form. The cross reveals His infinite love, far beyond any imaginable love or sacrifice of man. The only worthy response that we can make is obedience.

All our horizontal social relationships are determined by the primary vertical relationship, between God and ourselves. Therefore, we need something more than a social philosophy, a revolutionary cause, a political ideal, or a crusade for a better world. We are commanded to seek above all the rule of God. Man—including Communist man—is made by God, is responsible to God, is in need of God.

When the Communist devotee calls our faith unscientific, superstitious, and antisocial, we do not answer him with a denunciation of his atheism. There is too much practical atheism outside of the Communist camp. Rather, we endeavor to make real to the Communist our faith that gives true meaning and value to life, a faith that is not measured by mortal minds alone, but dares to trust in the holy mysteries of infinity and eternity, a faith that rescues man from proud, self-righteous deification of his own achievements. We do not point with scornful finger at the Communist; we ask the Communist, if he will, to fold his hands along with the Christian, in worship of God who is also his God (though unrecognized) as much as ours. Some day, we pray, his antireligious scorn may change to humble and devout reverence.

2. Christianity has taken form in human structures and organizations; it has been enmeshed in history and culture; it has related itself to many different political and economic systems. We do not agree with the Marxist that religion is simply the reflection of unjust economic orders before the advent of Communist society. Certainly the Christian Gospel in its historical manifestations has both given to and received from its environment. We admit the unfortunate associations of the Christian Church with imperialism and other political evils of the past. At the same time we know that the Church has grown and changed through self-criticism, repentance, and inner purification. Christianity cannot be torn from the loom of history or from its social milieu today. Yet we must continually strive to set the Christian faith free from those inequalities and injustices with which it has been involved or is involved at the present time, and to present it in its essential purity to a sinful and suffering humanity. When Christians admit before God their sins in relation to society and the family of nations they ask the Communists to place themselves under the same judgment. We oppose new slaveries as well as old slaveries, aggression in the future as well as aggression in the past. The Christian call for radical repentance sounds throughout the world, to every nation and every

people. "All have sinned and come short of the glory of God. . . . Repent, for the kingdom of God is at hand."

3. As Christians we see God at work in history in many ways; He appears to the nations in many guises. He is Lord of history, of the history of Babylon and Egypt and Rome as well as of Judah and Israel. Assyria was the "rod of His anger, the staff of His fury." Cyrus was "His anointed, whose right hand He grasped," and "His shepherd" who would fulfill His purpose. He made the Caesars to serve the spread of the Gospel. He is in the turnings and overturnings of history; He rules over the rise and fall of empires. Communism is part of His domain. In God's providence Communism may be a teacher, a strange, harsh and unwelcome teacher, but nevertheless needed; in the words of Isaiah, "Though the Lord give you the bread of adversity, and the water of affliction, yet shall not thy teachers be removed." If God works through totalitarian Communism to bring about in some countries swift reconstruction, long-awaited social reforms, and the discipline of society, we must accept this as a judgment not only on these countries but also on us of the more privileged nations who have failed in our duty to the rest of humanity.

At the same time Christians should not shut their eyes to the cost of violent revolutions and the terrible physical and spiritual wounds that they inflict on the body politic. In long perspective these terrific upheavals may be necessary, even though the evil in them seems to outweigh the good. They, and all the social ferment of our time, show that God has placed tremendous creative powers in the hands of His creatures, to search out the secrets of nature, "to have dominion over the works of God's hands," and to influence the course of history, powers that may be used to construct or to destroy. This is the risk that God took when He gave freedom to man. The fallen angel may become a rebellious devil. Yet we are sure that God is the ultimate master and ruler of history, past, present, and future.

4. It is imperative for the Christian to try to understand Marxian Communism from within—its origins and development, its theories and structures, its religious features, its subtle appeals and dynamic force, as much as he tries to understand any religious or social movement of today. Ignorance is perilous. Understanding does not mean acceptance, but simply a wise discernment of the "signs of the times," and a clear insight into the thinking and feeling of

groups that are sharply different from us. We cannot be satisfied with a general condemnation of Communism. We must move beyond this to a deeper appreciation of those neglected truths and forgotten emphases of our Judeo-Christian heritage to which Communism is impelling us. "What do ye more than they?" would be Jesus' question to us today. The Christian Church may be subject to a sterner judgment because of the high faith that we profess and yet often fail to practice. And our understanding must extend farther than ideas and systems to the persons involved in Communism—those who have committed themselves to the Marxist cause, and the much larger number who, without fully supporting Communism or fully rejecting it, have to live and work daily under its control. Finally, if understanding is to be more than sentiment or knowledge it should lead us on to positive Christlike love, even for those whose philosophy and behavior may be repugnant to us.

5. Communist governments meet other governments on the political, cultural, economic, and military level, and out of these meetings come agreements, conflicts, or uneasy truce. Christians in both Communist and non-Communist lands have to judge the policies of their governments and take some stand with regard to these policies. Naturally, the Christian in the Soviet Union or the Chinese People's Republic looks at certain questions quite differently from his fellow Christian in the Western world or in neutral countries of Africa and Asia. The armament race and the "balance of terror" as both sides increase their stock piles of nuclear weapons and ballistic missiles, affect Christians everywhere, but we should not let the meeting of Christian minds and hearts be limited to political and economic channels. Christians in the West look on national defense and collective security as a rampart behind which certain freedoms may be protected and certain ideals be achieved; no doubt many Christians in the Communist empire look at us from behind ramparts which appear necessary to the protection of their liberties and aspirations. The important thing to remember is that fruitful meetings of Christianity and Communism, or of Christians in the two worlds, cannot take place on the level of government relations, economic competition, or military struggle; they must be on the ground of a common humanity and a common concern for all individuals and groups in society, linked on our part with steady faith in God's loving purpose for all His children. We must free ourselves from the hard stance of our governments, who bear the

responsibility of defending us, and work for spiritual encounters with Communists everywhere and with Christians in Communist nations.

6. The Christian finds his ethical presuppositions challenged again and again by the Communists, in the first place because contradictory interpretations are given to many old and familiar moral concepts. It is easy to repudiate the questionable means that Communists employ and justify because they serve the ends of revolution and a classless society. We do not as quickly admit that Communist regimes have effected some significant moral reforms: in China, for example, they have eliminated commercial prostitution and the gambling evil, and have elevated the status of women. We come to the encounter with firm belief in an "open society" which the Marxist, intent upon forcing his doctrinaire views and new system, does not share, and with a respect for the dignity and value of individuals which has deep roots in the Hebrew–Christian philosophy of man. Because we find a kind of stern Puritanism and group discipline among the Communists some may think it possible to harmonize our ethical principles with theirs. But we shall be doomed to disappointment. It will be necessary to hold firmly to essential Christian principles of right and wrong and to apply them the best we can in new and strange situations, resisting all temptations to moral compromise.

My own experience in Communist China revealed what seemed to me four serious moral weaknesses in the Communist system: deceitful propaganda and false accusations; hatred and an almost demonic brutality toward those who are considered "enemies of socialism"; tyranny over the mind and spirit of men; and idolatry—not so much the official atheism as the worship of false, man-made gods and the absolutizing of human power. We must avoid identification of Christian morals with the standards of our Western middle-class society, without accepting at face value the distorted Communist picture of evil in the non-Communist world. Not merely in conversations but even more through demonstrations we need to make clear the truth and the power of the whole Christian ethic, for the individual and for society, recognizing that in God's mysterious purpose the Communist represents, as Emil Brunner says, "a great ethical urge, a powerful idea, a new way of thinking and willing," which we can only match with something higher and better.

7. The relation of religion—and in this discussion we mean the relation of Christianity—to the state is a crucial issue brought into sharp focus by a recent book, *How to Serve God in a Marxist Land.* Does Jesus' teaching about God and Caesar mean that the Christian in Russia or Communist China must serve two masters? Does the Pauline injunction about being subject to the governing authorities instituted by God apply under a Communist dictatorship? Is Communist government an order founded by God to which the Christian citizen owes allegiance? These are questions that mean different things to different people, and are answered in divergent ways, in Eastern and Western Europe, in India and China, in North America and in Africa. A neutral attitude does not appear possible in a Communist-dominated country, where certain accommodations must be made. In countries influenced by Communism, neutralism may result in the surrender of vital freedoms. Yet to some people freedom from hunger is more important than freedom from political autocracy.

The Bible was written on the background of Hebrew theocracy and ancient empires. It teaches no one pattern of government or economy, although we find in the last book of the New Testament an intense opposition to the despotism and injustices of the later Roman Empire. The prophetic message of the Scriptures seems to be fulfilled, as far as human civilization is concerned, in democratic rather than dictatorial rule. But the whole question of religious liberty is exceedingly difficult and complex. Christians need to approach it thoughtfully, earnestly, and with sensitive consciences, prepared to struggle and to sacrifice for basic human, God-given rights which people everywhere should enjoy. At the same time the Christian, when pressures are imposed or crucial tests come, must witness boldly to his supreme loyalty, and be ready always to say, "We must obey God rather than man," or the government of man.

8. Christianity and Communism meet also as organized communities of faith. The Christian Church, with nearly two millenniums of history, encounters a party, an army, a system, a world-wide organization, that is less than a hundred years old, yet overwhelmingly strong and fierce. Roman Catholicism is more similar to Communism in its centralized controls and totalitarian pattern than is Protestantism, but the Reformed churches, while freer from ecclesiastical rigidity and the shackles of tradition, are woefully disunited in the face of Communist power.

Christianity cannot hope to engage in effective dialogue with Communism or to influence, and evangelize, Communist followers and societies, unless its own organic life is healthy and vigorous, with all the characteristics of a true Church, a part of the "body of Christ." Its faith in the Triune God must be firm and sure. Corporate worship and personal devotions must be maintained (as is being done in Eastern Europe and on the Chinese mainland). The sacraments must be observed, and the Church must find ways of witnessing, at all costs, to the people around it, and ways of serving and suffering for society with the love of Christ.

In the crisis of our time the Church is called upon to recover its unique, God-given unity and mission, as a testimony to all nations and peoples. Every member must be an evangelist, from his own home to the ends of the earth. The Communists believe intensely in their cause; their faith will continue to march onward unless Christians believe yet more intensely in their cause and in their Lord, and form a community of faith, hope, and love that will inspire both the fanatical Communists and the doubtful and fearful world which wonders where to turn.

Christian coexistence with Communism on this planet is an undeniable fact today, hardly a subject for argument. Unless we can continue to live together we will perish together. If we can avoid a catastrophic war there may be increasing opportunities for us to meet, to talk, to work together instead of against each other, for a better world, and to bring about conditions for peace with a measure of justice. Let us be patient. A change may come in the next generation of Communists. Perhaps in a few decades, or centuries, Christianity and Communism will face one another as the Christian Church and Islam do today, different faiths and yet not intent each upon the destruction of the other. Meanwhile the Church of Jesus Christ must learn to live under all forms of political power, even as she has done in the past, and to testify to her divine, crucified, and risen Lord under the most favorable and also the most unfavorable circumstances.

The Communists' incessant and seemingly hypocritical talk about peace and brotherhood should not discourage the Christian Church from working in Christian ways for peace and brotherhood. Unless the Church can set the world a shining example of racial equality, of truth in political and social spheres, of wholesome family and community life, of sacrificial ministry by the stronger to the weaker;

unless she can maintain her fellowship across all the boundaries and barriers of our age; unless she can work with all good movements for freedom from hunger and want, unless she can help to redeem and transform our culture; she will seem to multitudes an irrelevant and expendable force. On the other hand, a new vision, a new dedication, a new united power in the world-wide Church of Christ, would give humanity new hope and courage.

9. We have said that twentieth-century Christianity is becoming more concerned about Communist power than about the major non-Christian religions. This does not mean a neglect of the other religions but rather a new phase in our relation to them. We see that Communist ideology and action challenge all religious faiths. To the orthodox Marxist every form of religion is an opiate and will ultimately disappear in the Communist society where the dialectic of history is resolved. Therefore, we find ourselves standing alongside Judaism, Buddhism, Islam, Hinduism, and other living religions in opposition to the self-sufficient secularism and atheistic creed of the Communist movement. Again, our study both of other religions and of the world-wide ideological struggle strengthens our conviction that Christianity has something unique to offer, as the way of salvation that mankind most needs, and as the highest ideal of personal and social living. Through a purified Christian Church, perhaps even a severely persecuted Church, God can work His will in our age. Communism will help to sweep away many superstitions and low forms of religion. It will destroy the wood, hay, and stubble, but the true gold will remain. And even if civilization comes crashing down around us, Christians can be the beginning of the new order that arises. Christianity should lead the believing world in its meek yet mighty encounter with Communist power, confident that we shall see new miracles in the spiritual as well as the scientific realm.

10. The Communist faith is eschatological. But its utopia lacks height and depth. It has been called a secularized form of the Christian apocalyptic. This is an oversimplification, but it is certainly able to fire the imagination and kindle the enthusiasm of multitudes. Even those who once were inspired and have been disillusioned admit its hypnotic power. But what does it promise us beyond this brief and earth-bound life? What hope do we have beyond human history with its darkness and tragedy along with its light and joy? The Communist government in China has forbidden

certain millennial sects from preaching crass interpretations of the imminent end of the world and final judgment. Yet, both under Communist power and regimentation and where there is greater freedom of worship and witness, we need to proclaim the Christian hope, as taught in the Scriptures, "till he come."

The Christian believes in personal immortality and not simply immortality of the human race or of the working class, as Marxism promises. He believes also in a social message and a social hope for the hungry, the sick, the illiterate, the oppressed, and the despairing; otherwise, Jesus' sermon in the synagogue of Nazareth has no relevance for us today. Christianity cannot afford to leave all further revolution and reform to nonreligious or antireligious movements. "The Christian Church," said Samuel Taylor Coleridge over a hundred years ago, "is the sustaining, correcting, befriending opposite of the world." While it is in the world, and while the world lasts, the Church must not for a moment cease its effort, by work and sacrifice and prayer, to bring society as well as individuals nearer to God and His purpose for mankind. Christianity is supported by its majestic hope, "Thy Kingdom come, Thy will be done on earth, as it is in heaven." What we earnestly strive for here, by God's grace, is a foretaste of the wonders that God has prepared for us in the life beyond, and for all His obedient children in the ages to come. Greater than any terrifying but transient Communist power is that which we invoke when we pray, "Thine is the kingdom and the power and the glory, for ever and ever, Amen."

The Nature of Encounter between Christianity and Other Religions as Witnessed on the Japanese Scene

BY MASATOSHI DOI

I

Professor Paul Tillich, in his *Interpretation of History,* has suggested that border lines are truly propitious places for acquiring knowledge, whereas if one stands in the interior, removed from the broad sphere beyond the boundaries, he is without an object of comparison with which to judge his own situation correctly.[1] If this be true, it may safely be said that Japan is one of the most propitious places for understanding the true nature of encounter between Christianity and other religions, and provides an excellent laboratory for the study of religions. In 1957 there were 142 Shinto denominations (including 15 Shrine–Shinto organizations), 170 Buddhist denominations, 36 Christian denominations, and 29 other religious organizations, making a total of 377, registered with the government.[2]

The postwar resurgence of new religions in Japan has been stupendous, with some 700 new religions registered with the government. About half of them disappeared after the enforce-

[1] (New York: Charles Scribner's Sons, 1936), p. 3.

[2] *The Year Book of Religion, 1957;* ed. by The Japanese Ministry of Education (Tokyo: The Finance Ministry's Printing Office, 1957).

ment of the new Religious Corporation Law of 1951, but others have made remarkable advances. At least five of them have won more than 600,000 adherents each. Reiyukai, a Nichiren sect, alone has gained a membership of 2,300,000, or more than four times the total Christian population.

The reasons for the burgeoning new religions are several. Marxist scholars ascribe them to the social unrest in postwar Japan. But this alone cannot explain the total phenomenon, because new religions are not necessarily thriving in the poverty-stricken areas. A more fundamental reason is to be found in the frustration of the whole nation by defeat in war. Every nation needs an object of devotion. For the Japanese it had been the destiny of the nation with the deified Emperor as its focal point. But now that the nation's destiny has run counter to their expectations, the Emperor himself disclaiming divinity, they have lost their object of devotion. It is very natural, then, that as they recover from their state of stupor, they look for a new religion that might heal their frustration and claim their total devotion. Such is the psychological situation in which the new religions have grown.

But this is only a recent development. In order to understand the situation correctly one must have adequate knowledge of the historical development leading up to it. I have no space here to deal with it in any considerable length, but I should like to describe briefly some basic mental traits of the Japanese which have contributed to the development of religion in Japan.

I propose to characterize the basic trait of the Japanese mentality as the absence of the sense of ultimacy. The original Japanese tribes were thoroughly optimistic. They were happy and contented with the present life. They had no ultimate viewpoint from which to judge the present. This is the reason why they had such a vague view of the future world. The future world, or Yomi, was only a shadowy, miserable place where the dead went. Even such contemporary Shinto sects with good standing as Konko-kyo and Kurozumi-kyo have no definite teaching concerning the future life.

This absence of the sense of ultimacy also explains why they lacked the consciousness of sin. In its place, they possessed a sense of ceremonial uncleanliness. But this referred to an external deficiency, while sin, in the Christian sense, is the moral sense of guilt.

Man cannot live without some standard of reference. When one lacks an ultimate point of view, he tends to lift up some part of the finite world as sacred, and in such a case there is no radical breach between the sacred and the secular. The relationship is understood in terms of continuity. Kami, the Japanese word for God, simply meant "what is above." Among the primitive Japanese, everything that was lifted a little above ordinary things, be it an animal or a stone, was worshiped as Kami. Any person who had done meritorious service for the ethnic group was enshrined as Kami.

This absence of the sense of ultimacy also leads to syncretism, which is characteristic of Japanese religions. On the Japanese scene syncretism means two things. One is the fusion of two or more religions into one system. This tendency has been very strong among the Japanese. The time was when Shinto gods were identified with Buddhist deities under the name of Two-Aspects Shinto. Even at present syncretic forms are prevalent among the "new religions." Syncretism also means man's split adherence to two or more religions. It is remarkable to note that in 1957, against a total population of 90 million, the total number of adherents reported by all religious organizations amounted to 123 million. Since the total number of those who had no religious beliefs at all was estimated at 24 million, this means roughly that each Japanese believed in two religions at a time.

This syncretistic attitude can be explained partly by the geographic position of the islands. Isolated from the continent by the sea, Japan has never experienced a sweeping invasion by a foreign religion. New religions never entered as radical antitheses to the old. They were introduced gradually and piecemeal, with the result that the old religions coexist with the new in layers, so to speak.

A great change came in the middle of the sixth century when Buddhism was introduced. The optimistic, life-affirming ancient Japanese for the first time learned to doubt the meaning of life. Their eyes were opened to the transitoriness of earthly things. "Contempt for this Polluted Land; Yearning after the Pure Land!" became their shibboleth. But the effect of this encounter was mutual. Buddhism accommodated itself to the life-affirming temper of the Japanese by developing esoteric practices. Doctrines with life-affirming implications were emphasized, for example, "Every person is Buddha in essence," "This world of life and death is in essence identical with Nirvana," and so forth. Nonetheless, it is true that the Japanese people, by virtue of Buddhist influence, have obtained a deeper insight into the meaning of life. Buddhism had a stronger sense of ultimacy than primitive Shintoism. This is proved by its power to relativize all spatial-temporal existence.

Confucianism entered Japan earlier than Buddhism, but its spiritual influence began to be felt much later, i.e., in the Tokugawa period. It is through and through a worldly religion, if it can be called a religion. It taught scarcely anything about the future life. Its greatest contribution was that it provided the nation with a system of morality which taught men to take universal laws pertaining to human relations more seriously. Thus far human relations had been dealt with in a rather spontaneous and emotional fashion. But Confucian morality, because of its feudalistic and legalistic character, could not do justice to the subjective and creative aspect of moral life. From the purely religious point of view it added little that was profound except the vague monotheistic idea of "the Heavenly Emperor" or "the Supreme Emperor."

When Christianity came into contact with the Japanese people for the first time in 1549, the Jesuit missionaries communicated their message in Buddhist terms because these were the only religious terms the Japanese could understand. The result was that Christianity was accepted by the Japanese as a religion of salvation.[3] But Christianity did not simply build upon the substructure which had been left unfinished by the Buddhists. This is proved by the fact that such important terms as "God" and "soul" were used in the Latin original because no equivalents could be found in Buddhist terms. For the Buddhist who understands the Ultimate Reality in terms of universal law or Dharma, God and soul as individual existences are something to be transcended. A personal God as the Ultimate Reality is foreign to the Buddhist philosopher, although there is a strong tendency in Japanese Buddhism, especially in Shingon Buddhism, to personify the Ultimate Reality. But in the final analysis this is only an expedient (*hoben*) to make it understandable to the common people. The Buddhist doctrine of transmigration seems implicitly to presuppose the permanence of individual souls, and some Buddhist scholars explicitly affirm the immortality of individual souls. But, after all, they are no more than

[3] Tadakazu Uoki, *The Spiritual Tradition of Japanese Christianity* (Tokyo: The Christian Literature Publishing Association, 1941), p. 30.

ripples in the water. All this seems to suggest that the relationship between Christianity and Buddhism is continuous and discontinuous at the same time.

The second encounter between Christianity and the Japanese people took place in 1859 when Protestant missionaries began their work. The first Japanese to be converted were sons and daughters of the samurai class who had been brought up in the Confucian tradition. Accordingly, what appealed to them most strongly was the puritan ethics introduced by the first Protestant missionaries. They felt that Christianity would give the nation power to fulfill the Confucian moral code. In translating the Christian concept of God they preferred the Confucian concept "the Supreme Emperor" to the Shinto concept "Kami," which had polytheistic connotations. This meant that they were better equipped than the Shintoists and Buddhists to understand the Christian concept of God. But considerable time elapsed before they understood fully the essence of Christianity as the Gospel of redemption.

The Shinto cosmogony and the Shinto concept of soul helped some Japanese to understand the Christian doctrine of creation and the Christian concept of soul, even though they had to overcome many discrepancies between the ethnic-naturalistic religion and the universal-revealed religion.

A deeper understanding of the Christian Gospel has been represented by those Christians who have been converted from Buddhism. They unanimously confess that the Christian Gospel is the fulfillment of Amida Buddhism. The Reverend Mr. Kamegai, a Christian minister converted from the Buddhist priesthood, says that nothing of the best in Buddhism is lost in Christianity, even though he admits there is a radical breach between Christianity as a revealed religion and Buddhism as a product of human reflection.

This brief sketch of the historical development of religion in Japan gives us a more realistic basis for a systematic discussion of "The Nature of Encounter between Christianity and Other Religions."

II

Scientific study of a subject presupposes a methodology, and determination of the method must come not from a preconceived dogma or logic, but from the true nature of the reality with which the student is to deal. The reality we are going to deal with here is not simply a psychological or cultural phenomenon, even though it has psychological, cultural, and even physical aspects. Instead, it is primarily a personal encounter between God who revealed Himself in Jesus Christ and man in his religion.

This excludes a type of dogmatic approach in which the objective knowledge of a group of dogmas is taken as the absolute presupposition and from which the experiencing subject is excluded. When a group of dogmas is taken in itself as the absolute truth, it becomes a closed system which can admit no element of truth or meaning in any other system, either religious or cultural. No one would imagine that such an attitude could do justice to the reality of other religions.

Hendrik Kraemer's Biblical realism is a marvelous attempt to do justice to the reality of other religions without drifting away from Biblical presuppositions. I agree with Dr. Kraemer in the conviction that the revelation in Jesus Christ is the ultimate standard of reference.[4] I also believe in principle that a theology of religion which investigates religions in the light of this revelation can understand their true nature more profoundly than a science of religion.[5] But I wonder if a theology of religion set forth by a theologian who has been brought up in a particular religious tradition may not involve limitations which prevent him from meeting with other religions in due fairness and openness. I am inclined to believe that a theology of religion alone cannot do justice to the reality of other religions. It needs objective knowledge of other religions as a corrective, even though I definitely reject the idea that the universal Logos is the final tribunal. The final decision must be made within the theological circle, after paying due attention to the objectively given knowledge of other religions. This is necessary because a theologian qua theologian cannot be flawless in his knowledge of other religions even if the revelation in the light of which he examines them be flawless.

Dr. Kraemer shows real wisdom when he says that Christianity as an historical religion is a distorted response to the divine act and as such stands under the judgment of God just as do all other religions.[6] This ability of Protestant Christianity to criticize itself

[4] Hendrik Kraemer, *The Christian Message in a Non-Christian World* (London: International Missionary Council, 1938), p. 110.

[5] *Ibid.*, p. 136.

[6] *Ibid.*, p. 109.

by the same standard as other religions constitutes the only door through which the theologian can communicate with other religions in due fairness and openness. This enables him to accept openheartedly such a corrective as I mentioned above. Faith gives him the ability to stand not only inside the theological circle but also outside it, as Professor Tillich would say. The stronger his faith is, the greater is his ability to step out of the circle without losing himself as a committed Christian.

Other objective approaches which are as inadequate as the above-mentioned type of dogmatic approach for dealing with our subject may generally be called *scientific*. By scientific approaches I mean those methods—by whatever name they may be called: comparative religion, history of religion, or science of religion—for which the universal Logos is the final tribunal and from which the existential involvement of the ego is excluded. Since faith is a matter of existential commitment it is clear that these objective approaches cannot do full justice to the real nature of religions. Yet it is also clear that there are such phenomena as similarities and dissimilarities between religions. In each religion there are strong points and deficiencies in comparison with other religions. Should these things be neglected or deemed insignificant because of the *sui generis* character of all religions?

In the Bossey document entitled "The Word of God and The Living Faiths of Men," fulfillment theory is discredited on the ground that religions are wholes and complete in themselves.[7] It is true that a religion is something more than the sum total of its parts; it has a principle or core which integrates the whole. But this integration should not be understood too much in biological terms. As a matter of fact, every historical religion is a synthesis of different elements from different cultures and religions as far as its historical expression is concerned. Christianity is no exception. Christianity in its present form is a synthesis of many elements from Judaism, the mystery religions, Hellenistic ideas, modern rationalism, and so forth.[8] Therefore, we must admit that there is some element of continuity between Christianity and other religions and cultures as far as their historical expressions are concerned, al-

[7] A document for study and discussion from the World Council of Churches Division of Studies, Geneva, 1958.

[8] See L. Harold DeWolf's essay on "The Interpenetration of Christianity and the Non-Christian Religions."—Ed.

though it is also true that there can be no conversion from one religion to the other unless there is some element of discontinuity between them.

In a survey conducted by the writer the majority of replies from converts gave support to the fulfillment theory. Out of 52 answers to the question, "Do you think Christianity is a fulfillment of the good points of your former religion or its total negation?", 25, or 48 per cent, were "fulfillment"; 19, or 37 per cent, were "total negation." Of the 19 who answered "total negation," 6 were fundamentalists who had been strongly indoctrinated with absolutist tenets. In addition to them, 4 answered, "Christianity is superior to my former religion"; 2 answered, "All other religions are implied in Christianity." If these latter are taken into account, the number supporting synthesis over negation is overwhelming. It may be asserted that this question is too sophisticated to be answered by average Christians. On the other hand it may be argued that these answers are valuable precisely because they have been given by laymen who are theologically unbiased. In any event, it can hardly be denied that the most natural answer Japanese Christians would give to this kind of question is the "fulfillment" type rather than the "negation" type.

My thesis, then, is that the central core of the religious experience, which is involved in the encounter between Christianity and other religions, is the existential commitment of a person, who has been brought up in a definite religious tradition, to God who revealed Himself in an historical event as the ultimately meaningful reality. This encounter is to be understood in terms of correlation between the ultimately meaningful event and the experiencing subject who accepts this event as ultimately meaningful. Where either pole of this correlation is lacking there can be no real encounter. No historical event can be ultimately meaningful unless there is an experiencing subject who accepts it as ultimately meaningful. And no experiencing subject can produce the ultimately meaningful event. Only what is *ultimately* meaningful can produce the consciousness of what is ultimately meaningful.

A genuine Christian faith must be absolute as far as it is an existential commitment within this correlation. But this absoluteness cannot be claimed as an objective truth because it cannot be proved objectively. It can be attested only through the total existence of the believer. I do not mean that the pragmatic test is the final tribunal, nor that there is an exact correspondence between the validity of the theological circle and its historical expressions. In so far as the subjective side of this correlation is relative to the social and psychological situation of the believer, there can be no final test in history. I simply mean that no better test is conceivable on the subjective side of the revelatory correlation.

The real experience of what is ultimately meaningful attests itself in its power to relativize everything which is preliminary, its power to say "no" to every attempt to elevate what is preliminary to the rank of ultimacy. This is the negative function of faith. There is an absolute gap between that to which faith testifies and everything else. But faith cannot testify to itself in this world except through that which is preliminary. The Christian message cannot be communicated to the Japanese without using terms and ideas understandable by them, whether these terms and ideas be Buddhistic, Shintoistic, or Confucian, and even though in the Christian's mind these terms and ideas may have different connotations than in the originals. Nevertheless when the Christian chooses one term from others there must be in the chosen term some quality by virtue of which it is more conformable than others to the reality to which he testifies. There must be an element of continuity between the two. It is the positive function of faith to choose between different terms.

We may state this in another way. When a Japanese Buddhist is touched by the Christian message, his existence within the Buddhist theological circle will be shaken. For a while he may remain within his original circle, retaining the power to resist the enticement of the new religion. The deeper he is involved in the original circle the stronger his resisting power will be. But the more he experiences the strength of the Word of God, the more he loses his power to resist. And finally he will surrender his total existence to the new reality, finding himself transferred into a new theological circle. At that moment he may be able to say, "But whatever gain I had [in Buddhism], I counted as loss for the sake of Christ" (Phil. 3:7).

However, no one can be sure that he is not still understanding some Christian doctrines in Buddhist terms. He may still be a hidden Buddhist. Buddhism is so deeply instilled within the lifeblood of the Japanese people that some Japanese Christians in critical moments invoke the name of Buddha instead of that of Christ. This suggests that they are Christians only on the conscious level while still remaining Buddhists in the subconscious. It might be that after a long process such a person's understanding of Christianity will be completely purged of Buddhist implications and he will become a real Christian from the bottom of his existence.

Now, faith in the Protestant sense is not simply the acceptance of a system of dogmas but a life which expresses itself through theological formulations, preaching, and social and cultural activities. In such expressions faith is not bound by any particular system of dogmas or ideas, nor is it restricted to a certain pattern of culture. As man's free response to the divine act it has the freedom to choose between various doctrines, ideas, and cultural patterns so that it may be able to create a new system of doctrines and ideas and a new cultural pattern in accordance with the historical situation in which the believer stands.

But in this process the man of faith is not left to his own discretion. He has to conform to the divine act to which he testifies. This involves, therefore, a double process of criticism and formation. In forming a new system of doctrines and a new cultural pattern he has to choose between different ideas and cultural values, and this criticizing process itself forms a new system and a new pattern. Emphasis can be either upon the critical side or upon the formative side. If too much emphasis is laid upon criticism for the sake of purity of doctrine, Christianity tends to become abstract and to remain aloof from the religious and cultural situation in which it stands. If, on the contrary, too much emphasis is laid upon formation for the sake of adaptation, it involves a danger of falling into distortion.

The much-retarded indigenization of Christianity in Japan may be partly explained from this angle. Since the beginning of Protestant missionary work a century ago, Christianity has pioneered in educational activities and social-welfare work. Even at present about one tenth of the colleges in Japan are Christian. Thus it may be said that the permeation of Japan by Christian culture has far exceeded the increase in church membership. But this "Christian culture" can hardly be said to be indigenous. For the mass of the people it is still something imported.

The Japanese church is noted for its high theological attainment in comparison with churches in other mission lands. Yet, as a matter of fact, we are still in a stage of importation. No theological system has ever been developed in Japan which can truly be called indigenous. This is partly due to the prevalence of a type of theology whose hairsplitting criticism tends to frighten theologians away from developing an apologetic theology that is pertinent to our boundary situation.

As a result, Protestant evangelism in postwar Japan, in spite of the slogan "Let the Gospel penetrate into the masses!", has not been as successful as it was intended to be, whereas hundreds of thousands of people are thronging to such fanatical religions as Risshokoseikai and Sokagakkai which promise to meet their immediate needs.

In response to my question, "Why have you given up your former religion?", 14, or 31 per cent, of 45 converts from other religions answered, "The teachers' personalities were debased"; 12, or 27 per cent answered, "The daily life of the believers was degraded"; 11, or 24 per cent, answered, "They were superstitious"; 5, or 11 per cent, were disgusted by corrupt religious management; only 3, or 6 per cent, were dissatisfied with their religious doctrines. This means that the Japanese people are more concerned with the value aspect of religion than its truth aspect. No religion can appeal to them unless it proves itself to be valuable or meaningful for them through creative and formative activities.

Of course, here lurks a danger. Too much accommodation to the value judgments of adherents of other religions would result in the suicide of Christianity. The true nature of Christian formation reveals itself in its power to transform the value system of a given culture. And yet, transformed values are also values. Christianity, because of the uniqueness of its revelation, cannot avoid competing with other religions in regard to this value aspect. Christianity is not the sum total of preliminarily meaningful things, but it cannot bear witness to the ultimately meaningful reality except through preliminarily meaningful things. When John the Baptist, through his disciples, asked Jesus, "Are you he who is to come, or shall we look for another?", Jesus answered neither "I am" nor "I am not." He simply said, "The blind receive their sight and the lame walk, lepers are cleansed and the deaf hear, and the dead are raised up, and the poor have good news preached to them" (Mt. 11:5).

Syncretism as a Theological Problem for Missions

BY HENDRIK KRAEMER

Driebergen, Netherlands

Dear Mr. Anderson:

When you asked me to be a collaborator in your volume *The Theology of the Christian Mission,* and assigned me the subject: "Syncretism as a Theological Problem for Missions," I showed considerable reluctance to accept. I attributed this reluctance to weariness, for I already have written considerably on syncretism as a missionary problem.[1] Your kind insistence to collaborate, nevertheless, caused me to accept.

Now, however, as I come to write the requested contribution I discover other roots in this reluctance. The conviction has grown in me that writing theoretical essays time and again on syncretism as a theological problem for missions has no use whatever. Such repeated essays are read, registered as the author's particular opinion, and then put on a shelf of one's library. In other words, it does not change missionary thinking or missionary strategy, but remains simply a museum piece.

This is connected with a strong tendency to treat "theological

[1] See *The Christian Message in a Non-Christian World* (London: Published for the International Missionary Council by Edinburgh House Press, and New York: Harper & Brothers, 1938); and *Religion and the Christian Faith* (London: Lutterworth Press, 1956), Chapters 24 "Syncretism as a Problem for Religion" and 25 "Syncretism as a Missionary Problem."

problems" essentially as theoretical affairs. With this tendency I heartily disagree. To me a "theological problem," if really of fundamental significance, is an eminently *practical* affair demanding new *decisions* and followed by new *action.*

When I had the privilege of being Director of the Ecumenical Institute, I frequently tried to hammer into the minds of conference participants a maxim which I consider an important truth. The maxim is that a sound theoretical idea (or a sound theological conception) is not simply a matter of intellectual delight and enjoyment but rather the most practical thing in the world. This indissoluble oneness of clear thought with vigorous action belongs to the essence of true theology, especially in relation to the Church's missionary calling. I am deeply convinced that the phenomenon of syncretism is a theological problem of fundamental importance to missions, both for sound missiological thinking and for missionary strategy. Therefore you are fully justified, from the point of view of missiology as an important branch of theology, in wanting to have a chapter on it in your symposium. But I fear that bracketed as such, that is as "a theological problem," it is a repetitious affair without much effect.

In my previous writings I have tried to put the above-mentioned maxim into practice. Having outlined the reasons why syncretism in recent decades has come so much to the fore in missionary thinking, I took care to point to the role played by the science of religion in sharpening our eyes to the significance of syncretism in religious and cultural life. The science of religion has aided us in seeing it as a *universal* phenomenon. Therefore I have emphasized that missionary people should not merely treat syncretism as a theological bogey but should acknowledge the fact that *all* historical religions in their concrete manifestations are syncretistic in different respects. This includes the three great religions which are *basically* antisyncretistic, Christianity, Judaism, and Islam. On the other hand I have emphasized equally that the great Oriental religions (Hinduism, Buddhism, Chinese) are *basically* syncretistic and therefore classical examples. Their *basic* syncretism penetrates their thinking, attitudes, and reactions in religious respect and blurs or relativizes the question of Truth. Because this basic fact operates without interruption and forms *the atmosphere in which the younger churches have to exist and grow,* it constitutes a perennial threat to the distinct character of the truth of the Christian message.

Syncretism as a theological problem concerns not only missions but all serious theological thinking in this time of increasing contact among the great religions. In fact, it is one of the most universal theological problems in which is implied the understanding of Truth (in the religious and philosophical sense), its authenticity and the source of its authority. As a theological and (I would add) philosophical problem, syncretism is, or at any rate should be, one of the truly great problems in the East-West dialogue. But it is not merely theoretical. It is eminently practical because it decides the whole attitude of life and its directive ultimates. For that reason I have tried to indicate methods of pastoral care, of religious instruction, and of theological training so that younger churches can develop and maintain a clear consciousness of the Christian Truth in the midst of an insidious syncretistic atmosphere that is constantly creeping in.

At the same time I appealed to Western and Eastern leaders of the missionary enterprise to develop a systematic effort for placing small bands of thoroughly trained experts in the service of the Church. They would serve in the great non-Christian religio-cultural areas and be experts in the respective religions and cultures of those areas. In describing these bands I used the term "watch-towers of thought," borrowing the expression from Professor William Ernest Hocking. When I first used this term, I said:

> To find them and *systematically* use them we must not only look to the ranks of the Christians in the Younger Churches or of the missionaries, but also to the Christian thinkers and scholars all over the world. A more deliberately thought-out marshalling and using of its forces in this respect on an ecumenical scale is an important concern for the world Christian community today.[2]

In the same writing I phrased the idea again in the following words: "*Every important region needs some men who on account of their ability and knowledge regularly sow the seed of new principles and methods*. This proposal is seriously recommended to the responsible agencies." [3]

I call to mind these examples from my previous writings to illustrate that, in my opinion, theology in itself (and that is what the isolated treatment of syncretism as a theological problem for mis-

[2] *The Christian Message in a Non-Christian World, op. cit.*, p. 306.
[3] *Ibid.*, p. 444.

sions often amounts to) is not theology in full but an amputated specimen of theology. Full theology includes expression in action and new forms of life, for the Christian truth, notwithstanding all its exclusiveness, is also all-inclusive.

D. T. Niles has said that all the talk about syncretism has led in India to an inclination toward ghettoism of the churches. If that is right, he justly protests against this. It proves that the discussion of syncretism as a theological problem for missions easily tends toward amputated theology as I have defined it, and consequently toward ghettoism, which is the exact opposite of what sound theological reflection on the life issue of syncretism should lead to, viz., missionary outreach and spiritual upbuilding. Therefore it is regrettable that D. T. Niles, in his rightful wrath about ghettoism, seems to ignore the necessity and inevitability of clear-sighted, Christian confrontation (*Auseinandersetzung*) with the creeping danger of syncretism. It is a subtle temptation that will continuously try to eat away the heart of the Christian Truth.

The "responsible agencies" to which I appealed in 1938 for these practical measures to combat syncretism have not responded even to this day. Missions continue without being appalled by the severe lack of sufficient forces to attend to fundamental issues, issues which require *competence* and not merely good will or zeal. We are investing in missions an enormous amount of money, energy, devotion, sacrifice, untiring zeal. This should be gladly and gratefully recognized. Yet if we look at the present world situation, in which our missions must deal with religions and cultures that are increasingly aware and jealous of their self-identity and spiritual achievement; and if we look at the dynamic world that, by its presuppositions and outlooks, is shaking Christianity to its very foundations, then we must realistically state that, by and large, missions are conceived and performed (without knowing or intending it) in an *amateurish* way. One more article on syncretism as a theological problem for missions will not cause the least change, because theology and spiritual strategy are usually kept neatly separate. For this reason I cannot overcome my aversion to write "one article more." I simply do not believe in its usefulness. What I do hope and pray for is the awakening of the "responsible agencies" to the fundamental necessities.

Sincerely yours,
H. Kraemer

Revelation and the Divine Logos

BY A. C. BOUQUET

The problem of the correct relationship between the Christian faith and non-Christian forms of religion has long ceased to be academic, and has indeed become pressing as never before, within the last twenty-five years, for many obvious reasons.

Yet the problem cannot be solved properly without some academic inquiry, since a merely popular attempt at tolerance may lead only too easily to mistaken conclusions, and may end by landing us either in a cynical skepticism or in an illogical and ill-considered syncretism coupled with hasty attempts at federation.

I make no apology therefore in putting forward a series of propositions, each to be considered in turn, but taken together forming as I would maintain, a logical sequence.

1. That the Christian movement, since it obviously did not arise *in vacuo,* must have been conditioned in its expression, as it moved out into the Hellenistic Jewish and Gentile world, and sought to evangelize it, by the language and thought-forms of that world, of which it must certainly have been aware.

2. That one of the principle language-and-thought-forms of that world was the Self-Expression of Ultimate Divinity, described as the divine Logos, and giving unity to the whole cosmos.

3. That this was certainly employed by the author of the Fourth Gospel, and by some of the chief early Greek patristic writers.

4. That the Christian Church eventually came to endorse such action, and showed its approval in certain ways.

5. That such endorsement must be regarded *either* as a fundamental mistake, *or* as a sign of growing into truth under the guidance of the Holy Spirit.

6. That if the second of these two alternatives be adopted, then it is right to carry it to its logical conclusion, in dealing with the sages and prophets of all non-Christian religious movements, both past and present.

Of these six propositions the first three are mainly concerned with the use of the term *Logos*. Protestant scholars to a varying extent have tried to show that its use in the Fourth Gospel prologue is to be regarded as having Jewish rather than Gentile significance. If they have not done this, they have, like Bultmann, sought to detach the prologue from the rest of the Gospel, and to regard it as of the nature of a Gentile accretion. Bultmann even goes so far as to say that it embodies a Gnostic myth. My own contention is that it is, on evidence, a deliberately planned introduction, composed by the writer of the succeeding chapters, and that if we approach it without prejudice, we are bound to see in it what was perhaps the first serious attempt at relating the Christian God-story to the religious beliefs of the Gentile world.

We must begin therefore by tracing the history of the term Logos up to the time of the emergence of the Christian movement.

It is usual to start with the Ionian thinker Heraclitus of Ephesus, whose main philosophical activity is centered traditionally about 504 to 501 B.C. and probably ended by about 480 B.C. Although the number of pre-Socratic thinkers is considerable, it is certainly a matter of observation that almost all the quotations from fragments which employ the word "Logos" come from Heraclitus. It is therefore reasonable to inquire what he meant by it. Perhaps the best description would be to say that it is to him an attribute of the Absolute. Recent scholars have rendered it in English as "formula" or "element of arrangement." All things happen in the universe κατὰ τὸν λόγον ("according to," or "in tune with," "the Logos") says Heraclitus, but he complains that most men do not realize this, but are αξύνετοι (uncomprehending). In a fragment quoted by Hippolytus,[1] Heraclitus says "Listening not to me but to the Logos,

[1] *Philosophumena* Bk. IX, para. 9.

it is wise to agree that all things are one." Sextus Empiricus in the second century A.D. quotes Heraclitus as saying, "although the Logos is common to all, most people live as though each has his own private and individual intelligence." In Diogenes Laertius [2] and in Clement of Alexandria [3] we find quotations which identify this Logos with ἕνσοφον (the One Wise Being), the one which is wise or the embodiment of wisdom; and Clement quotes Heraclitus as saying that this ἕνσοφον λέγεσθαι οὐκ ἐθέλει και ἐθέλει Ζηνὸς ὄνομα ("will not and yet will be called Zeus"). It is clear from this that Heraclitus oscillates between treating the Logos as an impersonal cosmic principle or formula, and identifying it with the Supreme Being in self-expression. One can hardly "listen" (ἀκόυειν) to a principle; one *can* listen to an Intelligent Being. It would seem then that Heraclitus, in thinking about the constitution of the universe, arrived at a unitary conception of it not unlike that of a much later thinker, Chu Hsi, who lived in China (A.D. 1130–1200) and who reduced the universe to the principles of *li* and *chi* (*chi* being matter, and *li,* cosmic principle), but who regarded *li* as possessing certain attributes which properly belong to some degree of personality.[4]

Later Greek philosophical thinkers than Heraclitus of course also used this term, and they came increasingly to attribute personality to the Logos. But for the moment I would only stress that in spite of the considerable antiquity of Heraclitus, and in spite of the disappearance of the bulk of his utterances, he was clearly known to many educated persons at the beginning of the Christian era as a famous thinker, and they were able to quote from what he said. It looks as though most of his deliverances must therefore have disappeared either through carelessness or lack of interest, or through the subsequent misguided hostility of Christians, for it is only the fragments remaining which show how important he was. But if in the second century A.D. it was known that he had written γινμένων γὰρ πάντων κατὰ τὸν λόγον (all things being made according to the Logos), it does not seem unreasonable to see an echo of this in the passage of the Johannine prologue where the writer, himself speaking of the Logos says: πάντα δὶ αὐτοῦ ἐγέντο, καὶ χωρὶς αὐτοῦ

[2] Bk. VIII.

[3] *Stromateis* Bk. V.

[4] See my *Comparative Religion* (London: Penguin Books, 1941), pp. 187–88.

ἐγένετο οὐδὲ ἕν.[5] It is as though a British writer of the twentieth century were to drive home some point by using a paraphrase of a quotation from Shakespeare.

We may now go on to see what other Greek writers of a later date than Heraclitus have said. This brings us immediately of course to Plato, whose philosophy has sometimes been described as "the old loving nurse" of Christianity. So far as I am aware there is only one place in the writings of Plato, apart from the generally agreed spurious epistles, where the Logos is referred to, and that is in the *Epinomis,* which, after having its authenticity questioned for a long time, now tends once again to be regarded as a genuine work of the philosopher. In this dialogue [6] we find that ὁ λόγος ὁ πάντων θεῖοτατος (the Logos, the most divine of all beings) is described as the orderer of the visible cosmos.

The Stoics appear to have taken over from Heraclitus most of his doctrine about the Logos, and from Zeno onwards they treat the universe as ordered by a central rational principle. The Logos is the immanent reason in the world, filling it from end to end, and assuring its unity. (Even Tertullian, who is a most anti-Hellenic Christian, in one passage accepts this idea and compares the Logos to honey filling all the cells of a honeycomb.) Cicero describes it as "The eternal truth which flows from all eternity." As Le Breton puts it: [For the Stoics] the Logos infallibly moves all beings, and is not a law foreign to their being, or a restraint externally imposed upon them; it is the most intimate force of their own nature.

But the later Stoics sought to come to terms with the ancient Hellenic mythology, and in Cornutus, an African of Leptis Magna, who flourished in the reign of Nero, we find the tendency to represent the Logos as personified in a number of mythical beings, who are what would be in Indian phraseology described as its *avatars.* Of these the most definite is Heracles, the others being mythical figures like the Titans, Pan, Chronos, Eros, Atlas, and Agathodemon. But later on a more definite step came to be taken, when Hermes, the god of reason and language, achieved recognition as the personification of the Logos, and is so described by Cornutus. Cornutus seems to assume *two* Logoi, the one incarnate in Hermes as the god of speech, the other the universal Logos who is the

[5] John 1:3, "all things were made through him, and without him was not anything made that was made."

[6] *Epinomis* para. 986C.

Reason of the world, so that in Hermes there is a kind of *kenosis* of the Logos. But about the same time as Cornutus there appears an apocryphal work by an anonymous Stoic writer, who actually conceals his identity under the name of Heraclitus, and calls his book *The Treatise on the Homeric Allegories;* and for him Hermes is the only deity who represents the Logos, and combines in himself the two attributes of language and reason.

Then we come to Plutarch. He, with considerable exegetical ingenuity, reads into the text of Plato references to the Logos which are perhaps not really there, and in his *Treatise on Destiny* declares that in the *Phaedrus* Plato says that destiny is the inevitable divine Logos acting through irresistible causes, and in the *Timaeus* that it is the law or formula (this is Heraclitean) in conformity with the nature of the universe, which regulates the sequence of all that happens.

In his *de Isidi et Osiride* Plutarch takes the myths of Horus and of Isis and interprets them in the following terms:

Of Isis he says: "She is the Female Principle in nature [thus like the Hindu *Sakti*] and is the One of numberless names, because she is converted by the Logos into, and receives, all appearances and forms."

Of Osiris he says that he is "the common Logos of all things in Heaven and Hell."

Of Horus he says: "Horus stands for the visible world. Unlike his parent, the Logos, he is not pure and unmixed, but bastardized by the corporeal element which is involved in it. Hermes stands for the Logos, who intervenes and declares that the visible world is truly the image of the world of ideas."

This kind of allegorization runs through the whole of Plutarch, and I hold no brief for it. *But the point to be emphasized is that some sort of incarnation of the Cosmic Logos,* albeit usually a mythical one,[7] *was a familiar idea to many educated Gentiles at the time when the Johannine writings came to be composed,* and that

[7] It was sometimes historical. Thus it is arguable that where the poet Horace treats Augustus Caesar as an incarnation of Hermes, he is being serious and not merely indulging in flattery. He is like the Brahman wrestlers who, at King George V's durbar, composed and recited a hymn in which His Majesty was invoked as Raghubasmani, a name for an avatar or incarnation of Vishnu. It must in fairness be admitted that both the author of the Epistle of Barnabas and also Origen employ the allegorical method in dealing with some passages of the Old Testament.

however the actual term Logos may have been misused, it represented a type of organic philosophy which the modern world cannot escape employing.

The submission is made therefore that to the Gentile world into which the Christian movement emerged, the existence and functions of the Logos were acceptable. This covers the first of my two propositions.

It follows that the Christians therefore must have had some awareness of the existence of such beliefs and doctrines. This immediately raises the question as to what use was made of the Logos concept by Jewish theologians. It has been usual to say that it was Philo of Alexandria who employed this conception in his interpretation of the Hebrew Scriptures. No doubt Philo's voluminous commentaries upon the *LXX* are the ones which are best known to Christians. But it is an error to suppose that Philo was the only Jew to write in this way. There were, beyond doubt, earlier commentators upon the *LXX* whose works no longer exist, although Philo refers to them; and one of these, Ezekiel the Tragic, in the second century B.C., said that it was the Logos who appeared to Moses in the burning bush. Origen quotes Celsus as saying that the Jews (plural) believed in a divine Logos, and he does not question the statement.

But of course it is Philo who is best known in this connection. For Philo himself the Logos, like Hermes, is the Messenger of God Most High. He appears to Hagar in exile, to Jacob on leaving Laban, and to the Israelites on their journey, conducting them through the desert. He is the Rock; a most tremendous assertion when we consider the use of the term to describe Yahweh, both in the Scriptures and liturgy of the Jews. He is the divine Name and the divine Dwelling Place, and there is one pregnant sentence in the commentary on the attempted sacrifice of Isaac by Abraham, where it is affirmed that the Logos appears and speaks. "But," says Philo, "where God speaks, He acts." There is no interval between His Word and His Action. His Word *is* His Action (ὁ λόγος, ἔργον ἦν αὐτοῦ). Moses, Abraham, and Melchizedek are all symbols of the Logos. In fact, just as Plutarch and Cornutus find the Logos in all sorts of episodes where supernatural or heroic beings have contact with mankind, so does Philo; only, since he is a monotheist, his Logos is always the manifestation of Yahweh. In his exegesis of Numbers 20:7 Philo makes "the king's highway" the equivalent of the Logos of God who is the Way of God. We are at once reminded of John 14:6.

Philo's Logos is eternal, is an essential part of Absolute Deity, and yet is subordinate to the latter, just as the Christ of the Fourth Gospel is represented as saying "My Father is greater than I." Philo's Logos is the Water of Life, and the Bread from Heaven. He is the Shepherd who leads His flock. He is sinless. He is called variously *παράκλητσς, ἀρχιερέυς, εἰκὼν θεοῦ, ἀνθρώπσς θεοῦ, πρεσβευτής*, and *πρωτόγονος*.[8] All but one of these epithets are applied to Jesus in the New Testament.

The relation of the foregoing evidence to the phenomenon of the Fourth Gospel needs but little emphasis. This is my third proposition. It must be clear that the object of its compiler, whatever primitive traditions, oral or otherwise, he may have used, was to communicate knowledge of the historical Jesus of Nazareth to the Hellenistic Gentile world. It is possible that he was looking in two directions, and hoped that he would also convince Hellenistic Jewish readers, if they were of the same school of thought as Philo and others like him, but the fact that he so consistently refers to "the Jews" in the *third* person instead of addressing them in the first person suggests that the people he wishes to reach are mostly Greek-speaking Gentiles. That in this he was a pioneer seems supported by the apparent slowness with which (as Dr. C. K. Barrett has observed) the Fourth Gospel was accepted by the early Church.

However it *did* in the end accept it, and by A.D. 180 Irenaeus can write that there are four and only four canonical Gospels, of which "John's" is one.

The Christian Church came to present the prologue of this Gospel as the main liturgical Scripture-reading for Christmas Day, the feast of the birth of the historical Jesus; and later to prescribe it as the "last Gospel" to be read by every priest before leaving the altar at the conclusion of mass. The main point of the Cana story (in chapter 2) which is so often missed, is that whatever happened at the wedding feast, the intelligent reader is expected to infer that Jesus was "greater than any mythical Dionysus": since Dionysus was alleged to turn water into wine in some of his temples, on certain of his festivals. At this point I would draw attention to the link between John 1:4 and John 12:35, which seems clearly

[8] Encourager or Comforter, High Priest, Image of God, Man of God, Elder, and First-Born.

to show that they are the work of the same author, since three words in both are used in the same connection, φῶς, σκοτία, and καταλαμβανεῶ ("light," "darkness," "overtake" or "overcome").

The next step after the composition of the Fourth Gospel seems to have been taken by Justin Martyr (d. A.D. 156) as is well recognized. Whether he knew the Fourth Gospel as we have it, can, I suppose, never be fully established, and it is possible that he could have worked on independent lines. Who the "ancient man" was who led him to Christ must forever remain uncertain. But one thing we know: Justin's cultural background was that of Greek philosophy, and like the writer of the Johannine prologue he accepts the Logos as "the light that enlightens every man." The famous passages in his *Apologies* in which he draws inferences from this are well known, though for the sake of completeness they shall be quoted here: "We have shown that Christ is the Logos of whom the whole human race are partakers; and those who lived κατὰ λόγον [in harmony with or in obedience to the Logos] are Christians even though associated atheists." Justin lists among those who lived κατὰ λόγον Heraclitus, Socrates, and Plato, and implies that he can think of many others. If pressed to give more names, he would doubtless have added to the list Anaxagoras, Empedocles, Zeno, Chrysippus, Cleanthes, and perhaps Epictetus, Seneca, Cicero, Cornutus, and Plutarch.

These statements have never been stigmatized as heretical, nor were they ever condemned by the undivided Church. It is only certain Protestant writers of the twentieth century who have called them in question. Moreover Justin, who sealed his discipleship with martyrdom, though never formally canonized, was venerated from the time of his death, and thus his canonization has always been accepted without question by subsequent generations.

Coming thus to my propositions four and five, we are faced with the dilemma: Either this treatment by the Johannine writer and Justin was part of a great mistake, which perhaps began with the acceptance of the Fourth Gospel as canonical, or it was part of that growing into truth which the Johannine Christ is represented as promising to his disciples.[9]

[9] It is not without significance that for the Gentile Christians in Rome at an early date the Fourth Gospel seems to have been their favorite. Apart from the visit of the Magi (with its obvious implications) most of the paintings in the early catacombs come from the Johannine narrative.

If we accept it as being the latter, then we are entitled to follow Justin's statements to their logical conclusion. This is my sixth and final proposition.

It is now well known that, not only in Hellas, but in many Asian countries, prophets and sages have arisen, both in the axial age and since, who, as Justin would have said, have endeavored steadfastly throughout their lives to live κατὰ λόγον.[10]

We can point to Zarathustra in Iran, in India to upanishadic teachers such as Yajnavalkya and Naciketas, as well as to the Buddha himself, to Nagarjuna, Sankara, and Ramanuja, to Bhakti saints such as Chaitanya and Tukaram, to mystics like Kabir, to Bodhidharma (if he is historical), to Chinese sages such as Kung Fu-tze, Mo Ti and Chuang-tzu, to Japanese sages like Nichiren and Shinran, to Mohammed in his earlier phase, to al-Ghazzali and to some of the great Sufis, and among famous Jews to Maimonides and the BEShT (the initiator of Hasidic Judaism), and even to that stern denouncer of religion and yet the apostle of the Dialectic Process, the self-styled atheist Karl Marx himself, so like an Amos *redivivus*.

Such an extrapolation of Justin's thesis is rejected by Karl Barth, Hendrik Kraemer, and all who stand on their side. But it would not have seemed improper to St. Thomas Aquinas, who wrote "if one explicitly believes in Providence, one must logically be held to believe in Christ, who is the supreme example of Providence," nor does it seem inconsistent with the teaching of the accredited modern Roman Catholic Theologian Père Jean Daniélou. Bishop Westcott in *The Gospel of Life* seems in effect to accept it. So do the writers in the Anglican nineteenth-century symposium *Lux Mundi*. So does William Temple, both in his Gifford Lectures, and in his commentary on the Fourth Gospel; so also does the great Swedish Lutheran archbishop and theologian, Nathan Söderblom of Uppsala.

Africa has so far not had time to produce any great philosophical thinkers; but no one who reads the account of African ideas of deity collected from many sources and expounded by Dr. E. W.

[10] It is possible to see in the *Philosophumena* of Hippolytus (A.D. 218–235) some rather clumsy attempts at developing the Logos-doctrine so as to include Asians. He is probably deriving some of his information from Megasthenes' *Indica,* and twice in Chapter 21 associates the Brahmans with the Logos.

Smith can doubt that in African minds the divine Logos has long been at work, and that the Christian doctrine of God appears congruous to Africans when they are confronted with it.

Nevertheless, when all is said and done, there seems always to be a gap between the sages and Jesus, which is not merely, as Neo-Protestantism seems to claim, a gap between transempirical naturalism and Biblical realism. We see the recognition operating in the first part of the anonymous second-century epistle *Ad Diognetum*, where the writer makes it clear that there is a distinction between the work of the Logos in Creation, and His work through Jesus in redemption. Something like the recognition of this seems to occur in Plutarch, who after all was not an explicit Christian. Plutarch, although he knows very well that, for his Stoic colleagues, the Logos is the one and only principle of being, governing, and directing the whole creaturely cosmos, differs from them in also recognizing (because he is too much of a realist not to do so), that nature, left to itself, is evil. Its own individualist tendencies, working on their own, only result in bringing disorder into the world. It is the supreme law of the Logos which can restore order and harmony, and make the individual members of the cosmos serve a higher end. The Christians would agree so far with Plutarch, but would add that this supreme law is not force, but Love. As the writer of the *Ad Diognetum* puts it βία οὐ πρόσεστι τῷ θεῷ (force is not present in the mind of God).

But this gap of course is not entirely due to evil, but to finitude. As Westcott pointed out, and as Evelyn Underhill in a later essay also emphasized, there is in many an individual sage or prophet an emphasis upon one aspect of divine Truth, whereas in the full Catholic Christian faith (which is perhaps rightly regarded as not yet complete) the supremacy of Jesus is linked with a recognition of all the many other aspects or facets of the one divine Truth. Bishop Westcott saw in Hindu philosophical theology a valuable stress upon the divine Immanence, while others have seen in Mohammed an equally valuable emphasis upon the divine Majesty and Transcendence. Yet both are exaggerations, and have need of Christian doctrine to bring Immanence and Transcendence into a balanced tension.

The foregoing considerations may serve to explain the undoubted fact that the teachings of some of the non-Christian sages seems to be actually at variance with the Christian proclamation.

It is not impossible that we shall find less disagreement when we come better to understand one another's use of terms. But it is only fair to suppose that some distortion or *brokenness* may occur in places, as the result of the human element, with its imperfection, finitude, and rebelliousness. There is certainly a good deal of philosophy which is not obedient to the Universal Logos, and which may therefore also contradict the Concrete Logos.

One of the very best points I think made by Tillich is that the divine Logos in this respect judges not only the disobedience of human wisdom, but also the disobedience *within* the Christian movement itself. Not even all Christians live κατὰ λόγον, to use the words of Justin Martyr in a different context. Hence the Logos concrete in Jesus gives to the Church a constant possibility of self-criticism, self-reformation, and self-renewal. This may well include the acquisition of a greater use of the *relatedness* which exists in *all* sincere religious activities, so that Christians may become more courageous in recognizing truth in other religions outside Christianity, and baptizing it into the service of the One Eternal Father of mankind. There is a very real sense in which the words of Justin are true and inspired: "Whatever men have uttered aright belongs to us Christians, for we worship and love, next to God Almighty, the Logos which is from the Unbegotten and Ineffable God." Certain questions have recently been put to me which seem fair ones, and which at this point I ought to try to answer.

Question 1. By what criterion do you judge whether any non-Christian sage or prophet is living κατὰ λόγον (according to, or in tune with, the Logos)?

Answer. I judge by the same criterion as the first Christians. What led them to formulate their doctrine was on the one hand the unique and overwhelming personality of the historical Jesus, and on the other hand the spectacle of good and earnest teachers who were not Christians. The idea of the Cosmic Logos, who acted in creation and then supremely once and for all in redemption, helped them to bring the two sides together. But they would not have thought of bringing them together if it had not been for the appearance in the world of the historical Jesus. Although the Johannine author seems to start from the Universal Logos and proceed toward Jesus, he would not have done so if he had not *first* known and remembered Jesus. It is only because of such knowledge and remembrance that he undertakes the statement of a case which leads from the general to the particular. This does not involve him in the adoption of what may be called a "neo-Hindu" position. Like all other Christians he believes that what has captured him is in the end bound to incorporate and supersede all other forms of religious belief and practice. He never expects them to survive in a state of merely peaceful coexistence. However gradual the process, it is not destined to be one of mere syncretism, but of displacement, accompanied, no doubt, by a measure of reconception, but of displacement in the end. The standard is largely one of sincerity, and provides for the recognition of the *partial* adherence to a life lived κατὰ λόγον.

To take one extreme case (perhaps the most extreme possible), that of Karl Marx. In his burning indignation against the exploitation of man by man, he is surely in line with the great Hebrew prophets whose work Jesus came not to destroy but to fulfill. In his tenderness for children (it is said he could never resist a child in distress) he comes very close to our Lord. But in his bitter hatred of opponents (perhaps due to his frequent affliction with carbuncles!), and in his rejection of the God of the Lord's Prayer, he falls short. The least in the kingdom of heaven—in the divine realm where Agape prevails—is greater than he.

Question 2. What do you do when you encounter a sage or prophet, e.g., Sankara in one of his aspects, in whose system there seems no place for the concept of the Logos?

Answer. This seems a formidable question, since what drew Justin toward Heraclitus and Plato in the first instance was that they appeared actually to use the same language about God as some learned Hellenistic Jews and Christians. But if we look more closely we shall see that what Justin really commends is *not* that they *taught* a Logos doctrine, but that they lived κατὰ λόγον (in itself, as we have seen, a Heraclitean phrase), i.e., that they strove after the discovery of the truth, believing that the universe was not in essence chaotic, but was only truly interpreted as the embodiment of a single supreme formula, moral and spiritual as well as physical. Now this is what almost all philosophers have striven after and believed, *and* in so far as they do so, whether they accept Christ or not, they are certainly living κατὰ λόγον.[11]

[11] Discussing this point with a Hindu professor who I think knows more about Sankara than any other living scholar and who is intimately acquainted with all his writings, I was interested to find that he felt that Sankara, in

It may be said that in this essay the actual idea of revelation (which occurs in its title), seems to get left out. The omission is only apparent. With the late Professor Gwatkin I would assert that all knowledge is in some sense revelation. The urge to know is implanted in us by the self-expression of the Living God which we have called here the divine Logos. Therefore the process of the acquisition of true knowledge about anything in the cosmos is rightly described as "God causing Himself to be understood"; and in the words of the Fourth Gospel, Life eternal [which can begin here and now] is *getting-to-know* the only True God, and His unique self-expression for this planet in the historical Jesus. But the contention of the Christian is that in Jesus it was not a case of God gradually causing Himself to be understood, but of a discontinuous action in history; not of *general* but of *special* revelation. Jesus himself wrote no book. He spoke much, it is true. But it was his life which pre-eminently proclaimed the nature of God, and it is through that life, extended in the *lives* of his followers (many of whom are either illiterate or inarticulate) that God is supremely known in His highest attribute of Holy Love.

This brings one finally to

Question 3. You say that the historical incarnation of the Logos spoken of in the Johannine prologue is superior to the mythical and fictional incarnations of Hermes, Rama, Krishna, or Pan. Why should this be so? If an idea is edifying, why need it be fact rather than fiction? Cannot God if He chooses reveal Himself by inspiring someone to tell a story which, even if not historical, symbolizes truth? (This was really a most important question, partly because it is one that is frequently asked in India.)

Answer. Let us consider first, not Jesus of Nazareth, but some of the sages who are alleged to have lived κατὰ λόγον. It obviously makes *some* difference whether these sages really lived, or not. It would be possible to make up any number of beautiful tales in which the hero lived κατὰ λόγον, but that would not prove that he existed, or even that anyone resembling him had so lived. It would only prove that the author or authors of the tales admired such a character. There is some doubt as to whether Lao-tzu ever lived,

---

one aspect of his thought, would have had no difficulty about accepting the idea of the Cosmic Logos; and he added that even in philosophical Buddhism there was a recognition of the Prajnaparamita, which was remarkably like the Stoic Logos.

but there can be no doubt that the Tao tê Ching represents doctrine which was certainly propagated by an early group of Taoists. There is also some doubt as to whether Bodhidharma, the reputed apostle of Zen Buddhism, ever lived. The Japanese Bodhisattva, Amitabha, is a purely mythical character; even if his successor Hozo be faintly historical, nothing is really known about him.

With regard to Rama and Krishna. In the original *Ramayana* of Valmiki (some centuries B.C.), Rama is merely a hero-king. There is not the slightest sign that he is thought of as a divine avatar. It is only centuries later (ca., A.D. 1530) that Tulsi Das invests him with supernatural attributes as the avatar of Vishnu; whereas from the very first there was a gospel about Jesus as well as a gospel by Jesus.

The story and sentiments of the Gita are extremely beautiful, but it is imaginative fiction. A teacher called Vasudeva, of whom nothing is known but his name, has become identified with Krishna, the god of a pastoral people, who somewhat resembles Pan or Dionysus; and the Gita discourses are put into his mouth. Moreover even the God of the Gita ends by being seen in a vision as the Destroyer. He too is only the personification of tropical nature, and is not the God of the Lord's Prayer. The influence of Rama and Vasudeva–Krishna upon the lives of Indian people is both profound and pathetic, and I should myself not feel disinclined to see the Logos at work in both.

But from the very first the essential point about Jesus of Nazareth is his *contemporary historicity*. He managed to replace all other cult personalities by being real instead of mythical. Even in the Fourth Gospel He is made to describe himself as "a man that hath told you the truth." His crucifixion when Pontius Pilate was procurator of Judea is completely attested; and whatever may have been and are the exact nature of the post-Resurrection appearances, the evidence is clear enough that they have taken place, and still take place, and that the fact of the Resurrection effected a reversal of the events of Calvary.

Thus the career of Jesus as the *Logos Incarnate* is not a record of what people would like to have happened, but of what *actually did happen.* It is not an edifying fiction, but a supreme event in the life of the Eternal Deity, and an event in the spatiotemporal order by which something decisive for the human race was achieved: and therefore it counts in a way which it never could have counted if it were dissolved into a corn myth, as Sir James Frazer and Mr. J. M. Robertson tried to dissolve it. The stark fact of the Gospels shows that the myths of dying gods are only evidence of the hunger of mankind for a redeemer. The assertion, ὁ λόγος σάρξ ἐγένετο (the Word became flesh) is the answer to human cravings.

I would wish to add that my emphasis upon Philo and other Jewish commentators and upon their Gentile predecessors and contemporaries does not mean that I am trying to pull to pieces the Gospel portrait of Jesus and to show how it was constructed as a sort of composite portrait, a synthetic attempt at creating a worshipful divine-human figure out of the desires, legends, and wishful thinking of the various races of mankind. My contention would be that *the synthesis was there first,* and that its nature was recognized afterwards. It is not because somebody wrote a book called *Poimandres,* or because Philo described the Logos as a Shepherd, or even because of the existence of the 23rd Psalm or of Ezekiel 34 that Jesus is *represented* in John 10 as saying "I am the good shepherd." On the contrary it was because his friends *remembered* that Jesus had *said* that, and because throughout his earthly ministry he *behaved* as a Good Pastor and commissioned Peter to feed his flock, that the link between Jesus and other representations of the divine Character came to be recognized.

In conclusion, one may be expected to say something about what one would wish the Asian convert to Christianity to do with regard to his sages. If the Logos doctrine be accepted, is there any precedent for his using these sages to give a kind of background to his theology?

Obviously there is. In the past history of the Christian Church one has not only the use made by the Alexandrian Fathers of their classical inheritance, but the use made by the medieval schoolmen and especially by Aquinas of the works of Aristotle. Further we have the phenomenon in England of the Christian Platonists of the seventeenth century, who were certainly Christians, and indulged in no foolish syncretism, but equally clearly paid respect to whatever value they found in the writings of Plato. And again there is good evidence that the late Stoic treatise known as the *Hortensius* of Cicero was read and valued by medieval Christians, although it is now known to us only in fragmentary quotations, while much earlier a great deal of Stoicism was absorbed into Christianity by such Latin teachers as Ambrose. I have therefore urged recently that it might not be impossible for there to be Christian Buddhists, Christian Moslems, Christian Vedantists, and Christian Confucians or Taoists, in the same sense that in the past there have been Christian Platonists, Aristotelians, and Stoics.

In this way the way the names of the great sages might be preserved and revered, yet without the essence of Christian doctrine being contaminated. One would not expect the Asian sages to be quoted where they were not in support of the Christian faith, or fell obviously below the level of it; but it would surely be foolish not to use (for example) the witness of such a document as the *Svetasvatara Upanishad* in the matter of theism, or the witness of an inspired teacher like Shinran to the doctrine of *sola fide,* even though trust in the merits of Amida is in itself only trust in a myth. The witness of a Koranic Sufi to the utter devotion of the human soul to the glory of God may be one-sided in its omission of the idea of any duty to one's neighbor, but it is a faithful witness of its kind, and is balanced, even in Islam, by the so-called "shepherd principle," which is clearly derived from Christianity. Similarly one would not endorse Plato's acceptance of the institution of slavery, or Epictetus's view of extramarital sex relations. Justin himself does not say: "Whatever men have said belongs to us Christians," but: "Whatever men have uttered aright, etc."

And further, to extrapolate the Logos doctrine of the Greek Fathers is to include not only pre-Christian sages, but wise and earnest men in every century who have lived and taught in isolation from or in ignorance of the true teaching of the Christian movement.

The Interpenetration of Christianity and the Non-Christian Religions

BY L. HAROLD DE WOLF

I

The Actual Interpenetration

1. In the First Century

Considering the manner in which the Christian faith was originated, we should expect to find much of Christian doctrine, ritual, ethical teaching, and mood to have been contributed by Judaism. It is sometimes forgotten by Christian people that Jesus not only was born and circumcised a Jew, but was a habitual attendant at services of the synagogue [1] and worked almost exclusively—though the exceptions are extremely significant—within the Jewish community.[2]

Apparently all of the twelve apostles were Jews and St. Paul called himself "a Hebrew born of Hebrews; as to the law a Pharisee." [3] The Church was founded in Jerusalem and there was a live question until the first council there whether anyone not a Jew could be a Christian. After that issue had been resolved it was still the almost invariable custom of St. Paul to begin his work in every city at the local synagogue. It would, indeed, be surprising if the

[1] Lk. 4:16.
[2] Cf. Mt. 10:6.
[3] Phil. 3:5.

Christian movement did not show from the beginning much evidence of Jewish influence within its own life.

To say that there is much of such evidence is a gross understatement. Within the brief compass of the Gospels alone there are literally hundreds of explicit or implied references to the Old Testament, including many quotations. Many such references are used as citations of authority. The sermons in the Book of Acts and the apostolic exhortations in the Epistles indicate that apostolic faith in Jesus was habitually represented as grounded in the Prophets, the Psalms, and the Pentateuch. Everywhere in the New Testament it is taken for granted that the God made known in Jesus is the God of Abraham, Isaac, and Jacob.

New Testament faith understands man to have been created in the image of God and to have fallen into sin so that the divine likeness has been corrupted. This doctrine of man is given on the authority of the Old Testament. So also is Jesus' teaching in support of the Pharisees' belief in the resurrection of the dead.[4]

Christian ethics was, from the beginning, a modified version of Hebrew ethics. Christians, like the Jews before them, understand the norms of human righteousness as grounded in the doctrine of God's own righteousness and of His law. When Jesus is asked what is the greatest commandment he replies by quoting from the *Shema,* then adds a second commandment quoted from Leviticus.[5] To be sure, he gives to the "neighbor" such a universal meaning as to transcend the national particularism of Leviticus, concerning both the neighbor to whom love is due and even more the person who is obliged to love.[6] Moreover, divine grace and forgiving love, which are prominent but secondary in the Old Testament, become central in New Testament ethics. The stress on purity of inner motive also characterizes the New Testament teaching to the point of repudiating various specific requirements of Hebrew law. Yet all these changes are in accord with some trends of teaching in the later Prophets and, together with the regrounding of ethics in the person of Jesus, constitute the fulfillment, not the abolition, of "the law and the prophets." [7] Even when Paul is glorying in Christian freedom from the old bondage of the law, he reaffirms the moral require-

[4] Mk. 12:18–27.
[5] Mt. 22:36–39; Deut. 6:5; Lev. 19:18.
[6] Lk. 10:29–37.
[7] Mt. 5:17.

ments of the spiritual life in terms clearly drawn from Hebrew teaching [8] and exhorts Christian believers to that brotherly love by which they "fulfill the law of Christ." [9]

Most Christian scholars would grant that their faith was a fulfillment rather than a radical displacement of Judaism. But what of other religions? Did any others contribute to the New Testament faith?

The relations of pre-Christian and first-century Judaism to non-Biblical religions are still much under investigation. However, few Old Testament scholars would defend the doctrine that no other religions contributed to the religion of the ancient Hebrews. Some aspects of Old Testament doctrine and practice are clearly characteristic of much primitive religion in widely distributed areas. Among such aspects are the close association between the forbidden or taboo and the sacred, the identification of strange and especially of terrifying natural phenomena with deity, and the offering of sacrifices on specially consecrated altars. The Hebrews well recognized such common elements. Not only were these elements a frequent source of temptation to leave Yahweh and worship other gods, but they serve also to provide the common frame of reference for appeals to worship Yahweh instead of other gods—as when Elijah and the priests of Baal call upon their respective deities to burn their offerings on Mount Carmel.[10] Often it is taken for granted that as Israel worships Yahweh, other peoples worship their own gods.[11]

More specifically, various scholars believe that they can find evidences in the ancient Old Testament religion of contributions from the Egyptians, Midianites, Canaanites, and Babylonians. In order to affirm the unrivaled originality of Israel's tradition, it is not necessary to deny such contributions.

It must be apparent to anyone whose mind is free to judge by the evidence that the Christian teachings in the New Testament include contributions from other religions in addition to the influences coming through and from Judaism. When it is considered that the New Testament books were written in Greek, in a period when there was much blending of Hellenic and Jewish thought, it

[8] Gal. 5:13–25.
[9] Gal. 5:2.
[10] 1 Kings 17:21–39.
[11] See especially Mic. 4:5.

is remarkable that there is actually so little evidence of influence from Greek sources in the New Testament. Yet there is some and it is important. The Stoic poet Aratus is quoted with approval in Acts 17:28. Only dogmatic prejudging of the issue can fail to find Hellenistic thought in the prologue of John.[12] The frequent occurrences of the symbols "light" and "darkness" in John and elsewhere tell us emphatically of Persian influence, whether direct or —more probably—indirect.

The acceptance of the Eucharist as a rite of purification, of identification with the life of the Saviour, and of admission to life after death show similarities to some rites of the Mysteries too close for mere coincidence. The Mysteries certainly included such rites earlier, so may be presumed to have influenced Christian interpretation of the Lord's Supper. Some of the references to Christian "mysteries" in the New Testament [13] and in patristic literature confirm this view.

2. *In Subsequent Church History*

Through its entire history the Church has held the Old Testament to be an integral part of its sacred Scriptures. This doctrine, with the consequent practice, has guaranteed that Old Testament religion would continue to exert a powerful influence on the Christian faith. At times it has even tended to submerge more distinctive aspects of the Gospel—as in the crusades, the various Calvinistic attempts to establish a legalistic theocracy, and some recent trends of African sectarianism.

It is the practice in some theological circles to deprecate the Christian apologetics of the second century as a betrayal, or at least a serious dilution, of the New Testament faith. But without such men as Justin, Clement of Alexandria, and then Origen there would have been no such formulations of Christian doctrine as appear in the ecumenical creeds, now usually regarded as the very symbols and norms of orthodoxy.

Justin and Clement used the Stoic doctrine of the *logos spermatikos* as the instrument for interpreting the relation between Christ and the best of pagan thought and life. The Logos which was incarnate in Jesus, they said, had implanted the seed of divine

[12] Cf. A. C. Bouquet, *The Christian Faith and the Non-Christian Religions* (New York: Harper & Brothers, 1958), pp. 146–49; cf. p. 158.

[13] E.g., see 1 Cor. 4:1.

truth in such men as Heraclitus and Socrates. All that was true and admirable, wherever found, the Apologists viewed as the work of Christ the eternal Word of God, and hence, they believed, should be welcomed with joy by the Church, but supplemented and fulfilled by the knowledge of Christ himself in all his fullness.

In the early Christian centuries, not only the works of Greek philosophers, but also such Greco-Roman religious literature as the Sibylline Oracles were sometimes recommended by the Fathers for edifying Christian reading.[14]

The early Christians found so much in paganism which was similar to elements of Christian doctrine and worship that they could not be content to regard the similarities as mere coincidence. When they did not explain them by reference to the wider activity of the Logos, they attributed them to devils who deliberately imitated the truth—sometimes even before it was revealed to men—in order to confuse and tempt men. This doctrine is highly significant, not because it commends itself as true—for certainly it does not—but because it testifies so emphatically to the presence of common elements in the paganism and the Christianity of those early centuries.

Much of the actual religious life of Europe remained a complex amalgam of Christian and pagan elements long after evangelization. Most of the European countries were "converted" as peoples, not individual by individual. Many old religious customs continued, with new names and interpretations. Often the names of saints—some of them probably not historical—took the place of the pagan deities and the familiar celebrations continued.

Of course the penetration has not been all from one side. Probably most Christian influence on orthodox Judaism has been negative. Modern orthodox Judaism is especially characterized by the rejection of Jesus Christ. This rejection encourages some interpretations of the Old Testament which are contrary to Christian doctrine, and it discourages other interpretations—especially of the later Prophets—which might lead some readers or hearers nearer to an acceptance of Christ. In the liberal Jewish community, on the other hand, there has been much infiltration of Christian thought and one may even hear, occasionally, favorable references to passages in the Gospels in Sabbath services. Liberal Judaism and

[14] See, e.g., Justin, *First Apology,* Chapter 44.

Unitarian Christianity sometimes become nearly identical in religious doctrine.

There have always been considerable Christian elements in Islam. The Koran teaches high respect for Jesus, as a true prophet of God, even though Mohammed is regarded as having superseded him, and though neither Mohammed nor most Moslems know much about the actual content of the New Testament. Christian influence is said to be more apparent in Sufism than in the rest of Islam.

Since a Christian church existed in South India at least as early as the ninth century, and perhaps even in the second century, subsequent similarities to Christianity found in the Indian religions may be due to Christian influence. The modern Christian penetration of Hinduism and Buddhism will be discussed in our next section.

3. The Contemporary Situation

The earlier Protestant missionaries to the lands of South and East Asia generally gave unfavorable reports of the religions encountered there. Those religions did not appear to offer any serious competition in high moral and spiritual values. This situation has radically changed. The more favorable contemporary assessment of the Eastern religions is doubtless due in considerable measure to more generous understanding by the missionaries at work. However, it is also apparent that the religions of Asia have changed radically and now offer much more that is morally and spiritually attractive to a sensitive Christian.

In Hinduism, the Brahma Samaj, Arya Samaj and Ramakrishna Society are all obviously syncretistic and include conspicuous Christian elements. To be sure, the Arya Samaj and many Ramakrishna devotees profess to find all their teachings in the Bhagavad Gita and the Vedas. However, these interpretations often seem highly strained, to say the least, and many were first brought forth in the nineteenth and twentieth centuries, under Christian stimulus. The Christian influence has been widely diffused in Hinduism, especially through C. F. Andrews and Mohandas K. Gandhi.[15]

Buddhism, too, provides many examples of Christian influence

[15] Cf. Bouquet, *op. cit.,* pp. 136, 276–77.

among the devotees and institutions of a non-Christian religion. Much of the present Buddhist activity in social work, hospital service, and other benevolent projects is obviously imitative of prior Christian activity or responsive to it. Sometimes the imitation is even more explicit, as in the Young Men's Buddhist Association in Japan and in the use of Christian hymns in worship, sometimes with the substitution of "Buddha" for "Christ." Some visitors in Polynesian Buddhist centers have been surprised to find that the Buddhists were even using hymnals and Sunday-school leaflets originally prepared for Christian churches.

What evidence is there that contemporary Christianity, in the United States, for example, has been influenced by non-Christian religions? Where the Nicene Creed is used, it bears witness to the ancient Hellenistic penetration of the Church already mentioned. The Old Testament lesson is a contribution of the ancient Hebrew faith. The sacraments of baptism and the Lord's Supper remind us of ancient Jewish rites, while the Lord's Supper is also reminiscent of the Mysteries.

The Church calendar bears emphatic witness to a syncretism of customary rites. Christmas is celebrated in the Church as the birthday of Jesus. However, the date of December 25 was originally the date of a celebration in honor of Mithras, Persian god of light widely popular in the Roman Empire in the early Christian centuries. The observance of Christmas obviously includes also elements of other pagan festivals, some of them Nordic, associated, like the Mithraic rites, with the winter solstice. Easter is historically related to the Jewish Passover and to pagan celebrations of spring, the time of nature's rebirth. The name Easter is derived from the Anglo-Saxon *Ēastre,* the Teutonic goddess of spring. Since the rest of the annual Church calendar is derived from the dates of Christmas and Easter, the whole Church calendar is continuing witness that the Church long ago took to itself various pagan religious rites, with appropriate changes in form and interpretation.

In American churches more recent non-Christian influences are evident. Preaching and Christian instruction show the effects of popular hedonism, individualism, nationalism, and other aspects of Americanism which in other times and places would be regarded as not only non-Christian, but even, in some instances, anti-Christian. These borrowings from our secular culture appear to be often accepted most uncritically in the Fundamentalist churches. On the other hand, liberal laymen and some ministers often accept the easygoing relativism of the Hindu syncretists. Their good-natured notion that all religions are right in their own way and that all take people to the same goal at last is doubtless due in part to a perversion of political religious tolerance and in part to loss of religious earnestness. But it has been affected also by the various forms of syncretistic Hinduism active in America, especially the Ramakrishna Society, and also by such related movements as Bahai and Theosophy. Such influences have been effective chiefly since the World Parliament of Religions, at Chicago in 1893, gave to Swami Vivekananda a platform from which his urbane message of universal religious acceptance was widely heard.

In Eastern Europe there has been a considerable penetration of many churches by Marxian ideas. Partly by the persuasive power of propaganda, and partly by coercive pressures, Communist governments are at times able to use churchmen as spokesmen for some Communist policies which are, to say the least, not implied by Christian faith. At the same time, American Christians are in a poor position to criticize such compromising of the Gospel so long as the churches here, with complete political freedom and with ready access to every kind of literature, still appear so often to be used as instruments of narrow nationalistic policy and, all too often, of special class interests besides.

II

The Theological Issues Concerning Interpenetration

1. Possible Attitudes and Policies

When we ask what is the proper Christian view of other religions, relative to interpenetration, we find that there are four main attitudes which have been recommended by various persons.

The first of these may be spoken of as *total rejection* with the purpose of *radical displacement*. This proposal is exemplified by most of the earlier Protestant missionaries. They regarded non-Christian religions as simply false and wholly evil. They thought that Hindus, Buddhists, and Moslems alike were in bondage to Satan and could escape the wrath of God only by repenting of their heathen practices *in toto* and accepting Christ. Few missionaries today, excepting some from the extreme Fundamentalist sects, would subscribe to so simple and extreme a view.[16]

Even fewer Christian missionaries of this or any age would subscribe to a *relativistic syncretism.* Its advocates would say that all religions were paths to the same Reality. No one path would be entitled to universal preference, since different paths may be better for different personal temperaments and social traditions. Such a view is represented by the Ramakrishna Society. It is deeply contrary to Christian tradition, to the New Testament, and to a thoroughly serious concern with truth. Some of those churches which have so far lost Christian identity as to debate the question whether they wish to be called Christian may find such views attractive, but relativistic syncretism can hardly be a live option to one who takes Christian discipleship or even truth seriously. Only an uninstructed or superficial sentimentality could regard the contrary teachings of Hinduism, Buddhism, Christianity, and Islam as all true and worthy of adherence. Good-natured assurances that good Buddhists will go to heaven by their own path just as Christians do by theirs will not please an intelligent Buddhist who is in earnest. He neither expects nor desires any such destiny as the Christian hope envisions.

A subtler and more sophisticated view than the two previously discussed is that represented with greatest distinction and impressive learning by Hendrik Kraemer. With E. C. Dewick, we may call this the doctrine of *discontinuity*.[17] Kraemer contends for Christian humility before adherents of other religions, and for appreciation of the high values to be found in them. He condemns efforts to mold the doctrines and practices of new churches in other lands after the image of our Western churches. However, while our Christian *religion* must be viewed in its finiteness and weakness, and stands under judgment as do the non-Christian religions, it is quite otherwise with the Christian *revelation.* All non-Christian religions are based solely on human effort and wisdom—often admirable—never on revelation. The Christian revelation is absolute, incomparable and *sui generis.* Moreover, even "Empirical Christianity has stood and stands under continuous and direct influence and judg-

[16] Some statements in support of such a view are quoted by E. C. Dewick in his book *The Christian Attitude to Other Religions* (Cambridge: Cambridge University Press, 1953), p. 41.

[17] See *ibid.*, p. 43.

ment of the revelation of Christ and is in virtue thereof in a different position from the other religions." [18] Therefore, Kraemer maintains, for the Church to cooperate with the non-Christian religions, or to engage in exchanges of views in search for further truth, would be simply a betrayal of the Word of God. In practical terms, then, Kraemer's view, too, implies a radical displacement, though with a somewhat more generous spirit and a different rationale than the view which we have designated by that name.

Kraemer shows no lack of confidence in his view, and his knowledge is formidable. But how do we know that he is right? We have only his word for it and the word of others holding similar views. To be sure, he insists that faithfulness to the revelation requires it; but he offers no proof. All the religions, including Christianity, he says, are relative; only the Christian revelation is absolute. Yet he assumes that he knows this revelation. But does not his interpretation of the revelation and its requirement of us constitute a part of religion, if not the religion of the Church, then at least the religion of Hendrik Kraemer? On what ground does Kraemer's understanding of the Word escape the relativism of all religion? If his understanding of the Word is, even in some respects, human and relative, then why should we accept this part of it, namely the doctrine of *discontinuity,* without the proofs required of any other human idea which claims identity with divine truth?

The principal contemporary competitor, within the Christian Church, to the doctrine of *discontinuity* is the doctrine of *fulfillment,* represented in especially discriminating and convincing fashion by such a man as A. C. Bouquet.[19] If Bouquet is right, then much as Jesus came long ago, not "to abolish the law and the prophets . . . but to fulfill them," [20] so his Gospel comes today to the laws and prophets of other religions. It is freely granted that the revelation to the Hebrews is forever uniquely related to Jesus and the Gospel, for that revelation prepared historically for the historical event of the Incarnation. No other revelation or religion

[18] Kraemer, *The Christian Message in a Non-Christian World* (New York: Harper & Brothers, 1938), p. 145. Kraemer's later book, *Religion and the Christian Faith* (London: Lutterworth Press, 1956) reaffirms this basic position.

[19] See his book, *The Christian Faith and Non-Christian Religions* (New York: Harper & Brothers, 1958).

[20] Mt. 5:17.

stood in this relationship, and, of course, no other ever can. It is also recognized that in some religions there is very much more that is contrary to the Gospel and much less in accordance with it than is to be found in the Old Testament. Nevertheless, it is insisted that as the Gospel is now brought to the people of non-Christian religions it does come to hearts more or less—however little in some instances—prepared for it by their former religions. This preparation should be viewed discriminatingly but gratefully by the missionary as a preparatory work of God. The Christian should, with alert, critical care, but also with outgoing, sympathetic understanding, cooperate with non-Christians wherever and however feasible without compromise of Christian principles. He should also be sensitively open to truth or grace which God may offer to him through the adherents of other religions. Always, looking to Christ as Lord, he welcomes or discards by reference to the norm of Christ.

2. *Arguments for a Carefully Discriminating Doctrine of Fulfillment*

It is impossible here to do more than outline in the briefest form some of the main considerations which the author believes should commend to the Church, and especially to Christian missionaries, the last of the four views which have been summarized. I hope to develop some of these considerations much more fully elsewhere.

A. THE BIBLICAL TESTIMONY We are assured in Acts 14:17 that God "did not leave himself without witness" even among peoples who knew none of the Biblical revelation. Moreover, the nature of this universal witness is suggested in the further words, "for he did good and gave you from heaven rains and fruitful seasons, satisfying your hearts with food and gladness." The non-Christian religions give compelling evidence that many peoples of the world have responded gratefully to these very disclosures of God's mercy. That many of the doctrines and practices which accompany their responses to God's material and spiritual gifts (for not all the "gladness" He has given has been induced by material blessings) are mistaken should not lead us to despise the truth and grace which have been vouchsafed to those peoples. We can be grateful that God does not reject all our worship as idolatry until all our doctrines are in proper order—else who could hope to stand before Him? If, as Kraemer would have us believe, God's revelation is given only through Jesus Christ, then how can the Gospel speak of "the true light that enlightens every man"? [21] There is much other Biblical testimony of similar import.

B. THE LOGOS DOCTRINE IN CHURCH HISTORY In the early Church it was believed that the Logos made flesh in Christ did, indeed, enlighten every man, whether or not that man had ever heard of Jesus. The apologists of the second century saw too clearly the truth and goodness in some of the teachings and some aspects of the lives of men like Socrates to regard them as evil. Yet, convinced as they were that the one true God was the source of all good, such men as Justin Martyr and Clement of Alexandria accounted for the wisdom of the nobler pagans as due to revelations of that same Logos. Considering both Justin's faithfulness unto death and the effectiveness of the Greek apologists in extending the Gospel, as well as the intrinsic persuasiveness of the doctrine, we should be slow to cast aside the doctrine of Christian fulfillment of which the Logos view is one specific form.

C. THE INEVITABLE MISSIONARY USE OF PREPARATION BY OTHER RELIGIONS Actually, among adherents of other religions, Christian missionaries always do build on selected concepts, understandings, and valuations previously provided by the other religions, whether they are aware of the fact or not—although they might often do better if they understood what was taking place. When the missionary speaks of God, or goodness, or life, or death, or spirit, he must use words which have been fashioned and given meaning in communication of the old religion. To be sure, the meaning must be corrected so that the words will become carriers of new meaning. Nevertheless, something of the old meaning is held to be sound, else there would be no means of communicating the new.

For example, in preaching the Gospel to the Mashona of Rhodesia (where I had most of my own brief missionary experience), as the missionaries preach and translate the Bible, they use the Shona word *Mwari* for God. Some ideas conveyed by the word are unchristian, as, for example, the notion of one who is not normally concerned for the individual person. Yet the word does imply, in the old religious culture of the people, the sovereign ruler of the universe who, when he acts, always acts justly. The meanings of just action, universe, and sovereign rule will also need correction. However, nearly everywhere in Africa the missionaries are

[21] Jn. 1:9.

grateful that the doctrine of a single sovereign high god has so well prepared the way for Christian preaching. This preparation must explain the fact on which H. A. Junod is quoted as commenting in the words, "It is wonderful to notice how easily the idea of the Christian God is accepted by the Bantus." [22] Of course it is not only the idea of God, but also ideas of spirit, holiness, goodness, prayer, love, and many others, which, through traditional religious teachings, have provided language by means of which the missionary can communicate the Christian message.

In several regions of Africa I asked first-generation Christians why they had accepted Christ. Various answers were given, all of them complex, but one element was included without exception. Every man questioned said that he had recognized that the Gospel offered a way to the actual living of the kind of life which he had dimly sensed before as the life which ought to be lived but of which he had never before held a clear idea or a lively hope. Many of the missionaries who had evangelized those regions had believed in radical displacement, but in the experience of their converts the Gospel had come, nevertheless, as fulfillment.

D. THE HOLY TRINITY What is needed in resolution of the problem before us is that we should understand anew and take more seriously the doctrine of the Trinity. If God has revealed Himself to men solely as the Son and only in Jesus of Nazareth, then we cannot hope to find any sign of His revelation of Himself where there is no knowledge of Jesus. Such a unitarianism of the Second Person implies the doctrine that God has left Himself without witness in most of the world through most of the centuries. Precisely such unitarianism of revelation is implied by the logic of Kraemer's theory.

But God is not only the Son, the Word spoken in Jesus. Even that Word was active in creation and "enlightens every man." But God is also the Father of all, who gives good gifts,[23] gladdens the heart [24] and convicts the conscience [25] of men and women everywhere.

Beneath the fearfulness with which some would seek to exclude all real exchange of communication between the Christian Church

[22] Bouquet, *op. cit.*, p. 262; cf. pp. 255–68.

[23] Cf. Mt. 4:45.

[24] Cf. Acts 14:17.

[25] Cf. Rom. 2:1–4, 14–16.

and the non-Christian religions is a lack of faith in the Holy Spirit. With a renewal of this faith we shall be eager to share our testimony to Christ—testimony both of word and deed—in every possible way with the people of other religions, entrusting to the present action of the Holy Spirit the guarding and nurturing of the precious seed.

In all of our homelands, even in all of our home churches, the wheat of Christian faith grows in the field with tares of every ungodly motive and thought. Yet we know that we must be in real and constant communication with our culture in all its depths. As Christians we cannot accept everything in Western culture. Much of it is hedonistic, materialistic, nationalistic, and hateful. All that must be condemned and rejected. But we do not reject all of Western secular culture. We seek to welcome every good element in it and to fulfill its best promise by bringing all into subjection to the lordship of Christ. Whether we are dealing with modern science, literature, industry, government, family life, or religious institutions, whether professedly Christian or not, this is the way of faith in the Triune God. It is He who made all men and is sovereign over all, who informed all creation by the Word of His active meaningful purpose, who disclosed Himself most fully in Jesus the embodiment of His Word, and who is actively seeking, by His loving Spirit, every one of His children everywhere.

His revelation, like all communication, depends on reception by the hearer, as well as on the disclosing by the one who speaks. Both in Christendom and in the non-Christian religions, His disclosure is clouded, distorted, and confused with illusions by the sin and ignorance of men. Yet nowhere has He left Himself without witness and everywhere we need to walk with quiet step and sensitive ear lest we miss some new disclosure of His grace. We must not presume to dictate to God the channel through which that disclosure may come.

The Christian Mission in Larger Dimension

BY FLOYD H. ROSS

Modern man is in serious trouble.

The last global time-space barriers to human intercourse have fallen to the jet age. The *physical* barriers to world community are gone. The crying need of the times is a world community in which people everywhere can participate productively and peacefully. Yet the walls of fear, prejudice, and anxiety stand all too firmly in the midst of our out-dated tribalisms. Modern Western man is at home neither with himself nor with the realm of nature. How can he become at home with his human brothers of other nationalities and creeds? In a sensitively written book, Van der Post has said, "The human tide of unreality is running full. The human being, the natural person, has never had so little honour from life and from himself as to-day. He is imprisoned in theories, in petrified religions, and above all, strangled in his own lack of self-awareness." [1]

Modern man is being forced to cross a new frontier.

This is the frontier of a greatly heightened awareness of what it means to be a *human being*. In the words of a member of the Jewish community, "I get tired of being continually reminded by my fellow Jews that I am a Jew. I would like to be reminded more often that I am a human being!" The problems of nationalism have

[1] Laurens Van der Post, *Venture to the Interior* (New York: Morrow, 1951), p. 213.

not been resolved, yet the problems of internationalism must now also be faced.

Modern *Christian* man is in serious trouble also.

He is prone to use the language of the nineteenth century, the period of great missionary expansionism, as he faces the ending of the twentieth century. His language is archaic; his arguments are usually unconvincing save to those already within the theological circle. The great issue of the hour is not Christian ecumenism but *human* ecumenism. Laudable as are the efforts of the World Council of Churches to bring some measure of understanding and charity into the relations of non-Roman Christian groups, the greater issue is practically untouched by that organization—namely, how to enter into a significant and mutually rewarding dialogue with the Asian faiths that are now beginning to show fresh life.

How rewarding these continuing conversations can become is determined to a large degree by the attitude of those seeking such conversations. In the words of a sensitive scholar whose spirit embraced both East and West, "We cannot establish human relationships with other peoples if we are convinced of our own superiority or superior wisdom, and only want to convert them to our way of thinking." His further admonition to the modern Christian is just as appropriate for the modern Hindu, Buddhist, or Moslem.

> The modern Christian, who thinks of the world as his parish, is faced with the painful necessity of becoming himself a citizen of the world; he is invited to participate in a symposium and a *convivium;* not to preside—for there is Another who presides unseen—but as one of many guests.[2]

The Christian mission today involves bearing witness to a profound search for living truth which can never be confined within any language, theological or nontheological, Christian or non-Christian. Certainly no one of us is qualified to preside in that search. Each can only hope to be a concerned participant.

In the effort to establish genuinely human relationships with thoughtful people of religious faiths other than our own, we need not fall into the trap of too many "Brotherhood Week" programs where politeness or a sweetness-and-light approach sometimes substitutes for persistent grappling with the important issues of human

[2] Ananda K. Coomaraswamy, *Am I My Brother's Keeper* (New York: John Day Company, 1947), p. 36.

diversity. Each of us who approaches the dialogue situation should be willing to set forth his presuppositions fairly frankly, but without brittleness, in order that they may be taken into account by those participating in the discussion. A few words revealing my own operational assumptions will suffice here.

Man's basic needs are fundamentally the same although they find radically different ways of coming to expression, both because of the suppleness of human nature and because of the diversities of geographical and cultural conditioning factors. The term *needs* is not to be confused with the term *wants*. By basic needs I refer to the need for orientation or a frame of reference, for self-worth, for self-transcendence. (Various writers use different terms here, depending on whether they are primarily psychologists, anthropologists, sociologists, theologians.) The conditions for growth toward physical and spiritual maturity are built into the structure of reality, from the simplest molecule to the complicated human brain. Growth, even in the religious life, is on the whole "carelesss" of man's formulas about the growth process; it goes on in spite of our misformulations. Man is never a purely passive agent, however. Responsiveness, capacity for deepened awareness, sensitivity, are all important personal qualities which seem to encourage the growth process.

The religions of mankind arise out of man's deeply felt need for self-transcendence, wholeness, reconciliation, expressed variously as the need for the beatific vision, for communion with God, moksha, nirvana, blessedness, etc. All religions are relative to man's specific condition or situation, though all religions seek to point beyond themselves to some transcendent dimension of meaning, power, or grace. The gods men worship reveal much more about the nature of man's search and the shape of his needs at the moment than they reveal about an ultimate reality. However, since man is a significant part of the totality of reality, what every religion "reveals" is never to be ignored.

The "God behind the gods" is always known relatively through his activities, theophanies, incarnations. What any man calls God or the will of God is subject to further clarification and possible repudiation in the light of deepened awareness. God is known in relative ways only, even in those traditions that claim special revelation or "the keys to the kingdom." In the language of Christian orthodoxy, God is ever known in partially distorted ways because of man's "sinful condition." Christians sometimes make a distinction between the "Gospel of Jesus Christ" and "Christianity," to avoid the relativities and ambiguities associated with the latter term. But the Gospel is not so delivered from the relativities of history; it too is known, professed, and interpreted in history by finite men.

Tillich reminds us of these things when he points out that Christianity is neither final nor universal, even though, according to him, it witnesses to that which is final and universal.[3] Another Christian scholar reminds us that Christianity "can never be more than a hint in history. Its subject is the eternal God, but its mode of communication is history, and in history nothing is evidently eternal." [4] And in a similar vein Berdyaev has written that Christianity has remained "an unfinished revelation about the absolute significance and calling of man." [5] To recognize that our best interpretations of the will of God for us in history are finite, not final, is to avoid one of the more subtle inducements to idolatry.

To approach the dialogue between the religions with open minds and hearts is not to succumb either to syncretism or to indifference. No Christian is asked to be untrue to his confession of faith and each participant must respect the right of the other to be true to his own integrity. If the conversations are approached with mutual respect and seriousness by all parties concerned, the circle of one's own faith may be deepened as well as broadened. There has been a tendency for Christians to underestimate the non-Christian religions at their deeper levels through concentrating on the more obvious features of the religious behavior and attitudes of "popular" religion. This is a practice which common courtesy demands that we eliminate. If a Protestant wants to be challenged by Roman Catholicism, he will normally pick out an alert Jesuit or Dominican teacher rather than enter into debate with a harried parish priest in a Mexican village, off the main track of theological conversation. Individual missionaries to non-Christian peoples have done

[3] Paul Tillich, *Systematic Theology* (Chicago: Univ. of Chicago Press, 1951), Vol. I, p. 134.

[4] Carl Michalson, "The Issue: Ultimate Meaning in History," *Religion in Life*, Vol. XXVIII (Summer 1959), p. 376.

[5] Nicolas Berdyaev, *The Meaning of the Creative Act* (New York: Harper & Brothers, 1954), p. 331.

this in notable cases, but most of the people in the home churches who finance the missionary programs have not been given the chance to listen to the case for Hinduism made by a Radhakrishnan, a Coomaraswamy, an Aurobindo, a Gandhi, or a swami of the Vedanta Society.

There are significant differences between the major Oriental religions on the one hand and the Semitic religions on the other. For example, attitudes toward nature are not the same. In general the Hindu has been taught to be wary of nature, her illusive and bewitching ways (described as maya); he tends to flee from her. The Buddhist traditionally has been inclined to try to make his peace with nature through finding a "middle way" between asceticism and self-indulgence. The Japanese Shintoist has felt both an esthetic and a divine dimension in nature, and has practiced living in loving interaction with her, as Shinto shrines, Japanese gardens, and the love of poetry illustrate. The Christian has been inclined to dominate nature, in an earlier period because he felt nature to be the abode of Satan and his demonic helpers. After the Renaissance and the Reformation, European Christian man sought to dominate nature "for the glory of God." Western man still tends to think of nature as something to be conquered—latterly, outer space.

Not only are there differing attitudes toward nature; there are also different attitudes regarding man, his nature, the nature of his predicament, the highest good which he should aspire to, and the techniques which he should use to actualize the *summum bonum.* In some cases the differences are greater than in others. But the search for differences should not displace the search for deeper-lying similarities. Research into all of these areas must draw increasingly upon the nontheological disciplines rather than being based primarily on Biblical studies. One's appreciation of his own heritage can be enriched by this kind of study even while he may become aware of the partial perspective which his own faith has supplied him. For the purposes of this chapter I shall confine myself primarily to treatments of the different attitudes toward history.

It has been stated repeatedly that it is the historical character of Christianity, its affirmation of "once-for-allness" in history, which sets it off from all other faiths, and thus undergirds its claim to exclusiveness. Something which was not true before became true in the once-for-all Incarnation in Jesus the Christ. "Something happened on Calvary for the first time. God's redemptive activity in history reached its culmination there." [6] God *became* flesh, once for all. This kind of incarnational doctrine cannot be paralleled in any other religion, the Christian usually hastens to add. He will admit that Hinduism in its Vishnuite form has a doctrine of incarnation (*avatara,* or "descents"), but he can point out that according to the Bhagavad Gita the deity descends whenever there is a decline of *dharma* ("righteousness" or, better, that which binds things together) and a rise of *adharma.*[7] Deity does not incarnate himself once for all, nor does deity *become* flesh.

I would agree with the Christians who stress that there is a distinction of fundamental importance here which should not be glossed over by a purely Vedantic interpretation. But it should be pointed out that what is *intended* by the Hindu teaching of recurring incarnations is not as far removed from the Christian doctrine of incarnation as is sometimes claimed. In each case, the intention is to say something significant about the nature of an ultimate reality that "cares" and "reaches out" toward men redemptively. The devotional path (*bhakti marga*) of Hinduism does affirm that the ultimate invades history, contrary to some Christian statements. However, Hinduism holds that the ultimate invades history in a variety of forms, places, and times; whereas the Christian's affirmation has been that the decisive invasion took place once for all. Niles has pointed out that in the Saiva Siddhanta form of Hinduism the claim is made that the truth of Saiva Siddhanta is the only saving truth, but "this truth is not pegged down in history

[6] D. T. Niles, *The Preacher's Task and the Stone of Stumbling* (New York: Harper & Brothers, 1958), p. 32.

Cf. Carl Michalson, *op. cit.*, p. 379: "In the New Testament a single event is endowed with finality by virtue of the presence of God in history. The possibility of an ultimately meaningful history is formed by that event."

Cf. Charles W. Forman, "The Challenge to Christian Exclusiveness," *Religion in Life,* Vol. XXVII (Summer 1958), pp. 355–56: "There can be no doubt that it is the historical character of Christianity that makes for exclusiveness. . . . The thing that is involved here is the exclusive character of history itself, and this can be overcome only by denying history or getting outside of history. If something has happened in history, then it is by its very nature exclusive. It can never be duplicated, repeated, substituted for, or recalled. It stands forever in its exclusive identity and all the ages are its heirs."

[7] The Bhagavad Gita 4.7–8.

as is the case with Jesus Christ." [8] For the Christian, speaking to Christians, there is no fault here. But in speaking to non-Christians, the Christian must bear in mind that truth is "pegged down" in different ways in different confessional points of view even within Christian circles. Does not the devout Roman Catholic find truth pegged down in a papal utterance bearing on faith and morals? Does not the Fundamentalist find truth pegged down in his interpretation of the Bible? Each of us runs the danger of self-deception in trying to peg down truth too decisively. It is a matter of human history, which the student of religious behavior must take seriously, that truth has been made real to persons in many ways and guises.

The early Christians did put forth the claim that "There is no other name given under heaven for the salvation of men." That the early Christians may have been overzealous in stating it in this way is a possibility the Christian must live with. For such a claim is subject neither to historical proof nor disproof. One either believes it or he does not. For the Christian, the decisive act of God is seen in the person and work of Jesus Christ. But believing this in faith does not rule out entertaining the possibility that this decisive act may point to that which has been experienced as reality in other modes and under other names. A faith experience cannot justify a particular concept or *interpretation* of that experience.[9]

The case for the distinctiveness of the Christian stress on history is also overstated when it is claimed that Jesus Christ is the only saviour in the history of religions who is a historical figure.[10] This would involve disproving the Hindu claim that behind the Lord Krishna of the Gita lies a historical figure, and proving the non-historicity of Gautama the Buddha who lies back of the many Buddhas and Bodhisattvas of Buddhist faith affirmations.[11]

Do the non-Christian religions find no ultimate meaning in life or history? According to Michalson the non-Christian cultures have

[8] *Op. cit.*, p. 38.

[9] Nor should we overlook what in Roman Catholic teaching is calling "invincible ignorance."

[10] Cf. Forman, *op. cit.*, p. 355.

[11] A. C. Bouquet has shown that the valuation of the historical is a variable, even in Asian lands in the past; it is a variable which is dependent upon culture and ideology and is not something which is permanently favored or discouraged by any particular geographical area. See his "The Evaluation of the Historical," in W. R. Inge et al., *Radhakrishnan: Comparative Studies in Philosophy* (New York: Harper & Brothers, n.d.).

been satisfied with less than ultimacy in history whereas the Christian proclamation has given rise to a history "in which it has been revealed that there is an absolute meaning in life." [12] The person who does not feel that there is any ultimacy in history, according to Michalson, falls either into revolt or resignation.

The human thirst for ultimate meaning, while felt in varying degrees, I would regard as universal. But I do not think evidence can be adduced to support the claim that only in Christianity can this thirst be satisfied. Arguments for the "ultimacy" of Christianity come perilously close to revealing a singular lack of feeling for ultimacy and a preoccupation with proximate concerns. The non-Christian religions at their best have, in their own way, been just as critical as prophetic Christianity in refusing to identify proximate goals with ultimate values. Or it might be more accurate to say that all the living religions have often fallen short of their own best insights in this area. In any event, faith in ultimacy can readily coexist with recognition of the purely relative and tentative character of one's arguments in support of ultimacy. Jew, Christian, and Moslem are now being invited to face up to some of the problems which arise when primarily Semitic (i.e., Near Eastern and European) categories of religious interpretation are used as though they alone can throw significant light on the divine–human encounter.[13]

The Christian would move more readily into a dialogue with non-Christians if he would recognize consciously the two levels on which he moves when he talks about his own faith. These two levels are the *confessional* and the *historical*. Historical here is to be understood in its more ordinary usage, involving the methods of historiography and the attempt to establish the occurrence or non-occurrence of objective events. "Sacred history" and historiography often are not talking about the same events at all, or, if they are talking about the same events, they talk about them in two radically different ways. "Sacred history" may make use of historical methods, but the "events" it seeks to establish can only be made to

[12] *Op. cit.*, p. 378.

[13] William S. Haas, *The Destiny of the Mind, East and West* (New York: The Macmillan Co., 1956), has made a contribution to the clarification of some of the issues. Haas sees many of the major differences between East and West as being rooted in different forms of consciousness. Hocking, Toynbee, Northrop, and Coomaraswamy have made interesting contributions in this area, though in widely differing modes and vocabularies.

appear to be established by such methods. Jesus of Nazareth is a historical fact or event. The Christ of faith is an inner reality. When a Christian says, "Jesus Christ is the only way," he is making a confession of faith just as he is when he testifies to his faith in the "once-for-allness." The confessional viewpoint may point to "outer events" in history as *vividly illustrating* inner response, but it cannot establish a logical or factual connection between them. A confession of faith always testifies to what has happened in *my* or *our* history, *not in history as such.*

The confessional viewpoint is intimately related to the mythic.

In myth and its correlated rituals mankind has ever sought to make his experience intelligible and meaningful to himself. The "language" of religion is the language of myth and poetry. Back of the myths which are reflected in narratives and rituals are mythic archetypes which are always operative in the life of faith. Philip Wheelwright has said that the very essence of myth is "that haunting awareness of transcendental forces peering through the cracks of the visible universe." [14] Myth relates to that which is felt to be "eternally true." The great mythic themes are timeless ones which have recurred again and again in human history—myths of the dying and rising god, of the great mother, of resurrection and rebirth, of the beatific vision, of salvation.[15] Tillich has written that "myths are symbols of faith combined in stories about divine-human encounters." [16] Myths wax and wane, but myth is never absent from man's spiritual life "for the myth is the combination of symbols of our ultimate concern. . . . There is no substitute for the use of symbols and myths: they are the language of faith." [17]

All of the early Christians' affirmations about Jesus the Christ were in the mythic dimension. They believed that Christ was in

[14] Quoted by Mark Schorer in "The Necessity of Myth," in *Daedalus* (Journal of the American Academy of Arts and Sciences), Spring 1959, p. 360.

[15] Cf. Mircea Eliade, *Birth and Rebirth* (New York: Harper & Brothers, 1958); *Myth of the Eternal Return* (New York: Pantheon, 1954); Joseph Campbell, *Hero with a Thousand Faces* (New York: Pantheon, 1949); *Masks of God* (New York: Viking, 1959); A. K. Coomaraswamy, *Hinduism and Buddhism* (New York: Philosophical Library, n.d.); Henrich Zimmer, *Myths and Symbols in Indian Art & Civilization* (New York: Pantheon, 1947).

[16] *Dynamics of Faith* (New York: Harper & Brothers, 1957), p. 49.

[17] *Ibid.*, pp. 49, 50.

some sense the "Messiah," or the "Son of Man," or the "Son of God." Some believed that he had a "virgin birth." All of these themes are ancient mythic themes, paralleled over and over again in the religions of mankind. That God "chose" one race to be "His people," that Jesus was a preexistent "divine being" whose coming marks the end of the "present age," that God let "His Son" die on a cross in order that the "Son's" death might obtain "atonement for the sins of man," that through Christ's "resurrection" the demonic powers of the world have been robbed of their dominion, that Christ will return on the clouds in his glory to finish his work of destroying sin, suffering, and death, that "there is no other name under heaven given among men by which we must be saved"—all of this is mythic.[18]

To say that it is myth is obviously not to say that it is fictitious. Myth is a vehicle of faith. Faith, myth, and poetry all refer to and reflect a dimension of life that is deeper than the purely historical, or the realm of objectification. The confessional viewpoint draws its vitality, not from the historical events to which it may point, but from the depths of the spirit where myth in the deeper sense always resides, though often partially sleeping, as it were. Interpreters of the Christian Gospel may think that they "demonstrate" its truth by an appeal to "history," but all of their language points to the primacy of the mythic. In ordinary history it can be said that every event is unique or once for all; but in "sacred history" once-for-allness refers to a dimension of *meaning* that is felt to be time-transcending and time-transforming.

Most statements regarding the "scandal" of Christianity thus miss the vital point.[19] The scandal lies in taking what is definitely

[18] Cf. Rudolf Bultmann, *Jesus Christ and Mythology* (New York: Charles Scribner's Sons, 1958); Karl Jaspers and Rudolf Bultmann, *Myth and Christianity* (New York: Noonday Press, 1958); Hans W. Bartsch, *Kerygma and Myth, A Theological Debate* (London: S.P.C.K., 1954); G. V. Jones, *Christology and Myth in the New Testament* (London: Allen & Unwin, 1956).

[19] Cf. Douglas Webster, *What Is A Missionary* (London: Highway Press, 1956), p. 13: "It is a scandal that God should be selective and choose just one race, the Jews, to be His own people and to receive special blessings and special knowledge. It is a scandal that God should take upon Himself our flesh and become a baby. It is a scandal that God should let His Son die on a cross. It is a scandal that He should count a man's attitude of faith in Jesus Christ as more important than his moral achievements. . . . It is a scandal that the Church should claim to have the only message that can

mythic-confessional language and treating it literally or historically, thus confusing many of those who stand outside the circle of faith and also excluding discussion of other temporal formulations of the eternal-mythic theme in other circles of faith, Hindu, Buddhist, and the like. The mythic theme underlying the New Testament is timeless but the language and forms of the New Testament definitely are not. They are archaic. To identify faith with a particular expression of faith is to fall into idolatry. No man's interpretations of the action of God should be canonized.

The appeal to history never establishes the validity of a religiously interpreted event even though certain events may have precipitated the faith response. There is no "objective" security for the man who lives by faith. What the Christian calls the "facts of redemption are themselves objects of faith and are apprehended as such only by the eye of faith. They cannot be perceived apart from faith. . . ." [20] The vitality of a religious experience is rooted in the mythic dimension of man's being, and is appropriated existentially in the living now, never in some "then." Faith expresses itself symbolically through mythological language and sacramentally through rituals and in the so-called fruits of the spirit. Christian *myth* is "truer" than Christian *history* for those who believe, for myth has its vitality prior to either the proof or disproof of any specific event or series of events. The vital outward expression of a profound myth is a life lived sacramentally. Whitehead has somewhere said that expression is the only sacrament. The expression of myth at its best is in art forms or poetry.

Why has there been this reluctance to state the case for the Christian myth? Part of it lies in pejorative uses of the term *myth* in nineteenth-century rationalism and so-called liberalism. Some of the hesitancy revolves in various uses of the terms *myth* and *mythological* by contemporary writers. Tillich seeks to introduce clarity into the picture by distinguishing between *natural* myths and *historical* myths. He refuses to follow those Christian theologians

---

save the world and that Christ is unique 'and that there is salvation in no one else, for there is no other name under heaven given among men by which we must be saved' (Acts 4:12)."

[20] R. Bultmann, *Jesus Christ and Mythology, op. cit.*, p. 72. Cf. p. 62: "The action of God is hidden from every eye except the eye of faith. Only the so-called natural, secular (worldly) events are visible to every man and capable of proof."

who would limit the term *myth* to repetitive natural processes understood in their ultimate meaning. Christianity for him roots in a historical myth—that Christ appears in the fullness of time, lives, dies, and is resurrected. But Christianity nonetheless speaks the mythological language, he insists, like every other religion.[21] I am not persuaded that the distinction is too fundamental. What one religion sees as cyclical or repetitive (a "natural" myth), for example, the struggle between the powers of good and evil, or incarnations, another religion may view in a once-for-all pattern ("historical" myth). A myth becomes "historical" by confessional proclamation: e.g., the Christian confession about "fullness of time" is a nonhistorical category growing out of Christian faith. If the mythic dimension is as important for the understanding of the religious life as it seems to be, it is important in spite of whatever adjectives we may choose to put in front of the term *myth*.

However, an additional source of the confusion over whether the Christian faith is mythic arises from Bultmann's use of the term "demythologizing" (*Entmythologisierung*). The term is subject to considerable confusion. Bultmann is concerned with discovering the deeper meanings behind the New Testament mythological conceptions. But in doing this he tends to equate mythology, or the myth, with one of its dimensions only, i.e., its objectifying tendency. He says, for example, that

> Mythology expresses a certain understanding of human existence. It believes that the world and human life have their ground and their limits in a power which is beyond all that we can calculate or control. Mythology speaks about this power *inadequately and insufficiently because it speaks about it as if it were a wordly power*. . . . Myths give worldly *objectivity* to that which is unworldly.[22]

Bultmann is not unaware that there is another, and deeper, dimension to the mythic; for in speaking of "God as acting," he

[21] Tillich, *op. cit.*, pp. 53–54: "Christianity is superior to those religions which are bound to a natural myth. But Christianity speaks the mythological language like every other religion. It is a broken myth, but it is a myth; otherwise Christianity would not be an expression of ultimate concern." Cf. Henderson, *op. cit.*, p. 54, where he makes a distinction between *transcendent* myths and *nontranscendent* myths (such as the Nazi myth of blood and soil).

[22] *Jesus Christ and Mythology* (New York: Charles Scribner's Sons, 1958), p. 19. (Italics mine.)

points out that it is *within* the so-called natural, secular events that God's hidden action takes place. This hidden action is visible only to the eye of faith.

> If someone now insists that to speak in this sense of God as acting is to speak mythologically, I have no objection, since *in this case myth is something very different* from what it is as the object of demythologizing. When we speak of God as acting, we do not speak mythologically in the objectifying sense.[23]

In attacking outdated mythic expressions in the New Testament, Bultmann has not been concerned to state the case for myth in this profound dimension. But vital demythologizing can only be carried on to the degree that the mythic, or faith, dimension has laid hold upon a man, inviting him to live ever more deeply by faith, not by fact.[24]

As it stands, Bultmann's process of demythologizing is incomplete. He regards the New Testament descriptions both of "the life without Christ" and of "the life with Christ" as mythological. But the transition from the one life to the other is brought about by the action of God through Jesus Christ, and this he refuses to regard as mythological.[25] His reason seems to be that because of the nature of sin, man cannot make the transition on his own. Man is "fallen" and every attempt to establish himself on his own power is doomed to failure. For Bultmann "fallen man" sees sin as mythological when he ought to see it as nonmythological.[26]

But if the "fall" is mythological, so also is "sin" or "fallenness."

Sin is a religious-mythological category and not an empirical-historical one. Immorality and morality are social-historical terms; sin and grace are religious-mythological terms. The man who says, "I have done a wrong" stands in an entirely different frame of reference than the man who says, "I have sinned." Sin carries the connotation of an offense against the transcendent source of being,

[23] *Op. cit.*, p. 62. (Italics mine.)

[24] In this sense the term "re-mythologizing" would be just as appropriate, for faith never appeals to history for its certitude though the faithful may make use of analogies from history.

[25] Cf. Henderson, *op. cit.*, p. 17.

[26] "Talk about sin ceases to be mythological as soon as man is met by the love of God . . . which accepts him for what he is not and so frees him from what he is." *Kerygma und Mythos,* p. 41, as quoted in Henderson, *op. cit.*, p. 18.

and thus is a category of religious faith. This is not to try to deny the actuality, for the religious man, of sin and of the love of God which redeems; but it is to point out that the language throughout is mythic and not historical.

For the person who may not find it possible to use the archaic language of the ancient mythic theme, it is not necessary to try to describe the transition from "old being" to "New Being" in any one specific fashion, nor necessarily with reference to the Christian event. *How* or *why* some people do, and some do not, make the transition from what, in New Testament language, is called "the life without Christ" to "the life with Christ" is still a mystery to both psychologist and theologian, sinner or saint! Like sin, "The work of God in Christ" is a mythological category, the significance of which cannot be grasped by the man who stands outside the circle of Christian faith. The transition from the state of no-faith to the state of faith is a mystery. Nothing is gained either for human understanding or for the Christian faith by claiming that the transition is nonmythological.[27]

For the Christian, the Jesus of history and the Christ of faith are inextricably intertwined, just as the entire Gospel is a mixture of the mythical and the historical. Both of these poles of the Christian faith must be kept in view. Neither should be ignored. When the historical has been practically denied, Christians have escaped into flights of allegory, fantastic speculations about emanations, and invidious forms of esotericism where the only canons applied have been those of private wish or private myth. Where the mythic has been denied or repressed, Christians have taken refuge in sterile literalisms, legalisms, fundamentalisms and brittle dogmatisms.

The quest for the historical Jesus can always contribute something not only to the Christian's interpretation of the historical setting of his faith but also to his own moral and religious life. But the deeper realms of the life of prayer and worship lie in the poetic and mythic depths of man's spirit, not dependent upon the historical knowledge that his studies may reveal. Most of the early Christians believed in the imminent end of the age and the return of the Christ. The nonfulfillment of that literal expectation did not kill off the

[27] The use of mythological categories very definitely does not hand over the Christian faith into the camp of nontheistic humanism. Study of the deeper dimension of myth can lead to a theistic position which is more acceptable than that of the older Christian apologetics.

Church, very probably because that belief, like others, was rooted in the mythic depths of their lives and was not tied to historical "fact."

To live by faith is not to live "by the facts" but by a power that has somehow seized one and transformed him from a person living in extreme self-centeredness to a person who can accept his finitude and live and work with others in compassion and understanding. Such a person does not demand final "answers." When we insist on the timeless significance of the basic Christian affirmations and then cling to time-bound parochial interpretations of the mythic theme, we take a loyalty oath to one interpretation of human history, thus denying our deeper humanity.

Early Christians said such things as "God so loved the world that he gave his only Son, that whoever believes in him should not perish but have eternal life," and "God was in Christ reconciling the world unto Himself." These confessions of faith, evoked by a man who had a place in history and who had an incomparable faith in God, were drawn from the same deep recesses of the human spirit as the ancient Chinese symbolism of the Yin-Yang, the Shiva-Shakti symbolism of Hinduism, the Yab-Yum symbolism of Tibet. All these seem to root in the human dream of a reconciliation, of a return to the source of all. Symbols and their local interpretations may periodically fade away, but the mythic theme goes on being reborn anew in seers and poets and sages.

Because of man's finitude, all interpretations of myths and symbols are relative. To be able to accept the relative as relative is one sign of the strength of the faith that is in a person. As Christians, we should go forth seeking converse with men of other faiths, not offering an absolute message but seeking to express the faith that is in us. In these conversations, one attitude which must be excluded is the attitude of exclusiveness. For he who feels he already "has" the truth does not enter fully into dialogue. He is much readier to speak than to listen.

As we learn to live more profoundly in faith, we talk less and less about "the only way" even though we nourish the hope that we may be "in the way." Hocking has pointed out that

> consciously or not, each one is seeking not "a" Way, but the "Only Way": just as any scientist is concerned to have not "a" truth, but The Truth, so the worshipper in whatever name will consider his way the Only Way, not as a proprietary nostrum but as The Truth indivisible and The Life, and as universal for just that reason.

But he adds significantly:

Thus understood, the Only Way, so far as its essence has by valid induction achieved finality, is no longer the Way that marks out one religion from all others: it is the Way *already present in all,* either explicitly or *in ovo.* The several universal religions *are already fused together, so to speak, at the top.*[28]

In all of our mission, whatever form it may take, we do well to keep in mind what Hocking in a much earlier writing called the nonintrusive work of God.[29] There is a human tendency to assume that God works best, or only, in the way in which we have been taught to see God's work. Semitic man generally has made much of the claims for the intrusive work of God, his "mighty actions"—actions that lend themselves all to readily to Hollywood Biblical dramas. The mystics of all faiths, and the living traditions at their highest, have been much more interested in the nonintrusive work of God.

Bultmann makes a comment in another context which is not radically out of line with Hocking's statement.

He who thinks that it is possible to speak of wonders as of demonstrable events capable of proof offends against the thought of God as acting in hidden ways. He subjects God's action to the control of objective observation. He delivers up the faith in wonders to the criticism of science and in so doing validates such criticism.[30]

In these times no man and no religious tradition suffer if we talk about "approaches" to God. All of us need to live more *in faith;* in this mood no one finds it necessary to cling to *the* faith. This includes our having more trust that God is ever making His nonintrusive approaches to all men everywhere. Our common humanity and our common need for reconciliation lie deeper within us than our Jewish, Christian, Buddhist, or Moslem confessions of faith. Where this profound feeling of our oneness with all humanity underlies our mission, instead of remaining primarily instruments of the institutions that have nourished us, we may become instruments of the living God.

[28] William E. Hocking, *The Coming World Civilization* (New York: Harper & Brothers, 1956), pp. 148–49.

[29] Review of "Is There a God," reprinted in above volume, p. 193.

[30] Bultmann, *op. cit.,* pp. 65–66.

PART FOUR
THEORY OF THE MISSION

The Meaning of Identification

BY MAX WARREN

Effective partnership between the Christians of the West and the Christians of Asia and Africa is one of the vital needs of the Christian mission of our time. But it is precisely now when it is most necessary that it is most difficult to realize. For one pattern of power in the world is disintegrating and the new pattern of power has not yet reached stability, and Christians by virtue of their involvement in history are inescapably related to one or other of these patterns of power. Here is the inner significance for the Christian mission of the revolt of Asia and Africa against the dominion of the West, of contemporary nationalism and racialism, in relation to the Church.

As might be expected it is among those who represent the most direct and immediate contact between the Church in the West and the Church in Asia and Africa that an awareness of this situation is most acute—that is, among missionaries from the West and some at least of their colleagues in the church in which they serve. This awareness has been reflected increasingly in recent years by the use of the phrase "identification with" as providing a clue to a new and creative relationship between East and West. There is, as we shall see, a shrewd Christian instinct at work in the choice of this word, a staking out of a claim that in a world of flux, in a world of power struggle, there is an incalculable potentiality in the power of love, the power to identify oneself with another in his hopes and fears, in his triumphs and failures, his generosity and his need, the power to break down separation, the power to be at one.

To speak of the power of love in a world of power struggle is to lay oneself open to the charge of sentimentality. This charge can only be met if it is clearly recognized and then translated into practice that love, Christianly understood, signifies an outward moving of the will in service, in service to which no limit is attached. The call to love is a call to a life of unlimited liability. The goal of this service in the common life of men is right living, which means a reflection of the divine righteousness. A just society is one in which this righteousness finds expression.

But where is the just society? In experience its realization is always being postponed. And the ground of postponement is man's refusal to love the highest when he sees it, in his preference for discovering the highest in the realization of his own desires. Society so organized needs redemption and rescue. The Christian reading of the meaning of life and history is that into this situation there has already come the power of love, that it is always at work, and that it is ceaselessly seeking to find outward expression in the acceptance of its dominion by individuals, groups, and societies. This is but to define in other words the Christian belief in revelation as the unveiling of the true meaning of creation, incarnation, redemption, resurrection, and the indwelling of Holy Spirit. And the focal point of revelation, now as always, is incarnation—the point where a principle becomes personal.

The best expression of this whole argument that I have met recently is found in a passage in that important contribution to our subject by Dr. Kenneth Cragg, entitled *The Call of the Minaret*. This book is an attempt to come near the world of Islam by way of identification—not the identification of Christianity with Islam, but the costly effort of the Christian to enter into a real conversation with the Moslem, never overlooking the cost this will also involve for the Moslem. This effort to establish communication, communion, involves for the Christian—and this must be our point of departure—a real attempt by the Christian to enter into the will of God for the Moslem, an entrance which will bring both Christian and Moslem to a new understanding of what that will demands. The need for a fresh approach to the world of Islam, the need for some new kind of initiative from the Christians of the West, would seem to be timely. Essentially the newness of this approach will be found in the humility which will be demanded, the self-emptying of much pride of possession which will be involved, and the readiness to take the form of a servant—a threefold attitude of mind seldom found as a natural endowment among the Christians of the West.

In Dr. Cragg's book, which develops this whole approach with great imagination and courage, there occurs the passage which I would quote as giving us a lead into our understanding of the phrase "identification with." He writes:

> In our time we may be unable to see the way out of the human problems of the world. But the way in is clearly evident. It is to invest our lives in the service of those problems as they bear upon people. Indeed the meaning of Christian compassion is that problems become persons, and cases people.[1]

The way in to the problems of our time, not the least of which is the struggle for power, is the way of incarnation, the following of the Incarnate Lord.

Let us clarify our Christian task as being a twofold one. The Church has to identify itself with the world as Christ did and with the same purpose of redemption and rescue. That is one part of the task. At the same time, as we have already seen, there is another task which lies *within* the life of the Church—the need to arrive at a new degree of identification between the Christians of the West and the Christians of Asia and Africa. In a special sense within the context of contemporary problems, success in the second operation is a precondition of success in the first.

We are dealing with a problem of reciprocal relationships, of genuine mutuality, which is by no means easy to define. Something will be achieved if we keep clearly in view the fact that at all times "identification with" must be an activity of persons. A church in the West cannot identify itself with a church in Asia or Africa otherwise than through the activity of persons. A lot of loose thinking would be avoided and much confusion of purpose and effort if that fact could be generally recognized.

"Identification with" becomes, then, in the first instance the adventurous meeting between the messenger from the Church in the West and certain particular members of the Church in Asia or Africa. Likewise the reverse is equally true when the messenger

[1] Kenneth Cragg, *The Call of the Minaret* (New York: Oxford University Press, 1956), p. 214.

of the Church in Asia or Africa comes over here to meet particular members of the Church in the West. If we in the West are more familiar with the first kind of meeting, that is an accident of history. It does not affect the principle. We may expect and hope that the latter kind of meeting will become increasingly common as messengers from Asia and Africa come in greater numbers to share in our domestic scene.

It should be obvious that in this interchange "identification with" must be mutual if it is to be a genuine partnership. This is often forgotten. "Identification with" does not mean loss of identity. It means the sympathetic entering into the life of another. Only by a deep mutuality of relationship can "identification with" be purged of a purely romantic and unreal significance. The missionary who leaves America or Britain for India does not go to meet his Indian colleague bearing all the burden of "identification with" on his own shoulders. Partnership involves for the Indian no less real an adventure of meeting, a no less difficult "identification with" the man from the West. The true dignity of relationship demands the recognition of mutuality.

But even that is not all. If identity is retained, as it must be if genuinely reciprocal relationships between church and church are to be realized, then both parties to the meeting have responsibilities back to those whom they represent. The man from the West retains with his identity his identification with those who have sent him, just as the Indian, in our illustration, has responsibilities born of his own identification with his own people. This applies *pari passu* if the Indian comes to the West. Beyond this still there is the responsibility of those who send to be identified with the one sent. In a word there is then a complex of relationships involved in all efforts at "identification with" which must be clearly understood and kept in mind by those who would engage in this spiritual adventure. There is nothing simple about incarnation. It stretches the imagination to the limit, and its sign is the sign of the cross.

All that I have said so far goes little beyond a general indication of what "identification with" must include within its range. As a first step toward understanding its deeper implications we must seek to understand the pattern set before us by Jesus Christ our Lord.

I would draw attention to three passages intimately linked with the life, conversation, and death of our Lord. The *first* passage is Philippians 2:5–8:

Have this mind among yourselves, which you have in Christ Jesus, who, though he was in the form of God, did not count equality with God a thing to be grasped, but emptied himself, taking the form of a servant, being born in the likeness of men. And being found in human form he humbled himself and became obedient unto death, even death on a cross.

That passage corresponds to *Bethlehem* in the historic life of our Lord—Bethlehem in its fullest meaning which includes the fact that "there was no room for them in the inn" *and* the offering not only of gold and frankincense but also of myrrh.

The *second* passage, Psalms 40:6–8, may be said to correspond with the *Temptation in the Wilderness and in the Garden of Gethsemane:*

Sacrifice and offering thou dost not desire; but thou hast given me an open ear. Burnt offering and sin offering thou hast not required. Then I said, "Lo, I come; in the roll of the book it is written of me; I delight to do thy will, O my God; thy law is within my heart."

The *third* passage is 2 Corinthians 5:21, which is linked with *Calvary:*

For our sake he made him to be sin who knew no sin, so that in him we might become the righteousness of God.

To this may be added by way of amplification the parallel passage from Galatians 3:13–14:

Christ redeemed us from the curse of the law, having become a curse for us—for it is written, "Cursed be everyone who hangs on a tree"—that in Christ Jesus the blessing of Abraham might come upon the Gentiles, that we might receive the promise of the Spirit through faith.

Those passages, linked as they are with Bethlehem, the ministry ushered in by the Temptation in the Wilderness and closed by Gethsemane, and the death upon the cross provide the theological foundation for any true appraisal of the Christian meaning of identification. Before, however, we draw from these passages certain inferences for practice let me add two other passages which provide for the superstructure to be raised upon that foundation.

The first of these passages is found in Romans 5:18–19:

> Then as one man's trespass led to condemnation for all men, so one man's act of righteousness leads to acquittal and life for all men. For as by one man's disobedience many were made sinners, so by one man's obedience many will be made righteous.

The other passage is from Ephesians 2:8–10:

> For by grace you have been saved through faith; and this is not your own doing, it is the gift of God—not because of works, lest any man should boast. For we are his workmanship, created in Christ Jesus for good works, which God prepared beforehand, that we should walk in them.

The foundation is laid in Jesus Christ. The superstructure built upon that foundation in human experience must take account of our human solidarity in sin and in grace and also the summons to partnership with God in which we discover the role of faith-obedience.

These five passages yield the following guides to action. (1) From Philippians 2:5–8 we learn that identification involves mutuality. The Revised Standard Version—"Have this mind among yourselves" is an important clue. Identification is essentially a social activity to which no bounds can be set. From the same passage we see that the abandonment of any privileged status is demanded. Self-emptying denotes this at least. And there has to be the positive acceptance of the role of the servant.

In this connection it is worth noting that the word *servant* in Scripture implies not only the idea of subordination but also the concept of service as the pattern of leadership. It has, indeed, to embrace the pattern presented by the figure, with the basin and the towel, washing the disciples' feet. But it has also to find room for Isaiah 53:11, "By his knowledge shall the righteous one, my servant, make many to be accounted righteous." Knowledge means much more than the possession of factual information. In its root meaning it contains the idea of bringing together, and hence the faculty of comprehension, the ability to give a balanced judgment. It is knowledge used perceptively. The man or woman who is called to be a servant may have his or her greatest contribution to make through the capacity to see things in perspective. This has a direct bearing on our theme. "Identification with" does *not* mean sharing a lack of perception or being unable to form sound judgments.

A final point from the passage in Philippians may be noted. What is called for is an attitude of humility—the ability to say "no" to oneself. That is the daily dying with Christ. Saying "no" to oneself, by the way, does not necessarily mean saying "yes" to everyone else!

Passage (2), Psalm 40, presents us with a number of additional pointers along the road. We may note first that striking double negative with which the passage starts:

> Sacrifice and offering thou dost not desire. . . . Burnt offering and sin offering thou hast not required.

That is, of course, hyperbole. What the Psalmist, who stands within the great prophetic tradition of Israel, is saying is that externals are not the essence of worship and that formal obedience to ritual law is no substitute for a right intention. Perhaps we can take a warning from these words that whatever the form which our identification with others may take there is no merit in the form itself. And if the form should generate a feeling either of martyrdom or of complacency then it will cease to be the vehicle of spiritual power.

"Thou hast given me an open ear" says the Psalmist. In so saying he reminds us that for identification with the will of God in any situation what is required above all else is the ability to listen—listen to God and listen to our fellow men. This, being translated, means the central importance of a time of quiet for prayer. It also means an openness to life in all its many-sidedness.

Obedience to the will of God is, of course, central to this passage. It is expressed in individual terms to remind us of an existentialist element in all obedience—the need for a response to a call, to a word spoken with an instantaneous demand. Such obedience will differ at different times and will not be the same for any two people, a thought which should save us from overready judgment of others. Incidentally, this would also seem to suggest that as we think of identification with others we should pause to consider what in them it is that we wish to identify ourselves with. The will which has to be done is God's will, not ours or the other man's.

A last word from the Psalmist reminds us that with our identification we are to bring a sense of joy. "I *delight* to do thy will, O my God."

The third passage, 2 Corinthians 5:21, and its parallel in

Galatians 3:13–14 show us the purposefulness of the Incarnation. It was for *our sakes*. Identification with others is never meant to be undertaken as a means to self-fulfillment, as an attempted escape from frustration.

The goal of that purposefulness was that those with whom the Christ identified himself "might become the righteousness of God." That is a tremendous phrase. There we see manhood being taken up into the Godhead. It suggests a transformation, a transfiguration. Surely this has something very pertinent to say to the practice of identification with others. Our goal is not to pass out of and beyond our own racial and national heritage, to try to be more African than the African, more Indian than the Indian, an attempt foredoomed to failure. Our goal is that *they* may become the righteousness of God. Their goal should be a like transformation of ourselves. If it helps to this supreme end to "go native" then let us "go native," but the proof of the value of "going native" will lie precisely, neither more or less, in the extent to which it helps to that end.

"Identification with" is, we see, a profoundly theological principle related to the divine activity of redemption.

In the fourth passage, Romans 5:18–19, we are reminded of the great truth of our human solidarity. In the first place there is the solidarity of a common need. In this we are already identified with those to whom we go, and they with us. I wonder if the failure of some missionary enterprises may not turn on the unwillingness to recognize in our feelings as well as with our minds that what we already have in common with those to whom we go, in our common sinfulness, is a solemn and inescapable bond of union.

And there is also the solidarity of mankind in grace. There is a deep and profound sense in which every man and woman we meet has already been redeemed. We address redeemed men and women. The difference between them and us, which is itself of grace, beyond our understanding, is that we know we are redeemed and they may not. It is a big difference. But the solidarity remains; they and we are both redeemed sinners. Inasmuch as we believe this our approach to others will be subtly different from the one which would see them as benighted heathen and ourselves as obviously enlightened from on high. The subtle difference makes all the difference because the look in the eye is different. Identification means sitting with men where they sit (Ezek. 3:15). The Revised Standard

Version of that passage from Ezekiel renders it: "I sat there overwhelmed among them." To be overwhelmed by one's share in a common sinfulness, and in the common need for forgiveness, and in the knowledge that grace of forgiveness is available for all, is a long first step toward true identification with our fellow men.

From this it follows that if we believe that redemption has already been decisively accomplished, if as a result of Calvary our total human situation has been changed, then our minds will be open to the possibility that God has already gone ahead of us into every place, cultural, religious, or political, to which we may find our way. We shall go then to meet God. There will be an air of expectancy about our identification.

From the last of our passages, Ephesians 2:8–10, we are reminded of two truths of great practical importance. "By grace you have been saved through faith." However much we may have been redeemed we only begin to enjoy redemption when we have made our own response to it by accepting it. This is, in fact, another aspect of mutuality. The response of faith means trust. And trust, in the religious sense, always expresses a mutual relationship. It is the establishment of partnership. All this is of grace, whether it be what comes to us from God and returns to Him in faith, or the response which we receive from our fellows and give to them. On this basis partnership between men can be built. On no other basis is it possible.

The second of the two truths from Ephesians is that "We are his workmanship." We do not set out on this adventure of identification with others as an act of supererogation, something which is an optional extra to which specially gifted persons are called. Rather it is something for which we have all been "created in Christ Jesus." It is the good way in which we have to walk, the highway of God in which the wayfaring men, however foolish, will be saved from stumbling and getting lost.

These inferences cumulatively considered provide us with the material for an attitude of mind such as can enter creatively into the human situation in which we find ourselves. "We may be unable to see our way out of the human problems of the world. But the way in is clearly evident." What we have attempted to discover in studying these passages from the Bible is clues to our equipment so that "going in" we may be the better qualified to be the kind of persons through whom the love of God can penetrate into the heart of the power struggle of our time. By "going in" we seek so to labor that our human society may in some measure be more able to reflect the will of God. This is not utopianism but obedience. We cannot tell how God will bring His purposes for mankind and man's world to a conclusion. But in so far as we identify ourselves with the will of God as revealed in Christ we can be certain that we shall be working along the line of that purpose and not against it. This gives meaning and direction and poise to life.

Fundamentals for a Philosophy of the Christian Mission

BY HAROLD LINDSELL

Every movement is undergirded by a basic philosophy whether that philosophy is known and expressed or unknown and unarticulated. The missionary activities of those who are wedded to a conservative theological viewpoint are founded on a basic philosophy which is generally known to them and which, while it has not appeared in print too often, has been adequately articulated in the minds of those who accept it. Although it is impossible here to delineate all of the presuppositions undergirding conservative missionary endeavor, there are five which are worthy of mention.

1. The Infallible Word of God

The foundation of all conservative missionary work is the concept of the Bible as the infallible Word of God. By this it is construed that the Bible, in the *autographa,* is without error of any kind, whether historical, geological, theological, etc. The view disavows mechanical dictation, and allows for differences in individual styles of writing. It embraces the idea that revelation progresses and adheres to the dictum that while all Scripture is inspired not all Scripture is necessarily true. Thus it holds that the Bible is inspired from cover to cover, but recognizes that many statements are simply accurate records of what wicked, lying, or sinful men are reported to have said.

Those who believe in an inspired Scripture acknowledge that the Bible was not entirely given by revelation (i.e., directly to men) through supernatural media even though parts of the Bible were so given. Rather it is a historical record and is thus not suprahistory but a record of God's dealings with men in concrete life situations. It contains all that man needs for salvation, providing a faith to live by, and commandments to be obeyed. The Bible is not only to be understood existentially, but also as a document which conveys propositional truth. This truth is above and beyond man. It stands outside of man so that its truth remains unchanging whether man bows before it or experiences it.

The Bible projects a world view. It is the source book from which man derives God's absolutes, which come from above and not from beneath. Its precepts are binding upon man and particularly upon those who are related to God in and through Jesus Christ. Thus any conservative philosophy of the Christian mission finds its rationale within the revelation of God in the Scriptures. Derivative truths, logically inferred from Biblical principles, are acceptable only as they find their ultimate validity in the Word of God written.

2. *The Gospel of Christ*

The Word of God written has for its purpose the unveiling of Jesus Christ to men. This means, of course, that propositional truth and one's assent to it has no meaning unless it leads to the person of Jesus Christ. The foci around which the plan of God unfolds are the two Words—the Word of God written and the Word of God incarnate, Jesus Christ. The incarnation of Christ had for its primary purpose the reconciliation of men to God. This reconciliation was effected in Christ through the Gospel. Thus the Gospel is the second presupposition underlying conservative missionary endeavor.

The Gospel itself has definite content; 1 Corinthians 15:1–4 is most frequently alluded to as defining the content of the Gospel. At the heart of the Gospel is the death of Christ. His death is looked upon as more than an example. Intrinsic in that death is the idea of atonement. The atonement itself embraces several elements. The first is the idea of satisfaction. An offended God whose being had been transgressed against by sin demanded that guilt be expiated. Christ, by his shed blood, did this very thing. He rendered satisfaction to a holy God who, in turn, was now able to forgive sin.

Paul expounds this theological concept when he speaks of God as the "just and the justifier" in Romans 3:26. The problem, of course, is posed by the nature of God when the question is asked, "How can a holy God forgive sin and let the sinner go free unless the demands of justice are met and satisfied?" Conservative theology believes that Christ's atonement on Calvary fulfilled these necessary conditions so that satisfaction was rendered which made possible the forgiveness of the sinner. The atonement of Christ was effective because Christ was the sinless Son of God of the same essence with the Father. Therefore the value of his death was infinite.

The second idea intrinsic in the Gospel is the fact of Christ's resurrection from the dead. Paul argued cogently that if Christ did not rise from the dead then there is no hope, no salvation, no eternal life (1 Cor. 15). Christ was "raised again for our justification." Thus resurrection and justification are inextricably linked together. If there was a resurrection there can be justification. But if there was no resurrection there can be no justification. The belief in the physical resurrection, then, leads to several conclusions. First, Christ is not a dead saviour but a risen and living Lord. Secondly, the resurrection is *prima-facie* evidence that his atoning work on Calvary was effective. It truly satisfied the justice and righteousness of God. Third, it demonstrates that there is victory over death and sin. Because Christ lives we shall live also. He is the first fruits which guarantee that we, like him, shall be raised from the dead incorruptible.

The Gospel does not simply comprise a set of doctrines. At its heart lie the death and resurrection of Christ. But the preaching of these doctrines will never bring spiritual life to man. Indeed unless the other two components of the Gospel are pressed into use the preaching of the first two will be sterile. When the facts of Christ's sacrifice and resurrection have been presented, man must then be faced with his great decision. Missionaries must confront him with the person of Jesus Christ and show him what action he must take. Simply, it is to urge upon man the necessity of Gospel repentance. Repentance consists in recognizing one's lost condition, having a godly sorrow of heart for sin, turning from that sin, and looking to Jesus Christ in faith for justification.

The preaching of the Gospel is only complete when the fourth aspect of that message has been presented. Knowing that Christ died and rose, and having repented, man is to be acquainted with the fact of the forgiveness of sins. The announcement of the forgiveness of sins when man has met the conditions of Gospel repentance is the capstone to the structure of the missionary message. Its inclusion makes possible a full-orbed Gospel. The significance of the last two constituent elements of the Gospel cannot be overstated. To preach Christ's death and resurrection alone is to emasculate the Gospel. These primary facts are designed to bring man to a place of decision. Alternatives are placed before him. Moral choices are propounded. Volition is called into play. He is informed of what he must do and what the results will be if he does it. Then he is urged to make the proper choice.

Following hard upon the message underlying missionary endeavor is the method or the means by which the message is made known to man. The message is the "what" of the Gospel; the means is the "how." Obviously the supreme method of communicating the Gospel is through preaching. Conservative missionary strategy has been largely devoted to this aspect of making the Gospel known. It has exalted evangelism and has been rightly criticized at times for its neglect of the social aspects of the Gospel. While one cannot excuse this oversight, nevertheless it can be explained in the context of the driving desire to make disciples of unbelievers as quickly as possible. This preoccupation with evangelism has been modified considerably over the past two decades and many changes in method have taken place.

Traditionally, conservative missionary methods have included medical missions and educational work in addition to evangelism. These means have been expanded across the years. But their usefulness has been consciously kept within narrow confines. Thus it is true that in principle and practice these two methods of communicating the Gospel have never been looked upon as ends in themselves. The humanitarian aspect of medicine and education is not considered to be a proper reason for their use. It is an incidental by-product of means which have for their primary objective the conversion of men. In other words, medicine and education are only means to an end. And the end in this instance is evangelism. To the extent they are useful in accomplishing the primary objective they are valued and employed. This view, obviously, runs at cross currents with that expressed in Hocking's *Re-Thinking Missions* in which the humanitarian element of medicine and education was accepted as a desirable goal and divorced from evangelism, as though the use of the former to attain the latter goal was an intrusion into the private lives of men.[1] Conservative missionary theory assumes that the nature of the Gospel supposes proselytism and any good means to this end is justifiable and desirable.

The means of spreading the Gospel have not been exhausted by the use of evangelism, medicine, and education. Translation work, colporteur endeavors, radio, tracts, Gospel trucks, book stores, literature, magazines, and other means are employed. Through these auxiliary means conservative mission agencies have performed prodigious feats but always with the same end in mind—evangelism. The greatest single agency whose work is devoted exclusively to translation work is that of the Wycliffe Bible Translators. More than eight hundred people are engaged in this strategic ministry, which is absolutely basic to evangelism proper. The work normally involves learning the languages, reducing them to writing, forming alphabets, translating the Scriptures, and then teaching the people to read their own languages. Furthermore, conservative missionary agencies have moved forward vigorously in the use of radio as a means of spreading the Gospel. A chain of such stations covers practically all the world, reaching even into Russia. Among the newest means is that of magazine distribution. Coordinated by the organization Evangelical Literature Overseas (ELO) publications have been brought into existence in many parts of the world. The Sudan Interior Mission publishes *Africa Challenge,* which runs into hundreds of thousands of copies for each edition. The substance of all this is the conviction that, while the message remains unchanged, the methods by which the message is communicated change from generation to generation. The only valid tests for any method are twofold: (1) Is it a legitimate means in itself; and (2) does it have a useful function as a means to the evangelistic end.

In this discussion of the Gospel, the theological content of it and the methods by which it may be spread have been unfolded. That

[1] An interesting exception to this generalization comes from the pen of R. Kenneth Strachan of the Latin America Mission who says: ". . . it becomes all the more important for true Christians to do good, to feed the hungering, to minister to the sick, without any other purpose than to express the compassion within them." "Is the Medical Missionary Obsolete?" *Missionary Mandate* (Chicago: Publication of the Student Foreign Missions Fellowship of the Inter-Varsity Christian Fellowship), Dec. 1959—Jan. 1960.

leaves for consideration the third aspect of this second presupposition—the objective of the Gospel. What precisely does the conservative expect to do with the Gospel? What goal lies before him? When has the missionary obligation been fulfilled?

First and foremost, conservative missionaries distinguish between *Christianization* and *evangelization.* The former supposes the possibility that the world will become Christian even though this objective may be immediately unrealizable. It looks for the permeative influence of the Gospel to leaven culture until the objective is fulfilled. Evangelization, on the other hand, presupposes that the world will never become distinctively Christian. Rather it understands the task of missions to be that of making the Gospel known to every creature. It accepts the fact that there will always be those who will reject the Gospel as well as those who will accept it. But it never envisions the possibility that all the world will embrace Christ and his teachings. Basically the difference derives from a variance in eschatological viewpoint. Conservative theology accepts the premise that the second advent of Christ is a necessary prerequisite to the ultimate triumph of God. This advent is related to the missionary task in that the Gospel must first be taken to all the world for a witness. Christ's second advent will occur when this task has been completed. The obvious fact that Christ has not come indicates that the Great Commission has not been fulfilled as yet. When it has been fulfilled Christ will come again.

Within the context of this vision—that the evangelization of the world is the single objective of the missionary mandate—there are two questions which are left unanswered with respect to the fulfillment of the Great Commission. And the Bible provides no clear answers to these questions. The first is the extent to which the Gospel must go before the mandate has been finished. Must every single person hear the Gospel or must there be simply a witness among every tribe and nation? The second is even more perplexing for this seeks to solve the problem, "When has a man heard the Gospel?" Has the Gospel been communicated when someone has heard John 3:16? Has the commission been fulfilled when a man has heard the Gospel once? Indeed, can we be sure that every time a missionary speaks he has given the Gospel? There are no ready solutions to these problems and they must be allowed to rest in the hands of a sovereign God.

3. Man's Condition, Need, and Destiny

The third basic presupposition underlying conservative missionary philosophy (besides the Word of God as the final foundation and the Gospel as the good news of God's redeeming grace) is man's essential predicament. Two components are involved in this problem. One has to do with man's condition and need, and the other with man's ultimate destiny if his need is not met.

Fundamental to a conservative philosophy of missions is the assumption that man is a sinner. He has been alienated from God by choice. He is irremediably lost in his natural estate. This is true whether one holds to federal theology which assumes that guilt is transmitted through Adam to Adam's helpless race so that by imputation all men are born both sinful and guilty, or whether one accepts the idea that Christ's death atoned for the guilt of the human race and that until a child reaches the age of accountability and commits overt sin (which all do who reach the age of accountability) he is without guilt.

Sinful man cannot redeem himself. His best efforts do no more than condemn him. He does not have within him the seed of everlasting life. This means that his greatest need is redemption, which is to be found only in Christ. Redemption does not consist in reformation, although it is intrinsic to redemption and obviously desirable. But a reformed sinner may not be a redeemed sinner, whereas a redeemed sinner is always a reformed sinner, too. Redemption, then, cannot spring from within the sinner. Rather it comes from God as a gift of His grace and is communicated through the Gospel by personal faith which results in regeneration. Thus regeneration is the vital need of the sinner. All other good traits and characteristics are desirable, but the best man with the finest of these is no better off than the most dissolute man because the criterion is not that of outward conformity to desirable traits and characteristics, but regeneration.

Man's desperate condition offers no realizable hope outside of Christ. But man still has within him a potential of what he can become in Christ. So no one need despair of man as though his situation were hopeless and irretrievable. Original sin and consequent guilt can never destroy the possibilities which are latent in man when he has been redeemed. Thus, to view the dilemma of man pessimistically is to forsake hope. To view it optimistically as though all men were to be saved is to embrace the unrealism of a Pollyanna. Somewhere between lies the true Christian concept. Not all men will be lost nor will all be saved. But all have possibilities, and for those who turn to Christ there is fulfillment and realization in part in this life and in full in the life to come.

Regeneration is the real need of man. But man may not be regenerated either because he has never heard the Gospel without which regeneration is impossible or because he has refused to avail himself of the benefits of the Gospel when he has heard it. Whichever it may be the end is the same. He is permanently separated from God. Heaven and hell, then, are the competing options which the unredeemed man faces. The knowledge that the man who has never heard of Christ is separated from God is a prime factor in stimulating conservative missionary zeal. Knowing that his only hope lies within the Gospel, it follows that man must be given the opportunity to make a rational choice.

4. The Inadequacy of the Non-Christian Religions

Implied in the statement of man's essential predicament is the fourth assumption which undergirds this philosophy of missions. All other religions, save Christianity, are inadequate and cannot provide salvation. All of them are under the judgment of God. No man who embraces any other religion and believes and practices what it teaches can entertain hope for a proper relationship to God. Neither ignorance nor effort toward a good life will suffice. No other way or road leads to everlasting life save Christianity. This is a highly dogmatic pronouncement, but it lies at the heart of all conservative missionary emphasis. Its adherents properly believe and claim that it is the teaching of the Scriptures; it is a "given" to which they subscribe without reservation. Eclecticism has no part in this theology and the exclusiveness of Christianity is assumed.

It should not be supposed that this idea of the inadequacy of the non-Christian religions is a view reserved to conservative theology alone. Hendrik Kraemer expressed a similar conclusion in different words. Despite individual dissent from this proposition the findings of the Madras Conference in 1938 reflected the same idea:

> We believe that Christ is the Way, the Truth and the Life for all, that He alone is adequate for the world's need. . . . There are many non-

Christian religions that claim the allegiance of multitudes. We see and readily recognize that in them are to be found values of deep religious experiences and great moral achievements. Yet we are bold enough to call men out from them to the feet of Christ. We do so because we believe that in Him alone is the full salvation which man needs.[2]

Elements of a primitive revelation may be found in all of these non-Christian religions. But they are so marred and defaced that no one can find salvation in and through them. Similarities do exist but all of them are radical dissimilarities when examined against the backdrop of the Biblical revelation. The existence of the real always supposes the possibility of the counterfeit. And the counterfeit itself supposes there must be a reality which it simulates. At best, then, all non-Christian religions are counterfeits of the one true faith.

5. The Church in the Plan of God

This brings us to the final assumption in the philosophy of the Christian mission. It has to do with the Church in the plan of God for the world. The Church is a redemptive fellowship which exists in the world for the sake of believers. Within this first purpose of the Church it is the will of God for His people to be of one mind, united in the faith, and using the means of grace for growth as well as for fellowship. But the Church exists not only for the benefit of those who are properly related to Christ. It exists also for those who are not properly related to him. It is to this second purpose for the Church that we address ourselves.

The Church is a witnessing fellowship living in the world for the sake of the world. It is not of the world, but it is in the world. Hence it is never the business of the Church to withdraw itself from the world. Rather it is to find its mission in the world while refusing to identify itself with anything that is of the world and the spirit of evil. It is called upon to go to the depths in its identification with lost mankind, having for its one goal the evangelization of the world. It is not the function of the Church to be a witness-bearer as though this were but one strand of its corporate business. The Church *is* witness. And when this is not true the Church is not the Church. The motivation of the Church as the bearer of the Gospel derives from the nature of the body, the command of the risen Lord to go,

[2] *The Authority of the Faith,* Vol. I in *The Tambaram, Madras Series* (London: Oxford University Press, 1939), p. 210.

the love of Christ which constrains his people, and the moral, physical, and spiritual needs of the world.

There is no room for pride or boasting in the Church. The treasure which it possesses is held in earthen vessels. It can never communicate the Gospel as though the recipients were in any sense indebted to those who bear the Gospel. Rather those who have the Gospel are indebted to those who have it not, and this because Christ is Lord of the Church. Such an attitude suggests that the Gospel bearers will never be concerned with the treatment they receive nor be discouraged when their message is rejected. Their sole business is to bring the message, suffer the indignities, and leave the results to God. The twofold function of the bearers of the light is to bring man into the same fellowship of the Gospel and build him up in the holy faith until he has been conformed to Jesus Christ.

Unfortunately there is one vital disjunction. Individuals who willingly subscribe to commitments for the Church as a whole do so as long as they are not personally involved. Hence hardly anyone will dispute the corporate responsibility of the Church as mission. But few will accept individual responsibility. The commands of Scripture, however, are not only addressed to the Church at large but to individuals as well. Thus there is personal and individual responsibility which no believer may escape. Clergy and laity alike are bound by Scripture to this responsibility. Every believer, therefore, has a threefold responsibility for the evangelization of the world: to go, to give, and to pray. Those who do not go abroad (they are still witness-bearers at home) because they are not called must still give and pray. It is only when the Church *in toto* takes seriously the command of Christ and involves itself seriously in these three ways that true dimension is given to the mission. And the compelling sanction for members of the body of Christ is the final judgment of believers when an account of one's stewardship must be rendered.

These are the five basic presuppositions which underlie a conservative philosophy of the Christian mission. Their validity stems from the conviction that they constitute a Biblical "given" and can be regarded as absolutes which bind the consciences of concerned believers. The history of missions is replete with notable examples of individuals and agencies who have performed yeoman service for the cause of Christ precisely because they believed these presuppositions and lived in accordance with them. Men like Carey, Judson, Livingstone, Taylor, and Studd, are such. The continued conviction that these presuppositions are true will produce now and in the years to come men who will do likewise for God in fulfilling the Great Commission. The acceptance of these standards will ever result in lives of devotion and self-sacrifice which alone are true evidences of belief in them.

The Missionary Imperative in the Orthodox Tradition

BY ALEXANDER SCHMEMANN

I

Until quite recently the Eastern Orthodox Church was regarded in the West as a *nonmissionary* church. It was an opinion commonly held that the great missionary movement which marked so deeply the Christian West during the last centuries by-passed somehow the "static" Christianity of the East. Today this view seems to have lost some of its strength: new historical research has made it quite clear that the Orthodox achievements in the field of mission, although somewhat different from those of the West, are nonetheless important and impressive.[1] Our purpose in this brief essay, however, is not to present a historical or statistical survey of the Orthodox missionary expansion. It is much more important to try to understand and to analyze, be it only tentatively and partially—the missionary *imperative* in the Orthodox tradition, or, in other terms, the relation in it between mission, on the one hand, and the faith, the life and the whole spiritual "vision" of Orthodoxy, on the other hand. A theology of mission is always the fruit of the total

[1] Josef Glazik, *Die Russisch-Orthodoxe Heidenmission seit Peter dem Grossen.* Ein missionsgeschichtlicher Versuch nach russischen Quellen und Darstellungen (Münster: Aschendorffsche Verlagsbuchhandlung, 1954). By the same author: *Die Islammission der Russisch-Orthodoxen Kirche* (Münster: Aschendorffsche Verlagsbuchhandlung, 1959).

"being" of the Church and not a mere specialty for those who receive a particular missionary calling. But for the Orthodox Church there is a special need to reflect upon its basic missionary motivations, because its presumably nonmissionary character has been too often explained by, and ascribed to, the very essence, the "holy of holies" of Orthodoxy: its sacramental, liturgical, mystical ethos. Even now, as the study of Orthodox missions seems to correct the traditional view, there remains the temptation to explain these missions as a marginal "epiphenomenon" in the history of Orthodoxy, as something that happened in spite of its general tendencies and trends. This is why a *theological* clarification is necessary. Can a church whose life is centered almost exclusively on the liturgy and the sacraments, whose spirituality is primarily mystical and ascetical, be truly missionary? And if it is, where in its faith are the deepest motivations of the missionary zeal to be found? In somewhat simplified terms this is the question addressed, explicitly or implicitly, to the Orthodox Church by all those for whom "ecumenical" means necessarily and unescapably "missionary."

II

It is without any doubt in Orthodox ecclesiology, i.e., in the doctrine and experience of the Church, that we find the basic elements of an answer. To formulate them, however, is not an easy task. It must be kept in mind that the Orthodox Church has never been challenged by an ecclesiological or doctrinal crisis comparable to the Reformation or Counter-Reformation. And because of this it had no compelling reason to reflect upon itself, upon the traditional structures of its life and doctrine. There was no theological elaboration of the doctrine of the Church, this doctrine having been never questioned or opposed. It was in the ecumenical encounter with the West, an encounter whose beginnings must be traced back to the early twenties (Stockholm, 1925 and Lausanne, 1927) that for the first time the Orthodox were requested not only to *state* their ecclesiological beliefs, but also to *explain* them, i.e., to express them in consistent theological terms. But at this point there appeared an additional difficulty which has remained ever since as the major difficulty of the Orthodox participation in the ecumenical movement. A dialogue presupposes necessarily an agreement on the terms that are being used, a common language. Yet, from the Orthodox point of view it was precisely the rupture in theological understanding, the theological alienation of the West from the East that, first, made the "schism" so deep and, then, all attempts to heal it—from 1054 to the Council of Florence in 1438–1439—so hopelessly inadequate. Therefore, in the ecumenical encounter, the Orthodox Church had to face a Christian world with several centuries of "autonomous" theological and spiritual development behind it, with a mind and thought-forms radically different from those of the East. The questions it asked of the Orthodox were formulated in Western terms, were conditioned very often by specifically Western experience and developments. The Orthodox answers were classified according to Western patterns, "reduced" to categories familiar to the West, but hardly adequate to Orthodoxy. This situation, although years of contacts and conversations have no doubt improved it, is still far from being overcome completely. The "catholic language" has not yet been recovered. All this, in addition to basic dogmatical differences, explains the "agony" of Orthodox participation in the ecumenical movement and constitutes a very real obstacle not only to an agreement, but to a simple understanding. One must remember this when trying to grasp the Orthodox approach to missions.

III

"Heaven on earth": this formula familiar to every Orthodox expresses rather well the fundamental Orthodox experience of the Church. The Church is first of all and before everything else a God-created and God-given reality, the presence of Christ's new life, the manifestation of the new "eon" of the Holy Spirit. An Orthodox in his contemplation of the Church sees it as the divine Gift before he thinks of the Church as human response to this gift. One can rightly describe the Church as an eschatological reality, for its essential function is to manifest and to actualize in this world the *eschaton,* the ultimate reality of salvation and redemption. In and through the Church the kingdom of God is made already present, is communicated to men. And it is this eschatological, God-given fullness of Church (not any juridical theory of mediation) that constitutes the root of the ecclesiological "absolutism" of Eastern Orthodoxy, absolutism which is so often misunderstood and misinterpreted by the Protestants. The Church as a whole is means of grace, the sacrament of the kingdom. Therefore its structure: hierarchical, sacramental, liturgical, has no other function but of making the Church ever capable of fulfilling itself as the body of Christ, as the temple of the Holy Spirit, to actualize its very nature as grace. For the God-given fullness of the Church, or rather the Church as fullness—and this is an essential aspect of Orthodox ecclesiology—cannot be manifested outside these ecclesiastical structures. There is no separation, no division, between the Church invisible (*in statu patriae*) and the visible Church (*in statu viae*), the latter being the expression and the actualization of the former, the sacramental sign of its reality. Hence the unique, the central, ecclesiological significance of the Eucharist, which is the all-embracing sacrament of the Church. In the Eucharist "the Church becomes what it is," fulfills itself as the body of Christ, as the divine *parousia*—the presence and the communication of Christ and of his kingdom. Orthodox ecclesiology is indeed eucharistic ecclesiology. For in the Eucharist the Church accomplishes the *passage* from this world into the world to come, into the *eschaton;* participates in the Ascension of its Lord and in his messianic banquet, tastes of the "joy and peace" of the kingdom. "And Thou didst not cease to do all things until thou hadst brought us back to heaven, and hadst endowed us with Thy kingdom. . . ." (Eucharistic prayer in the Liturgy of St. John Chrysostom). Thus the whole life of the Church is rooted in the Eucharist, is the fruition of this eucharistic fullness in the time of this world whose "image passeth by. . . ." This is indeed the *mission* of the Church.

The Church is also *human response* to the divine Gift, its acceptance and appropriation by man and humanity. If the order of the Church is shaped and conditioned by the eschatological fullness of the Gift, is its sacramental sign, it is the acceptance of the Gift and the growth into its fullness that is the purpose of the Christian community. The Church is fullness and the Church is also increase and growth in faith and love, knowledge and *koinonia.* This response has two aspects, neither of which can be separated from the other, because they condition each other and together constitute the dynamics of Christian life and action. The first one is *God-centered:* it is the sanctification, the growth in holiness, of both the Christian individual and the Christian community, the "acquisition by them of the Holy Spirit," as the ultimate goal of Christian life was defined by one of the last and the greatest Orthodox saints, St. Seraphim of Sarov (d. 1836). It is the slow transformation of the old Adam in us into the new one, the restoration of the pristine beauty, which was lost in sin, the illumination with the noncreated light of Mount Tabor. It is also the slow victory over the demonic powers of the cosmos, the "joy and peace" which *hinc et nunc* make us partakers of the kingdom and of life eternal. The Orthodox spiritual tradition has always stressed the mystical nature of Christian life, as life "hidden with Christ in God." And the great monastic movement which started in the fourth century after the Church was officially recognized by the Roman Empire, given a "status" in this world, was nothing else but a new expression of the early Christian eschatologism, the affirmation of Christianity as belonging ontologically to the life of the "world to come," the negation of any permanent home and identification in this world.

The second aspect of the Church as *response* is *man- or world-centered*. It is the understanding of the Church as being left in this world, in its time, space, and history, with a specific task or mission: "to walk in the same way in which he walked" (1 Jn. 2:6). The Church is fullness and its home is in heaven. But this fullness is given to the world, sent into the world as its salvation and redemption. The eschatological nature of the Church is not the negation of the world, but, on the contrary, its affirmation and acceptance as the object of divine love. Or, in other terms, the whole "otherworldliness" of the Church is nothing but the sign and the reality of the love of God for this world, the very condition of the Church's mission to the world. The Church thus is not a "self-centered" community but precisely a missionary community, salvation not from, but of, the world. In the Orthodox experience and faith it is the Church-sacrament that makes possible the Church-mission.

IV

We can try now to formulate with more precision the various aspects of the "missionary imperative," as implied in the Orthodox experience of the Church. This imperative is the essential expression of the Church as gift and fullness, its projection in time and space of this world. For if, on the one hand, nothing can be *added* to the Church—its fullness is that of Christ himself—the manifestation and the communication of this fullness constitute, on the other hand, the very life of the Church in this "eon." On the day of Pentecost, when the fullness of the Church was realized once for all, began the *time of the Church,* the last and the crucial segment of the history of salvation. Ontologically the only *newness* and, therefore, the only *soteriological content* of this segment is precisely *mission:* the proclamation and the communication of the *eschaton,* which is already the being of the Church and indeed its only being. It is the Church as mission that gives to this time its real significance and to history its meaning. And it is mission that gives to the human response in the Church its validity, makes us real co-workers in the work of Christ.

Nothing reveals better the relation between the Church as fullness and the Church as mission than the Eucharist, the central act of the Church's *leiturgia,* the sacrament of the Church itself. There are two complementary movements in the eucharistic rite: *the movement of ascension* and the *movement of return.* The Eucharist begins as an ascension toward the throne of God, toward the kingdom. "Let us put aside all earthly care" says the hymn of offertory, and we prepare ourselves to ascend into heaven with Christ and in Christ, and offer in him—his Eucharist. This first movement, which finds its fulfillment in the consecration of the elements, the sign of the acceptance by God of our Eucharist, is, to be sure, already an act of mission. The Eucharist is offered "on behalf of all and for all," it is the fulfillment by the Church of its priestly function: the reconciliation of the whole creation with God, the sacrifice of the whole world to God, the intercession for the whole world before God. All this *in Christ,* the God-man, the Unique Priest of the new creation, the "One who offers and the One who is offered. . . ." But this is accomplished by a total separation of the Church from the world ("The doors, the doors!" proclaims the deacon as the Eucharistic prayer begins), by its ascension to heaven, its entrance into the new "eon." And then, precisely at the moment when this state of fullness has been reached and consummated at the table of the Lord in his kingdom, when "we have seen the true Light and partaken of the Holy Spirit," the second movement begins—that of the *return into the world.* "Let us depart in peace" says the celebrant as he leaves the altar and leads the congregation outside the temple—and this is the last, the ultimate, commandment. The Eucharist is always the End, the sacrament of the *parousia,* and, yet, it is always the *beginning,* the *starting point:* now the mission begins. "We have seen the true Light, we have enjoyed life eternal" but this Life, this Light, are given us in order to "transform" us into Christ's witnesses in this world. Without this ascension into the kingdom we would have had nothing to witness to; now, having once more become "his people and his inheritance," we can do what Christ wants us to do: "you are witnesses of these things" (Lk. 24:48). The Eucharist, transforming "the Church into what it is"—transforms it into mission.

V

What are the objects, the goals, of mission? The Orthodox Church answers without hesitation: these objects are *man* and *world.* Not man alone, in an artificially "religious" isolation from the world, and not "world" as an entity of which man would be nothing but "part." Man not only comes first, but is indeed the essential object of mission. And yet, the Orthodox idea of evangelism is free from individualistic and spiritualistic connotations. The Church, the sacrament of Christ, is not a "religious" society of converts, an organization to satisfy the "religious" needs of man. It is *new life* and redeems therefore the whole life, the total being of man. And this whole life of man is precisely the world in which and by which he lives. Through man the Church saves and redeems the world. One can say that "this world" is saved and redeemed every time a man responds to the divine Gift, accepts it and lives by it. This does not transform the world into the kingdom or the society into the Church. The ontological abyss between the *old* and the *new* remains unchanged and cannot be filled in this "eon." The kingdom is yet *to come* and the Church is not *of* this world. And yet this kingdom to come is already present and the Church is fulfilled *in* this world. They are present not only as "proclamation," but in their very reality, and through the divine *agape,* which is their fruit, they *perform* all the time the same sacramental transformation of the *old* into the *new,* they make possible a real action, a real "doing" in this world.

All this gives the mission of the Church a *cosmical* and a *historical* dimension that in the Orthodox tradition and experience are essential. State, society, culture, nature itself, are real *objects* of mission and not a neutral "milieu" in which the only task of the Church is to preserve its own inner freedom, to maintain its "religious life." It would require a whole volume to tell the story of the Orthodox Church from this point of view: of its concrete *participation* in the societies and cultures, of which Orthodoxy became the total expression of their whole existence; of its *identification* with nations and peoples, yet without betrayal of its "otherworldliness," of the eschatological communion with the heavenly Jerusalem. It would require a long theological analysis to express adequately the Orthodox idea of the *sanctification of matter,* or precisely the cosmical aspect of its sacramental vision. Here we can only state that all this is the object of Christian mission, because all this is assumed and offered to God in the sacrament. In the world of incarnation nothing "neutral" remains, nothing can be taken away from the Son of Man.

The *Apostolate of the Church*

BY R. PIERCE BEAVER

The apostolate is the ministry of reconciliation.[1] It is the Church's office or function of bearing witness to the Good News that God has in Christ reconciled the world unto himself and that as a consequence of the unity of men with God in Christ, men may be reconciled with one another. This testifying was the prime function of the Twelve. This is the chief function of the whole body of Christ, his Church, which was commissioned by the risen Lord to be his witnesses "in Jerusalem and in all Judea and Samaria and to the end of the earth" (Acts 1:8). It was for this task and privilege that the power of the Holy Spirit was promised and given. It was for this that our Lord also promised his abiding presence. The Church is to be simultaneously the herald of the kingdom and the demonstrable first fruit of that kingdom. This is why God has put the Church in the world, and in His providence "this gospel of the kingdom will be preached throughout the whole world, as a testimony to all nations; and then the end will come" (Mt. 24:14).

The term *apostolate* is a proper and useful designation of this central function of the Church of Christ. The Church in most of

[1] It is with great reluctance that the writer deals with the theme of the apostolate in such brief space. A fuller treatment is in progress in a small book on "The Eucharist and Apostolate." Some aspects of this subject are treated more adequately in the writer's William Carey Lecture for 1957: *The Christian World Mission: A Reconsideration* (Calcutta, Baptist Mission Press, 1957).

its branches and divisions has usually acknowledged its apostolic character, but often only a minority of the members have been zealously devoted to the witnessing. Frequently, too, sectarian and partial definitions of the apostolate have deprived the proclamation of sufficient scope and power. Now and again the Holy Spirit has called the Church to new obedience and there have been great periods of expansion and of transformation of social life. The Roman Catholics have long used the word apostolate both for the total mission of the Church and for special forms of witnessing. Various Protestant writers have been employing the term for more than a decade, but Professor J. C. Hoekendijk of Utrecht probably introduced it most powerfully.[2] The thinking and writing of the Dutch, German, and Swiss mission theologians, during and since World War II, about the relationship of the mission of the Church to the End and the writings of Max Warren have summoned the Church and the member disciples to accept the apostolate as their required task and to cease regarding it as the "elective" which it has been since the Reformation, although most of these writers have not used the term.

The apostolate or mission of the Church has its roots in the creative, the revelatory-illuminating, and the redemptive-revelatory work of God. It is one form of God's love reaching out to all men. The creation will not be complete until the advent of the new heavens and new earth in the kingdom which the Church proclaims. Moreover, through all the painful consequences of man's rebellion against God, the Holy Spirit ever brings new light about the purposes of God, the nature of man, and the ultimate liberation that will come with the kingdom. Despite all its miserable failure and imperfections, there can be seen in the household of faith the fruits of the divine reconciliation and a foretaste of the redeemed humanity. As God sent His Son, so the Son has sent his body, the Church, empowered by the Holy Spirit, to preach the Gospel of reconciliation to the whole world. The Church exists primarily to witness to this good news, and every other function of the Church is subsidiary and contributory to this purpose. Although secondary to the apostolate and contributory to it, the other functions, such as worship and nurture, in no way lose stature and importance

[2] Unfortunately very little of Professor Hoekendijk's writings are available to most American readers. See a few articles in the *International Review of Missions.*

in this relationship. The missionary ministry of Jesus Christ is the prototype of the Church's ministry of witness, as Bishop Newbigin has forcefully pointed out in the booklet, *One Body, One Gospel, One World.*[3] Yet it must be noted that the Gospel comprises not only the teaching of Jesus Christ, but also the teaching of the early Church about him—about what God has done in the Crucifixion, Resurrection, Ascension, and giving of the Holy Spirit, namely, the reconciling of the world to Himself.

The Disciple and Baptism

Since the Church, Christ's mystical body, is sent out into the world to undertake the apostolate, this life of witnessing is also the vocation of every member in that body. St. Paul instructs Christians in the unity of the body and the singleness of its manifold ministry. He reminded the young church in Rome of the diversity of ministries that make up the witnessing to God's saving work. A special measure of faithfulness might be required of the commissioned apostolic ministers, such as himself, as he instructed the Corinthians—but all members share in the apostolate of the body. "Because there is one loaf, we who are many are one body, for we all partake of the same loaf"—the Eucharistic bread of our Lord's own body broken for the remission of sins and the healing of the broken society of men estranged from God. One frequently hears in missionary circles today the assertion that every church member is meant to be a missionary. This is an exaggeration. Only some are sent, but all are called to make their witness. This is the most fundamental function of the layman in his ministry, but in our clergy-dominated churches the disciple is usually even more neglectful of this office than of his other duties implied by the doctrine of the priesthood of all believers. The apostolic vocation of laymen so evident in the churches of Korea is seldom found elsewhere. The establishment of seventy-three new churches by the staff of the Presbyterian Hospital in Taegu ought not to be so extraordinary, as it most certainly is in fact. Every Christian in a congregation of believers is first and foremost a disciple, that is, a pupil-companion and an apprentice co-worker, learning from and serving his Lord in a joint ministry with him. Witnessing is the first of his many functions of ministry, in which the ordained

[3] Lesslie Newbigin, *One Body, One Gospel, One World: The Christian Mission Today* (London and New York: I.M.C., 1958), p. 17 especially.

pastor is intended to inspire and guide him and set him an example.

The sacrament of baptism, to which the rite of confirmation must be joined if infant baptism is practiced, clearly reveals the place of witnessing in the Christian profession. The emphasis of this sacrament is by no means as much upon individual salvation as upon the incorporation of the disciple into mystical union with our Lord and his body the Church for sharing in Christ's mission and in the corporate life of the body. Note the difference between the pronouns of the baptismal and Eucharistic creeds of the Western Church, the Apostles' and the Nicene Creeds respectively. The singular "I" of the former and the plural "we" of the latter are significant. It is on the basis of his individual act of witnessing to his faith that the disciple may be by God's grace joined mystically with his Lord in the master-disciple relationship and be incorporated into the common life and ministry of the body. Thereafter the disciple says "we" in the Eucharistic feast when the congregation is renewed in its union with Christ for his saving work among men, and the common life and commitment strengthen the individual in his personal witnessing.

It is on the basis of the example of Jesus' own baptism and the injunction in the Great Commission about baptizing the nations that the Church has made baptism a sacrament. Neither has to do primarily with personal forgiveness of sins nor personal security in boarding the ark of salvation, which generally receive the primary emphasis. Emulation of the prototype and obedience to the Commission lay stress upon life commitment to Christ in faith, upon following him, taking up the cross of discipleship, participation in his ministry, and upon identification with the sinners to whom the Gospel is proclaimed. The disciple facing his sinless Lord does confess his sin and throws himself upon the love and mercy of God for forgiveness, but he also emulates Jesus' identification of himself with sinners in need of reconciliation; for when our Lord was baptized by John in the Jordan he was making such an identification, not confessing his sins. Baptism and confirmation are an offering up of the self upon the altar of the Gospel to be used of Christ in his mission. God's gift of the Holy Spirit in the sacrament and rite is a repetition of the original bestowal on Pentecost. It is for power in witnessing (Acts 1:8). This complete reorientation of life in emulation of Christ and in joint service with him is the "dying unto the world" that is mentioned in the baptismal orders. The believer publicly testifies to his faith in what God is doing for him and will do for all men. It is the disciple's first act of witness in what is henceforth to be a life of witness in the witnessing community of all believers. Professor Marcus Barth has written:

> But when those baptized throw themselves at the feet of, and implore the mercy of the Father, Son, and Holy Ghost, then they do not separate themselves from the accursed world. But they confess in the midst of, and for sinful, maybe grinning, maybe blaspheming, maybe stone-throwing men that God wants *all,* not the few only, to be saved and to come to the knowledge of truth. A Christian's life will day by day be a witness to God's fatherhood over all, Christ's death for all, the Spirit's promise to all. Baptism is the unique, necessary, public beginning, pledge, investiture into the ministry of witnesses.[4]

Moreover, since it is primarily due to the command about baptism in the Great Commission that the Church has made this rite to be the required sacramental act of entrance into the household of faith, its meaning ought to be seen in that context. "Go therefore and make disciples of all nations, baptizing them in the name of the Father and of the Son and of the Holy Spirit, teaching them to observe all that I have commanded you; and lo, I am with you always, to the close of the age" (Mt. 28:19–20). The baptizing is thus inseparably connected with the discipling of the nations. "All that I have commanded" surely must include the discipling of the nations. Our Lord's abiding presence is promised in this task, and, according to Luke in Acts 1:8, the Holy Spirit is bestowed above all for power in the witnessing.

Evangelism and Sending

The apostolate or ministry of proclamation of the reconciliation God has made with the world in Christ is the Church's main purpose until God brings His kingdom in all its fullness. The "End" awaits this faithful performance. Dedication to the apostolate would take emphasis off the Church as an institution and stress its nature as a community of reconciliation. It would make every form of order and polity expendable and allow again that freedom of organizational form (but within a genuine unity) that marked

[4] In a paper on evangelism read to the Federated Theological Faculty of the University of Chicago.

the apostolic and postapostolic ages. It would cut the root of ecclesiolatry and remove men's fears for the safety and prestige of the Church. It would make the Church and the disciple-members ready to lose their lives in bearing the cross of Gospel witness. It would put stress on the relevance of preaching to the contemporary needs of men and society. Each local congregation devoted to the apostolate would spend itself in proclamation, sustained by the memory of the cross and Resurrection, empowered by the Holy Spirit, recognizing the presence of the risen Lord who makes the Church his body, and made joyous by the hope of the glorious coming of the kingdom. It would lose no opportunity and neglect no medium for preaching the Gospel. It would preach by word and deed and by the quality of the personal and corporate life of the believers. The timeless message would be made timely and relevant to every man in his family, his vocation, his culture, his nation, his world order. Then the worship, the nurture and fellowship, and the service of the congregation would authenticate and validate the message that is preached.

There are two supplementary and complementary parts to the apostolate which can be separated or the one of them neglected only to the hurt of the Church's health and to disobedience to the Great Commission. One is the local apostolate, *evangelism.* This is witness to Christ's reconciling saviourhood and lordship and the exercise of the ministry of reconciliation where the congregation worships and the disciple-members earn their daily bread in their several vocations. It includes personal testimony about God's act in Christ and the fellowship of the kingdom in the Church that is given to friends, neighbors, and those engaged in daily contact by the disciples. Such witness is made in the discharge of a Christian vocation in craft, profession, or business. It is effected also in the quality of the Christian family, which may be the Church in microcosm, and in the responsible stand which the congregation of disciples takes on community and social issues and in the demonstration of the relevance of the Gospel to these issues. And it is made in the preaching in the house of God where its truth is attested by the company of believers assembled in the unity of reconciliation with God and with men.

The other aspect of the apostolate is the *sending*—mission in the more traditional sense. It is the evangelistic outreach beyond the congregation and home locality, involving the commissioning and sending of some representative agent who makes witness on behalf of the sending church and its disciples. The distance in miles or kilometers which the missionary agent travels to his place of witnessing is not significant. But be it near or far, that missionary must go to some place that is a distant "end of the earth" to the sending group and himself. Geographical ends of the earth have disappeared in a time of jet travel and a world-wide Church, but there are social, cultural, ideological, and spiritual "far ends" of human society in profusion. There is a frontier of strangeness to be crossed to the place where the missionary can proclaim Jesus Christ as Lord to unreconciled people who have not known and accepted him. Bishop Newbigin, in discussing what activity can be called "missionary" in the context of a world-wide Church, states:

> *The differentium lies in the crossing of the frontier between faith in Christ as Lord and unbelief.* To make clear and to keep clear this, the distinctive meaning of the word "missionary" is one of the most important requirements of the present discussion. He who is sent to make Christ known and obeyed as Lord among those who do not know and obey Him is a missionary, whether his journey be long or short. The missionary frontier runs through every land where there are communities living without the knowledge of Christ as Lord.[5]

The lending of personnel within the Christian community is not in itself sending, but rather fraternal aid, which is mutual burden-bearing by members of Christ's body, a requirement of the common life. However, a church in one land can send its representative to aid another church in another land in the work of the apostolate, and, if the proclamation of the Gospel is the chief end in view, that agent becomes the missionary of both branches of the Church. When he crosses over the frontier of faith in Christ to give witness to those who do not know and believe, then he crosses the most important of all the frontiers of strangeness.

"Sending" is intimately bound up with "evangelism." When the sending to the "ends of the earth" is neglected, the wellsprings of evangelism dry up. This has been demonstrated too often in the history of the Church. Neither half of the apostolate is an elective. "You shall be witnesses in Jerusalem and in all Judea and Samaria,

[5] Newbigin, *op. cit.*, p. 29.

and to the end of the earth." Evangelism and mission are the two poles of the apostolate. Every congregation is a front-line post in a world mission; and every disciple is meant to be a witness and to share in the sending of witnesses.

The Lord's Supper and the Apostolate

The functions of the Church in addition to the apostolate are many. They include the priestly office of worship, the shepherding of souls, teaching, prophesying, the ordering of the common spiritual life, nurture, fellowship, mutual aid of the brethren in their needs, healing, works of mercy and compassion, peacemaking, and a dozen others. They all, however, derive from one or another of three main functions: witnessing, worship, and fellowship; both of which latter are closely related to the first. Christian worship is offered to God through Jesus Christ in the Holy Spirit by a corporate body of priests, the congregation representing the whole Church, not by a mediating priesthood of a different order, because the mystical body of Christ by God's grace shares in our Lord's high priesthood and with him enters into the holy of holies. The office of a priest is to offer "gifts and sacrifices" (1 Pet. 2:9)—namely, praise and thanksgiving, the sacrifices for sin, and the intercession for the household of faith and for all men. This priestly office which the mystical body of Christ performs while it is in the world busy with the apostolate keeps it in right relation to God, dedicated to the doing of His will, joyous in His service, and empowered by His Holy Spirit. Moreover, were there space enough, it could be shown how each involves witness to God's deeds in Christ and his coming kingdom. Above all, the center and "inmost sanctuary" of worship is the Eucharist or Lord's Supper, which is the means by which the Church's mystical union with Christ is renewed and affirmed and by which she is offered up in identification with him to be broken with him in the healing of the unreconciled world. It is, moreover, the dramatic enactment of the Word that is preached, the Gospel of reconciliation.

The Lord's Supper is too profound and mysterious for any man or the whole Church to define and describe in all its significance, and here the writer lifts up only what he believes to be its primary—and most neglected—meaning. In stressing its corporate nature and action he does not deny the personal, individualistic aspects of forgiveness, communion, and bestowal of peace to the disciple, but he would affirm that these are subordinate and are by-products of the chief action of the sacrament.

This memorial which our Lord commanded (Lk. 22:19) does "proclaim the Lord's death until he comes" (1 Cor. 11:26), and proclaims, even when the Church forgets verbally to make witness, "For God so loved the world that he gave his only Son, that whoever believes in him should not perish but have eternal life" (Jn. 3:16). God's reconciling act in history is declared to be ever present and ever relevant, and it holds the promise of the eschatological fulfillment. The whole world of mankind and the redemption of the entire race are within the scope of the sacrament: in the confession of sins and promise of forgiveness, in the prayers for the days and season that set forth the Gospel to be preached to all the world, in the creed which affirms a faith to be offered to all; for the reconciling Saviour is one "who for *us men* and our salvation came down from heaven." The alms, oblations, and intercessions which are offered and consecrated together represent a sacrifice of concern and compassion for the brethren and the world. The Lord's Prayer, with its petition for the coming of the kingdom, gathers together and climaxes all the intercessions. But the Supper is much more than an act of commemoration and proclamation of an historic event. It is a present gathering of the disciples of Christ with him around his banquet table where he is truly present with them. Gathered there in the one fold with the one Shepherd, they are reminded that this family feast is incomplete until all for whom Christ died be brought to that festive board. This is the place of ingathering. This meal is also the "messianic banquet" where he who was crucified, dead, buried, and rose again keeps his promise to drink with his disciples the new wine in the new age of the kingdom. Here the first fruit of the redeemed and reconciled new community is visible to the world—a company that is only a token of the great assembly yet to be brought together "from east and west, from north and south, and sit at the table in the kingdom of God" (Lk. 13:29). Surely no disciple can at that table eat and drink, rest and repose for himself and be unconcerned about the ingathering. And here the nourishment is provided which gives the disciple strength to go forth in order to make the ingathering. Above all, as baptism makes the new disciple an evangelist, so the Lord's Supper is the means by which participation in the mission of Christ is repeatedly renewed.

St. Paul instructed the Corinthian Christians (1 Cor. 10) that even as the Hebrews who ate of the sacrifices of the altar in the Temple were partakers of the altar of God, so those who eat of food sacrified to idols on pagan altars have fellowship with, *and participate in the life of,* devils. Similarly, he declared, partaking of the table of the Lord means sharing in our Lord's person and his mission. "The cup of blessing which we bless, is it not a participation in the blood of Christ? The bread which we break, is it not a participation in the body of Christ?" And it is the blood that was *shed* and the body that was *broken.* Eating this bread and drinking this cup for participation in Christ and his mission effects identification and that effects unity. "Because there is one loaf, we who are many are one body, for we all partake of the same loaf." Unity comes not from any creedal statement or common practice, but is effected through this unstinted devotion to our Lord in his mission of reconciliation. The congregation, making the Eucharistic offering for the whole Church, is accepted by God and made one mystically with the Eucharistic bread. Then the Church is truly the body of Christ and in him and with him may be broken for the reconciliation of estranged men and women with God. The ever-abiding Presence in the apostolate and the peace for power in witness are then imparted to the congregation and the disciples as they make their communion. "Go therefore, and make disciples of all nations, baptizing them . . . and lo, I am with you always, even to the close of the age."

Unity, Fellowship, Service, and Witness

The unity in Christ effected in the breaking of the Eucharistic bread is then to be demonstrated in the fellowship of the Church so that men may see that God does actually effect the reconciliation of men with Him and with one another in the bonds of Christ's love. Unifying, mutual burden-bearing love visible to all beholders is the only pragmatic proof of the claims of Christ that a skeptical world will accept. Our Lord prayed, "that they may all be one; even as thou, Father, art in me, and I in thee, that they also may be in us, so that the world may believe that thou hast sent me" (Jn. 17:21). The purpose of Christian fellowship is, then, not so much mutual enjoyment as evangelistic proclamation. Segregation, caste, schism, unbrotherliness in the Church negate the claims made for Christ by the evangelist. Unity is shown in love that bears the fellow members' burdens in the Church through *diakonia,* which is originally and still should be the practical extension of the alms and intercessions offered in the Eucharist, and in the bridging of personal, racial, cultural, and other differences in one comprehensive community. But *diakonia* never knows when and where to stop. The ministry of compassion is never confined to the members of the household of faith but spills over into ministry to all others in need and becomes overtly an act of witness. The Gospel is preached, and the Eucharistic loaf is broken and cup spilled out, when even a cup of cold water is lovingly given in the name of Christ. The disciple's love must embrace the whole world, for it is God's love in his heart.

The Holy Spirit

It is the Holy Spirit who is the Great Apostle and who leads and empowers the Church in its witnessing. It is the presence of the Holy Spirit, the Illuminator, the Lord and Giver of life, that makes the body of Christ a living organism. He is the bond of union with our Lord and in him worship is directed to God. He crowns faithful witness with fruitfulness, for he goes before every evangelist and missionary preparing hearts and minds to hear. It is only by him that a man can call Jesus "Lord" (1 Cor. 12:13). It is by his power that the Gospel of reconciliation is preached effectively and relevantly and then authentically shown forth in the unity, fellowship, and service of the Church.

The *Holy Spirit and the Christian Mission*

BY F. W. DILLISTONE

The very title Holy Spirit presents us with a startling paradox. Since the publication of Rudolf Otto's *The Idea of the Holy* we have come to think of the "Holy" as the awe-inspiring, the withdrawn, the mysterious, that which can only be approached with reverence and godly fear. On the other hand our greater familiarity with the Hebrew background of the conception of Spirit leads us to think in terms of a wonderful power invading human life and bringing vitality, inspiration, energy. But how can that which is infinitely beyond the common touch of man be received into his common life? How can the everlasting burning enter the realm of the temporal and the sinful without destroying all that falls within its path?

I

For an expansion of this paradox I turn to the book of Isaiah. In the earlier part of the prophecy the title "The Holy One of Israel" becomes established for the first time as an altogether distinctive title of Deity, and its implications are disclosed not by formal definition but by the famous story of the call of the prophet in chapter 6. There our imaginations are lifted to the vision of One who is high and exalted and far beyond the common gaze. We sense the glory of eternal light, the purity of eternal fire, and the threefold cry of "Holy" finds its meaning within the fullness of the revelation.

Yet although the Holy One of Israel is so far removed from sinful man, the gulf is not absolute. He sends the fire of cleansing. He sends the word of challenge. And the prophet, energized but not consumed by the communications from the divine Presence, goes forth to announce judgment and doom on everything that is opposed to the divine purpose. Man is not cut off entirely from the divine concern but if his only hope was to be set between the fire of purging and the fire of judgment—then indeed he could but go in fear and trembling all the days of his life.

But if it is in the first part of the book that the name of the Holy One of Israel stands revealed, it is in the second part that the nature of Spirit is revealed through the call of God's Servant. Here the key passage is Isaiah 61 and the whole emphasis is upon grace. The Spirit comes not as fire of cleansing but as the oil of refreshing. Instead of the coal that scorches there is the anointing that re-creates. And the purpose of the Spirit's activity is all of grace. To bring good tidings to the afflicted, to bind up the brokenhearted, to proclaim liberty to the captives, to comfort all who mourn, to build up ancient ruins, to raise up former devastations, to proclaim the year of the Lord's favor and through it all to glorify His name —this is the work of the Spirit and, as another passage shows, it stretches beyond the boundaries of Israel to the very ends of the earth.

Yet even in the light of this revelation man has no right to presume. The very nature of the situation from which he is being rescued is sufficient testimony to the precariousness of his life upon the earth and to the poverty of his existence apart from the movement of the divine grace. He is not entirely powerless to order and direct his own life, but if his only hope is in his own efforts then indeed he must go in disillusionment and anxiety all the days of his life.

The Holy—the Spirit. The symbol of an intense purity—the symbol of a boundless grace. The Old Testament linked the two together on only three occasions and even then with the note of holiness altogether determining the significance of the title. It was left to the New Testament to bring the new revelation of Holy Spirit, a revelation only made possible through the fusing of the Holy and the Spirit in the person and activity of Jesus the Christ.

II

The two elements of which I have been speaking are brought together in a remarkable way in the story of Jesus' baptism. The whole setting of John's baptism proclaims the holiness of the God of Israel. He is about to act in judgment. His fan is in His hand. He will throughly purge His floor. His agent, the Messiah, will come as the fire to destroy sinners and to separate a holy remnant capable of surviving the judgment and entering God's holy kingdom. In submitting himself to John's baptism Jesus acknowledged the holiness and the burning activity of the God whose representative he was.

Yet in the record of the actual moment of baptism a different note is struck. The heavens are opened. Jesus is acclaimed as the Son, the Well-beloved. He is addressed with words taken from the calling of God's Servant. He is to fulfill a mission which will not only raise up the fallen in Israel but extend God's salvation to the ends of the earth. Here is a new revelation that the ineffably holy is also the unboundedly gracious: that the one who confesses the holy judgment of God at the same time bears witness to His gracious salvation.

The dialectic continues in the stories of the Temptation and early ministry which immediately follow. As Jesus withdraws to the wilderness he stands again before the Holy. His mission is to be grounded in the word of the Holy, the worship of the Holy, the waiting for the Holy. Yet returning in the power of the Spirit he declares his mission in terms of the great proclamation of Isaiah 61: "The Spirit of the Lord is upon me because he has anointed me to proclaim the acceptable year of the Lord." And all wondered at the gracious words which proceeded out of his mouth.

Still further the Lucan narrative shows him in conflict with the spirit of evil. Even the demonic man recognizes a more-than-human presence. "I know who you are, the Holy One of God." Holiness confronts the unclean and the demonic with the fire of destruction. Yet in immediate succession comes the narrative of his reception of the sick and the diseased: "and he laid his hands upon every one of them and healed them." Or to give one further example, Jesus teaches his disciples to pray that God will sanctify His name ("Hallowed be thy name"). Did not this imply that it was at the very heart of Jesus' mission to act in God's name against all that was opposed to His purpose? Yet when the disciples thought to call down fire from heaven to consume those who refused to receive Jesus on his way to Jerusalem, he turned and rebuked them saying "You do not know what manner of spirit you are of," and went on to define this Spirit in fuller terms as that which does not destroy men's lives but saves them.

So in the life and ministry of Jesus the double-sidedness of the Holy Spirit is constantly set forth. That he was the authoritative representative of the Holy God—the God who searches the perversions and iniquities of mankind with His fire of judgment—of that there could be no doubt. At the same time that he was the authentic bearer of the divine Spirit—the Spirit who binds up the wounds of mankind with His grace and salvation—of that also there could be no doubt. It was only when the nature of Holy Spirit had been once-for-all disclosed through the words and deeds of the Messiah, that it was possible for the Christian missionary vocation to receive its classic expression: "Receive the Holy Spirit. As the Father has sent me, even so I send you."

III

The author of the Acts of the Apostles must be regarded as the foremost interpreter of the work of the Holy Spirit in the Christian mission. At the very outset he shows that the mission of witness is entirely dependent upon the coming of the Holy Spirit in new power. What could be more forceful than Acts 1:8: "You shall receive power when the Holy Spirit has come upon you; and you shall be my witnesses in Jerusalem and in all Judea and Samaria and to the end of the earth." What could be more vivid than the record of the fulfillment of this promise in Acts 2:1–11?

In this record particular emphasis is laid upon three symbols. An event which could not be described in ordinary human terms is mediated to us through (a) a sound of a rushing wind, (b) tongues of fire resting upon individuals, and (c) speech in other tongues. In this initial stage there is an overwhelming sense of the pressure of the Holy in the new situation. There is already a foretaste of the last days, with God enthroned in His universe and the exalted Christ pouring out His Spirit upon men. It is for those who are awake to what is happening to turn to God in order that they may receive His Holy Spirit and be incorporated into the body of God's elect.

This is the initial emphasis—a group of men energized by the divine Spirit, cleansed and enkindled by the divine fire, bearing witness to the wonderful works of God "as the Spirit gave them utterance." But as the first emphasis is so clearly upon the Holy, the second movement, as in the Gospel story, is toward that *service* which the Spirit so characteristically inspires. We see the Apostles succoring the needy, healing the lame, preaching the Gospel to the poor, bringing release to the captives, proclaiming the acceptable year of the Lord. Through their common prayers and fellowship they refreshed themselves again and again in the presence of the Holy: through their testimony in word and deed to the name of God's holy servant Jesus (Acts 4:31) they extended his saving work further and further afield.

So the course of the Church's missionary task was set. It was to hold together two profound movements of the divine Spirit which have often seemed to be mutually exclusive. On the one side God ever moves toward man as the Holy: transcending man's littleness, shaming his selfishness, challenging his complacency, stretching his boundedness, condemning his perversity. On the other side God ever moves toward man in the Spirit of the Servant: understanding man's weaknesses, feeling his temptations, healing his wounds, loosing his bonds, restoring his confidence and hope. It is possible to have an awareness of the first and to bow down in awe and contrition; it is possible to recognize the second and to expand in sympathy and good will. But to receive the Holy Spirit revealed in Jesus the Christ, to die constantly to sin and self-will in the presence of the Holy while at the same time the saving compassion of Jesus is constantly made manifest in the power of the Spirit—this is beyond the possibilities of flesh and blood but not beyond the range of the grace of God. This alone is the missionary pattern of the Church of Christ.

IV

The keynote of the Acts of the Apostles is the expansion of the Church through the power of the Holy Spirit. But when we turn to the Epistles of St. Paul another aspect of the Spirit's work comes prominently into view. Now it is not so much extension outward as sanctification inward. The life of the infant churches has to be stabilized and deepened and this can only come about through the continuing operation of the Holy Spirit.

The Epistle to the Romans reveals the new confidence in relation to physical death now open to those who walk in the Spirit. It reveals, too, the pattern of the life of prayer in the Spirit with the children of God being guided to make their intercessions according to the mind and purpose of God. The Epistles to the Corinthians reveal the nature of the worship and the moral life which belong to the Spirit-filled body of Christ. The Spirit inspires order, not confusion; purity, not license; edification, not meaningless excitement; cohesion, not blind individualism. As he deals with concrete problems that have arisen in the Christian community, Paul makes it clear that not every inspiration and impulse comes from the divine Spirit. The Holy Spirit is ever working to produce a pattern of corporate life in the Church conformable to that once-for-all revealed in the incarnate life of Jesus the Christ.

Through the Epistles, then, we see the sanctifying work of the Spirit in progress, assuring men of their divine sonship, purifying their relationships, intensifying their intercessions, interpreting their worship experiences. The body of Christ is indwelt by the Spirit who is Holy—and this means the Spirit who is not only powerful to drive forward as wind and to spread outward as the fire but also strong to release from the down-drag of evil and death and to lift up into the realm of pure being and eternal life. That a new note has come into Christian proclamation can hardly be doubted. Will the concern for the purity and the otherworldliness of the Christian family undermine the urgency of the commission to evangelize the nations?

The history of the Christian Church since the end of the first century can be regarded as a continuing dialectic between what today might be called the inner-directed and the outer-directed, between, that is to say, the concern for inner sanctification and the urge to outward service. One may regret that the earlier dialectic between the Holy as burning judgment and the Spirit as healing salvation has been replaced and yet the very nature of the problems with which an expanding Church had to grapple made the change almost inevitable. For as the Church moved out beyond an environment which had been impregnated by the Hebrew tradition it found itself in the midst of peoples who lacked both ethical disciplines and any kind of ordered religious life. In response to a Gospel preached in the power of the Spirit they might indeed turn from idols to serve the living God. But the power of the Spirit was now needed above all to draw them away from the works of the flesh and to lift them to a regular experience of filial communion with a Holy Father in the Spirit of His Son.

So it came about that from the second century onwards there was little conscious connection made in the Church between the gift of the Spirit and the call to evangelize. The Spirit had been given to the Church, it was believed, to build it up in sanctity. Through the Spirit-endued ministers of the Church, through the words of Scripture interpreted by the Spirit, through the sacraments made effectual by the Spirit, the Church could grow in holiness and rise to its true life in God Himself. The Church was, in fact, life in the Spirit, and the work of the Spirit was above all to purify and illumine every soul within the Church.

This view of the Spirit's function has been characteristic of the Eastern Church throughout its history. The Spirit is proclaimed through catechesis and liturgy as the Spirit of truth, of light, of life, of love. He completes the work of Christ and brings every several member of the Church into a personal union with the Triune God. Those who are received into the Church come immediately within the area of the Spirit's sanctifying power: but that the Spirit is ever moving outwards to bring good tidings to a wider world—of this there is little consciousness in the Eastern tradition.

The Western Church has always been concerned to extend the borders of its influence and to bring the heathen within its fold. Doubtless a variety of motives have been active within this mission, but it is at least open to question how far it has been directly related to the continuing work of the Holy Spirit. It is true that a fine early twelfth-century sculpture above the portal of a church in North Burgundy shows the reigning Christ bestowing his Spirit upon the apostles and beneath them there are representatives of the many nations to whom they were being sent. Again in Langland's fourteenth-century poem "Piers Plowman" there is a striking reference to the coming of "one *Spiritus Paraclitus*" to Piers and to his followers. This Spirit, coming as light and fire, made them masters of all men's language and promised to go with them in the mission of dealing grace and dividing it wisely "among all kinds and conditions who can use five senses." But in the work of the great theologians the Spirit is, above all, the moving agent who directs the soul of man into union with God. The Spirit leads man to contemplate the image of God, to delight in Him, to consent to His will, to be joined to Him in love. The Spirit as sanctifier in the fellowship of the Church is beautifully expressed; the Spirit as moving in the hearts of men with a divine compulsion to go out and seek the lost can less easily be found.

V

Even the coming of the Reformation did not immediately lead to a rediscovery of Pentecost and of the world-wide Commission of the Church. There were indeed particular circumstances, social and geographical, which would have precluded any extensive overseas missionary activity. But besides this the great churches of the Reformation were at first seriously beset by the problem of extremists who in so many cases appealed to the Spirit as the inspirer of their social and political activities. In response to such claims the Reformers gave almost exclusive emphasis to the work of the Spirit as bearing witness to and interpreting the Word. The Bible was the very constitution of the new order and it was the constant task of the Spirit to take of the things of Christ therein contained and to reveal them to men. The sixteenth and seventeenth centuries were a time of major upheaval and strife in Europe, and until a reasonable social order had been established it was unlikely that any real freedom of movement would be allowed to those who, conscious of the Spirit's urging to new adventure, desired to go at his bidding to the regions beyond.

But gradually the changing conditions of the eighteenth century began to lift men's horizons. An expanding world brought back to their consciousness the risen Lord's Commission and the Holy Spirit's enabling. How difficult were the obstacles to be overcome may be seen for example in the record of John Eliot, the pioneer missionary to the Indians. It was in 1646 that he preached his first sermon to them in their own language, after a long period spent in trying to win their confidence and speak their tongue. "Certainly," Increase Mather wrote afterwards, "it was the Holy Spirit who inspired him to hear and obey that call"—though to many of his brethren at the time there was no such certainty, seeing that in their view the Indians were nothing more than wild beasts whom God had called them to fear and fight. In the mid-eighteenth century it was William Carey who had to persuade his brethren that God was calling His Church to action and that the way was open for a new obedience to the charge to be witnesses to the uttermost parts of the earth.

As is well known, it was at first left to individuals, groups, societies, to be the agents of the Holy Spirit in this renewed missionary activity. In more official church circles there was a strong suspicion of enthusiasm, a reluctance to go beyond the traditional patterns of parochial life, and no ready recognition of responsibility toward the inhabitants of remote heathen lands. Yet the few were conscious of the movement of the Spirit, both in their own hearts as motivating power and in the hearts of the heathen as convicting and converting power. One may take, for example, some words from a sermon preached in London in the year 1810 by a certain Claudius Buchanan, lately returned from India. "What," he asks, "were the ordained means of conversion?" He answers:

> The Apostle informed the judgment with facts, and addressed the conscience with doctrines, and the holy spirit "guided their minds into all truth." This influence of the holy spirit was the miracle which produced the conversion of the heathen world, and of the Jewish world. And the influence of the same spirit exists at this day, though less in degree, agreeably to the promise, that it should "abide for ever"; and is manifest, in every case, of the conversion of a sinner, whether he belong to the heathen or the Christian world.
>
> Our duty then, my brethren, in regard to the Gentiles in this age, is to do what was done in the first age; to assert the truth of revelation by oral preaching, or by writings sent among them; praying that God would do honour to his own word by the witness of the spirit; and depending on "the author and finisher of our faith," for a blessing on the work which he hath commanded.
>
> But you are to understand, that those who disbelieve the doctrine of the atonement, and of the influence of the holy spirit, will never be solicitous to communicate Christianity to heathen nations; and, for this obvious reason, they have no motives. Survey the whole body of men, now employed in the four quarters of the globe, in promoting the Gospel of Christ, whether societies or individuals, and whether by preaching, by writing, by pecuniary contribution, or by personal exertion, and you will find that they ALL, or nearly all, believe in the doctrines of divine grace, and of atonement by "the blood of the Lamb." For these are the doctrines which engage the heart and affections; and, when men have felt there power and consolation, then they have found MOTIVES for diffusing them. When we shall have

learned to consider the Gospel as "the UNSEARCHABLE RICHES," and the INESTIMABLE GIFT, then shall we earnestly desire to impart it to others.

In such a sermon we see the main emphases of evangelical life and thought. The central doctrine to be proclaimed is that of God's gracious act of atonement in and through the saving work of Christ. The central influence moving men to make the proclamation and moving sinners to receive and believe it is that of the Holy Spirit himself. It is the Holy Spirit who motivates the missionary; it is the Holy Spirit who convicts the sinner and leads him to repentance and faith. The recognition of the work of the Spirit in sanctification and in the creating of fellowship is by no means lost but throughout the century the awareness of his concomitant activity in moving the children of God to share in his witness to the saving work of Christ grew stronger and clearer. The way was being prepared for a more comprehensive theology of the Church's mission which the twentieth century would bring. By the time of the World Missionary Conference at Madras in 1938 it had come to be understood, at least on the official level, that missionary activity is not simply the task of a small number of people seized by a special concern, but rather the task of the Church as a whole. If the Church is the body of Christ animated by his Spirit, then it must be of its very nature to continue his mission of salvation to the ends of the earth.

VI

At the Willingen Conference in 1952 the theological presuppositions of the whole missionary movement were clearly and forcefully expressed. This movement, it was affirmed, has its source in the Triune God Himself. He has sent forth one Saviour to seek and save all the lost, one Redeemer who by his death, resurrection, and ascension has accomplished a full and perfect atonement and created in himself one new humanity, the body of which Christ is the exalted Head. This is followed by a fine statement:

> On the foundation of this accomplished work God has sent forth His Spirit, the Spirit of Jesus, to gather us together in one Body in Him . . . to empower us for the continuance of His mission as His witnesses and ambassadors. By the Spirit we are enabled both to press forward as ambassadors of Christ, beseeching all men to be reconciled to God, and also to wait with sure confidence for the final victory of His love. . . .

There is no participation in Christ without participation in His mission to the world. That by which the Church receives its existence is that by which it is also given its world mission. "As the Father hath sent me, even so send I you."[1]

This is a simple and yet profound statement of the theology of the Church's missionary task. It brings us back to the Holy God whose Spirit must always strive with a world estranged and alienated from its true life and destiny. It focuses attention upon the Servant anointed by the Spirit for his work of healing and salvation. It reminds us of the sending forth of the Holy Spirit of him who through death and resurrection had opened the kingdom of heaven to all believers. Henceforward the Church has its task and its enabling. To bear witness to the uttermost parts of the earth is its continuing obligation: to receive power through the Holy Spirit is its constant privilege.

To sum up. There have been times in the history of the Christian Church when the emphasis on the *holy* in the title *Holy Spirit* has been altogether dominant. Then men have been concerned for holiness, for purity, for separation, for aspiration heavenwards in the corporate life and worship of the Church, and in the striving for individual sanctity. Again there have been times when the emphasis on *spirit* has been altogether dominant. Then the concern has been for power, for spiritual energy, for expansion, for urgent proclamation, as constituting the marks of God's true servants who are endued by His Spirit. But if the Church is indeed the instrument of *Holy Spirit* then the duality of the title must surely be revealed in a dual pattern of life. On the one side there must be witness to the fire that is never quenched, to the light that cannot be approached, to the glorious majesty of a Holy God. On the other side there must be witness to the energy that is never exhausted, to the grace that has no bounds, to the patient involvement of the divine Spirit in every framework of human culture.

And to this end the Christian's prayers will also be twofold. He will pray that the Comforter may bestow the "holy flame."

O let it freely burn
Till earthly passions turn

[1] "A Statement on the Missionary Calling of the Church," in *Missions Under the Cross*, ed. Norman Goodall (London: Edinburgh House Press, 1953), pp. 189–90. This statement arose out of the report of Group I on "The Missionary Obligation of the Church" at Willingen.

To dust and ashes in its heat consuming
And let thy glorious light
Shine ever on my sight
And clothe me round, the while my path illuming.

He will also pray that the love of God may be shed abroad in his heart by the same Holy Spirit.

Enlarge, inflame and fill my heart
With boundless charity divine:
So shall I all my strength exert,
And love them with a zeal like thine;
And lead them to thy open side,
The sheep for whom their Shepherd died.

Missions and World History

BY PAUL TILLICH

Every activity of the Church must be derived from the foundation of the Church itself. It must be an activity which follows *necessarily* from the very nature of the Church. It is not the accidental but the necessary functions of the Church which are the subject of theological consideration.

The theological problem of missions belongs to two groups of theological problems: first, to those which deal with the doctrine of the Church, and secondly, to those which deal with the Christian interpretation of history. The following discussion is not that of an expert. I am not a specialist in missions, but a systematic theologian who is trying to bring the great reality of missions into the framework of a Christian interpretation of history and a Christian doctrine of the Church.

For the Christian interpretation of history, the meaning of history is the kingdom of God.

There are three main riddles of history. History runs toward a goal which is never actualized in history. History runs in one direction, and this direction is irreversible. Historical time moves ahead toward something new. To the question, "toward what does history run?" the Christian answer is, "toward the realization of the kingdom of God through and above history."

History is disrupted into innumerable large and small, comparatively independent, historical movements, in different sections of the world, in different periods of time. The question is: If we say "the history," do we not presuppose a unity of history? But this unity is never actual. There are always divergent tendencies. There is always human freedom, which has the power and the possibility of disrupting any preliminary unity of history. Nevertheless, this unity is always intended, and the kingdom of God is a symbol for the unity of history in and above history.

In history there is always a struggle going on between the forces which try to drive toward fulfillment in the kingdom of God and its unity and the forces which try to disrupt this unity and prevent history from moving toward the kingdom of God; or in a religious-mythological language, there are always conflicts going on in history between divine and demonic forces.

From this it follows that in history there is a continuous mixture of good and evil in every group, in every agency which carries the historical process, in every period, in every historical actualization. History has a tragic ambiguity; but the kingdom of God is the symbol for an *un*ambiguous situation, a purification of history, something in which the demonic is conquered, the fulfillment is reached, and the ambiguous is thrown out. In this threefold sense, as fulfillment, unification, and purification of history, the kingdom of God is the answer to the riddles of history.

Of course, the kingdom of God seen in this light is not a *stage* of history. It is not a utopia which is somewhere and nowhere. There is no such stage, even in the farthest future of history, because history is always a battlefield of divine and demonic forces. However, history is running *toward* the kingdom of God. Fulfillment transcends history, but it is fulfilled *through* history.

The second statement about the Christian interpretation of history is that the historical representative of the kingdom of God, in so far as it fights in history, is the Christian Church. The Christian Church, the embodiment of the New Being in a community, represents the kingdom of God in history. The Church itself is not the kingdom of God, but it is its agent, its anticipation, its fragmentary realization. It is fighting in history, and since it represents the kingdom of God it can be distorted but it can never be conquered.

The third statement about the Christian interpretation of history is that the moment in which the meaning of history becomes fully manifest is to be called the center of history, and that this center is the New Being in Jesus as the Christ. In this center the contradictions of historical existence are overcome, in "beginning and power."

The fourth statement about the Christian interpretation of history is that history is divided by the center of history into two main sections, the period before the center and the period after the center. However, this is true in a different way for different people and different nations. Many people, even today, are still living *before* the event of Jesus as the Christ; others, those who have accepted Jesus as the Christ, are living *after* the center of history. The period before the manifestation of the center of history either in history universally, or in particular individuals, nations, and groups, can be called the period in which the bearer of the kingdom of God in history is latent. It is the period of the latency of the Church, the period in which the coming of the Church is prepared in all nations. This is true of paganism, of Judaism, and of humanism. In all three groups and forms of human existence, the Church is not yet manifest, but it is latently present, and it prepares for the coming of the center of history. Then, after the center of history has come and after it has been received by pagans, Jews, and humanists, there is a Christian church in its manifest state, in a state which is no longer preparation, but reception, namely reception of the New Being in Jesus as the Christ.

From this fundamental statement issues directly the meaning of missions. Missions is that activity of the Church by which it works for the transformation of its own latency into its own manifestation all over the world. This is a statement with many implications.

The first consequences are critical consequences, namely, critical against misinterpretations of the meaning of missions. One should not understand missions in a lower sense than this just mentioned. First of all, one should not misunderstand missions as an attempt to save from eternal damnation as many individuals as possible among the nations of the world. Such an interpretation of the meaning of missions presupposes a separation of individual from individual, a separation of the individual from the social group to which he belongs, and it presupposes an idea of predestination which actually excludes most human beings from eternal salvation and gives hope for salvation only to the few—comparatively few, even if it is millions—who are actually reached by the message of Jesus as the Christ. Such an idea is unworthy of the glory and of the love of God and must be rejected in the name of the true relationship of God to his world.

An attempt to interpret the meaning of missions was made by nineteenth-century liberal theology in the idea that missions is a cross-fertilization of cultures. With the primitive cultures it is not so much a cross-fertilization as a transformation into higher cultures. But missions is not a *cultural* function; it is rather the function of the Church to spread all over the world. It is one of the functions of extension of the Church, of its growth; and it is—as growth is generally—an element of a living being without which he finally must die. This is quite different from the idea of cross-fertilization. Cross-fertilization can only claim that the limited values of one culture should be completed by the limited values of another culture. But cultures come and go, and the question of the meaning of history transcends any culture and any cultural cross-fertilization. Therefore, since missions is supposed to contribute an *answer* to the meaning of history, the suggested answer of "cross-fertilization" becomes utterly inadequate.

Moreover, missions is not an attempt to unite the different religions. If this were the function of missions, a uniting point, or center, would have to exist. Then, however, *this* uniting center would be the center of history, and the Christ would become "decentralized." He would no longer be the center; but the center would be that which is above him and also above Buddha, Mohammed, and Confucius. The Christian Church would then be *one* religious group among others, but it would not be the agency of the kingdom of God, as we have described it and as it has always felt itself to be.

According to Christian conviction, the Christ is *the* center of history and therefore the uniting point in which all religions can be united after they have been subjected to the criticism of the power of the New Being which is in the Christ. Therefore, we must say that missions is neither the attempt to save individual souls, nor an attempt at cultural cross-fertilization, nor an attempt to unite the world religions. Rather, it is the attempt to transform the latent Church—which is present in the world religions, in paganism, Judaism, and humanism—into something new: the New Reality in Jesus as the Christ. Transformation is the meaning of missions. Thus the mission is a function which belongs to the Church itself, and it is a basic element in the life of the Church.

This transformation is one from the Church in its latency, in its hiddenness under the forms of paganism, Judaism, and humanism, into its manifestation. This refers not only to the nations and groups *outside* of the Christian nations but also to the Christian nations themselves. There must always be missions—or attempts to transform the preparatory state into the manifest state of the Church, not only outside but within the Christian orbit. This is because there is always paganism, Judaism, and humanism in the midst of the Christian nations themselves.

The transformation of the state of latency into one of actualization is a necessary function of the Church. It is a function which is always present and which has never been missing. There were periods, of course, in which there were no official institutions for missions. However, while institutions are historically changing, functions are unchangeable as long as there is a Church, because functions belong to the essence of the Church. Even in periods in which the mission toward those outside the Christian orbit was very small, it was never completely lacking, because there were always contacts between Christians and non-Christians. Where there are contacts, there is witness to Christianity, and where there is witness to Christianity, implicitly there is missionary activity. In this sense it can be said that the process of transformation is always going on; it is going on both within and outside the Christian nations and cultures. The claim of the Church that Jesus as the Christ is the bringer of the New Reality for mankind is identical with the demand made upon the Church to spread itself all over the world. And that is what missions does.

Now we consider this transformation in its theological meaning. There was a discussion, especially in the last period of liberal theology, about the absoluteness of Christianity. Is Christianity the absolute religion? Is Christ the center of history? Is he the bringer of the New Being? Or are the other religions of equal value and does each culture have its own proper religion? According to these ideas, Christianity belongs to the Western world and it should not interfere with the religious developments of the Eastern world. This, of course, would deny the claim that Jesus is the Christ, the bringer of the New Being. It would make this statement obsolete, because he who brings the New Being is not a relative figure but an absolute figure of an all-embracing character. The New Being is one, as being-itself is one.

The universality of the Christian message, its universal claim, includes what has been called by a not-too-happy term, the "absoluteness of Christianity." Let me call it its *universality*. Now how can you prove today as a Christian, or as a theologian, that the Christian message is universal and valid for all cultures and religions so that Christ must become what he potentially is, the center of history for *all* historical developments? How can you prove this? Obviously the answer is that you cannot prove it at all in terms of a theoretical analysis, for the criteria used in order to prove that Christianity is universal are themselves taken from Christianity. Therefore, they do not prove anything except for those who are within the Christian circle. There is no theoretical argument which can give the proof of the universality of Christianity and the claim that Jesus is the Christ. Only missions can provide that proof. Missionary work is that work in which the potential universality of Christianity becomes evident day by day, in which the universality is actualized with every new success of the missionary endeavor. The action of missions gives the pragmatic proof of the universality of Christianity. It is a *pragmatic* proof. It is the proof, as the Bible calls it, of power and Spirit. It is not a theoretical proof which you can give sitting in your chair, looking at history; but if you are in the same historical situation as missions, then you offer a *continuous* proof, one which is never finished. The element of faith is always present, and faith is a risk. But a risk must be justified, and that is what missions does. It shows that Jesus as the Christ and the New Being in him has the power to conquer the world. In conquering the world, missions is the continuous pragmatic test of the universality of the Christ, of the truth of the Christian assertion that Jesus is the Christ.

In the same way, missions bears witness on behalf of the Church as the agency of the conquering kingdom of God. This also cannot be proved in abstract theoretical concepts. Only missions can prove that the Church is the agent through which the kingdom of God continuously actualizes itself in history. Missionaries come to a country in which the Church is still in latency. In this situation the manifest Church opens up what is potentially given in the different religions and cultures outside Christianity. In some way and on some level, every human being is longing for a new reality in contrast to the distorted reality in which he is living. People are not *outside* of God; they are *grasped* by God on the level in which they *can* be grasped—in their experience of the Divine, in the realm of holiness in which they are living, in which they are educated, in which they have performed acts of faith and adoration and prayer and cult, even though the symbols in which the Holy is expressed may seem extremely primitive and idolatrous. It is distorted religion, but it is not nonreligion. It is the reality of the Divine preparing in paganism for the coming of the manifest Church, and, through the manifest Church, the coming of the kingdom of God. This alone makes missions possible. One might call this preparation —which we find in all nations—the "Old Testament" for these nations. But I hesitate to do so, because the term "Old Testament" is used ordinarily, and rightly, for a very special preparation, namely for the preparation of the coming of Christ as the center of history through the elected nation.

This leads me to the second consideration: the Church is latent also in the elected nation, i.e., in Judaism. It is prepared in it so that it can become manifest in it, but it is not yet manifest in it in the full sense of the word. It drives toward manifestation; and certainly the community of the Jewish nation and the community of the synagogue into which Jesus was born are preparatory stages for the coming of the center of history, the Church, and the kingdom of God. But they remain preparatory. They anticipate, in prophetism; and they actualize, fragmentarily and with many distortions, in legalism. However, they are not the manifest Church; they are still the latent Church. If Christianity comes to them, they might or might not accept the transformation out of latency into manifestation. We know that what in some forms of paganism is comparatively easy is in Judaism almost impossible. Paul had this experience. He writes in Romans 9–11 (one of the great and rare pieces of an interpretation of history in the New Testament) about the question of missions toward the Jews. He believed that this mission to the Jews would not succeed until the pagans would have become members of the manifest Church. One of the great problems of missions toward the Jews today is that we often have the feeling that it is by historical providence that the Jews have an everlasting function in history. "Ever" means as long as there is still history and, therefore, paganism. The function of Judaism would be to criticize, in the power of the prophetic spirit, those tendencies in Christianity which drive toward paganism and idolatry. Judaism always stood against them as a witness and as a critic, and perhaps it is the meaning of historical providence that this shall remain so, as long as there is history. Individual Jews will always come to Christianity; but the question whether Christianity should try to convert Judaism as a whole is at least an open question, and a question about which many Biblical theologians of today are extremely skeptical. I leave that question open. I myself, in the light of my many contacts and friendships with Jews, am inclined to take the position that one should be open to the Jews who come to us wanting to become Christians. Yet one should not try to convert them; rather, we should subject ourselves as Christians to the criticism of their prophetic tradition.

The third group in which we have the latent Church is humanism. I think not only of Greek, Roman, and Asiatic humanism but also of humanism within the Christian nations. There are many people who are critical of Church, Christianity, and religion generally. Many times this criticism comes from the latent Church, is directed against the manifest Church, and is often effected through the power of principles which belong to, and should be effective in, the manifest Church itself. Nevertheless, in spite of the important function of the latent Church, it is never the last stage. That which is latent must become manifest, and there is often a hidden desire on the part of people who belong to the latent Church to become members of the manifest Church. This can happen, however, only if the manifest Church accepts the criticism which comes from the latent Church.

These foregoing remarks show that missions is by no means one-sided. There is also missions to the Christians by those non-Christians to whom Christian missions are addressed. What Christian missions have to offer is not Christianity—certainly not American, German, or British Christianity—but the message of Jesus as the Christ, of the New Being. It is the message about Jesus as the center of history which, day by day, is confirmed by missions. However, it is *not* Christianity as a historical reality that is this center of history. The goal of missions is the mediation of a reality which is the criterion for *all* human history. This criterion not only stands critically against paganism, Judaism, and humanism wherever it may be, but it also stands critically against Christianity, outside and inside the Christian nations. All mankind stands under the judgment of the New Being in Christ.

A final point must be made in praise of what missions has done, and is doing, in creating churches in sections of the world which are outside the Western cultural orbit, making it possible to offset the unconscious arrogance of much Christian missionary work. This is that unconscious arrogance which assumes that Christianity, as it has developed in the Western world, is the reality of the New Being in Christ. It is only *one* of its expressions, a preliminary one, a transitory one, as was Greek Christianity, Roman Christianity, and Medieval Christianity. It is not the end. These new Christian churches provide another great proof for Jesus' being the center of history. They demonstrate that his message and the New Being in him is able to overcome not only the resistance of those outside Christianity but also the unconscious and almost unavoidable arrogance of those churches which carry out the missionary work. The fact that there are new churches in another cultural orbit, developing their independence and resisting the identification of the kingdom of God with any special form of Christianity, is perhaps the greatest triumph of Christian missions.

Conflict in Mission: Historical and Separatist Churches

BY CHRISTIAN G. BAËTA

In this essay, which is written against the general background of West Africa, with Ghana particularly in mind, the term *historical churches* is used to indicate the older, on the whole larger and more firmly established, churches that have resulted from the labors of Western missions over the past century and a half or so. They have been constituted as African churches with preponderantly African leadership. The term *separatist churches* signifies those bodies that have more recently come into being and exhibit certain special features which make them stand apart from the main stream of Christianity as known and practiced across the world and through the centuries. They are usually referred to as "sects," but this designation is avoided here because it is known to be repugnant to their leaders, who much prefer them to be known as "churches."

Of the separatist churches there are those which have been initiated and are still supported, even actually run, by foreign agencies (American and British), while others have arisen from indigenous African prophetism. In order not to blur the confrontation, only the latter are taken into account in the present essay, since they are furthest removed from the historical churches. It is here intended neither to attempt a full characterization of these churches nor to discuss any of the topics of general interest that are usually raised in regard to them, such as their relation to the impact of modern Western civilization and to emergent African nationalism. The sole object of this writing is merely to try to clarify some of the problems which confront the historical churches as they consider what their attitude should be toward this other important and rapidly growing group.

On the whole the separatist churches lean so heavily on the strong personalities of their leaders that some have judged them to be only a passing phenomenon. Indeed, several have already come and gone. It must be borne in mind, however, that whatever the stability and duration of particular churches might be, there is no reason to suppose that the end of the separatist movement itself, as such, it anywhere in sight. On the contrary, if the perennial rise and fall of new cults within African paganism is a true parallel, then we are only at the beginning of this sort of development. However, there is immediate and urgent need for the historical churches to make up their minds about the separatist churches and to find a carefully thought-out, acceptable, and Christian *modus vivendi* with them, quite apart from any considerations relating to the future.

On this subject a great wealth of friendly good counsel has already been forthcoming. Generally it has been to the effect that the historical churches should do all in their power to preserve or to attain fellowship with the separatists. The nature of most of this advice suggests, however, that perhaps the real points of difficulty have not been spotted or have not been quite fully understood. To be specific, there have been warnings against adopting attitudes of pharisaic self-righteousness and spiritual superiority; exhortations to a greater humility; to Christian love rather than legal-mindedness; to repentance of all the sins, failures and inadequacies that have driven so many, deeply dissatisfied, right into the arms of the separatist churches; to emulation of the latter's evangelistic zeal and their use of indigenous worship symbols, instead of clinging to quite unsuitable Western patterns. . . . These criticisms doubtless have their justification, but by themselves they can hardly be said to meet the case. As regards the temptation to spiritual pride, in particular, a sufficient chastening and corrective already exists in the sheer apparent success of the groups in question!

This whole matter of what the historical churches are to do about the separatist ones comes to a head, of course, when one or other of the latter seeks admission to a national Christian Council.

This happened in Ghana in 1957, and the reactions on that occasion are perhaps significant and instructive.

At its May sitting of that year, the Executive of the Christian Council of Ghana had before it applications for membership from two of the most important separatist churches in the country. There was no evidence whatever of any of the unchristian and uncharitable attitudes, which are so often feared, for the historical churches; certainly nothing was said even remotely suggesting that the applications should be rejected out of hand. There was rather a sense of embarrassment, of almost complete unpreparedness for the question, and uncertainty about the best line of answer. A proposal that the applicants should be requested to submit statements of their doctrinal positions was soon abandoned. It was felt that this would not be a fruitful approach since, as a rule, separatist churches simply continued to profess the doctrine taught by the historical church with which their founder was connected, without strict regard to its relation with their practice.

It was emphasized that, whatever the final decision eventually reached on the applications, the Council had a plain and inescapable duty to help these bodies find their way into the main stream of Christian faith and practice, if only they would be willing to accept such help.[1] Then, in view of the quite obvious lack of any information on them beyond vague generalizations and impressions, it was decided that the Council should seek, both by observation and by interviewing the leaders, to acquaint itself fully with all the relevant facts before the matter was further discussed.

These applications still await a definite decision and reply. While the Council is eager to exercise Christian charity and to seize the proffered hand of fellowship, it must take into serious considera-

[1] In fact, this thought was only a pious hope. It is hard to see how the historical churches could have afforded any such assistance without appearing to condemn and to instruct. Since self-confidence and even pride in one's own religious convictions is no monopoly of any group, and bearing in mind the well-known temper of the separatist churches in disputation, anyone can see how no positive result could be expected from such an approach. The Professor of Divinity of the University College, Dr. N. Q. King, came to the rescue by inviting leaders of the more prominent separatist churches to attend the annual Refresher Course held for ministers and clergy and any others with an interest in theological studies. Again, although at first there were looks of frank surprise and puzzlement, no "superior airs" were discernible. The first-timers were pleasant but uncommunicative.

tion the far-reaching implications of such an association as is proposed. It is quite clear that, apart from greatly enhancing the standing of the suppliant churches in the eyes of their own people and of the general public, thus lending support to their views, their affiliation with the Council cannot do otherwise than cause ordinary Christians to conclude that the differences between the two groups of churches are of small importance and may be ignored. Obviously the Council would not be acting responsibly if it permitted this opinion to be formed without itself being fully convinced of its truth.

A closer look would reveal that, although both groups use the common Christian name, the substance of the religion taught by each is so different from the other that the question seems justified: are they even basically engaged upon the same business? The Christianity taught by the historical churches is a message calling men to repentance of their sin and to a life of faith. If sin is in essence rebellion against God, faith is complete trust in Him through our Lord Jesus Christ, and absolute dependence upon him in all one's affairs, both for this world and for the hereafter. This faith expresses itself in a life lived in God's forgiveness and grace (which are made available to man through the atoning work of Christ) and dedicated to the performing of God's will. Its objective is man's constant fellowship and communion with God, and the means of its nurture are the Word of God, worship, and (with most churches) the sacraments. As St. Paul sums it up, the "Gospel," i.e., Christianity, "is the power of God for salvation" (Rom. 1:16), in other words, God's answer to man's true and deepest need.

The Christianity offered by the separatist churches may be described as a power for overcoming the ills of the secular aspect of life. Human need is conceived almost entirely in terms of these ills. While such terms as "sin," "grace," "the precious blood of our Lord and Saviour Jesus Christ," and other Christian themes are constantly spoken about, the central preoccupation is and remains how to cope effectively with the ills of worldly life. For instance, "sin" is really relevant only in so far as it is a potent cause of bodily, mental, and social disorders; the significance of "the blood of Christ" resides in the fact that, by doing away with sin, it prepares the way for, or itself directly effects, bodily healing; "faith" is to entertain no inward doubt whatsoever that the particular help sought will be received. The "Gospel" here may be summed up in the actual words of a very typical separatist-church public invitation:

> Bring all your worries of unemployment, poverty, witch troubles, ill-luck, enemy, barrenness, sickness, blindness, lameness, sorrow. Jesus is ready to save all who come to him in belief and faith. "Let him who hears say, 'Come.' And let him who is thirsty come, let him who desires take the Water of life [2] without price" (Rev. 22:17). "Him who comes to me I will not cast out" (Jn. 6:37b).

The petitions which are brought to the separatist churches, and with which they concern themselves above everything else, are precisely the same as those traditionally submitted in indigenous African religion, whether in its unadulterated form or in such modern syncretistic forms as the Tigari cult.[3] Church services of "witness" are regularly held in which members give testimonies about the granting of such requests. The nature of the hopes held out must provide an answer to those who wonder why historical church workers do not appear to be able to attract such large crowds as the separatists can draw. But the far more important questions are, of course: Is this the true essence of Christianity? Is it legitimate to present what are merely some of the beneficial by-products, as the whole thing?

Again the separatist churches observe a large number of special customs, rites, and ceremonies, particularly ecstatic dancing and various fasts and taboos. Now if these were considered as mere aids to worship, or forms of giving expression to religious sentiment, or esthetics, there would not be any difficulty at all, and the only problem presented would be how to "baptize into Christianity" such of them as might not be considered to be quite suitable at first. However, that is not so; rather, a very special meaning attaches to these practices. They are looked upon as necessary techniques whereby the coveted blessings are secured. For example, ecstasy

[2] In the particular separatist church concerned, as in several others, "blessed" or "holy" water plays a crucial role, and the public advertisement quoted goes on to ask all comers to bring each "one white bottle filled with water." This is blessed in the service and then taken home for use.

[3] An account of this cult is given in James B. Christensen: "The Tigari Cult of West Africa," in *Papers of the Michigan Academy of Science, Arts and Letters* (1953 meeting), Vol. XXXIX (1954).

is necessary because it is in this condition that contact is made with the supernatural power and the desired healing is obtained. The dance which induces ecstasy is therefore no mere jubilation before the Lord, but a calculated means of obtaining a benefit. These ideas, familiar in indigenous African religion, are regarded by the historical churches as false.

As in African religion, the blame for failure to obtain requests is firmly fixed on some fault in the petitioner himself or in the performance of the observances prescribed for him. With the separatist churches failure is chiefly ascribed to lack of "faith" in the sense above described, or to refusal by the petitioner to confess some secret sin. But it is confidently taught that, if all is in order on the petitioner's side, then his wish cannot otherwise but be granted.

It must be clearly understood, however, that the separatist churches name and appeal to the Christian God alone, whereas in African religion, naturally, it is the various deities and other supernatural forces recognized that are addressed. This is the big and a very real difference, but it is also perhaps the only one discernible.

Another great stumbling block to fellowship between the two groups of churches is the question of polygamy. This was a sore point when Christianity was first preached in Africa south of the Sahara. It is still a sore point today. As far back as 1938, on the occasion of the Tambaram Conference of the International Missionary Council, the historical churches instructed their delegate to get a clear ruling from this world assembly of Christians on this burning issue. The question went right to the heart of the matter and the answer was unequivocal.

> At the instance of the churches in the Gold Coast . . . the question is raised as to whether monogamy is essential to Christianity or is merely a factor in European civilisation—whether in the practice of polygamy there is something radically incompatible with a vital faith in Christ, and living of a true life in fellowship with Him. . . . Monogamy is not a mere factor of civilisation; it is vital to the life of the Church and its value has been realised in its own experiences; it was taught by the Lord Himself and has Scriptural authority behind it (Eph. 5:31–33; 1 Tim. 3:12, 5:9). Both for men and for women polygamy militates against the attainment of the fulness of life which is in Christ. . . .[4]

[4] From *The World Mission of the Church* (London: I.M.C., 1939), pp. 157 f.

All the separatist churches admit polygamy,[5] not indeed as a concession or in order to seduce members from the historical churches, but because they believe that the position of the latter is in this regard, within the African context, entirely mistaken. In a statement of faith one of them, the Musama Disco Christo Church, declares: "We believe that (as an African Church) polygamy is not a moral sin."

Of course this debate goes on; it has recently called forth some rethinking on the part of missionaries and ex-missionaries. For example, Gunnar Helander writes: "Is monogamy an inalienable part of Christianity, or is it founded on a historical development, a Roman-European tradition?", which would appear to be precisely the same question as was put at Tambaram. He goes on to say: "What have we done to the Africans in the name of Christianity? Polygamy, which Christ does not forbid, we have fought against as the greatest of all evils, but divorce and remarriage, which He does forbid, we have introduced." [6] In a private letter my attention has been drawn to a recent book in German in which Traugott Bachmann, a former missionary to the Nyika in Eastern Africa, appears to have expressed identical or very similar views.[7] There have been others who have done the same.

A striking contribution to the discussion, not only of the polygamy issue but also of the main subject of the present essay, was recently made in an interchange of views privately circulated.[8] Questioning whether polygamy could be more important than other issues between the churches—religious ones such as the ministry and the sacraments, and moral ones such as ("the not-so-distant") slavery and war—it points out that whereas the churches holding opposing views might regard each other's positions as defective, dangerous, and in need of improvement, yet they do not for that

[5] From my reading I gather that in some West African countries some separatist churches do not permit polygamy. That is not the case in Ghana. The only possible exception is a body which insists that it is merely a society within one of the historical churches, though it has adopted several of the practices which are features of separatist churches. But it continues in communion with its mother historical church, and thus cannot be counted with the separatist churches.

[6] In *Must We Introduce Monogamy* (Pietermaritzburg: 1958).

[7] *Ich gab manchen Anstoss* (Leipzig: Verlag Koehler & Amelang, 1957).

[8] I refrain from quoting author and source because there has not been time to seek and obtain permission to do so.

reason unchurch one another by refusing to sit together in joint councils. In other words, on what grounds are polygamists shut out of councils in which Quakers and Church of England, Salvation Army, pacifist and nonpacifist churches are equally admitted?

If Christian Europe has not yet been able to abandon the system of war, have the churches from Europe (or America, etc.) any clear grounds for demanding that all African churches must abandon the system of polygamy before they can be recognized as churches? If we make this demand, then by what theological criteria are we defining the Church? Are we making monogamy into a new "note" or "mark" of the Church, as One, Holy, Catholic, Apostolic, and Monogamous?

This author proceeds, doubtless with his tongue in his cheek:

Recognition of churches *as* churches must be made at the proper theological level, with due realization that we are churches by the grace of God and in spite of our many defects. In fact, to believe that the Church is One, and to describe it in terms of the Biblical image as the Bride of Christ, invites the devastating suggestion that our very multiplicity is a form of blasphemous polygamy, wherein we are all seeking to be the separate bride of Christ! And if we are so sure of Christ's attitude to monogamous marriage, are we equally sure of his attitude to our present ecclesiastically polygamous state?

Another writer opines that all the early missionaries needed to do was to get their converts to admit that monogamy was the "goal"; they should never have gone beyond that to attempt to interfere with and control the matrimonial customs of people of a different culture.

Of course all this is interesting and thought-provoking. At Tambaram the representatives of African churches asked for a thorough research to be undertaken into the whole field of African marriage and its relation to the Christian Church. In due course a scholarly volume was produced.[9] In the light of the apparent new trend in missionary thinking indicated above, perhaps there is room for a competent reexamination of the entire subject of the theology of Christian marriage. For their part, however, the historical churches face two quite simple but very hard facts. In

[9] *Survey of African Marriage and Family Life,* ed. and with an introduction by Arthur Phillips (Oxford University Press, 1953). A summary and brief discussion of some points in this volume is provided in the I.M.C. Research Pamphlets No. 1, *African Marriage* by T. Price (London: SCM Press, 1954).

the first place, whatever the early missions should have done, actually they unanimously and consistently taught monogamy as an essential element of the Christian family. In fact this is one of the few points upon which there was no dissension among them at all. It is the heritage, it is that which the historical churches have received and seek to pass on, and this fact is not altered even by pointing out that probably the reason was merely the common Western cultural background.

Secondly, there can be no reasonable doubt that the affiliation of the separatist churches would mean the acceptance of the practice of polygamy for all church members. How could there be an association of churches in the same council, in which some approved polygamy and others did not permit it?

Thus the divergency between the positions of the two groups, both in religious belief and in morality, is very serious indeed. Doctrinally it is not merely a matter of holding different views on certain particular aspects (e.g., the ministry and sacraments) of fundamentally the same faith, rather it is two totally different understandings of what the Christian religion is, to start with, and of precisely what men are about when they set out to practice it. In other words, it is not a case of parting company somewhere along the road and coming together again further on, but one of starting from two entirely different points and never really meeting at all. To represent a minor part as the whole is impermissible because the resulting distortion may be very bad and most harmful. In this case, it threatens to stunt spiritual growth.

Furthermore, in the ethical sphere, dissension on such an all-important matter as the family, the continuing, God-ordained basis and source of the presence of the human race upon earth, may not rightly be regarded as being of the same level of significance as differences of opinion upon such an abnormal thing as war, or upon a passing economic and social fashion as was slavery, very wicked though it certainly was.

These deep disagreements at utterly crucial points, each by itself and cumulatively, indeed made it seem unlikely that the proposed association will be judged to be feasible at the present stage. Yet the search continues for some answer other than a simple rejection. It is a painful and burdensome thing not to be able to join up with brothers calling upon the same Name, who are so earnest in their purpose, so devoted to the Bible, so persevering in many good works, so eagerly expectant for the miracles of God to happen. Hard thinking on these matters must go on, but more needed still are many prayers that God would grant ever deeper insights on both sides, which, working from within each group, will gradually cause the existing barriers to crumble.

Further Toward a Theology of Mission *

BY WILHELM ANDERSEN

The theme of this essay refers to the theological discussion which took place in connection with the World Missionary Conference in Willingen, Germany (1952) and which is still continuing.[1] Willingen took a decisive step further on the way toward a reformulation of the theology of mission. Recognitions were expressed there that are valid for the missionary activity of all of Christianity. Therefore they must not be left forgotten in the past, but they must be thought through and discussed again and again so that they bear fruit in the life of the Church and for her service in the world.

The special formulation of the theme, "*Further* Toward a Theology of Mission," directs our thoughts, however, at the same time in another direction. We must go forward on the way which Willingen started. Many questions remained unanswered there. This may be because there was not enough time for discussing them. On the other hand it must be taken into account that there was not yet any unanimity for answering them. The precondition for further fruitful work on these remaining open questions is that all the churches and missions that participated in the conference at

* Translated by Joseph Cottrell Weber

[1] This essay is directly related to the writer's study for the International Missionary Council entitled *Towards a Theology of Mission* (London: SCM Press, 1955).

Willingen remain concerned with the matter and in contact with one another. Remaining concerned with the matter means that the results of Willingen must be recognized and assimilated. The contact between the various churches and confessions must be maintained so that they can mutually help one another to go the way which the living God through his Holy Spirit wants to lead the Church in the world. For the following exposition there is then a double task. We will recall once again the result of Willingen. In the second part we will attempt to indicate some milestones along the future way.

I

The basic and decisive recognition for a theology of missions consists in this: *Mission has its source in the Triune God.*

> Out of the depths of his love for us, the Father has sent forth his own beloved Son to reconcile all things to himself, that we and all men might, through the Spirit, be made one in him with the Father in that perfect love which is the very nature of God.[2]

The sentence "Mission is the work of the Triune God" must not be understood, however, as an abstract, timeless truth. Mission is as *missio Dei,*[3] the original and at the same time the continually new working of the Triune God who turns to man and to the world. God is the living God, who is Himself Light and Life. As such, He is also a movement toward man and the world, spreading light and life.

It should not be forgotten that this sentence also contains a certain criticism of the theme of Willingen, which was "The Missionary Obligation of the Church." But it is a constructive criticism and, therefore, one which leads further. The proclamation of "the missionary obligation of the Church" should in no way be revoked. It is valid and urgent. But it is decisive that it be understood in the right relationship and in the context which is valid for it. The admonition of J. C. Hoekendijk that "Every Church-centered theory of mission is bound to go astray because it revolves around

[2] "A Statement on the Missionary Calling of the Church," in *Missions Under the Cross,* edited by Norman Goodall (London: Edinburgh House Press, 1953), p. 189. This statement arose out of the report of Group I at Willingen.

[3] See the introduction to a theology of mission under this title: *Missio Dei* by Georg F. Vicedom (München: Chr. Kaiser Verlag, 1958).

an illegitimate center,"[4] will always remain connected with the conference in Willingen. Willingen has taught us to see mission, "the missionary obligation of the Church," from the standpoint where it is valid: from the Triune God, whose creation and instrument in the world is the Church of Jesus Christ.

If this recognition is rightly respected and thought through in its consequences, it can be effective in opening up the way for the future. This is particularly true for the proposed integration of the International Missionary Council with the World Council of Churches. There must be no opportunity for human claims to rule or for attempts at guardianship. Mission is the work of God and takes place only under God's guardianship. There must be room in the Church only for that striving which calls for submission in obedience to God's working.

The sentence which characterizes mission as the work of the Triune God was interpreted at Willingen in an important way: *the decisive act of God, the fulfillment of His missionary will, is the Cross of Jesus Christ.* The center of a theology of mission is, therefore, faith in the crucified and risen Christ. The address of Canon Max A. C. Warren on "The Christian Mission and the Cross" was one of the high points of the Willingen Conference. At no other of the earlier international conferences on missions did the Cross of Jesus Christ stand so very much in the center as at Willingen. If we want to recognize mission as the work of God and if we want to let it be true and valid, then we must learn ever anew to see it from the standpoint of the Cross. Karl Hartenstein, one of the German participants, expressed what this means in a report on Willingen shortly before his death:

> The Cross of Christ is both the sign of God's grace and power, the divine act of forgiveness and of conquest over the opposing powers and spirits. The Crucified is the victor. The Christian fellowship [*Gemeinde*] is caught up into his victory and is commissioned with the proclamation of that victory. The Cross as the sign of the hiddenness of the lordship of God is at the same time the sign of the coming triumph of God and as such is the only key to the interpretation of the present world situation.[5]

[4] "The Church in Missionary Thinking," *International Review of Missions,* Vol. XLI (1952), p. 332.

[5] Walter Freytag, Karl Hartenstein, et al., *Mission zwischen Gestern und Morgen* (Stuttgart: Evangelischer Missionsverlag, 1952), p. 61.

These two sentences, "Mission is *missio Dei*" and "The Cross of Jesus Christ is the center of mission," belong indissolubly together. They mutually explain and interpret each other. If the second sentence does not follow the first, there exists the danger of making a timeless speculation out of the truth of *missio Dei*. The Cross stands in the middle of history and calls us to take and accept history seriously. We can only talk about the source of mission in the Triune God because He has intervened in history through the death and resurrection of Jesus Christ to change the fate of the world. And thereby He has allowed faith to look into His heart.

> The Cross is the illuminating center of the mystery of God's redemptive purpose. It is there that we begin to look into the heart of God, begin to believe that some understanding is possible, even for us, of the mystery of redemption. And it is by way of the Cross that we are compelled to see both the necessity for showing forth that redemption and also the manner of the showing.[6]

For a theology of mission, then, the limits are set. Mission is completely and fully the work of God. It is His work that He has carried out and is carrying out in our world. It is directed to us men and allows no one the possibility of neutrality. It is above all the work for which the Triune God alone is responsible. He guarantees its final success. Through the incarnation, crucifixion, and resurrection of Jesus Christ God has created realities in the course of this world which are immovable. After God followed the sending of His Son with the sending of His Holy Spirit, He began with the founding of the Church to free and claim men for His coming kingdom. Therefore all the mission work of the Church lives in a certainty which can be shaken neither by human omission nor guilt, neither by any earthly failure: He will gloriously carry out His work. It is one of the happy tasks of a theology of mission to communicate to the work of the world mission something of the confidence with which the Apostle Paul embraces the way and the future of God's people (Rom. 11). God remains true to Himself; He has founded His covenant (Rom. 11:27). He cannot revoke His gifts nor His call (Rom. 11:29). "For from him and through him and to him are all things. To him be glory forever. Amen" (Rom. 11:36).

[6] Max A. C. Warren, "The Christian Mission and the Cross," in *Missions Under the Cross, op. cit.*, p. 25.

But mission is at the same time the work of God in the world which He shares with men as His instruments. Not as if God needed a human counselor or a human assistant. It is rather much more a sign of His greatness which condescends to man, when God not only wins men for His kingdom, but even takes them into His service, bestowing upon them and honoring them with His Spirit to be His fellow workers (1 Cor. 3:9).

Here in a theology of mission is the context in which one must speak about the Church. The Church is both a coming together and a sending forth (*Sammlung und Sendung*). As the people of God which have been assembled among the peoples of the earth for the coming kingdom, we may speak—with reservation—of the Church as the goal of mission. In her services of worship, where the praise of God is already being sung, we see that for which God wishes to redeem creation. The final and real goal of the *missio Dei,* however, is not the Church, but the establishment of God's kingdom, to which the Church as *ecclesia viatorem* is on its way. Therefore, the Church does not understand herself and misses the meaning of her existence if she is not at the same time a sending forth. She is God's summons in the world, the company of followers who assemble around the flag of Christ, whom they believe and confess as the real Lord among lords and King of kings. She is—not out of her own strength but in the authority of the Holy Spirit—His mouthpiece in the world, through which He himself wishes to speak; His instrument through which He carries out His work. And in this sense it is essential to speak of the missionary obligation of the Church, because it pleases God through the Church to lead His mission to its goal.

Thus the theology of mission is presented with its other task. It must be for the thought and life of the Church the same thing that movement is for the works of a clock. The Church of Jesus Christ lives only in movement. She stops being what she through the will of God is and should be if she no longer lives in sending forth and no longer carries out mission. She herself lives from the fact—and only from this fact—that she is on her way with the Word which God has entrusted to her and which addresses the world and which presses its way through to all peoples.

Not only do the present organized churches need such a service through a theology of mission, but also the institutions, societies, and officials which have in times past taken up the cause of mission.

Bishop L. Newbigin in his essay, "One Body, One Gospel, One World," [7] has pointed to this with great emphasis and seriousness: "There is a very natural human desire that things should always remain unchanged." From this desire no human society or organization is excepted. "But to succumb to this is death." This must be considered above all in regard to the planned integration of the International Missionary Council with the World Council of Churches. Here is presented—we dare to say, here God Himself presents—a great chance for the Church and mission. But here also lurk grave dangers.

> There is a real danger that the discussion of the proposal for integration should become entirely absorbed in the details of organization, and that the larger questions concerning the Church's faithfulness to its missionary calling should be forgotten.[8]

It certainly does not lie in the power of man to avoid these threatening temptations. If God Himself were not active here, and if we could no longer have the certainty that God Himself comes closest to His goal through the Church and mission which have existed in history, we would stand before a hopeless undertaking. But this confidence is assured us. And therefore the theology of mission has now in the time before us a task full of promise.

II

After having discussed mainly the results of Willingen in the first part of this essay, we now turn our attention in another direction. The theme "Further Toward a Theology of Mission" reminds us that we cannot look back to the theology of mission as to a task that has in every aspect been completed. That will never be the case, or only when we have come from believing to seeing, when our understanding is no longer in part, but when we understand as we are understood (1 Cor. 13:12). The theology of mission is, like all theological thinking, a kind of reflection (*Nachdenken*), a miserable sketching of the ways of God which is never fully adequate nor directly to the point. But God has bid us do it and God does not let it take place without His promise.

We agree with Bishop L. Newbigin when he says that a theology

[7] Lesslie Newbigin, *One Body, One Gospel, One World: the Christian Mission Today* (London: I.M.C., 1958).

[8] *Ibid.*, p. 7.

of mission lives from studying the Bible. It must continually carry on this study and thereby prove itself authentic. "In every age we have to go back to God's revelation of Himself to learn afresh, by the guiding of the Spirit, what is our duty for today." [9] That, naturally, cannot mean that the trinitarian source, the Christological realization, nor the pneumatic fulfillment of mission, i.e., the foundations of mission, must continually be theologically questioned. This foundation has been laid; it rests in the power of God. And as surely as the Bible is the witness to the speaking and acting of the Triune God, so surely does the study of the Scriptures—and this above everything else—help us to perceive that this foundation alone is firm and sturdy.

But it is still the task of a theology of mission to assist in building upon this foundation in obedience to the Spirit; or, to speak with another metaphor, to see that the road which has been prepared is traveled. Dr. Norman Goodall, in his report on Willingen, has named several problems which this conference did not solve and to which a theology of mission should turn its attention.[10] This must be done now for the sake of the missionary enterprise of the Church. The theology of mission wishes to serve the obedient fulfillment of mission. But this service has beyond itself yet another significance. There are a number of problems by which the Church in general is confronted and which can be solved meaningfully only by a theology of mission. This appears to us to be true for two of those problems named by Dr. Goodall with which we wish to deal: the question of the relation between history and salvation-history (*Geschichte und Heilsgeschichte*), and the question of eschatology.

The importance of these two themes becomes apparent in the recent history of the ecumenical movement. At the Evanston Assembly of the World Council of Churches in 1954 eschatology was a central point in the discussions. And the theological preparations for the next plenary session of the World Council, which—God willing—will bring about the integration of the World Council and the International Missionary Council, have already shown that the problem of history and salvation-history forces itself more and more into the foreground. It is true that missionary thinking shows the way both problems can be overcome.

[9] *Ibid.*, p. 17.
[10] *Missions Under the Cross, op. cit.*, pp. 20–22.

We will begin with the first problem named by Dr. Goodall, which will lead us then to the second problem. What relationship and what difference exist between history and salvation-history? We will not deal with this in general, but will specify it as the question of the relation between God's act in creation and God's act in redemption. In my report on Willingen I have already indicated how the two lurking dangers here (i.e., an identification of the act of creation with the act of redemption on one hand, or the assumption of a juxtaposition more or less without any relation, on the other hand) are encountered by a theology of mission which is grounded in the Trinity and made concrete in Christ.[11] But it became clear at the conference in Willingen that there are still unanswered questions here among the churches and missions. It is, therefore, understandable when these questions call for attention in the work of the preparation for the coming conference at New Delhi in 1961. For whoever asks about the Lordship of Christ over the world and the Church cannot escape the question: "How is God's act of creation related to His act of redemption?"

The ecumenical study document on this matter rightly points out that questions are touched here which are closely associated with the various traditional positions and with confessional decisions that have already been made.[12] This makes them difficult, but promising. The various churches have entered into conversation with one another with such an intensity as has never before been the case. This clarification must be carried on theologically. In their discussions the various confessional partners in the conversation are mutually responsible for giving insight into the theological recognitions which they have won and into the spiritual experiences which they have had. If this discussion results in a coming together which is determined by a readiness to learn from one another, then the whole Church can penetrate more deeply into the perception of Truth and, thereby, be led further on the way of Truth.

The assertion of an overlapping unity of God's action upon man and in the world can be variously motivated. It is characteristic of the Anglican position and is theologically grounded in the Incarnation. Naturally, such an opinion is schematic and generalized.

[11] Andersen, *op. cit.*, pp. 50 ff.

[12] See *The Lordship of Christ over the World and the Church,* Documents for an Ecumenical Study (Geneva: World Council of Churches, 1957).

But for a clarification of positions such a simplification is hardly to be avoided. We must, therefore, be concerned to recognize the intention of the respective positions so that we do them justice.

It is a very impressive conception when from the standpoint of the Incarnation, which is understood as the declaration of God's solidarity with the world, the solidarity of the Church with the world is claimed and secular history itself is evaluated as salvation-history. The Church, thereby, becomes in a certain sense a continuation of the Incarnation of Christ. The Church and the kingdom of God draw close together. For in Christ the kingdom has drawn near, he is the *αὐτοβασιλεία*.

The significant lecture by Max A. C. Warren, "The Christian Mission and the Cross," shows the fruitfulness of such thinking for a theology of mission. For Warren, however, something else is characteristic. And this may be helpful in the ecumenical conversation. He sees the Incarnation closely related to the Cross. The Incarnation as declaration of God's solidarity with man has become valid through the power of His oneness with sinners, established and upheld by Christ in his obedience to death on the Cross. One can speak of a solidarity of the Church with the world, and, therefore, of an indissoluble connection between salvation-history and secular history, only in looking at the Cross. The Cross is to be seen as "the place of judgment and of grace, where both the world and the Church are judged and receive forgiveness."

Let it be suggested that a one-sided incarnational theology can conjure up dangerous misunderstandings. The attempt to understand history through the theology of mission should not lead to a general philosophy of history. We *believe* in the *missio Dei* as the meaning and motive of history, but this truth cannot be illuminated by the ways of philosophy. In Warren's thinking, through his strong emphasis on the Cross, such dangerous reflections are subdued but are not completely shut out. Incarnational theology can also lead to shallowness. That takes place when the fact of the Cross of Jesus Christ has only a marginal significance. Mission, which has at its very center the testimony to the act of God in the Cross and resurrection of Jesus Christ, is reduced to a general human declaration of solidarity with the world. It becomes social gospel and falls victim to the secularization against which Warren so emphatically warns us.

In the deliberations at Willingen still another position made its appearance. It was presented by J. C. Hoekendijk, who strongly criticized Anglican mission theology, which is thought out from the standpoint of the Church and the Incarnation. In his opinion a decisive dimension is overlooked, or limited in a way that is inadmissible by the Church: the eschatological dimension of the kingdom of God. According to Hoekendijk, mission means that the Gospel of the kingdom must be proclaimed to the world. This confrontation of the world with the kingdom of God, according to Hoekendijk for a reason different from the Anglican position, leaves no room for a distinction between God's act in creation and redemption. Certainly, the God who lets His kingdom break in upon us with the resurrection of the Crucified is the Creator of the world. He reclaims the world for Himself and for His kingdom with the victory of Christ over sin, death, and the devil. Since the coming of Christ, however, a distinction between history and salvation-history, between the act of creation and the act of redemption, is unreal.

When we attempt to evaluate these respective positions, we perceive a difference of emphasis in Christology. On the one side (in Warren's position, to be sure, wisely corrected), the Incarnation, God's declaration of solidarity with the world in His becoming man in Christ, is evaluated as God's decisive act. Thus the assumption of a continuity of God's action in the world is made possible, which is basic for the Anglican doctrine of Church and Order. At least one component of the doctrine of the historic episcopacy can be seen here. On the other side, all that happened in Christ is interpreted from the standpoint of Easter and the Ascension. This makes necessary an emphatic accentuation of discontinuity. The kingdom of God is breaking in. It calls forth its own witnesses and will succeed in itself through the power of God. But it is the great eschatological factor which corresponds to nothing that is already in the world. The other doctrine of Church and Order which comes from this position is obvious.

If this theological evaluation of the differences is correct, then the way is indicated by which they can be overcome or consolidated. Because Jesus Christ is both the Incarnate Word of God and the Lord who has been raised from the dead and elevated to the right hand of God, both of these positions have the same point of reference. This point of reference, however, is no idea, but the real Jesus Christ. As long as he is considered on both sides, the assurance is given that in the witness to him through the preaching of the Gospel and in the administration of the sacraments the mission of God will continue in the world.

This is a valid consolation. But it does not relieve us of the task of attacking theologically the discrepancy which is apparent here. The theological and missionary insights which were achieved at Willingen can point the way. But they necessitate, on the basis of their trinitarian affirmation, a stronger differentiation in God's action than can be perceived in the two positions sketched above. The endeavor to distinguish correctly between history and salvation-history or between the act of God in creation and in redemption (the two questions, although closely related, are by no means synonymous) has an element of truth in it which cannot be relinquished.

At first it must be said that we cannot expect any theoretical instruction from the Holy Scriptures. The history of God's dealings with men, to which the Scriptures witness, is salvation from the very beginnings which are known to us. God is the Saviour and Redeemer of the people whom He has chosen to be partner in covenant. That is the dominating point of view in the New Testament as well as in the Old Testament.[13] But this very history is only then perceived in its special significance when its vicarious character comes to our view.[14] We see this already in the way in which Genesis 12 explains the beginnings of God's history with Abraham. God called him out of his homeland, away from his friends, out of his father's house, and that means at the same time out of his heathen environment, because He wanted to begin with him a history that would bring about the salvation of all peoples. This history has the character of vicariousness. God is the Creator of heaven and of the earth. Nothing happens without His will. "And he made from one every nation of men to live on all the face of the earth, having determined allotted periods and the boundaries

[13] Cf. Hans Lehmann, "Schöpfergott und Heilsgott im Zeugnis der Bibel," *Evangelische Theologie*, 1951, pp. 97 ff.

[14] See the important study by C. H. Ratshow on "Das Heilshandeln und das Welthandeln Gottes: Gedanken zur Lehrgestaltung des Providentia-Glaubens in der evangelischen Dogmatik," *Neue Zeitschrift für Systematische Theologie*, 1959 (1). This article became known to me only after I had finished the manuscript for this essay. It is very closely concerned with the results of our work and has considerable significance for a reformulation of the theology of mission.

of their habitation" (Acts 17:26). The meaning of the story (or history) of Noah is to testify to the will of God that He wants to spare man his creaturely life in spite of man's evil heart and disobedience against his Creator. This expression of God's will, of course, does not empower us to develop an independent theology of history or a theory of a special action of God in creation. This is not what is meant by the distinction at which Goodall is aiming. The Bible is not interested in this. Whoever asks in such a manner is using false criteria.

But we cannot get around the actuality of a distinction. The history of God with Israel, which reached its culmination and goal in Jesus Christ, is salvation-history in distinction from the history of other peoples, which we believe also to be originally and finally determined by God. It has in its basic structure and in its point of culmination a vicarious character. For, according to the will of God, it documents that the Creator and Lord of all the world has accomplished His salvation through reconciliation.

Thereby we come in another way to the fact to which the above positions were related: the reality of Jesus Christ. But our way points us to the very center, to the Cross. What takes place here cannot be expressed without the help of the concepts of vicariousness and reconciliation. The decisive missionary kerygma to the world begins, then, with the report: "Christ died for our sins in accordance with the scriptures" (1 Cor. 15:3).

Now a healthy theology of mission will not commit the error of isolating the view of the Cross from the Incarnation on the one side, nor from the Resurrection on the other side. Only when it does not do that does it have any hope of overcoming the antitheses which we mentioned. A theology formed from the whole Christ—the incarnate, crucified, and resurrected—offers a place for the just concern of the first position. It not only empowers but it obliges the Church to declare her solidarity with the world. The Church knows that she is the salt of the earth and the light of the world. She knows this not because she considers herself to be the continuation of the Incarnation, but because she believes on the elevated Lord who is present in her midst. She lives from his declaration of solidarity with the sinner. And it is his solidarity to which she testifies.

This is certainly no chance solidarity. It is true and real. But it is true and real in such a way that one cannot forget that the Church is indeed in the world, but not of the world (Jn. 17:11, 16). Therefore the nature of the Church and the nature of mission, in whose service the Church is used, cannot be described without giving full due to that which is the particular in God's act of redemption. The Church is no institution which is supposed to make the life of man on earth more bearable and livable. She is the measure which God has taken to serve the accomplishment of His final will for salvation. Let no one misinterpret this consciously one-sided sentence as a disparagement of social and welfare work of Christian love. This has its place in the Church. The Church would not be the Church of the God who has mercy on His whole creation if her secular environment did not experience the love which lives in her. She makes a place on earth where once again life becomes worth living. But the Church is primarily and ultimately the people whom God has won for His kingdom and is leading to His coming kingdom.

We are now already at the point where it becomes clear that the first problem mentioned by Goodall is closely connected with the second one of mission and eschatology. The solution of the one contains the solution of the other. A theology of mission that is determined from the standpoint of the whole Christ does justice to the eschatological dimension. Thus we have turned our attention to the other side. But here also we cannot be uncritical. We believe that we must warn against Hoekendijk's eschatological leveling of Church and world. The Church is not only that which is sent forth (*Sendung*) to the world, but also, without ceasing to be that which is sent forth, that which is gathered together (*Sammlung*) in the world. She is the people of God gathered from all peoples. She participates in the structure of the people of Israel. Even in the New Covenant she remains the wandering people of God, that is on the way toward God's goal. God has claimed her for His work of redemption which will come to its goal and conclusion.

The question of mission and eschatology is connected closely with the theme of Evanston (1954). This is further proof of how important the participation of the theology of mission is in the general theological reflection of all of Christianity in the whole world. And it can contribute decisively to this reflection specifically in this problem. Perhaps this contribution does not consist primarily in a deepening of theological perception. This must necessarily remain piecemeal. The eschatological dimension has two components: the *already* and the *not yet*. The kingdom of God has come in Christ, but we nevertheless are waiting for its appearance in glory. We cannot escape this tension as long as it is certain that Christ is and was and is to come. The conference in Evanston made this clear. In this it did not lead beyond Willingen. But the greatest task for a theology of mission is indeed not to communicate knowledge. Instead, it should be the great agitation in the life of the Church. The Church should never become fixed at any one place in the world. She must be on her way to the ends of the earth in the certainty that His time is pressing. In this manner mission calls forth the end, the coming of the Lord himself. The theology of mission is then, also, at its goal. Then it also becomes adoration of the Triune God.

BIBLIOGRAPHY

Compiled by the Editor

1. BIBLIOGRAPHIES

Anderson, Gerald H. (compiler). *Bibliography of the Theology of Missions in the Twentieth Century*. 2nd ed. revised and enlarged. New York: Missionary Research Library, 1960. Paperback.

Benz, Ernst and Nambara, Minoru. *Das Christentum und die nicht-christlichen Hochreligionen: Begegnung und Auseinandersetzung. Eine Internationale Bibliographie*. Leiden: E. J. Brill, 1960. Paperback.

An excellent bibliography of Christianity and the non-Christian religions; does not include Judaism.

Bibliografia Missionaria. Compilata dal P. Giovanni Rommerskirchen O.M.I., Bibliotecario della Pontificia Biblioteca Missionaria; coll'assistenza del P. Nicola Kowalsky O.M.I., Archivista della S.C. de Propaganda Fide; e del P. Giuseppe Metzler O.M.I., Professore del Pontificio Istituto Missionario. Rome: Pontificia Università di Propaganda Fide, Piazza di Spagna, 48. Paperback.

This is an exhaustive bibliography of current Catholic literature; published annually. Section I deals with "Mission Theory."

The International Review of Missions (London).

Each issue (quarterly) contains the "International Missionary Bibliography," which is the best bibliographical source for non-Roman Christians.

Het Missiewerk (Nijmegen).

The last issue every year has a bibliographical survey of mission literature, compiled by Dr. Alph. Mulders, with primary attention to Catholic publications.

Parole et mission; revue de théologie missionnaire (Paris).

This Catholic quarterly has a bibliographical section in each issue.

Vriens, Livinus, O.F.M. Cap., with the collaboration of Disch, Anastasius, O.F.M. Cap., and Wils, J. *Critical Bibliography of Missiology* (Bibliographia ad Usum Seminariorum Vol. E 2.) Translated from the Dutch by Deodatus Tummers O.F.M. Nijmegen, Holland: Bestelcentrale der V.S.K.B. Publ., 1960. Paperback.

An admirable, annotated bibliography of Catholic missiological literature.

2. JOURNALS (with publishing addresses)

Canadian Journal of Theology. 75 Queen's Park Crescent, Toronto 5, Ontario, Canada. Quarterly. $3.

The Christian Century. 407 S. Dearborn St., Chicago 5, Ill. Weekly. $7.50.

Christianity Today. 1014 Washington Building, Washington 5, D.C. Fortnightly. $5.

Church History. (The American Society of Church History.) 520 Witherspoon Building, Philadelphia, Pa. Quarterly. $5.

The Ecumenical Review. World Council of Churches, 17 Route de Malagnou, Geneva, Switzerland; or 475 Riverside Drive, New York 27, N.Y. Quarterly. $3., 14s.

Église Vivante. Société des Auxiliaires des Missions, 44 rue des Bernardins, Paris 5ᵉ, France; or 61 Boulevard Schreurs, Louvain, Belgium. Bimonthly. $5., 28s.

Euntes Docete. Commentarii Pontificiae Universitatis de Propaganda Fide. Editiones Urbanianae, 16, via Urbano VIII, Rome, Italy. Quarterly. $5.

Evangelische Missions-Magazin. Basler Missionsbuchhandlung G.m.b.H., Basel 3, Missionsstrasse, 21, Switzerland. Quarterly. $2.

Evangelische Missions-Zeitschrift. Evang. Missionsverlag G.m.b.H., Stuttgart S., Heusteigstrasse, 34, Germany. Bimonthly. $2.

De Heerbaan. Nederlandsche Zendingsraad, Amsterdam, Herengracht, 368, Netherlands. Bimonthly. $1.50.

The Indian Journal of Theology. William Carey Road, Serampore, West Bengal, India. Quarterly. $2.50, 10s.

The International Review of Missions. Edinburgh House, 2 Eaton Gate, London, S.W. 1, England; or 475 Riverside Drive, Room 440, New York 27, N.Y. Quarterly. $3.50, 15s. 6d.

The Japan Christian Quarterly. Kyo Bun Kwan, 2 Ginza 4-chrome, Chuo-ku, Tokyo, Japan. Quarterly. $3.50.

Het Missiewerk. Laan Copes van Cattenburch 127, 's Gravenhage, Netherlands. Quarterly. $1.25.

Le Monde non chrétien. 17, rue Saint-Antoine, Paris 4ᵉ, France. Quarterly. $2.

The Muslim World. Hartford Seminary Foundation, Hartford 5, Conn. Quarterly. $3.

National Christian Council Review. The Wesley Press, Post Box 37, Mysore City, India. Monthly. $2.50, 10s.

Neue Zeitschrift für Missionswissenschaft (*Nouvelle Revue de science missionnaire*). Seminary Schöneck/Beckenried, Switzerland. Quarterly. $4.

Nordisk Missions Tidsskrift. Lohses forlag, Bernstorffsgade, 21, Copenhagen 5, Denmark. Quarterly. $2.

Norsk Tidsskrift for Misjon. Egede Institute of Missionary Study and Research, Theresegt. 51 B., Oslo, Norway. Quarterly. $2.

Occasional Bulletin. The Missionary Research Library, 3041 Broadway, New York 27, N.Y. Published 10–16 times each year. $2.

Parole et mission; revue de théologie missionnaire. Éditions du Cerf, 29, boulevard Latour-Maubourg, Paris 7ᵉ, France. Quarterly. $3.

Religion and Society. Christian Institute for the Study of Religion and Society, Post Box No. 57, 19 Miller Road, Bangalore 1, India. Quarterly. $5., 20s.

Religion in Life. 201 Eighth Avenue South, Nashville 3, Tenn. Quarterly. $4.

The South East Asia Journal of Theology. 6 Mount Sophia, Singapore 9. Quarterly. $3.

The Student World. World's Student Christian Federation, 13, rue Calvin, Geneva, Switzerland; or National Student Christian Federation, 475 Riverside Drive, New York 27, N.Y. Quarterly. $2.50, 15s.

Studia Missionalia. Pontificia Universitas Gregoriana, Piazza della Pilotta, Rome, Italy. Annual.

Svensk Missionstidskrift. Domkyrkoplan, 2, Uppsala, Sweden. Quarterly. $1.60.

Theology Today. P.O. Box 29, Princeton, N.J. Quarterly. $3.

Worldmission. National Office of the Society for the Propagation of the Faith, 366 Fifth Avenue, New York 1, N.Y. Quarterly. $5.

Zeitschrift für Missionswissenschaft und Religionswissenschaft. Aschendorffsche Verlagsbuchhandlung, Münster/Westf., Germany. Quarterly. $3.75.

Zeitschrift für Religions- und Geistesgeschichte. Verlag E. J. Brill G.m.b.H., Köln, Haus am Friesenplatz, Germany. Quarterly. $6.50.

3. THE BIBLICAL BASIS FOR THE CHRISTIAN MISSION

Baird, William. *Paul's Mission and Message.* New York: Abingdon Press, 1960.

Bible, The Holy. Revised Standard Version. New York: Thomas Nelson and Sons, 1952.

Blauw, Johannes. *Goden en Mensen: plaats en betekenis van de heidenen in de Heilige Schrift.* Groningen: J. Niemeijer in Samenwerking met de Ned. Zendingsraad, 1950. (Bijdragen tot de Zendingswetenschap, III.) Paperback.

A Biblical study of Christianity and the religions.

Brunner, Emil. *Die Unentbehrlichkeit des Alten Testamentes für die missionierende Kirche.* Basel: Evang. Missionsverlag, 1934. (Basler Missionsstudien, Heft 12.) Paperback.

The indispensability of the Old Testament for the missionary Church.

Carver, William O. *The Bible a Missionary Message.* New York: Fleming H. Revell Company, 1921.

A Southern Baptist approach to the Biblical basis for missions.

Chirgwin, A. M. *The Bible in World Evangelism.* New York: Friendship Press, 1954. Paperback.

The use of the Bible through the ages as an instrument of evangelism.

de Dietrich, Suzanne. *The Witnessing Community. The Biblical Record of God's Purpose.* Philadelphia: The Westminster Press, 1958.

Using the methods of Biblical theology, the author deals with the question of how God's People should face the world of their time and how they should fulfill their function in it.

DeWolf, L. Harold. *The Enduring Message of the Bible.* New York: Harper & Brothers, 1960.

A Biblical theology for laymen, with much illustration from the mission field and with relevance to the theology of mission.

Freytag, Walter. *The Gospel and the Religions.* London: SCM Press, 1957. (I.M.C. Research Pamphlets, No. 5.) Paperback. Original title: *Das*

Rätsel der Religionen und die Biblische Antwort. Wuppertal-Barmen: Jugenddienst-Verlag, [1957].

A Biblical inquiry into the issues which arise in the confrontation between Christianity and the non-Christian religions.

Glover, Robert Hall. *The Bible Basis of Missions.* Los Angeles: Bible House of Los Angeles, 1946.

A very influential book in conservative circles.

Henry, Carl F. H. (ed.). *Revelation and the Bible.* Grand Rapids, Mich.: Baker Book House, 1958.

Written by leading authorities in the conservative evangelical tradition.

Jeremias, Joachim. *Jesu Verheissung für die Völker.* Stuttgart: Verlag W. Kohlhammer, 1956. (The Franz Delitzsch Lectures for 1953.) Translated into English by S. H. Hooke, *Jesus' Promise to the Nations.* London: SCM Press; Naperville, Illinois: Alec R. Allenson, Inc., 1958. (Studies in Biblical Theology, No. 24.) Paperback.

An important study for the theology of mission, dealing with the place of the Gentile nations in the promises of Jesus; includes valuable bibliographical references.

Love, Julian Price. *The Missionary Message of the Bible.* New York: The Macmillan Company, 1941.

Martin-Achard, Robert. *Israël et les nations. La perspective missionnaire de l'Ancien Testament.* Neuchatel & Paris: Delachaux & Niestlé, 1959. (Cahiers Théologiques, 42.) Paperback.

Missionary perspective of the Old Testament; includes bibliography. An English translation, *Israel and the Nations,* is in process of preparation.

Mathews, James K. *To the End of the Earth. A Study in Luke–Acts on the Life and Mission of the Church.* Nashville: National Methodist Student Movement, 1959. Paperback.

A Biblical study by the Methodist Bishop of the Boston Area, who was formerly a missionary in India and later an executive secretary of the Methodist Board of Missions.

May, Peter. "Towards a Biblical Theology of Mission," in *The Indian Journal of Theology* (Serampore), Vol. VIII (Jan.–March 1959), pp. 21–28.

Phillips, Godfrey Edward. *The Old Testament in the World Church; With Special Reference to the Younger Churches.* London: Lutterworth Press, 1942.

The importance of the Old Testament for missionaries and national leaders.

Raguin, Yves. *Théologie missionnaire de l'Ancien Testament.* Paris: Éditions du Seuil, 1947. Paperback.

A study of Old Testament mission theology by a Catholic scholar.

Rétif, André, S.J. *Foi au Christ et Mission; d'après les Actes des Apôtres.* Paris: Le Cerf, 1953.

A study of the doctrinal basis for mission in the Acts of the Apostles, in which the author deals with the apostolic *kerygma* and the Lord's place in it, and the part played by signs and missionary work as God's judgment.

Rowley, Harold Henry. *The Missionary Message of the Old Testament.* London: Carey Press, [1945].

A valuable contribution, now out of print, by a leading Old Testament scholar who formerly served as a missionary overseas.

Schick, Erich. *Mission und Missionsverantwortung im Licht der Bibel.* Basel: Basler Missionsbuchhandlung, 1955. (Die Sammlung der Gemeinde, Heft 10). Paperback.

Missions and the responsibility to proclaim the Gospel, in the light of the Bible.

Shillito, Edward. *The Way of the Witnesses.* London: The Livingstone Press; New York: Friendship Press, 1936. Paperback.

A New Testament study in missionary motive.

Soper, Edmund Davison. *The Biblical Background of the Christian World Mission.* New York: Abingdon-Cokesbury Press, [1951]. Paperback.

A good introductory study by an American Methodist scholar.

Sundkler, Bengt and Fridrichsen, Anton. *Contributions à l'étude de la pensée Missionnaire dans le Nouveau Testament.* Uppsala: Das Neutestamentliche Seminar zu Uppsala, 1937.

Studies of missionary thought in the New Testament. The two essays in this work are "Jésus et les païens," and "La pensée missionnaire dans le Quatrième Évangile."

Warren, Max A. C. *The Gospel of Victory.* London: SCM Press, 1955.

A study in the relevance of the Epistle to the Galatians for the Christian mission today.

Wiersinga, H. A. *Zendingsperspectief in het Oude Testament.* Baarn: Bosch en Keuning, 1954.

The mission perspective in the Old Testament.

Wright, G. Ernest. *The God Who Acts. Biblical Theology as Recital.* London: SCM Press, 1952.

4. HISTORICAL STUDIES

Addison, James Thayer. *The Medieval Missionary.* New York: International Missionary Council, 1936.

A scholarly, well-written study of mission methods, motives, and message during the medieval period.

Benz, Ernst. "Pietist and Puritan Sources of Early Protestant World Missions (Cotton Mather and A. H. Francke)," in *Church History* (Philadelphia), Vol. XX (June 1951), pp. 28–55.

Dürr, Johannes. *Sendende und werdende Kirche in der Missionstheologie Gustav Warneck's.* Basel: Basler Missionsbuchhandlung, 1947. Paperback.

A critical study of Gustav Warneck's mission theology.

Glazik, Josef, M.S.C. *Die Russisch-Orthodoxe Heidenmission seit Peter dem Grossen. Ein missionsgeschichtlicher Versuch nach russischen Quellen und Darstellungen.* Münster: Aschendorffsche Verlagsbuchhandlung, 1954.

An important historical study of the Russian Orthodox mission to the heathen since Peter the Great, with twenty-five pages of valuable bibliography.

Harnack, Adolf von. *Die Mission und Ausbreitung des Christentums in den ersten drei Jahrhunderten.* 2 vols. 4th ed. Leipzig: J. C. Hinrichs'sche Buchhandlung, 1924. Translated into English and edited by James Moffatt, *The Mission and Expansion of Christianity in the First Three Centuries.* 2 vols. 2nd ed. New York: G. P. Putnam's Sons, 1908.

The standard history of missions in the early Church.

History's Lessons for Tomorrow's Mission: Milestones in the History of Missionary Thinking. Geneva: World's Student Christian Federation, 1960.

Essays by Latourette, Hogg, Margull, Gensichen, Neill, Rétif, Philippe Maury and others. Includes extensive annotated bibliography.

Hogg, William Richey. *Ecumenical Foundations. A History of the International Missionary Council and Its Nineteenth-Century Background.* New York: Harper & Brothers, 1952.

A classic study which gives the necessary understanding of background developments in this period. Extensive footnotes and bibliography.

Holsten, Walter. *Christentum und nichtchristliche Religion nach der Auffassung Luthers.* Gütersloh: C. Bertelsmann, 1932.

Luther's understanding of Christianity and non-Christian religion, in a study by the Professor of Missiology at the University of Mainz.

———. "Reformation und Mission," in *Archiv für Reformationsgeschichte* (Gütersloh), Vol. XLIV (1–2, 1953), pp. 1–32.

A positive and sympathetic appraisal of the Reformers' concept and contribution in missionary thinking, with a summary in English and bibliographical notes.

Kübler, Otto. *Mission und Theologie: Eine Untersuchung über den Missionsgedanken in der systematischen Theologie seit Schleiermacher.* Leipzig: T. C. Hinrichs'sche Buchhandlung, 1929.

A valuable study, now out of print, of missionary thought in German systematic theology from Schleiermacher to 1927.

Latourette, Kenneth Scott. *A History of the Expansion of Christianity.* 7 vols. New York: Harper & Brothers, 1937–45.

A monumental work; important in establishing the history of missions as a recognized field of theological study.

Liechtenhan, Rudolf. *Die urchristliche Mission: Voraussetzungen, Motive und Methoden.* Zürich: Zwingli-Verlag, 1946. (Abhandlungen zur Theologie des Alten und Neuen Testaments.) Paperback.

An historical study of the Christian mission as founded in the message and lifework of Jesus, and carried forth by the primitive Church and St. Paul.

Littell, Franklin Hamlin. *The Anabaptist View of the Church: A Study on the Origins of Sectarian Protestantism.* 2nd ed. Boston: Starr King Press, 1958.

See Chapter 5, "The Great Commission."

———. *The Free Church.* Boston: Starr King Press, 1957.

See Chapter 7, "The Free Churches and Ecumenics." In the chapters cited from both of these books the author relates the theology of mission in the Free Church tradition to the ecumenical movement, and attempts to develop a new interpretation of the significant place which missions play in the doctrine of the Church as understood by the Free Churches.

Myklebust, Olav Guttorm. *The Study of Missions in Theological Education.* 2 vols. Oslo: Hovedkommisjon Forlaget Land og Kirke, 1955–57. (Studies of the Egede Institute, 6–7.) Paperback.

A definitive work on the history (1800–1950) of the study of missions as a theological subject.

Nieden, Ernst zur. *Der Missionsgedanke in der systematischen Theologie seit Schleiermacher.* Gütersloh: C. Bertelsmann, 1928.

A critical study, now out of print, of missionary thought in German systematic theology from Schleiermacher down to 1927.

Pietsch, P. Johannes, O.M.I. *P. Robert Streit O.M.I. Ein Pionier der katholischen Missionswissenschaft.* Schöneck/Beckenried, Schweiz: Administration der Neuen Zeitschrift für Missionswissenschaft, 1952.

A survey-study of the contribution made by Father Streit, who was a pioneer in Catholic missiology in the early twentieth century; includes a bibliography of his writings.

Richter, Martin. *Der Missionsgedanke im evangelischen Deutschland des 18. Jahrhunderts.* Leipzig: T. C. Hinrichs'sche Buchhandlung, 1928.

A study, now out of print, of missionary thought in Protestant Germany during the eighteenth century. Includes eleven pages of bibliography.

Schärer, Hans. *Die Begründung der Mission in der katholischen und evangelischen Missionswissenschaft.* Zollikon–Zürich: Evang. Verlag, 1944. (Theologische Studien, Heft 16.) Paperback.

The foundation of the mission in Catholic and Protestant missiology.

Schmidt, Martin. *Der junge Wesley als Heidenmissionar und Missionstheologe.* Gütersloh: C. Bertelsmann, 1955. Translated into English by L. A. Fletcher, *The Young Wesley: Missionary and Theologian of Missions.* London: Epworth Press, 1958. Paperback.

Van den Berg, Johannes. *Constrained by Jesus' Love. An Inquiry into the Motives of the Missionary Awakening in Great Britain in the Period between 1698 and 1815.* Kampen: J. H. Kok, 1956. Paperback.

A valuable historico-theological assessment of missionary motives, with extensive bibliographical footnotes.

Warneck, Gustav. *Abriss einer Geschichte der protestantischen Missionen von der Reformation bis auf die Gegenwart. Mit einem Anhang über die katholischen Missionen.* 10. Aufl. Berlin: Verlag von Martin Warneck, 1913. Third English edition translated from the eighth German edition by George Robson, *Outline of a History of Protestant Missions from the Reformation to the Present Time.* New York: Fleming H. Revell Co., [1906].

A standard work by the German "father" of Protestant missiology

[Missionswissenschaft]; especially valuable today for his appraisal of missionary thought and motivation from the Reformation through the founding of the Protestant missionary societies.

Zwemer, Samuel M. "Calvinism and the Missionary Enterprise," in *Theology Today* (Princeton), Vol. VII (July 1950), pp. 206–16.

5. CHRISTIANITY AND OTHER FAITHS

Appleton, George. *Glad Encounter: Jesus Christ and the Living Faiths of Men.* London: Edinburgh House Press, 1959. Paperback.

Beginning with the great doctrines of the Christian faith, the author tries to interpret Jesus Christ as good news to men of other faiths.

Ashby, Philip H. *The Conflict of Religions.* New York: Charles Scribner's Sons, 1955.

A challenging appeal for a united witness of the major religions in meeting the problems of mankind.

The Authority of the Faith. Vol. I in *The Tambaram-Madras Series.* 7 vols. London: Oxford University Press, 1939.

This important symposium continued the Tambaram debate concerning "discontinuity" and "Biblical realism," with essays by Hendrik Kraemer, Walter Marshall Horton, Karl Hartenstein, David G. Moses, H. H. Farmer, and others.

Baillie, John. *The Idea of Revelation in Recent Thought.* New York: Columbia University Press, 1956.

———. *The Interpretation of Religion.* New York: Charles Scribner's Sons, 1928.

———, and Martin, Hugh (eds.). *Revelation.* London: Faber and Faber, 1937.

A symposium, now out of print, with essays by Gustaf Aulen, Karl Barth, Sergium Bulgakoff, M. C. D'Arcy, T. S. Eliot, Walter M. Horton, and William Temple.

Bavinck, John H. *The Impact of Christianity on the Non-Christian World.* Grand Rapids, Michigan: W. B. Eerdmans Publishing Co., 1948.

A scholarly study by a conservative Dutch missionary theologian.

Bennett, John C. *Christianity and Communism Today.* New York: Association Press, 1960. (A Haddam House Book.)

A penetrating Christian analysis by the Dean of Union Theological Seminary in New York.

Bouquet, A. C. *The Christian Faith and Non-Christian Religions.* London: James Nisbet and Co.; New York: Harper and Brothers, 1958.

The author has a preference for the larger view of revelation "supported by Söderblom and William Temple, as against the opinions of Witte and Kraemer."

———. *Is Christianity the Final Religion?* London: Macmillan and Co., 1921.

———. *The Christian Religion and its Competitors.* Cambridge: Cambridge University Press, 1924.

Braden, Charles S. *Jesus Compared. A Study of Jesus and Other Great Founders of Religions.* Englewood Cliffs, N.J.: Prentice-Hall, Inc., 1957.

Brunner, Emil. *Die Christusbotschaft im Kampf mit den Religionen.* Stuttgart u. Basel: Evang. Missionsverlag, 1931.

The struggle of the Christian message with the religions.

The Christian Life and Message in Relation to Non-Christian Systems of Thought and Life. Vol. I of *The Jerusalem Meeting of the International Missionary Council, March 24–April 8, 1928.* 8 vols. London: Oxford University Press, 1928.

A symposium of essays and reports that are important for an understanding of the evolution of mission theology among Protestants in the twentieth century.

Cragg, Kenneth. *The Call of the Minaret.* New York: Oxford University Press, 1956.

———. *Sandals at the Mosque. Christian Presence Amid Islam.* New York: Oxford University Press, 1959.

Both these books, by an Anglican missionary scholar, are concerned with the Christian understanding of Islam in the modern world and the Christian response to it.

Devanandan, Paul D. *The Gospel and Renascent Hinduism.* London: SCM Press, 1959. (I.M.C. Research Pamphlets, No. 8.) Paperback.

A study of the Hindu approach to Christianity and the Christian concern in renascent Hinduism.

Dewick, E. C. *The Christian Attitude to Other Religions.* Cambridge: Cambridge University Press, 1953.

This English scholar reminds Christians not to exclude the possibility that God may also have truly spoken to men through other channels.

———. *The Gospel and Other Faiths.* London: The Canterbury Press, 1948.

Eckhardt, A. Roy. *Christianity and the Children of Israel.* New York: King's Crown Press, 1948.

A scholarly survey of the Christian relationship to the Children of Israel and a suggested theological basis for a Christian approach to the Jewish question. Extensive bibliographical references.

Eliade, Mircea and Kitagawa, Joseph M. (eds.). *The History of Religions: Essays in Methodology.* Chicago: University of Chicago Press, 1959.

Essays by Benz, Daniélou, W. C. Smith, Heiler, and others, that point out the new significance and relevance of studies in the history of religions for the theology of mission.

Farmer, Herbert H. *Revelation and Religion. Studies in the Theological Interpretation of Religious Types.* London: James Nisbet and Co., 1954.

Farquhar, John N. *The Crown of Hinduism.* London: Oxford University Press, 1913.

The thesis of this controversial study was that Christ can create a substitute which would preserve and "crown" all that is good in Hinduism.

Forman, Charles W. *A Christian's Handbook on Communism.* Rev. ed. New York: Committee on World Literacy and Christian Literature, National Council of the Churches of Christ in the U.S.A., 1955. Paperback.

A concise treatment with suggested reading list.

Hedenquist, Göte (ed.). *The Church and the Jewish People.* London: Edinburgh House Press, 1954.

Essays by Christians and Jews, prepared under the auspices of the I.M.C. to impress upon Christians their continuing responsibility in relation to the Jewish people of today.

Hermelink, Jan. *Verstehen und Bezeugen. Der theologische Ertrag der "Phänomenologie der Religion" von Gerardus van der Leeuw.* München: Chr. Kaiser Verlag, 1960. (Beiträge zur evangelischen Theologie, Band 30.) Paperback.

The author's doctoral dissertation; a study in Gerardus van der Leeuw's concept of "The Phenomenology of Religion."

Hocking, William Ernest. *Living Religions and a World Faith.* London: Allen & Unwin; New York: The Macmillan Company, 1940.

In a fuller statement of his basic position in *Re-Thinking Missions,* Dr. Hocking suggests the way toward a world faith, not by means of "radical displacement," but by "synthesis" leading to "reconception."

———. *The Coming World Civilization.* New York: Harper & Brothers, 1956.

A philosopher's approach to history, in which he gives attention to the character and future role of Christianity among the religions of the world.

Hogg, A. G. *The Christian Message to the Hindu.* London: SCM Press, 1947.

A respected and retired missionary theologian from India deals with the challenge of the Gospel in India.

Horton, Walter Marshall. *Christian Theology: An Ecumenical Approach.* Rev. and enlarged ed. New York: Harper & Brothers, 1958.

See the Appendix: "Christianity and Other Living Faiths," pp. 293–308.

Hume, Robert Ernest. *The World's Living Religions. With Special Reference to Their Sacred Scriptures and in Comparison with Christianity.* Rev. ed. New York: Charles Scribner's Sons, 1959.

An outstanding study, first published in 1924, issued now in a new edition, revised by Charles S. Braden.

Jones, E. Stanley. *The Christ of the Indian Road.* New York: Abingdon Press, 1925.

A thoughtful presentation of the Christian mission, especially as related to the challenge in India, by the noted American Methodist missionary evangelist.

———. *Christ at the Round Table.* New York: Abingdon Press, 1928.

Jurji, Edward J. *The Christian Interpretation of Religion. Christianity in Its Human and Creative Relationships with the World's Cultures and Faiths.* New York: The Macmillan Company, 1952.

Kraemer, Hendrik. *The Christian Message in a Non-Christian World.* Published for the International Missionary Council in London: Edinburgh House Press; New York: Harper & Brothers, 1938.

One of the most important books in the evolution of mission theology among Protestants in the twentieth century, this was written for the

I.M.C. meeting at Madras in 1938 and emphasized "Biblical realism" and "discontinuity."

———. *Religion and the Christian Faith.* London: Lutterworth Press, [1956].

The approach and material are new, the author's exegetical study of the Biblical data is especially valuable, but his position is basically unchanged from that in his earlier book.

———. *World Cultures and World Religions: The Coming Dialogue.* London: Lutterworth Press, 1960.

Manikam, Rajah B. (ed.). *Christianity and the Asian Revolution.* Madras: Diocesan Press for Christian Literature Society, Madras and Friendship Press, New York, 1954; reprinted [1955].

Studies which assess the Christian mission in Asia. See especially the chapter by J. Russell Chandran, "The Christian Approach to non-Christian Religions," pp. 185–209.

Moses, David G. *Religious Truth and the Relation between Religions.* Madras: The Christian Literature Society for India, 1950. (Indian Research Series, No. 5.) Paperback.

A challenging study by an Indian scholar who maintains that the criterion of religious truth must be sought in the essential nature of religion itself, in terms of the fundamental needs which it satisfies, in the conservation, creation, and practical realization in life of values. Bibliography included.

Niles, Daniel T. *The Preacher's Task and the Stone of Stumbling.* New York: Harper & Brothers, 1958. (The Lyman Beecher Lectures for 1957.)

An ecumenical leader from Ceylon deals with the question "What is the nature of the existence of the Christian message in a non-Christian world?"

Ohm, Thomas, O.S.B. *Die Liebe zu Gott in den nichtchristlichen Religionen. Die Tatsachen der Religionsgeschichte und die christliche Theologie.* Krailling vor München: Erich Wewel Verlag, 1950.

The noted Catholic missiologist in Münster presents in this massive volume, rich in bibliographical references, a masterful study on the love of God in non-Christian religions.

Perry, Edmund. *The Gospel in Dispute. The Relation of Christian Faith to Other Missionary Religions.* Garden City, New York: Doubleday and Co., 1958.

The author is an American Methodist who says that all non-Christian faiths "not only are unable to bring men to God, they actually lead men away from God and hold them captive from God."

Phillips, Godfrey Edward. *The Transmission of the Faith.* London: Lutterworth Press, 1946.

A study in the process of communication to non-Christians, by an English missiologist.

Price, Frank Wilson. *Marx Meets Christ.* Philadelphia: The Westminster Press, 1957.

A contrast of the two persons, the two ideas, the two systems, the two faiths, by one who faced Communism in China.

Radhakrishnan, Sarvepalli. *East and West in Religion.* London: George Allen & Unwin Ltd., 1933.

The philosophy of religion treated from the comparative point of view by a non-Christian who is Vice-President of India and former Professor of Eastern Religions at Oxford University.

———. *Eastern Religions and Western Thought.* 2nd ed. London: Oxford University Press, 1940.

———. *Recovery of Faith.* New York: Harper & Brothers, 1955.

The author seeks a transcendent unity of religions.

Rosenkranz, Gerhard. *Evangelische Religionskunde. Einführung in eine theologische Schau der Religionen.* Tübingen: J. C. B. Mohr (Paul Siebeck), 1951.

An effort toward understanding the living religions in light of the Christian truth; includes seven pages of bibliography.

Ross, Floyd H. *Addressed to Christians: Isolationism vs. World Community.* New York: Harper & Brothers, 1950.

A challenging approach to the problem of world community and the question of the Christian relation to the other religions of the world, by one who questions the adequacy of any one religious symbol for all peoples of the world.

Schuon, Frithjof. *The Transcendent Unity of Religions.* London: Faber and Faber; New York: Pantheon Books [1953].

A Study of Oriental and Occidental religions in which the author seeks to prove that there is a transcendent unity underlying all the great religions.

Schweitzer, Albert. *Christianity and the Religions of the World.* Translated by Johanna Powers, with a Foreword by Nathaniel Micklem. New York: Henry Holt, 1939; The Macmillan Co., 1951. Original title: *Das Christentum und die Weltreligionen.* 2nd ed. München: C. H. Beck, 1925.

Smith, Wilfred Cantwell. "Christianity's Third Great Challenge," in *Christian Century,* Vol. LXXVII (April 27, 1960), pp. 505–08. See "Reader's Response to the W. C. Smith Thesis," by the Anglican Bishop of Nagpur (J. W. Sadiq), in *Christian Century,* August 24, 1960, p. 974.

Steere, Douglas V. "Mutual Irradiation," in *Religion in Life* (Nashville), Vol. XXVIII (Summer 1959), pp. 395–405.

An American Quaker view.

Toynbee, Arnold. *Christianity Among the Religions of the World.* New York: Charles Scribner's Sons, 1957.

The author suggests that Christians should recognize that, in some measure, all the living higher religions are also revelations of what is true and right, and that Christianity should be purged of the exclusive-mindedness and intolerance that follows from a belief in Christianity's uniqueness.

Vicedom, Georg F. *Die Weltreligionen im Angriff auf die Christenheit.* 2nd ed. München: Chr. Kaiser Verlag, 1957. Paperback.

An analysis of the present world situation, of the threat to Christianity from the revival of other religions, and a call for a spiritual revival within Christianity to meet the challenge.

———. *Die Mission der Weltreligionen.* München: Chr. Kaiser Verlag, 1959. Paperback.

Wach, Joachim. *The Comparative Study of Religions.* Edited with an Introduction by Joseph M. Kitagawa. New York: Columbia University Press, 1958.

Includes twenty-six pages of bibliography.

———. *Types of Religious Experience: Christian and Non-Christian.* London: Routledge & Kegan Paul Ltd.; Chicago: University of Chicago Press, 1951.

West, Charles C. *Communism and the Theologians: Study of an Encounter.* London: SCM Press; Philadelphia: Westminster Press, 1958.

A solid study of the Christian encounter with Communism as seen in the theology of Tillich, Niebuhr, Barth, and others.

6. THEORY OF THE MISSION

Allen, Geoffrey. *The Theology of Missions.* London: SCM Press, 1943. Paperback.

A concise introductory survey of missionary motive, outreach, and method by an Anglican with missionary experience in China.

Allen, Roland. *Missionary Methods: St. Paul's or Ours.* London: Robert Scott, 1912.

———. *Essential Missionary Principles.* New York: Fleming H. Revell Company, 1913.

———. *The Spontaneous Expansion of the Church and the Causes which Hinder It.* London: World Dominion Press, [1927].

Andersen, Wilhelm. *Auf dem Weg zu einer Theologie der Mission.* Gütersloh: C. Bertelsmann, 1957. Translated into English by Bishop Stephen Neill, *Towards a Theology of Mission: A Study of the Encounter between the Missionary Enterprise and the Church and Its Theology.* London: SCM Press, 1955. (I.M.C. Research Pamphlets, No. 2.) Paperback.

The most valuable single item one could read for a succinct survey of the developments from Edinburgh 1910 through Willingen 1952, with indications of further possible lines of development in the discussion concerning the missionary obligation of the Church.

Baker, Archibald G. *Christian Missions and a New World Culture.* Chicago: Willett, Clark & Co., 1934.

A culture-centered approach with the cross-fertilization of cultures as the objective of the missionary enterprise.

Bavinck, John H. *Inleiding in de Zendingswetenschap.* Kampen: J. H. Kok, 1954. English translation by David H. Freeman, *An Introduction to the Science of Missions.* Philadelphia: The Presbyterian and Reformed Publishing Company, 1960.

A basic introduction by a conservative Dutch scholar.

Beaver, R. Pierce. *The Christian World Mission: A Reconsideration.* Calcutta: Baptist Mission Press, 1957. (The William Carey Lectures of 1957 at Serampore College, West Bengal, India.) Paperback.

The writer summarizes the situation today, challenges traditional concepts of Church and mission, and suggests further lines of development for the future.

Beaver, R. Pierce. "North American Thoughts on the Fundamental Principles of Missions," in *Church History* (Philadelphia), Vol. XXI (Dec. 1952), pp. 345–64.

Catarzi, Dan, S.X. *Lineamenti di Dommatica Missionaria. Teologia delle Missioni Estere.* 2 vols. Parma: Istituto Saveriano Missioni Estere, 1958.

A careful Catholic exposition of mission theology.

Champagne, Joseph Etienne, O.M.I. *Manuel d'Action Missionnaire.* Ottawa: l'Université d'Ottawa, 1947. Translated into English by Roy L. Laberge, *Manual of Missionary Action.* Ottawa: University of Ottawa Press, [1948].

A basic general manual in Catholic missiology.

Charles, Pierre, S.J. *Les Dossiers de l'Action Missionnaire. Manuel de Missiologie.* 2nd ed. Louvain: Éditions de l'Aucam, 1938.

The late Père Charles was a leading Catholic missiologist for whom mission was the primary function of the Church, by the Church, to plant the Church; and the specific object of missionary activity was to make the Church grow to the ends of the earth.

———. *Missiologie. Études, Rapports, Conférences.* I. Louvain: Éditions de l'Aucam, 1939.

———. *Études Missiologiques.* [Paris]: Desclée De Brouwer, 1956.

The Christian Mission Today. Edited by the Joint Section of Education and Cultivation of the Board of Missions of the Methodist Church. New York: Abingdon Press, 1960. Paperback.

Essays by twenty-one contemporary leaders who consider: (1) motives for the Christian mission; (2) the Church in America; (3) Methodism and the mission overseas; (4) the mission faces a world of change; (5) the task of minister and people.

The Church's Witness to God's Design. Vol. II in *Man's Disorder and God's Design: The Amsterdam Assembly Series.* London: SCM Press; New York: Harper & Brothers, 1948.

An ecumenical study prepared under the auspices of the World Council of Churches in preparation for the Amsterdam Assembly, with important essays and the official findings of the preparatory commission.

Cook, Harold R. *An Introduction to the Study of Christian Missions.* Chicago: Moody Press, 1954.

A thoughtful presentation from the conservative evangelical viewpoint.

Daniélou, Jean, S.J. *The Salvation of the Nations.* Translated from the French by Angeline Bouchard. London: Sheed & Ward, 1949. Original title: *Le mystère du salut des nations.* Paris: Éditions du Seuil, [1946]. German edition: *Vom Heil der Völker.* Frankfort/M: Verlag Josef Knecht Carolusdruckerei, 1952.

A popular little book by a noted Catholic missiologist.

DeWolf, L. Harold. *The Case for Theology in Liberal Perspective.* Philadelphia: Westminster Press, 1959.

See Chapter XI, "The Mission," pp. 182–89.

Dillistone, F. W. *Christianity and Communication.* London: Collins; New York: Charles Scribner's Sons, 1956.

A study of the principles and practices of effective communication of the Christian Gospel.

———. *Revelation and Evangelism.* London: Lutterworth Press, 1948.

The theology of revelation and its implications for the evangelistic activity of the Church.

Ferré, Nels F. S. *The Christian Faith: An Inquiry into Its Adequacy as Man's Ultimate Religion.* New York: Harper & Brothers, 1942.

Fison, J. E. *The Blessing of the Holy Spirit.* London: Longmans, Green and Co., 1950.

This study, by an Anglican scholar, points to the essential place and significance of the Holy Spirit for the Christian mission.

———. *The Christian Hope: The Presence and the Parousia.* London: Longmans, Green and Co., 1954.

Forman, Charles W. *A Faith for the Nations.* Philadelphia: Westminster Press, 1957. (Layman's Theological Library.)

A helpful introductory study for laymen and ministers, by the Professor of Missions at Yale Divinity School.

Freytag, Walter. "Vom Sinn der Weltmission," in *Evangelische Missions-Zeitschrift* (Stuttgart), Vol. VII (1950), pp. 1–8; also in *Evangelisches Missions-Magazin* (Basel), Vol. XCIV (1950), pp. 67–75; English tr. "The Meaning and Purpose of the Christian Mission," *International Review of Missions* (London), Vol. XXXIX (1950), pp. 153–61; Swedish tr. "Världsmissionens innebörd," *Svensk Missionstidskrift* (Uppsala), Vol. XXXVIII (1950), pp. 11–22; Danish tr. in *Nordisk Missions Tidsskrift* (Copenhagen), Vol. LXI (1950), pp. 3–15.

Goodall, Norman (ed.). *Missions Under the Cross.* Addresses Delivered at the Enlarged Meeting of the Committee of the I.M.C. at Willingen, Germany, in 1952; with Statements issued by the Meeting. London: Published for the I.M.C. by Edinburgh House Press and distributed in the U.S.A. by Friendship Press, New York, 1953.

Contains important essays on mission theory by a cross section of ecumenical mission leaders.

Hartenstein, Karl. *Die Mission als theologisches Problem. Beiträge zum grundsätzlichen Verständnis der Mission.* Berlin: Furche-Verlag, 1933.

Dr. Hartenstein was Missions-Director in Basel and a leading spokesman for the Continental viewpoint on the theology of missions.

Hartt, Julian N. *Toward a Theology of Evangelism.* New York: Abingdon Press, 1955.

An interpretation of the Church's mission in terms of the basic theological beliefs upon which every evangelistic effort must build.

Hebert, Gabriel. *Fundamentalism and the Church.* London: SCM Press; Philadelphia: Westminster Press, 1957.

A critical study of the strengths and weaknesses of Fundamentalist theology and its implications for the missionary movement.

Henry, A. M., O.P. *Esquisse d'une théologie de la mission.* Paris: Éd. du Cerf, 1959.

Theological speculation on the missionary activity of the Church, its aim, its means, and its progressive phases.

Hermelink, Jan and Margull, Hans Jochen (eds.). *Basileia: Walter Freytag zum 60. Geburtstag*. Stuttgart: Evang. Missionsverlag, 1959.

Essays in German and English on missions, the Church, and ecumenics from fifty-two scholars in honor of the late Professor Walter Freytag.

Hoekendijk, Johannes C. *Kerk en Volk in de Duitse Zendingswetenschap*. [Amsterdam: Drukkerij Kampert en Helm, 1948]. Paperback.

A critical study of German mission theory, centering upon the two concepts of Church and nation [*Volk*].

———. "Die Kirche im Missionsdenken," in *Evangelische Missions-Zeitschrift* (Stuttgart), Vol. IX (1952), pp. 1–13; English tr. "The Church in Missionary Thinking," in *International Review of Missions* (London), Vol. XLI (1952), pp. 324–36; French tr. "L'Eglise dans la Pensée Missionnaire," in *Le Monde non chrétien* (Paris), 1951, pp. 415–33; Danish tr. "Kirken i missionstaenkningen," in *Nordisk Missions Tidsskrift* (Copenhagen), Vol. LXIII (1952), pp. 3–19.

This critical essay prior to the Willingen Meeting of the I.M.C., by a noted Dutch missionary theologian, stimulated deeper reflection upon the relation of the Church to mission.

Hogg, William Richey. *One World, One Mission*. New York: Friendship Press, 1960. Paperback.

This interdenominational study book on the theme "Into all the world together" presents a substantial introduction to the foundations, the history and problems of the Christian mission; includes bibliography.

Holsten, Walter. *Das Kerygma und der Mensch. Einführung in die Religions- und Missionswissenschaft*. München: Chr. Kaiser Verlag, 1953. Paperback.

A summary study of missionary thinking to the present time, with exhaustive bibliographical references, by the Professor of Missiology at the University of Mainz.

James, Athanasius Coucouzes. "The Orthodox Concept of Mission and Missions," (pp. 76–80) in *Basileia,* edited by Jan Hermelink and Hans Jochen Margull. Stuttgart: Evang. Missionsverlag, 1959.

A valuable statement by the Archbishop of the Greek Orthodox Church in North and South America.

Jurji, Edward J. (ed.). *The Ecumenical Era in Church and Society. A Symposium in Honor of John A. Mackay*. New York: The Macmillan Company, 1959.

Essays by Kraemer, Goodall, Devanandan, Dillistone, Niles, and others, that consider crucial issues relevant to the theology of mission.

Kantonen, T. A. *The Theology of Evangelism*. Philadelphia: Muhlenberg Press, 1954.

A conservative Lutheran scholar seeks to clarify the central truths of the Gospel in their relation to the actual work of evangelism.

Kraemer, Hendrik. *The Communication of the Christian Faith*. Philadelphia: Westminster Press, 1956.

A study of communication in Biblical, historical, and contemporary perspective; with a critical consideration of possible answers to the breakdown of communicating the Christian faith.

———. *A Theology of the Laity*. London: Lutterworth Press; Philadelphia: Westminster Press, 1958.

Fundamental rethinking of the place and responsibility of the laity in the Church and in the world.

Latourette, Kenneth Scott. *Toward a World Christian Fellowship*. New York: Association Press, [1938]. (Hazen Books on Religion.)

A concise introductory study dealing with the questions and criticisms put to the missionary enterprise most frequently.

Laymen's Foreign Missions Inquiry, Commission of Appraisal; William Ernest Hocking, Chairman. *Re-Thinking Missions: A Laymen's Inquiry After One Hundred Years*. New York: Harper & Brothers, 1932.

This report stimulated recognition of the missionary problem as a theological problem. It provoked basic rethinking of the issues on all sides, but was itself widely criticized for its tone of optimism and relativism.

Levai, Blaise (ed.). *Revolution in Missions*. 2nd ed. Calcutta: YMCA Publishing House, 1958.

An important symposium by Indians and Westerners who examine the Christian mission today.

Lindsell, Harold. *A Christian Philosophy of Missions*. Wheaton, Illinois: Van Kampen Press, 1949.

A systematic exposition from the Biblically conservative American point of view.

———. *Missionary Principles and Practice*. Westwood, N.J.: Fleming H. Revell Co., 1955.

Loffeld, Edouard. *Le problème cardinal de la missiologie et des missions catholiques*. Rhenan, Holland: Éditions Spiritus, 1956.

The Professor of Missions at the Roman Catholic University of Nijmegen deals with the question "What is the purpose of missions?" as the cardinal question of missiology, and gives major attention to the relation of the Church to mission.

de Lubac, Henri. *Le fondement théologique des missions*. Paris: Éditions du Seuil, 1946. Paperback.

A Catholic study of the theological foundation for missions.

La lumière des nations: les problèmes actuels de l'Eglise et de la mission en Asie et en Afrique. Neuchatel: Éditions Delachaux & Niestlé, 1944. (Collection "l'Actualité Protestante.")

A symposium on mission theory and strategy. See especially the essay by Théo Preiss, "L'Eglise et la mission," pp. 9–34.

McGavaran, Donald Anderson. *The Bridges of God: A Study in the Strategy of Missions*. London: World Dominion Press; New York: Friendship Press, 1955.

A contrast between the "People Movement" and the "Mission Station Approach."

———. *How Churches Grow: The New Frontiers of Mission*. London:

World Dominion Press, and distributed in the U.S.A. by Friendship Press, New York, 1959.

The author favors winning the winnable now, pouring all available mission resources into existing responsive populations.

Mackay, John A. "Theology, Christ, and the Missionary Obligation," in *Theology Today* (Princeton), Vol. VII (January 1951), pp. 429–36.

A Christ-centered approach to the theology of mission by a distinguished Presbyterian missionary theologian.

Margull, Hans Jochen. *Theologie der missionarischen Verkündigung: Evangelisation als oekumenisches Problem.* Stuttgart: Evangelisches Verlagswerk, 1959.

The theology of mission as an ecumenical problem; includes thirty-four pages of bibliography. An English translation is in preparation.

Michalson, Carl. *The Hinge of History.* New York: Charles Scribner's Sons, 1959.

See Chapter X, "The Mission of the Church," pp. 235–46.

Miller, Donald G. *The Nature and Mission of the Church.* Richmond, Va.: John Knox Press, 1957. Paperback.

da Mondreganes, Pio Maria, O.F.M. Cap. *Manuale di Missionologia.* Rome: Marietti, 1950.

A standard Catholic work on mission theory, with extensive bibliographical references.

Morgan, E. R. *The Mission of the Church.* London: The Centenary Press, 1946.

Written by an Anglican bishop who says that the Church's mission is to be the Body of Christ, to proclaim and recall the Presence.

——— (ed.). *Essays Catholic and Missionary.* London: SPCK, 1928.

An Anglican symposium on the theory and practice of missions.

———, and Lloyd, Roger (eds.). *The Mission of the Anglican Communion.* London: SPCK and SPG, 1948.

Predominantly "high church."

Mulders, Alphons. *Inleiding tot de Missiewetenschap.* Bussum: Uitgeverij Paul Brand N.V., 1950.

A basic Roman Catholic introduction to missiology, by the Director of the Missiological Institute at the University of Nijmegen, Netherlands, and editor of *Het Missiewerk.*

Murphy, Edward L., S.J. *Teach Ye All Nations. The Principles of Catholic Missionary Work.* New York: Benziger Brothers, Inc., [1958].

A popular introduction to Catholic mission theory.

Neill, Stephen. *The Unfinished Task.* London: Edinburgh House Press; Lutterworth Press, 1957.

———. *Creative Tension.* London: Edinburgh House Press, 1959. (The Duff Lectures, 1958.)

Both of these books by an Anglican bishop with missionary and ecumenical experience deal with the state of the Church and theology in mission at mid-twentieth century.

Newbigin, Lesslie. *The Household of God.* New York: Friendship Press, 1954.

A dynamic study of the Christian community, its nature and its mission.

———. *One Body, One Gospel, One World: The Christian Mission Today.* London: Edinburgh House Press, 1958. Paperback. German ed.; *Die eine Kirche, das eine Evangelium, die eine Welt: die christliche Mission heute.* Stuttgart: Evang. Missionsverlag, 1959. Paperback.

A provocative presentation of problems facing the mission today.

Niles, Daniel T. *That They May Have Life.* New York: Published in Association with the SVM by Harper & Brothers, 1951.

The author seeks to trace the connection between God's work in creation and redemption and God's call to all men, through the Church, to share in His work.

Ohm, Thomas, O.S.B. *Machet alle Völker zu Jünger; eine katholische Missionstheorie.* Freiburg: Wewel, [to be published soon].

This new extensive theory of missions, by the noted Catholic missiologist in Münster, is certain to be a major contribution of benefit to all.

Orchard, Ronald K. *Out of Every Nation. A discussion of the internationalization of missions.* London: SCM Press, 1959. (I.M.C. Research Pamphlets, No. 7.)

——— (ed.). *The Ghana Assembly of the International Missionary Council; December 28, 1957, to January 8, 1958, in Accra, Ghana. Selected Papers with an Essay on the Role of the I.M.C.* London: Published for the I.M.C. by Edinburgh House Press and distributed in the U.S.A. by Friendship Press, New York, 1958.

Paton, David M. *Christian Missions and the Judgment of God.* London: SCM Press, 1953.

An Anglican missionary writes concerning what is to be learned about the Church's mission and for her missionary strategy from "the missionary debacle in China."

Paton, William. *A Faith for the World.* London: Edinburgh House Press, 1929.

Written by a former secretary of the I.M.C. and editor of the *International Review of Missions,* this study still merits careful reading.

——— (ed.). *The Missionary Motive.* London: SCM Press, 1913.

Paventi, Saverio. *La Chiesa Missionaria.* 2 vols. Rome: Unione Missionaria del Clero in Italia, [1949–50].

See Volume I: *Manuale de Missionsologia Dottrinale;* a standard Catholic work, with bibliographical footnotes.

Perbal, Albert, O.M.I. *Premières leçons de théologie missionnaire.* Paris: Dillen, 1937.

An important Catholic study of the fundamentals in mission theology.

Phillips, Godfrey Edward. *The Gospel in the World: A Restatement of Missionary Principles.* London: Gerald Duckworth and Co., 1939; abridgment, 1947.

A stocktaking of the principles governing the Christian mission.

Pickhard, Elsie C. and Shotwell, Louisa R. (eds.). *Every Tribe and Tongue.* New York: Friendship Press, 1960. Paperback.

Records the search of six hundred delegates from thirty-six denominations for the meaning of the mission in today's world; includes essays by E. L. Smith, Niles, Espy, Lazareth, Perry, and others.

Price, Frank Wilson. *As the Lightning Flashes.* (The Sprunt Lectures for 1948.) Richmond, Virginia: John Knox Press, 1948.

A reinterpretation of the missionary purpose for a new era.

Ranson, Charles W. *That the World May Know.* New York: Friendship Press, 1953.

Written by an ecumenical leader at the request of the National Council of Churches in the U.S.A. to interpret the life and task of the Church in the world.

——— (ed.). *Renewal and Advance: Christian Witness in a Revolutionary World.* London: Edinburgh House Press, 1948.

Addresses and statements from the meeting of the I.M.C. at Whitby, Ontario, Canada, July, 1947.

Rétif, André, S.J. *Introduction à la doctrine pontificale des missions.* Paris: Éditions du Seuil, 1953.

A study of the pontifical doctrine of missions as seen in the official statements of the supreme authorities, i.e., the Popes, the Papal Congregations, and in the statements of the Congregatio de Propaganda Fide.

Richter, Julius. *Evangelische Missionskunde.* 2 vols. Vol. I: *Evangelische Missionsgeschichte.* Vol. II: *Evangelische Missionslehre und Apologetik.* Leipzig: A. Deichertsche Verlagsbuchhandlung, 1927.

A standard German work on the history and theory of Protestant missions.

Roux, Hébert. *Eglise et mission.* Paris: Société des Missions Évangéliques de Paris, 1956. (Collection Présence de la Mission.) Paperback.

A study in the relation between Church and mission.

Rowlingson, Donald T. " 'No Other Name'—In What Sense?" in *Christian Century,* Vol. LXXVII (Sept. 14, 1960), pp. 1055–57.

Schlunk, Martin (ed.). *Botschafter an Christi Statt: von Wesen und Werk deutscher Missionsarbeit.* Gütersloh: C. Bertelsmann, 1932.

An important symposium by eminent German and Swiss scholars, dealing with various aspects of mission theory.

Schmidlin, Joseph. *Katholische Missionslehre im Grundriss.* Münster: Aschendorffsche Verlagsbuchhandlung, 1919; 2nd ed. 1923. Translated into English by Matthias Braun, *Catholic Mission Theory.* Techny, Illinois: Mission Press, S.V.D., 1931.

The first systematic approach to the theology of missions among Roman Catholics. Extensive bibliography, pp. 462–79.

———. *Einführung in die Missionswissenschaft.* 2nd ed. Münster: Aschendorffsche Verlagsbuchhandlung, 1925.

An introduction to the science of missions.

Seumois, Andr. V., O.M.I. *Vers une définition de l'Activité Missionnaire.* Schöneck/Beckenried, Suisse: Administration de la Nouvelle Revue de Science Missionnaire, 1948. (Cahiers de la Nouvelle Revue de Science

Missionnaire, Nr. 5.) Translated into German by Joseph Peters, *Auf dem Wege zu einer Definition der Missionstätigkeit*. Gladbach: B. Kühlen Kunst und Verlagsanstalt, 1948.

A succinct survey of developments toward a definition of the Christian mission among Roman Catholics from 1910 to the present.

———. *Introduction à la Missiologie*. Schöneck/Beckenried: Suisse: Administration de la Nouvelle Revue de Science Missionnaire, 1952.

The author summarizes past developments and points toward new advances in this introduction, the most substantial available, to Catholic mission theory. Includes extensive bibliographical footnotes.

Soper, Edmund Davison. *The Philosophy of the Christian World Mission*. New York: Abingdon-Cokesbury Press, 1943.

This writer's position, midway between Hocking and Kraemer, is still probably the most representative view of American thought on the subject.

Speer, Robert E. *Missionary Principles and Practice*. New York: Fleming H. Revell Co., 1902.

Dr. Speer was a leading spokesman during the first half of the century.

———. *Christianity and the Nations*. (The Duff Lectures for 1910.) New York: Fleming H. Revell Co., 1910.

Considerable attention is devoted to the aim and motive of missions.

———. *The Finality of Jesus Christ*. New York: Fleming H. Revell Co., 1933.

Stewart, James S. *Thine Is the Kingdom: The Church's Mission in Our Time*. New York: Charles Scribner's Sons, [1957].

Lectures on the missionary aim and motive by a noted Scottish theologian.

Thomson, James Sutherland. *The Divine Mission*. (The R. P. MacKay Memorial Lectures for 1956–57.) Toronto: The United Church Publishing House, 1957. Paperback.

The author seeks to restate the missionary character of the Christian faith in terms of the Christian doctrine of God, stressing the theological basis for missions as over against the humanistic and sociological.

Vicedom, Georg F. *Missio Dei: Einführung in eine Theologie der Mission*. München: Chr. Kaiser Verlag, 1958. Paperback.

A valuable new approach to the theology of mission from the theocentric point of view.

Visser't Hooft, W. A. *The Pressure of Our Common Calling*. Garden City, N.Y.: Doubleday & Co., Inc., 1959.

An approach to the theology of the ecumenical movement, by the General Secretary of the World Council of Churches.

Walker, Alan. *The Whole Gospel for the Whole World*. With an Introduction by E. G. Homrighausen. New York: Abingdon Press, 1957.

Written by an Australian Methodist with ecumenical perspective, this book challenges contemporary concepts of evangelism.

Warneck, Gustav. *Evangelische Missionslehre: Ein missionstheoretischer Versuch*. 2 vols. Gotha: F. A. Perthes, 1897.

Professor Warneck was the great German missiologist; this was his famous work which, for the first time, gave a systematic exposition of Protestant mission theory.

Warren, Max A. C. *The Christian Mission.* London: SCM Press, 1951.

Canon Warren is the General Secretary of the Church Missionary Society, London, and editor of the well-known *CMS News-Letter.*

———. *The Christian Imperative.* New York: Charles Scribner's Sons, 1955.

———. *Caesar the Beloved Enemy.* London: SCM Press, 1955.

———. *The Truth of Vision. A study in the nature of the Christian Hope.* London: The Canterbury Press, 1948.

———. *Partnership: The Study of an Idea.* London: SCM Press, 1956.

Webber, George W. *God's Colony in Man's World.* New York: Abingdon Press, 1960.

The life and mission of the Church in the inner city, as experienced in the East Harlem Protestant Parish, New York.

West, Charles C. and Paton, David M. (eds.). *The Missionary Church in East and West.* London: SCM Press, 1959. (Studies in Ministry and Worship, No. 13.) Paperback.

Studies that aim to erase the boundary line which divides "mission" from "ecclesiology," and ask the basic question, "What does it mean to believe that the Church itself is a missionary body?"

White, Hugh Vernon. *A Theology for Christian Missions.* Chicago: Willett, Clark and Co., 1937.

The author suggests the service of man as the regulative aim of Christian missions.

World Council of Churches, Division of Studies. "A Theological Reflection on the Work of Evangelism," in *The Bulletin* (Geneva: World Council of Churches, Division of Studies), Vol. III (November 1959), pp. 1–46.

A document on the theology of evangelism drawn up by the World Council of Churches, Department of Evangelism; Canon Theodore O. Wedel, Chairman.

Zwemer, Samuel M. *"Into All the World": The Great Commission, a Vindication and an Interpretation.* Grand Rapids, Michigan: Zondervan Publishing House, 1943.

Dr. Zwemer was Professor of the History of Religion and Christian Missions at Princeton Theological Seminary, an authority on Islam, founder of *The Muslim World* journal, and was representative of a conservative, scholarly approach to the theology of mission.

———. *Thinking Missions with Christ. Some Basic Aspects of World-Evangelism; Our Message, Our Motive, and Our Goal.* Grand Rapids, Michigan: Zondervan Publishing House, 1934.

INDEX OF NAMES AND SUBJECTS

(See also Contents and Bibliography)